AF379293

Seeing through Stone

Seeing through Stone

Edited by
Gina Dent
Lauren Schell Dickens
Rachel Nelson

Published by
Institute of the Arts and Sciences at UC Santa Cruz
and San José Museum of Art

Contents

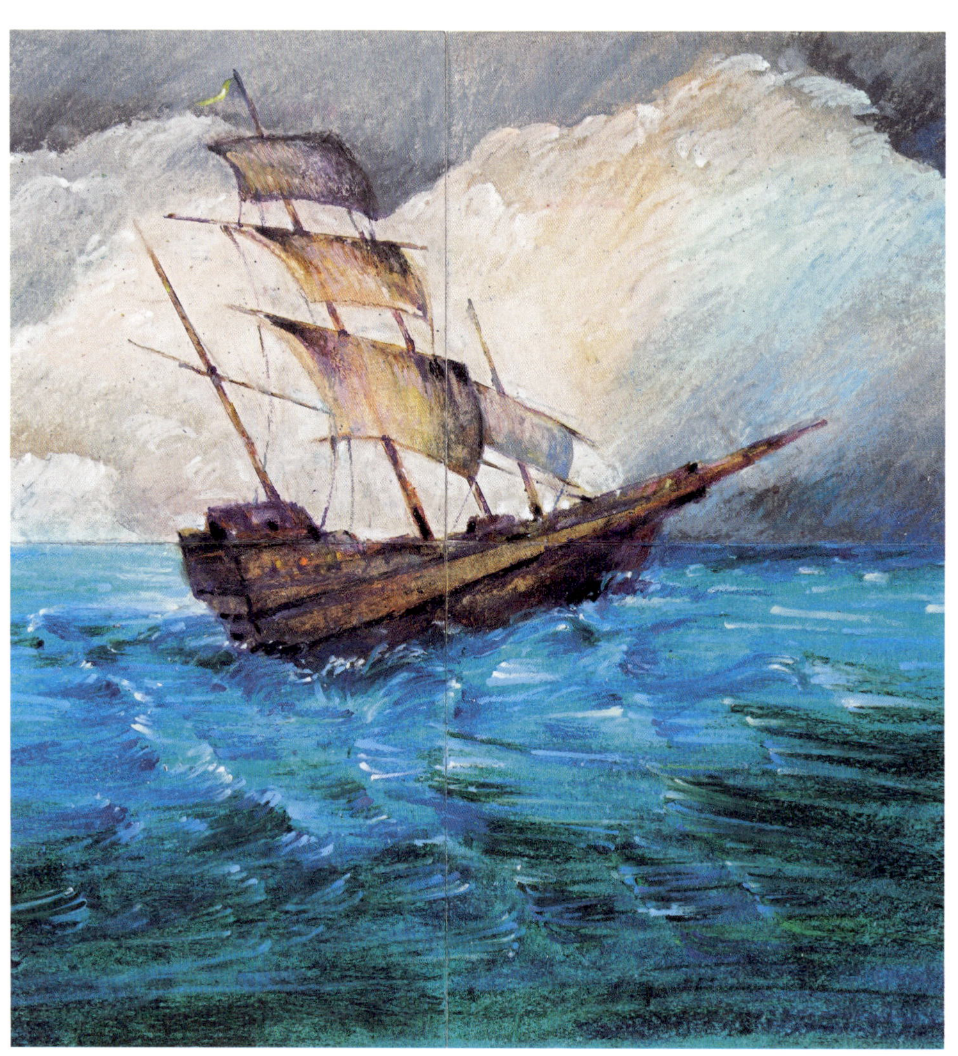

In the Artists' Words

I learned to make candy from a fellow prisoner in 1962. His name was Joseph Montgomery, but we called him Cap Pistol. He had a job in the kitchen and so did I, on the cook shift. I was fascinated with the way Cap Pistol made things, like cinnamon rolls and candy. I was fascinated watching him make pralines, how he stirred the mixture of sugar, butter, and evaporated milk, how he whipped it up and got out all the air bubbles, added his ingredients, and then how it caramelized. And when he pulled it, I was fascinated watching it harden. Anyway, I said, "Man, I got to learn how to make this candy."

If I remember correctly, it was my friend Herman Wallace who first used a cold drink can to make some candy in his cell. And it dawned on me that you could make a whole bunch. The way I would do it was, first, I would peel the top off of one cold drink can, and open that up and then take another cold drink and take the top off that. Then you take the bottom and you put that bottom into the top of the can. You leave the bottom of the first can. That's a base. And then you would take another can, and you would cut the bottom and you would fold it, and then you would take another can and do the same thing. The cans are made of aluminum and thin, so we could heat them up. We'd use toilet paper for our burners. We'd just roll it up and light it. And that would last for ten minutes sometimes, depending on how thick or how big you made the toilet paper wad. We had people who used to work out in the field sometimes, and they used to gather pecans. But I started making so much I didn't always wait for pecan season, and I started making it with peanuts. The peanuts were a good substitute. The only things I needed were milk, sugar, butter, and salt.

While confined, you become creative. The mind is constantly at work, and you come up with ways to overcome your confinement. Someone else might restrict you physically and mentally, but you don't have to do that to yourself. When you're in prison like that, you have to come up with ideas to do the thing that your space and your environment restrict you from doing—that you are not allowed to do. And that was why I learned how to make candy. Like I said, Herman put that idea out there, and I didn't want it to die. I extended it. I started making the candy all the time, every week. I was giving it to the dudes on death row and it was something that we could kind of look forward to.

There's no limit to what people collectively really
can do. I think people place limitations on themselves. I think they do it more leisurely out here
in the free world, but in prison, it's a concentrated
thing. So you have to get hold of something, and it
becomes a gem, a precious stone. Just the feeling of
having that kind of freedom, I think it does wonders
for the psyche. You're in a hopeless situation, but in
a hopeless situation you still could envision hope.

When I started making candy, I saw myself getting
out of prison and saying with candy, "Now that I'm
free, I can make life a little freer for you." The concepts of candy and freedom converged.

Robert Hillary King

Memories of Keraniganj Jail is a series of quite small architectural models I made based on my uncle's memories of jail. My uncle is Shahidul Alam, a Bangladeshi activist and photographer. He was jailed by the government of Bangladesh after reporting on student protests. He spent 107 days in jail, and there was a campaign to release him. As an architect, while he was in jail, I imagined the spaces he was in and constructed them in my mind. I wanted to go in and hold his hand. After he came out, he described the spaces in more detail, and I built the models based on his memories and my imagination.

It was an interesting process to construct the models of the jail without drawing surveys or the materials I'm used to working with. I had to grapple with, for instance, whether it mattered if I got the scale and the dimensions of the room right or not. Matters of scale were important because of how it came into my dreams. From the day my uncle was abducted, I was campaigning and writing letters during the day, and at night, I dreamed. I knew he'd been tortured and made to walk up and down stairs with heavy objects on his head. And in my dreams, I began to see spaces, but they were suddenly scaleless. They were unlike spaces I had ever seen before. Sometimes they would expand and contract and expand again. And sometimes they were mainly color and raw emotion. I wondered: Is that what happens to space if you're confined or you're in pain? What happens to your sense of scale or space if you are hurt or you're frightened or blindfolded?

When I made the models, I wasn't compelled to make something so abstract, however. Those spaces in my mind were interesting, but I didn't think I could even achieve those dream sensations through art. And I don't really want to make abstract works about my uncle's pain. His pain is his pain. So the models show many of the elements that I drew from stories my aunt would tell me after visiting him. When my uncle was released, our conversations about the jail were full of stories about other prisoners and their experiences—the vegetable garden they grew, the music they made, or the animals they had. As my uncle said to me, "There's no one experience of prison. And even within the cell I was in, various prisoners would have different experiences." So the models became more about narrating his and his fellow prisoners' stories and memories.

I wasn't an activist until my uncle went to jail, but after he was released, I began campaigning for other political prisoners in India. For the last four years, I've been campaigning for G. N. Saibaba, who is a professor of English at Delhi University, and now

I am making work based on letters that we have exchanged. Professor Saibaba is accused of being a Maoist under the terror laws. He is serving a life sentence and has gone through periods of solitary confinement,[1] and he is 90 percent physically disabled.

During my communication with Saibaba and my work on his campaign, I have had to carry on with my day job as an architect, often working on pretty mundane projects. But Saibaba's letters began to change the way I drew my construction drawings and the details for those very regular projects. When I am working on building projects, sometimes, for instance, I'll do something like put a red window in a very boring kitchen extension. And then I realize that this is because the prisoners I am campaigning for often talk about the red exit gate, which is their overriding symbol of hope and despair in prison.

I think one half of my work could be described as didactic, and clearly part of the resistance movement: the messaging is quite clear and direct, because it is about life and death. That art is about getting people out. For example, when I made the models about my uncle, I needed to get out his story and the story of the other prisoners he'd left behind. I really saw the weight on him about who he had left behind—even the sparrows that he had left behind.

I can't help but have this other side of my work, which is much more inward, in which meaning is not as clear. The diptych drawings are part of this. Viewers see black-and-white projections of architectural sketches. These are projections of drawings I have sent to Saibaba and his fellow prisoners. I drew these works, the ones sent to the jail, by hand in luminous colors: the colors that prisoners described to me and that they long to see. The two halves of these diptychs will never be seen together. And the truth is, the ones that I send to him in jail, I don't even know if he'll receive them. They may be confiscated and destroyed.

I am not always sure where these works are taking me, but I know that I am trying to articulate architecture as a language of struggle and resistance. With painting, music, or poetry, there's a tradition of these media being used as the art of dissent. But I'm not a painter. I'm not a poet. My language of expression is still architecture. It's really the only language I know.

1. Professor Saibaba was released from prison on March 5, 2024, after almost ten years of imprisonment, based on a finding of "insufficient evidence."

Sofia Karim

I actually never thought I would be getting my nails as dirty as they are. I definitely identify more as a builder and a maker than a gardener, but now I love it. I've learned so much from the gardens and the plants, just in terms of ways of living, ways to be, ways to love, ways to have hope, ways to be generative, ways to be better, ways to be less of a jerk.

My slow path to being a gardener started when I asked Herman Wallace what kind of house does a man dream of who's lived in a six-foot by nine-foot cell for decades.[1] The first thing he said was, "I can clearly see the gardens. They will be full of gloxinia, delphiniums, and roses, and I wish for guests to be able to smile and walk through flowers all year round." When he joined the ancestors just three days after his physical freedom from prison, at that point we had twelve years of writing letters and visits. And the prison actually gave me back the letters I had sent him. When I read back through all the letters, I recognized how much Herman talked about nature and plants and gardens and flowers throughout those twelve years. And I knew that gardens would be a way to uphold Herman Wallace's life and legacy. Eventually that led to the Solitary Gardens project, through which we grow gardens in collaboration with folks who are still inside, and to all the work we are doing with plants, gardening, and the movement for abolition.

There's an adaptation of a quote by Thich Nhat Hanh that says something like, "If you plant lettuce and it doesn't do well, do you blame the lettuce?" No, right? You figure out if it needs more water, you figure out if it needs more sun, maybe you move it to another place inside the garden. It is the whole ecosystem that needs to be shifted and changed for the lettuce to thrive. The ways that the garden teaches us about abolition are vast, because, of course, when we think about abolition, it comes down to the same thing. If a human being is not doing well and that is manifesting in them causing harm, we blame them. However, we should be thinking about how and why that person needs more water, needs more light, or needs to be moved to a different spot.

The plants do a lot of teaching. For instance, I grow a lot of okra, being in Louisiana. Okra is part of the mallow family and has an edible seedpod. But this seedpod, you have to harvest it when it's small. You can't let it grow to its fullest potential, to its biggest, to when the plant has the most pods, or it becomes too fibrous and too hard to eat. This is very counterintuitive to the ways that we've been conditioned in the West and by capitalism, where the emphasis is always on growth—things should be the biggest, the largest, the most productive. And okras refuse that. They teach us that sometimes less is enough, pushing back against the logic of racial capitalism.

Or think about yarrow. When yarrow is planted near tulsi (a basil), it encourages the oil production in the tulsi. It doesn't compromise its own growth, it's just encouraging the plants around it to become their fullest selves. And I've learned a lot from that.

At a certain point in growing gardens in collaboration with folks for years, I realized I have this abundance of plant material. And I began to think about all that plants can teach us, and about how our relationship to the plants can allow us to be better people, and to make a better world. I started making some teas and tinctures, sort of experimenting, having that foundation of wonder and curiosity. That grew into further curiosity when one of the solitary gardeners was super into plant medicine. Now we have an apothecary of plant medicine that's been designed by incarcerated individuals, we call it the Prisoner's Apothecary.

To bring the apothecary to the people—and to facilitate public-facing conversations at the intersection of health care sovereignty, plant medicine, and abolition—the Abolitionist's Apothecarts (mobile apothecary carts) came into being.

In every single interview that I've ever given over the last nineteen years, I've found myself including this: Mwalimu Johnson, who was one of my most beloved elders, used to say, "It takes all the tiny grains of sand to hold back the oceans of oppression." We all have meaningful roles to play when we see ourselves with a unity of purpose.

jackie sumell

I'm a co-founder of SAKA, an artist alliance for genuine agrarian reform and rural development in the Philippines. SAKA was founded in 2016 around the idea that cultural work is a form of organizing people that recognizes the different frequencies on which we can contribute to focusing attention on critical issues. *Feudal Fields* is the first tapestry I made; it's a map of Hacienda Luisita. Haciendas are essentially sugarcane plantations, although in the postcolonial context of the Philippines, the term has come to mean something more like "private estate," or "land held by the ruling class." Hacienda Luisita is in Central Luzon, north of Manila, which is where the Communist Party was founded. The region has a long history of peasant disenfranchisement, from colonial times, when lands were sequestered and controlled by the church, to after Spanish colonization, when the same lands were passed on to local elite families. Now, Hacienda Luisita is owned by the Cojuangco family, which is among the most powerful families in the Philippines. In 2004, the plantation workers at the hacienda organized and staged a protest outside the central sugar mill. They were met with violence by state forces, and fourteen people died, including children, in an incident now known as the Hacienda Luisita massacre. This happened when I was in high school and was a turning point for me. By the time I was getting out of college, I understood the massacre at Hacienda Luisita to be part of an ongoing historical continuum of peasant struggles in the Philippines. I made *Feudal Fields* as a narrative of this history, showing the violence of the massacre not as a discrete event but as continuous and recurrent in different spaces and in different times.

Feudal Fields II: Tinang is my newest tapestry. Tinang is a smaller hacienda within the same region. Most, if not all, of the farmworkers who are working the land have been doing so for generations, yet they do not have ownership of the land. This is despite the fact that the Comprehensive Agrarian Reform Program (CARP) was drafted in 1987, mandating the redistribution of private and public agricultural lands to the farmworkers. CARP has so many loopholes that beneficiaries can barely claim their lands because of all the bureaucracy. At Hacienda Tinang, the beneficiaries have been able to acquire all the legal documents that were kept from them by the original landowner, who also coincidentally happens to be the mayor of the town, and have gone through all the necessary steps to legally assert their rights on the land. In 2022, as a form of protest in support of these legal efforts, a collective I am involved in collaborated with the farmworkers to organize a gesture of collective land cultivation, colloquially known as *bungkalan*. For collective land cultivation, the cash crops—in this case, sugarcane —are removed and replaced with food crops. A large contingent of advocates, including foreign students, was present for the *bungkalan* at Hacienda Tinang, as was the media. The mayor called in the state forces, and ninety of us were rounded up and detained. Foreigners were let go first, and the remaining eighty-three of us were charged with two cases: land usurpation and illegal assembly. These are policies that were made during martial law times and have not been used for decades. This gave me firsthand experience of the faults in the different layers of policy that compose the agrarian reform program and how the judicial system bends based on the whims of those in power, which informs *Feudal Fields II*. In the tapestry, I've also incorporated personal narratives and maps drawn by other people I was arrested with, continuing the process of counter-mapping that has been part of my practice since 2017.

Translating these stories into textile work is a way of drawing on different languages of visual and material culture that reflect the context of their production. In *Monuments of Great Divide*, I've incorporated small sculptures made in a town called Paete. *Paete* means "chisel," and the town is named for the carving of wooden religious imagery, for which it is known. We are witnessing the decline of this industry due to the mass production of cheap, plastic versions attained through the global supply chain, the effects of which are experienced as a continuation of colonization economically and culturally.

Having a carver who is used to making figurines of saints make a wall instead, as is the case in *Monuments of Great Divide*, seems to me a kind of poetry; a wall could be either protection or a barrier. One of the sculptures, for instance, looks like a medieval bamboo barricade. At banana plantations in some areas, the fruits are hung on these medieval-looking structures. Landless farmers have repurposed these structures during protests, using them to hang banners and slogans about the lack of proper wages and conditions on plantations. I have also seen them used by the plantation owners to control generationally marginalized farmworkers. In one instance, there was a sign hung saying, "Trespassers will be shot. Survivors will be shot again."

The economic and land policies that inform my artworks create a kind of social incarceration—a general suspended state that is experienced like incarceration. I think about how many generations of not just landlessness but also debt affect culture, the social fabric, and even the body. In Negros Island, there is this word, *tigkiriwi*, which means something beyond starving. When you're starving, hunger is felt in your stomach. But tigkiriwi is when hunger also gnaws at your mind. It's the long-internalized starvation that just eats at you.

Cian Dayrit

There is an image from the 2004 Critical Resistance South Conference that I keep returning to when I think about my work. Critical Resistance is an organization that works to bring attention to the prison-industrial complex (PIC). The first conference was at UC Berkeley in 1998. The expectation was that, like, three hundred people would show up. Instead, thousands of people from around the country came. This was a real testament to how much prisons affect people's lives and communities. It also marked how much work was already taking place against the PIC, and the huge potential for movement building in that moment. When I look at the image from the 2004 conference, which also was attended by thousands of people (and I'm in the picture too), I see the people, the community that is important to my work—and that I work within. This community is always expanding. It is composed of different organizations and different people from different parts of the country and sometimes from different parts of the world.

The potential for movement building still exists— we have not completed that work. I've seen that space of trying to build that movement, trying to help make those connections, trying to collaborate with different organizations at different times. And

I think about how our work as artists can contribute. We can help create spaces in which to build the movement, help make connections, and work to collaborate according to different organizations' capacities. We can also ensure the movement is influencing the art world, to some degree, and making an impact on art schools and things like that. This is how I think about the space I'm trying to hold and the audience I am imagining through my practice.

I have a long-running project called *Degrees of Visibility*, for which I have been taking pictures from publicly accessible viewpoints of prisons, jails, and detention centers since 2012. Once, at an exhibition, someone asked me if I had been to the Old Atlanta Prison Farm, an abandoned city-owned prison complex in southwest DeKalb County. I went and visited the next day, and I took my camera. That raised a lot of questions for me in relation to *Degrees of Visibility*. Because the whole logic of that series is showing particular carceral spaces and titling them according to the number of people who are locked up in them, I wasn't sure how a prison that was closed down, and empty, would fit. And I also started to wonder if the space could really be called empty. I started thinking about what happens to a prison after it's no longer used for its carceral purposes. How do closed prisons open up to different possible futures, different possible uses, or different possible imaginations? So this became a kind of abolitionist exercise for me that seeded a new series of film works.

Ashes, Ashes, the first in what has now become a trilogy of films, was made at the time when officials were promising that Rikers Island, the prison island in the East River in the Bronx, was going to be closed. The piece consists primarily of footage of the shoreline, looking at the weeds and the plant life and the birds and other things that are there that would potentially replace the prison on the island, if it was gone. The audio for the piece features different organizers and activists talking about what they envision taking its place.

The second film is called *Double Time*. It was made in 2021 around the so-far partial closing of the Arizona State Prison Complex in Florence, Arizona, and is a similar kind of landscape study, while also dealing with the relationships between prisons and the history of imperialism and western expansion in the United States.

And Water Brings Tomorrow is the third piece in the trilogy. When I was filming it, in California where I live, we had a series of major rain events. There were historic floods, and the old Tulare lakebed, which was drained for farming more than a hundred years ago, became a lake again. In the small city of Corcoran, where the lake once was and now is again, there are two state prisons. While officials rushed to create a levee to keep the prisons from being submerged by the lake, I used the potential of that moment of reclamation as my point of departure for *And Water Brings Tomorrow*.

Ashley Hunt

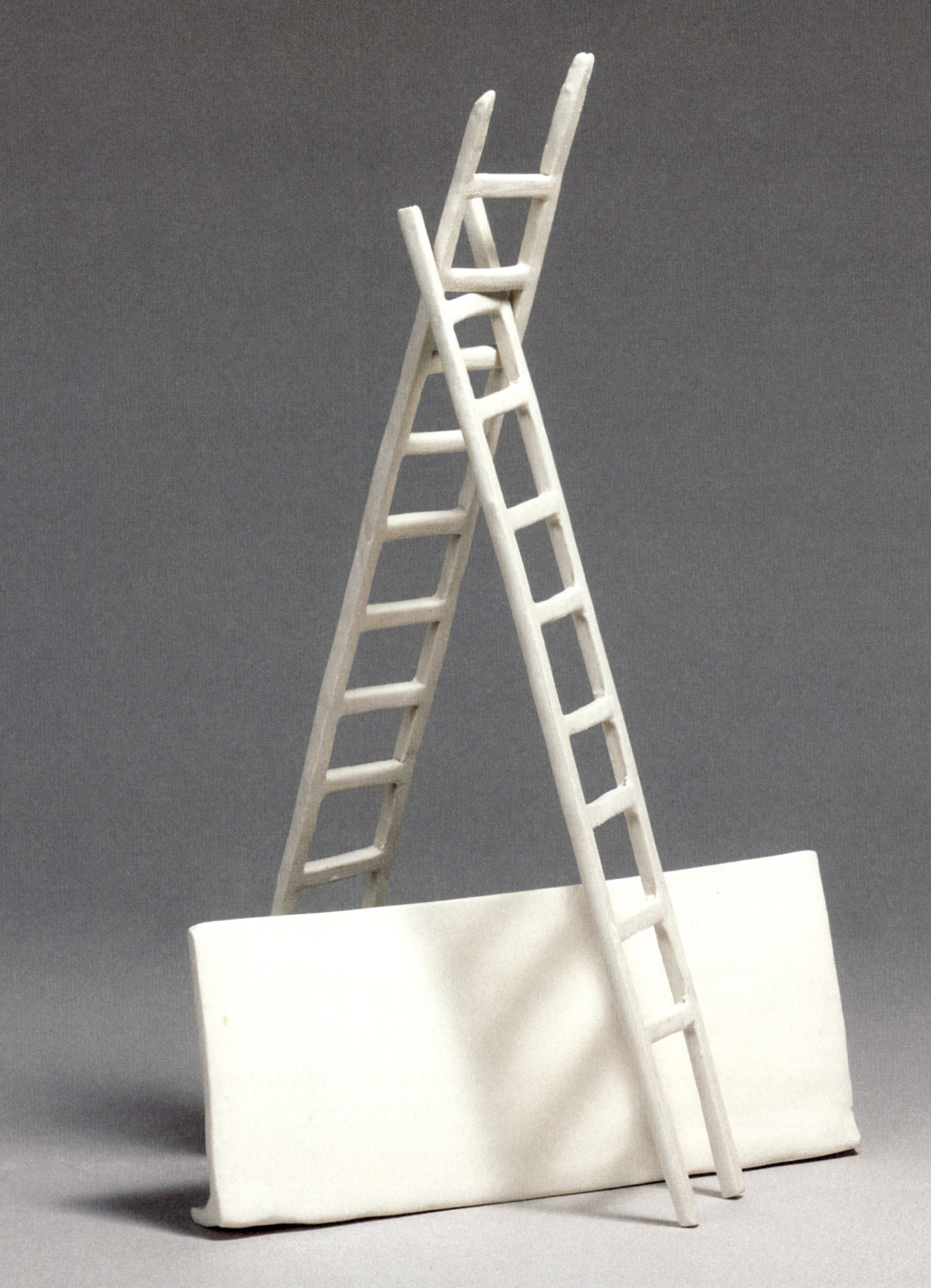

Preface

Robin D. G. Kelley

This remarkable exhibition takes its title from Etheridge Knight Jr.'s poem "He Sees through Stone." The poem, written while Knight was in prison, describes an older Black prisoner who, in his infinite wisdom, assumes the form of a seer or diviner of sorts. Evoking images of the prayer grounds where enslaved people found refuge and communed with God, Knight tells of being led "into the dark forest," where the seer

> taught me the secret rites
> to take a woman
> to be true to my brothers
> to make my spear drink
> the blood of my enemies

The old man teaches the narrator the rituals of love and war and uses his "secret eyes" to defend himself from snarling "black cats" on the yard ready to pounce.[1]

Seeing through Stone brings together artists whose secret eyes invite us not only to see through carceral walls so as to imagine liberatory futures but also to see our enemies and adversaries, to prepare for war while learning to love, to contemplate the meaning of abolition and freedom with accountability. These artists are multidirectional seers. To see through stone is to penetrate prison walls and enclosures from inside; it is also to see in from the outside—whether through walls built with state bonds or private capital, or through enclosures regulated by states or nations. And it means seeing flashes of freedom through the walls and ceilings of our globally enclosed reality. The carceral landscape envisioned in these works extends beyond prisons to include plantations, reservations, labor camps, border walls, black sites, and residential schools. Carceral spaces are by nature extractive, in that they extract people from communities; they extract state surpluses from our collective sweat and blood; they extract land and resources, arrest life, and make "holes in the earth," to quote the title of Imani Jacqueline Brown's work included in the exhibition.[2] But the artists in this exhibition show us that holes can be filled with seeds, enclosures blown up and remapped, a starry night read as a guide to freedom, a jailhouse repurposed as a safe house, the prison yard turned into a freedom square. They invite us to imagine jail wings that fly, bars and walls made of glass, a quilt depicting the history of state-sanctioned racist violence on one side and abolition democracy on the other, and a walking stick that serves as a lifeline to community and a tether to ancestors.

Stone makes for a powerful metaphor: it is organic, prehistoric; it is earth before prisons, before private property, before commodification, before humans. When I was a kid growing up in Harlem in the 1960s, incarceration was colloquially referred to as "making big rocks into little rocks." And while stone may be the materialization of enclosure, the act of working stone sometimes serves as punishment. I am reminded of the startling irony of Palestinian laborers in the West Bank extracting and cutting stone from its quarries, or crushing stone to make concrete, to build all manner of Israeli dwellings, shopping malls, and prisons, not to mention the apartheid wall dividing the occupied from the occupier. Similar to Gaza, the West Bank is itself a kind of open-air prison, with the Palestinian Authority and Israeli occupation forces functioning as prison guards.[3]

Etheridge Knight looms over *Seeing through Stone* in ways that may not be readily apparent. He represented a generation of imprisoned intellectuals radicalized by the insurgencies of the 1960s, especially the Black liberation movement. They recognized the revolutionary rather than rehabilitative possibilities of art, prefiguring the kinds of collaborative abolitionist projects reflected here. Born in Mississippi, Knight came of age in Kentucky, enlisted in the army in 1947 at the age of sixteen, experienced the brutalities of war in Korea, and returned to the United States addicted to heroin. In 1960, a robbery conviction landed him in the Indiana State Prison, where he proved to be a brilliant autodidact, a disciplined reader, and an

extraordinarily talented poet. Hoyt W. Fuller, editor of *Negro Digest*, began publishing Knight's poems in 1965, and this caught the attention of poets Gwendolyn Brooks and Dudley Randall, founding publisher of Broadside Press. In 1968, Broadside published Knight's first collection, *Poems from Prison*, with a preface by Brooks, who discovered in these poems "blackness, inclusive, possessed, and given; freed and terrible and beautiful."[4] In addition to "He Sees through Stone," the book includes poems about prison, love, death, and the myth of universalism, along with poems for Malcolm X, Dinah Washington, Langston Hughes, and Gwendolyn Brooks. Knight used poetry to break through walls and connect. He explained in an interview, "Prison is a very oppressive, painful, alienating world. You've been, not exiled, you've been in-ziled. You've been cut off from your community . . . The purpose of art, any poetry is for communication. To bring about a communion, a community."[5]

In 1968, the same year *Poems from Prison* came out, four formerly incarcerated Black artists—Ben Bey, Bill Beal, Bill Ross, and William Montgomery—secured a grant from the W. Clement and Jessie V. Stone Foundation to support incarcerated artists as well as artists recently released from prison. In January of 1970, they launched an art guild called Looking Toward Freedom, which offered some training but mainly established

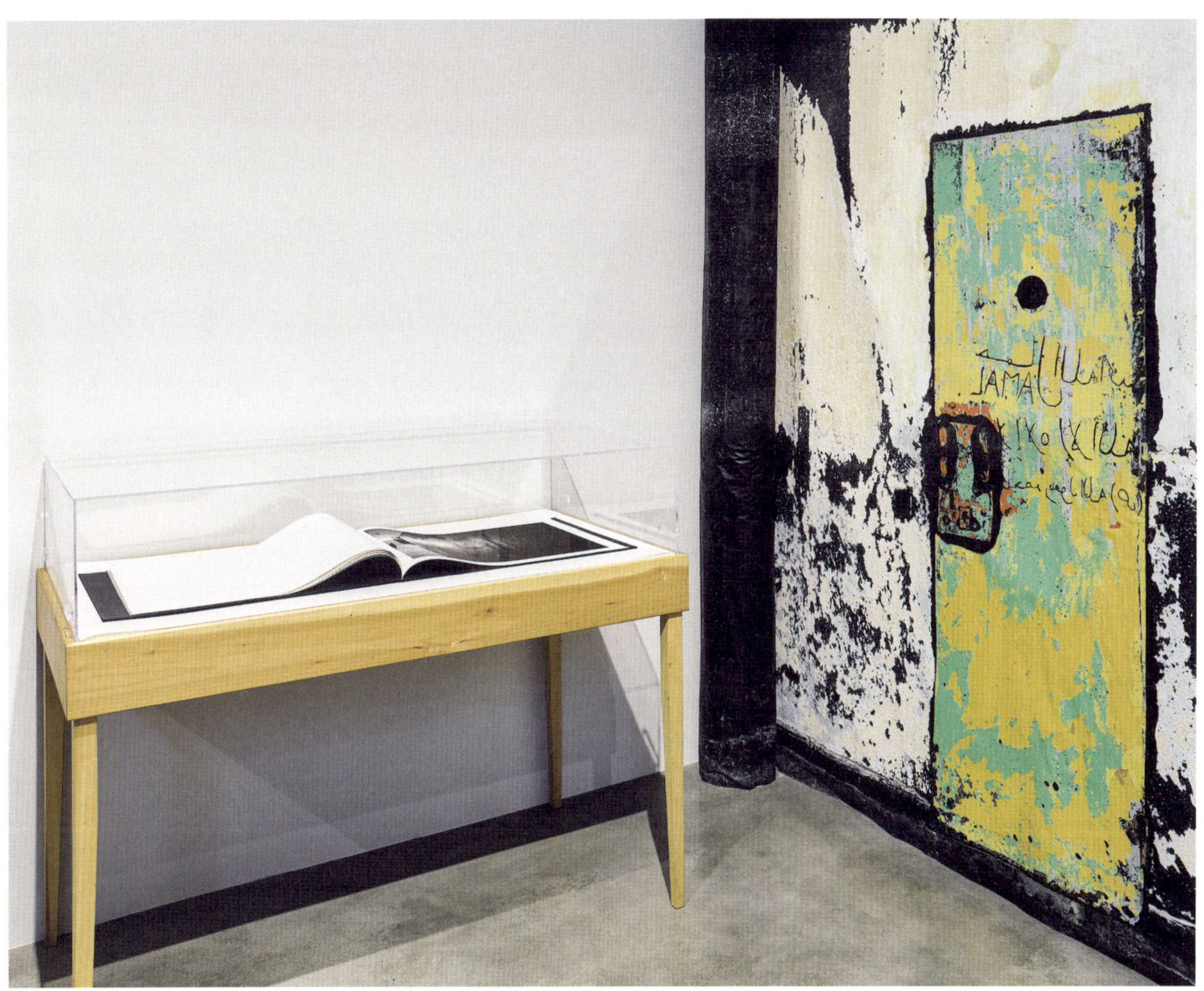

Patricia Gómez and María Jesús González, *Las 7 puertas* (detail), from the series "Tiempo Muerto, Proyecto para Sección Abierta (Cárcel de Palma de Mallorca)," 2011–13. Courtesy of the artists.

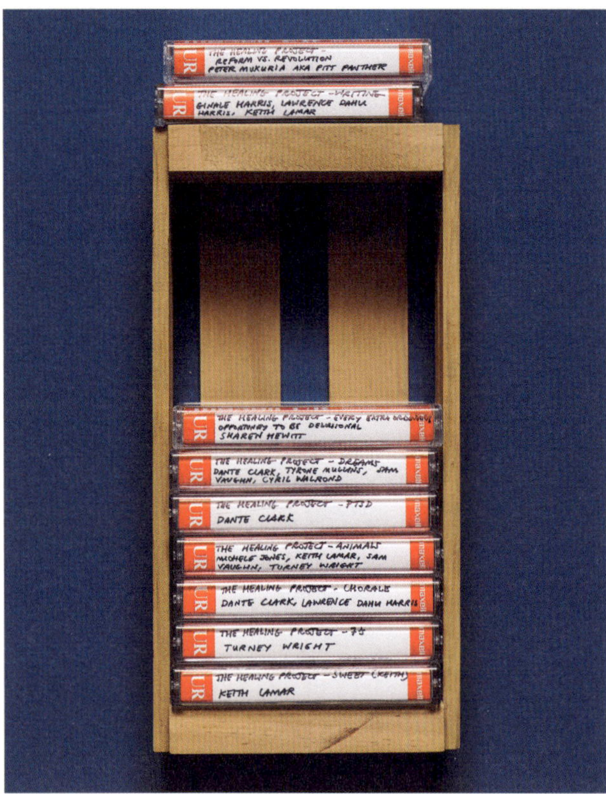

Samora Abayomi Pinderhughes, *Listening Station* (excerpt), from *The Healing Project*, 2016–ongoing. Audiocassettes. Collection of The Healing Project.

a market for members to sell their work and make a living. Obviously, these artists did not identify as "abolitionists," but they did regard Looking Toward Freedom as more than an employment scheme. It was a political project to strengthen movement and community ties, celebrate Black culture, and visually express what genuine freedom might look like. Bey, for example, became a major figure in Chicago's Black Arts Movement, working with the South Side Community Art Center alongside artists Lorenzo Pace and the center's founder, Margaret Burroughs.[6]

The Stone Foundation's commitment to supporting imprisoned artists gives the concept of "seeing through stone" a different meaning—one that relates to the distinction between art as rehabilitative labor and art as, in the words of cultural studies scholar Nicole Fleetwood, "an abolitionist vision to end human caging and the conditions that produce prisons."[7] W. Clement Stone built his fortune selling insurance, authored three books on positive thinking as the key to success, and was a lifelong conservative. He donated a cool $10 million to Richard Nixon's presidential campaigns in 1968 and 1972.[8] Like his president, Stone believed in law and order, but he also supported decarceration and prison art programs as a surefire way to reduce recidivism rates. He believed prison art programs served a dual purpose. First, making art could provide a steady source of income. Stone financed a national survey in 1969 that identified about seven thousand incarcerated artists, many of whom had participated in prison art programs. In the course of five years, sales from the artists' work came to nearly $1.2 million—with the prisons taking a large proportion of the proceeds to fund their programs.[9] Second, Stone and his associate Harry H. Woodward Jr. believed that the stereotype of incarcerated men as "tough, callous and not very bright, thus suitable only for hard, physical labor programs" undermined efforts to fund treatment and educational initiatives: "One of the most salient factors that took place at our nationwide prison art show was the surprise of viewers that such fine, creative work could be done behind high walls."[10]

Stone was strongly influenced by Karl Menninger's *The Crime of Punishment*, which argued that criminal behavior was essentially a mental health matter and ought to be treated with therapy rather than prison. The book was touted by liberals, conservatives, Christians, and mental health professionals, especially as drug addiction became a primary focus of law enforcement, and as white youths increasingly became the face of addiction. Stone purchased the book in bulk and sent copies "to influential people in the field of corrections."[11] *The Crime of Punishment*, like *Poems from Prison*, was published in 1968—the year, as abolitionist

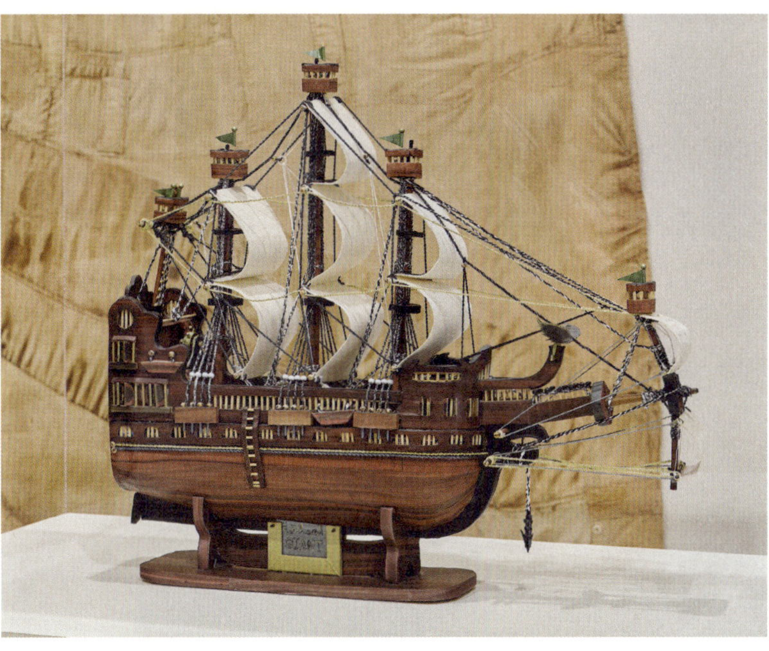

Moath al-Alwi, *Untitled (GIANT)*, 2017, from the Tea Project's *Ode to the Sea*, 2023/24. Cardboard, rope, fabric, plastic, and acrylic, 24 × 36 × 9 in. Courtesy of the artist.

scholar and activist Ruth Wilson Gilmore trenchantly observed, when radical insurgencies reached a peak and met stunning defeats, and when "the crumbling foundations of the old order . . . gave way to the possibility of astonishing prison growth."[12] In other words, 1968 marked a pivotal push for decarceral solutions, which enjoyed surprising support only to be crushed under the weight of a global economic crisis, ideologically driven crime fears, and what Gilmore calls the "prison fix" in the form of an acceleration of prison construction.[13] But she also reminds us that the prison abolition movement emerged precisely out of the ashes of these defeats, marking a qualitative leap from rehabilitation and liberal decarceration to the radical vision of abolition that animates *Seeing through Stone*.

This radical vision is the foundation for Visualizing Abolition, the initiative responsible for conceiving and curating the exhibition. Launched by feminist-abolitionist scholars Gina Dent and Rachel Nelson at the University of California, Santa Cruz Institute of the Arts and Sciences, Visualizing Abolition is a multidisciplinary, multiyear project that, unlike liberal prison art programs, interrogates, disrupts, and seeks to dismantle our carceral culture through a dynamic collaboration between artists (inside and outside prison walls), abolitionists, institutions of higher education, art museums, performing arts venues, and the wider public. Since its founding in 2020, Visualizing Abolition has organized several exhibitions; commissioned new works; sponsored a "Music for Abolition" series curated by composer, drummer, and educator Terri Lyne Carrington; offered postdoctoral fellowships, artist residencies, and graduate workshops; developed new curricula; and hosted a wide array of public programming. According to Dent and Nelson, the project's overall objective "is to change the narrative that links prisons to justice, contributing instead to the unfolding collective story and alternative imagining underway to create a future free of prisons."[14]

The work of constructing and representing the "collective story" of the movement toward abolition does not treat art as an escape from carceral realities or the violence those realities have wrought upon all of us. The artists in *Seeing through Stone* do not assume abolition is merely about cages and walls and arms, nor do they erase the trauma endured by family, friends, lovers, and generations that follow when one is incarcerated or disappeared. As abolitionist and disability justice organizer Mia Mingus puts it, "Abolition [is] a much larger project than just no prisons. It's also about how we abolish the prison state inside of us too, so that we're not just throwing people away or using punitive measures even in our own relationships and worlds."[15] Again, Etheridge Knight stalks the exhibition,

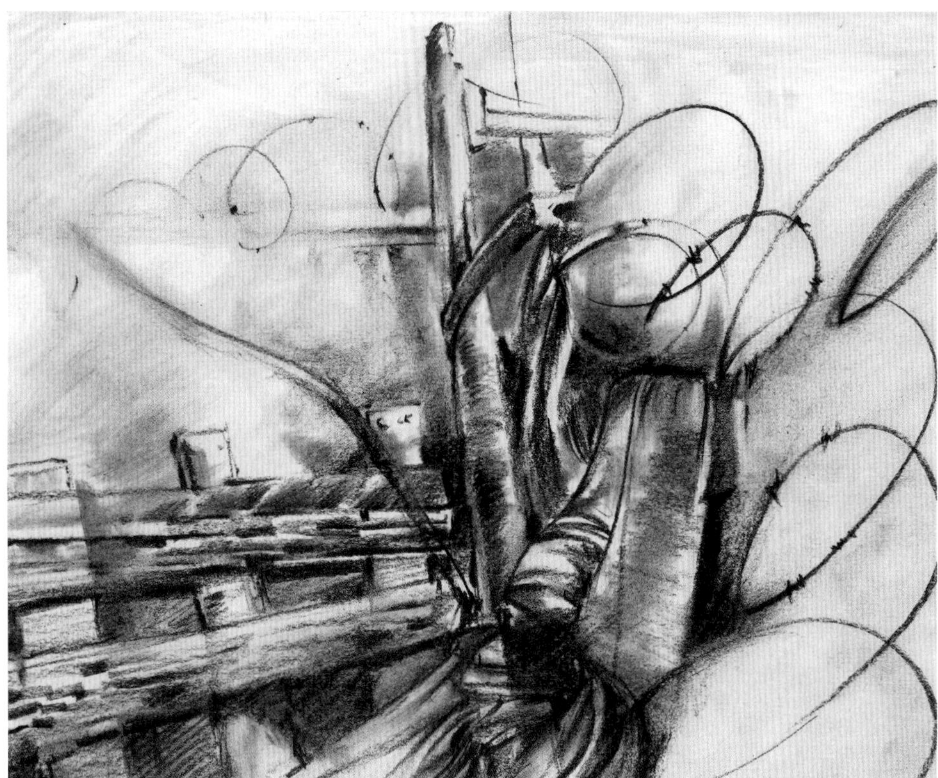

Ghaleb Al-Bihani, *Untitled*, 2014, from the Tea Project's *Ode to the Sea*, 2023/24. Charcoal on paper, 9¾ × 11⅞ in. Courtesy of the Tea Project.

reminding us that what one sees through stone is not always pretty or hopeful or liberating. He said as much in "To Make a Poem in Prison," confessing that "the air lends itself not / to the singer."[16] And he revealed as much in the trajectories of his life. Even at the very height of his fame, as he navigated a world beyond prison walls, he struggled with addiction, returned to jails and prisons and rehab, and frequently abused those he loved.

Samora Abayomi Pinderhughes' *The Healing Project*, a collective multimedia project, addresses the kinds of challenges that dogged Knight and so many others. It asks: How do we create art (in all genres and expressions) that can combat structural violence and end the prison-industrial complex, while attending to the injuries of such violence? For Pinderhughes, as with Knight, the key is communication—seeing and hearing through stone. *The Healing Project* brings us the voices and stories of incarcerated people on their terms, collaged with music and images in ways that resist both normalizing and spectacularizing the prison. It is a beautiful expression of Visualizing Abolition's imperative to promote work that is collaborative rather than extractive, and that crosses and ultimately demolishes what Gina Dent identifies as the "prison as a border" —"the distinction between the 'free world' and the space behind the walls of the prison."[17] This is what it

means to see through stone. It is what abolitionist art is supposed to do—imagine freedom while struggling to get free.

1. Etheridge Knight, *Black Voices from Prison* (New York: Pathfinder Press, 1970), 154.

2. Imani Jacqueline Brown, *The holes in the earth mirror the holes in our souls (and from them we can grow trees)*, 2023.

3. See Andrew Ross, *Stone Men: The Palestinians Who Built Israel* (New York: Verso, 2019).

4. Gwendolyn Brooks, preface to *Poems from Prison*, by Etheridge Knight (Detroit: Broadside Press, 1968), 9. On Knight's biography, see Michael S. Collins, *Understanding Etheridge Knight* (Columbia: University of South Carolina Press, 2012); Jean Anaporte-Easton, "Etheridge Knight: Poet and Prisoner—An Introduction," *Callaloo* 19, no. 4 (Autumn 1996): 940–46; and Charles H. Rowell, "An Interview with Etheridge Knight," *Callaloo* 19, no. 4 (Autumn 1996): 966–81.

5. Etheridge Knight, "Interview: Etheridge Knight," by Steven C. Tracy, *MELUS* 12, no. 2 (Summer 1985): 21.

6. Judy Roberts, "Ex-convict Artists Find Freedom Has Many Forms," *Chicago Tribune*, July 1, 1971; "Stone Protégé to Stage One Man Art Show Here," *Chicago Defender*, December 15, 1971; "Ben Bey, Chicago and New York Artist, Passes," *Chicago Crusader*, February 26, 2020, https://chicagocrusader.com/ben-bey-chicago-and-new-york-artist-passes/.

7. Nicole R. Fleetwood, *Marking Time: Art in the Age of Mass Incarceration* (Cambridge, MA: Harvard University Press, 2020), 8.

8. Douglas Martin, "Clement Stone Dies at 100. Built Empire on Optimism," *New York Times*, September 5, 2002. Stone founded Combined Insurance Company of America.

9. "Stone-Brandel Center Show Prison Art," *Chicago Defender*, January 8, 1970.

10. Harry H. Woodward and W. Clement Stone, "Art in Correctional Institutions," *Journal of Correctional Education* 22, no. 1 (Winter 1970): 5. Woodward was a political scientist and prison reformer who directed the Correctional Programs Achievement Motivation Systems at Chicago's Stone-Brandel Center, an institution founded by W. Clement Stone and attorney Paul Brandel.

11. Harry H. Woodward and W. Clement Stone, "Guides for Better Living," *Journal of Correctional Education* 21, no. 3 (Summer 1969): 15. Coincidentally, one of the books influenced by Menninger's argument happened to include a long interview with a friend Etheridge Knight made in prison, Art Powers, who talks about Knight's evolution as a poet. See Art Powers, "The Prison Artist," in *An Eye for an Eye: Four Inmates on the Crime of American Prisons Today*, ed. H. Jack Griswold et al. (New York: Holt, Rinehart and Winston, 1970), 112–22.

12. Ruth Wilson Gilmore, *Golden Gulag: Prisons, Surplus, Crisis, and Opposition in Globalizing California* (Oakland: University of California Press, 2007), 26.

13. Gilmore, *Golden Gulag*, 87–127.

14. "Visualizing Abolition," Institute of the Arts and Sciences, UC Santa Cruz, https://ias.ucsc.edu/visualizing-abolition/.

15. "Beyond Punishment: The Movement for Transformative Justice," *Rustbelt Abolition Radio*, July 10, 2017, https://rustbeltradio.org/2017/07/10/ep07/.

16. Knight, *Black Voices from Prison*, 160.

17. Angela Davis and Gina Dent, "Prison as a Border: A Conversation on Gender, Globalization, and Punishment," *Signs* 26, no. 4 (2001): 1236–37.

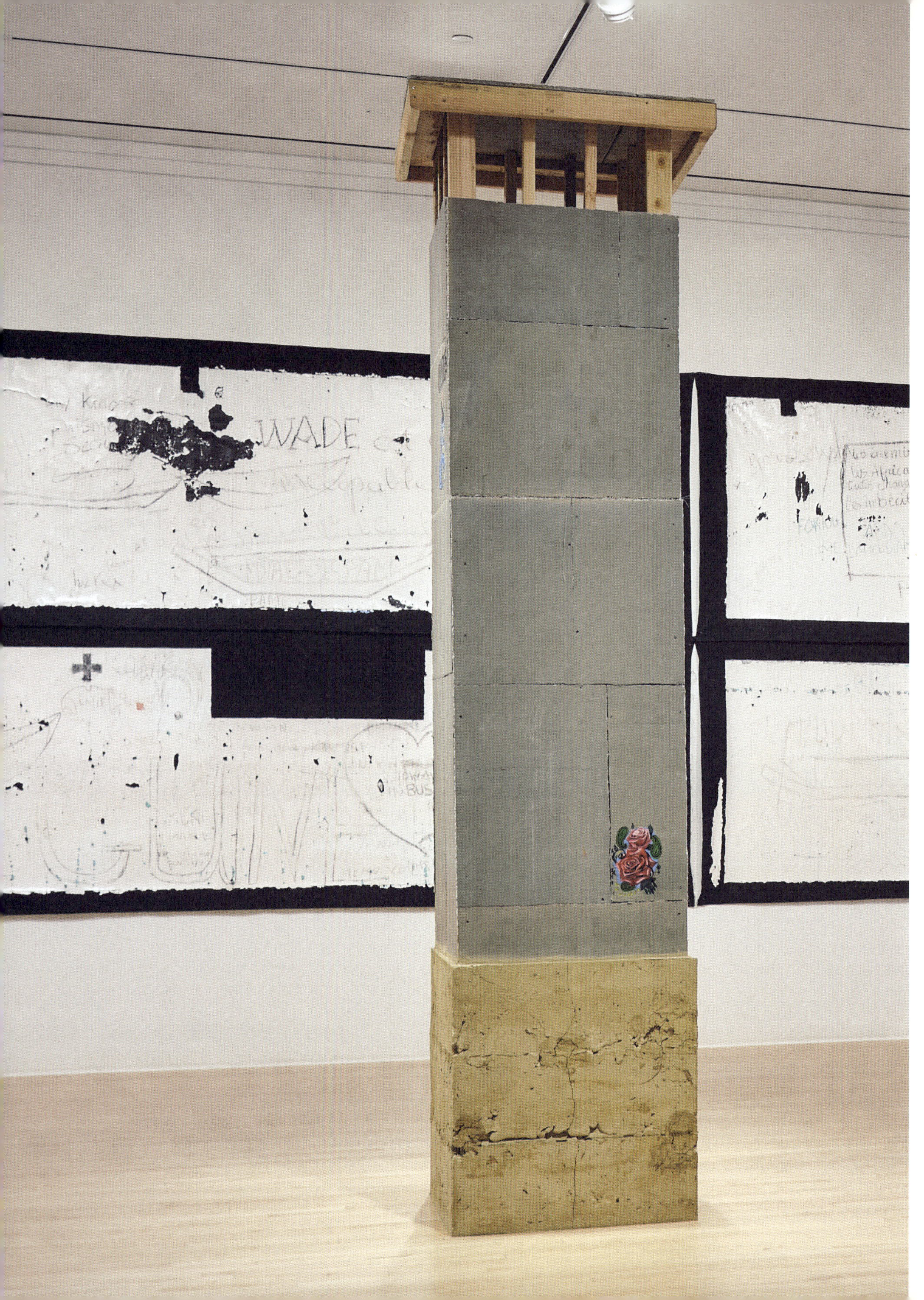

Introduction:
Seeing through Stone

Gina Dent, Lauren Schell Dickens, and Rachel Nelson

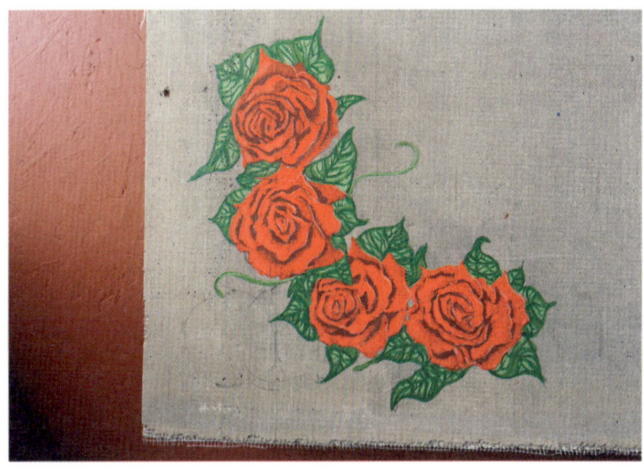

He sees through stone
he has the secret eyes
—Etheridge Knight, "He Sees through Stone"[1]

A twelve-foot prison surveillance tower anchors each of the three sites of the sweeping exhibition *Seeing through Stone*: the Institute of the Arts and Sciences (IAS) at the University of California, Santa Cruz; the San José Museum of Art (SJMA); and Santa Cruz Barrios Unidos (SCBU). The towers are constructed of concrete walls with compressed dirt as their support. Over the course of the exhibition, these surveillance towers are transformed—their gray concrete walls disappear beneath vividly colored paintings collectively made from the wall murals that enliven SCBU, a culturally oriented community organization run by formerly incarcerated and system-impacted people, or by artists participating in workshops there. The multi-site artwork, *Tres Terrenos*, was born of a series of workshops at SCBU led by artist Caleb Duarte as part of the regular community-building practices of the center, which also operates a food pantry, a tiny-house village, reentry services, a recording studio, education spaces, after-school programs, and more to create a space of belonging—a home—for those who have been marginalized. *Tres Terrenos* brings aspects of the care work done at SCBU into material form. Green leaves and flowers bloom across the concrete. Hands clasp in solidarity. And towers built to control and divide are transformed, reshaped by the actions of the people into beacons of hope.

Tres Terrenos materializes the world-building work of prison abolition. In this context, the word "prison" references different kinds of carceral institutions, including not only prisons but also jails, penitentiaries, detention centers, and the legal systems that support them. The prison abolition movement advocates for the end of all carceral institutions because of the relationship between prisons (understood here in the term's broad usage) and historical systems of racism, economic disenfranchisement, and heteropatriarchy. The idea of abolition is sometimes dismissed as utopian, because it is difficult to imagine prisons as anything less than a permanent fixture of society. Yet with *Tres Terrenos*, as guard towers become beacons of social transformation, what comes into view is a surprisingly clear vision of the possibilities for abolition. As this collective artwork reminds us, abolitionists are committed to doing the hard work of shifting public perceptions of existing systems to create a world without these structures of unfreedom. They do this even as they work to create new social, economic, political, and aesthetic conditions that do not re-create historical oppressions.

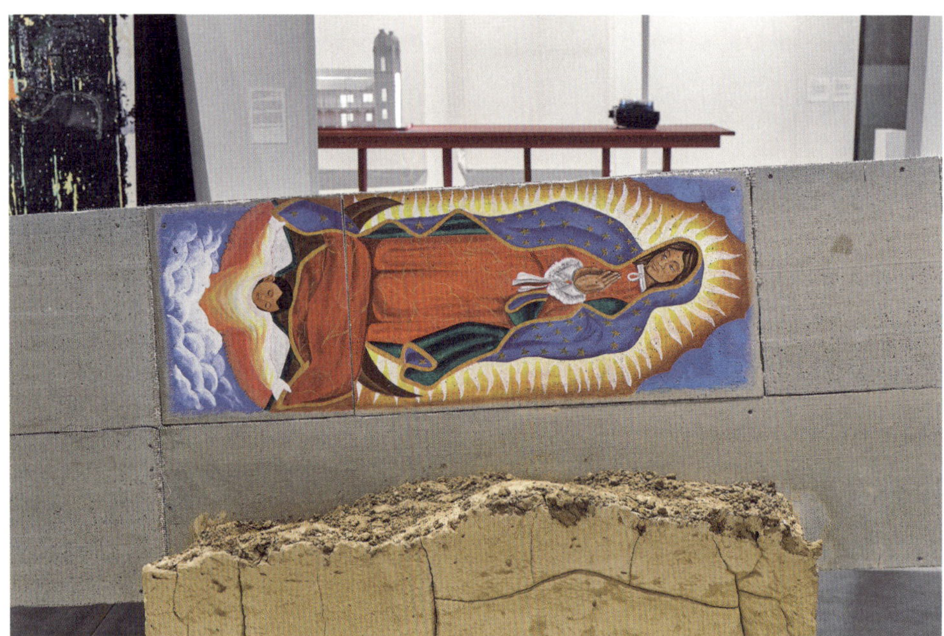

Caleb Duarte with Santa Cruz Barrios Unidos, *Tres Terrenos* (detail), 2024. Courtesy of the artist and Santa Cruz Barrios Unidos.

Tres Terrenos is one of sixteen newly commissioned artworks in the exhibition, which includes works by over eighty artists. Together, these works begin to map what some refer to as the "expanding constellation" of prison abolition—the organizing, dreaming, world-making, and activism that offer ways to see and live apart from carceral structures. The participating artists work in different contexts and forms, including social practice and conceptual aesthetics, and also circulate differently, with some primarily sharing their work with loved ones inside and outside of prisons and others exhibiting in galleries, museums, and global biennials. Although this might seem an unlikely gathering of artists, they are united by the critical importance they place on communities and collaborative orbits. *Seeing through Stone* responds to this shared emphasis. The making of the exhibition was itself a way to nurture global communities, facilitating introductions between artists working in different parts of the world and under different conditions, building solidarity for future work. It was undertaken as part of the larger art and education initiative Visualizing Abolition, housed at UC Santa Cruz and grounded in the methodologies of the prison abolition movement. Exhibitions and programs are created in collaboration with the SJMA, SCBU, and other organizations and individuals to explore possible (if imperfect) modes of institutional collectivity as alternatives to standard practices that prioritize the interests of individuals and single organizations. Reflecting the values of the abolitionist movement, and negotiating complicated prison bureaucracies, *Seeing through Stone* centers those most impacted by the criminal legal system, bringing them together with a vibrant and growing consortium of people outside of prisons to collectively imagine new worlds.

The exhibition takes its title from the poem "He Sees through Stone," written by Etheridge Knight in 1968, while he was being held in the Indiana State Prison. In the poem, Knight writes of the one who has "secret eyes" and is able to see through the opacity of stone, grasping the true nature of these institutions. What does it mean to see inside of prisons—to really see and hear the people held in cages? What does it mean for incarcerated people to see out and beyond, to a world without walls? Following Knight's provocation, the exhibition is organized to highlight creative practices taking place both inside and outside of prisons, as well as across prison walls. We have eschewed some of the tropes of representation that are commonly used by prison reform initiatives—for example, an emphasis on portraiture or figuration—to avoid reinscribing labor on particular bodies and reducing structural harms to narratives of individual guilt and redemption. Instead, we focus on the act, process,

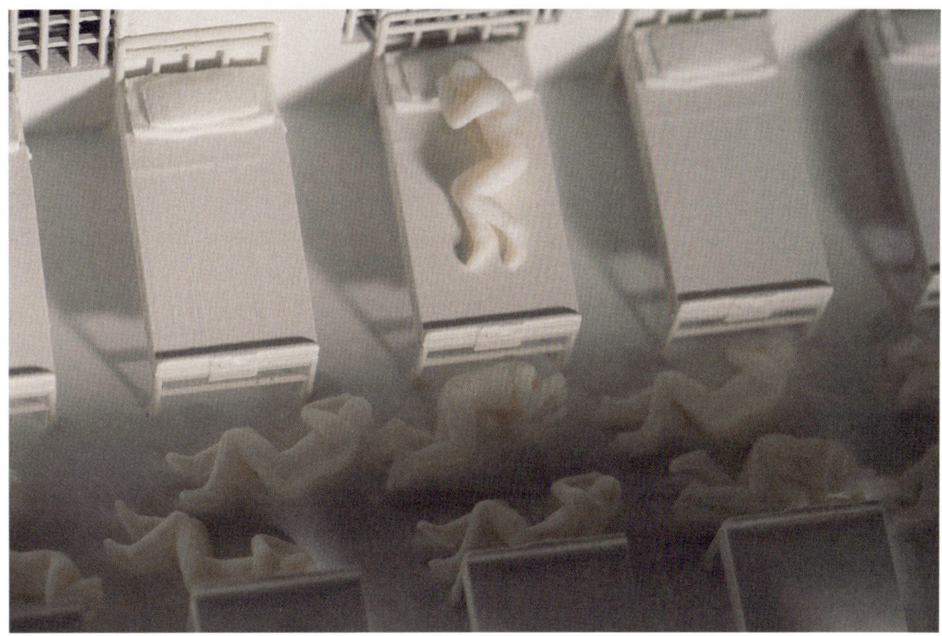

Sofia Karim, *Memories of Kerani-ganj Jail* (detail), 2019. Courtesy of the artist.

and practice of seeing, bringing together artists and artworks that cultivate a collective, global vision of a world otherwise, built on non-carceral values and logics. Through creative practices of social infrastructure building, like the work of SCBU, as well as more poetic and conceptual projects engaging an aesthetics of abolition, these artists use their "secret eyes" to bring into sight the imaginative and practical efforts flourishing around us.

The relationship between prisons and perception —including, as some in visual culture studies have argued, even the physical act of seeing—is complex. Scholar and curator Nicole Fleetwood points out that "prison thrives on limiting the field of vision of imprisoned people and the nonincarcerated public":[2]

The carceral state not only removes people from their homes and neighborhoods [but] also shapes how prisons and people confined to them are viewed in public life. This power to reveal and to hide prisons and the imprisoned has an enormous influence on how the larger public comes to understand the function of the prison and to justify the removal and incapacitation of millions.[3]

The organized and delimited field of vision that Fleetwood describes is key to the machinations of the criminal legal system. Prisons and the people held within them are disappeared from sight, based both on the location of facilities in rural regions and on the outsize impact on the most minoritized populations. At the same time, prisons and crime are spectacularized through televisual, filmic, and other entertainment media, shaping the public perception both of how these systems work and of the people they enclose.

The artists in *Seeing through Stone* challenge this dynamic, bringing into view that which is made to vanish behind prison walls while also troubling the popular representations that allow people to unsee the deep social harms of these systems. Timothy James Young's *Disposition*, for instance, is a record of the systemic oppression hidden within the bureaucracy of the criminal legal system. The title of the work refers to the legal meaning of the word in the United States: a disposition on a criminal record is the current status or final outcome of an arrest or prosecution. Young has created a disposition against this system by compiling some of the writs and grievances he has filed over his almost three decades of incarceration in the San Quentin State Prison (recently renamed the San Quentin Rehabilitation Center) to request medical care, adequate legal representation, and repairs to his property damaged by prison guards.

Khalid Qasim, *Untitled*, 2016, from the Tea Project's *Ode to the Sea*, 2023/24. Instant coffee and paint on paper, 17 × 14 in. Courtesy of Khalid Qasim's attorney, Shelby Sullivan-Bennis.

Sofia Karim, a practicing architect, works from a place of practicalities—concerned with gravity, structural endurance, and building regulations—to create a space of architectural care and reimagining. Made in collaboration with her uncle, photographer and activist Shahidul Alam, *Memories of Keraniganj Jail* is a detailed rendering of the time Alam spent as a political prisoner in Bangladesh, comprising small 3D-printed models made from his descriptions of the jail. One model depicts a cell in which individuals are made to lie, according to Alam, like "packed sardines," vividly evoking the now familiar historical images of slave ships—forging another link between geographies, struggles, and times. Another model reveals an overflowing prison hospital. Beyond re-creating the oppressive spaces and revealing the workings of systems normally hidden, the models revel in tiny details, such as the shelves Alam improvised in his cell to serve as bird feeders, that resist the built environment of repression.

The global scope of the exhibition, of which Karim's depiction of the prison in Bangladesh is just one example, is a reflection of the proliferation of carceral conditions: there are 11.5 million people in prisons worldwide, a number that only grows when considering all carceral forms. *Seeing through Stone* takes as its premise the understanding that the world is being violently stitched together through prisons, refugee camps, detention centers, and surveillance infrastructures fueled by global capitalism. Carceral systems do not take identical forms across the globe, yet they are often shaped by the same contours and through coordinated systems; the well-documented relationship between prisons, racism, and poverty in the United States is not an isolated phenomenon. Prisons are part of the widespread politics of disposability that has become a global export through histories of colonialism, slavery, Indigenous dispossession, and genocide, normalizing the lack of social welfare and systems of care available to people marginalized by class, race, gender, sexuality, ability, and other factors. The exhibition also acknowledges that carceral systems and military systems are deeply intertwined—hence the evolution from a focus on the term "military-industrial complex" to the development of an analysis of the prison-industrial complex. The movement for prison abolition is connected to struggles worldwide against war, military operations, and ongoing colonial violence. In Palestine, as an urgent example, the use of collective punishment by the State of Israel manifests not only in obscene rates of incarceration (since 1967, Israel has detained approximately one million Palestinians in the occupied territory, including tens of thousands of children) but also in the wholesale, genocidal

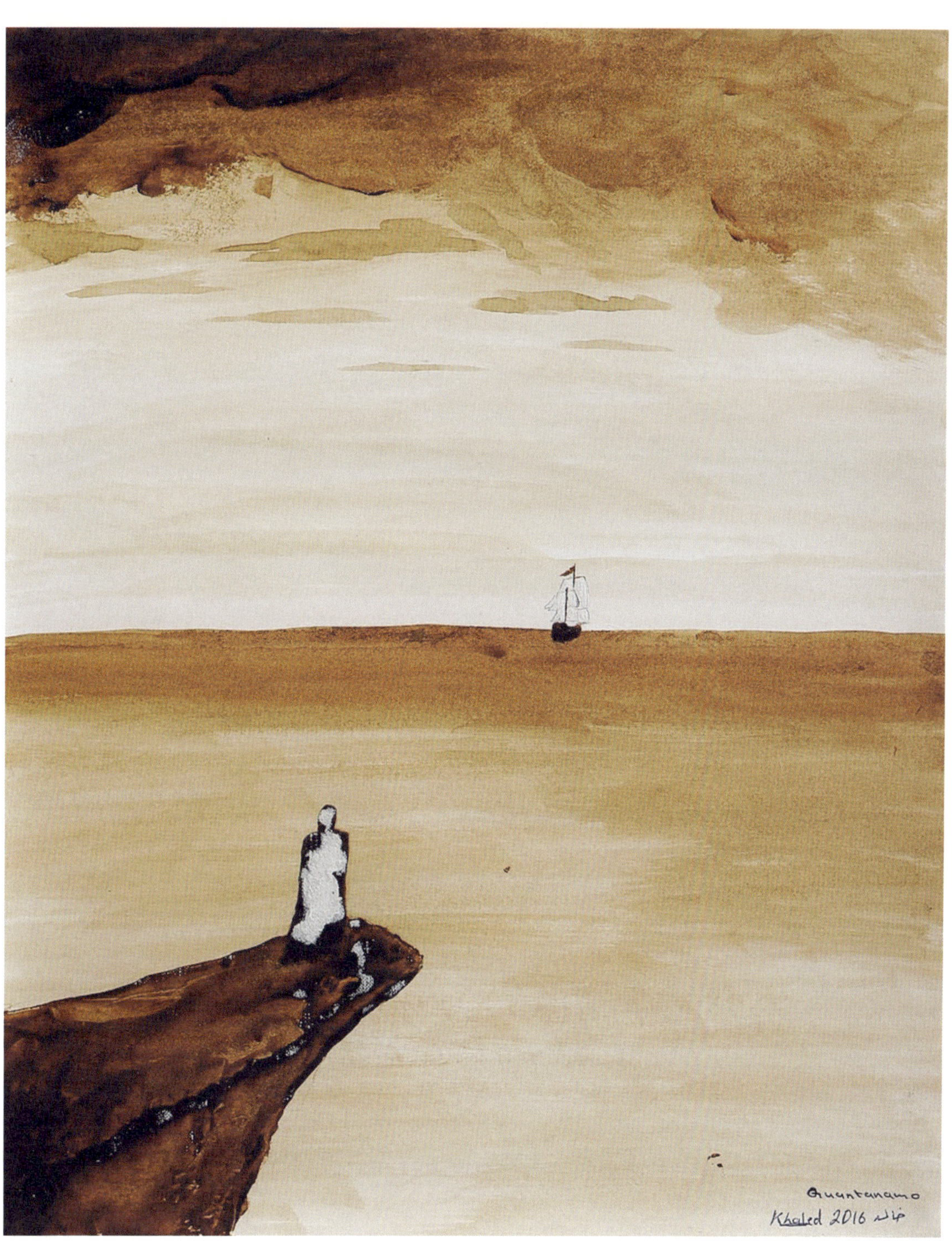

Quantanamo
Khaled 2016 خالد

militarized assault on Gaza and the occupied territory that is unfolding even as we write.[4]

Reflecting this global complexity and deepening our understanding of it, some of the artworks in *Seeing through Stone* are highly localized and historically specific—such as the video work by The Freedom Theatre, a Palestinian community-based theater and cultural center located in the Jenin refugee camp in the northern part of the West Bank, which not only calls attention to the situation in Palestine but also allows us to glimpse the practice of freedom-making under some of the most dire circumstances. For *Your Time Is Not Your Time*, members of The Freedom Theatre staged a conversation while Jenin was under siege, risking their lives to talk about their experiences with incarceration and living under occupation as a challenge to the ways of life imposed on them. Cian Dayrit's work with landless farmworkers in the Philippines has a similarly unflinching focus. Through elaborate tapestries and other works, Dayrit connects the three-hundred-year Spanish colonial period in the Philippines with its contemporary vestiges: peasant farming communities denied access to their legally owned agricultural land. *Feudal Fields II: Tinang*, Dayrit's most recent tapestry, diagrams a protest in 2022 in which farmers and activists uprooted cash crops and replaced them with food crops in Hacienda Tinang, a sugarcane plantation in the province of Tarlac. The protest led to the arrest of some ninety people, including the artist.

Other artists map global constellations within their projects. Working as the Tea Project, Amber Ginsburg and Aaron Hughes collaborate with artists currently or formerly held in Guantánamo Bay to trace the ongoing ties between the military prison and Chicago's jails, while São Paulo–based collective Frente 3 de Fevereiro connects public collective actions and protests against racism and police brutality in Brazil to similar events in Haiti, Colombia, and the United States. And the difficult work of forging and sustaining transnational solidarities is taken up by Explode! Platform (Cláudio Bueno and João Simões), also based in São Paulo. For their intervention at the IAS, the collective collaborated with other Brazilian activists and artists working against carceral systems to select books in Portuguese about prisons and abolition in Brazil. These books, with select passages emphasized, have been introduced into the institute's existing collection of books about the same subjects in the United States, foregrounding the untranslatability, nuance, and opacity of concepts produced in geopolitically specific contexts.

Without eliding the different contexts in which these works operate, *Seeing through Stone* casts an intentionally wide net, gathering together the many strands and locations, peoples and movements, that constitute abolitionism. Moving from artwork to artwork, struggle to struggle, the exhibition argues that the historical trajectories that have led to contemporary prisons must be understood—and disrupted—if abolition is to be realized. The act of seeing through stone does not render the stone invisible; rather, it calls attention to its structure, weight, and mineral composition as we bore holes through it.

This resonates with the relationship between critique and liberation that Robin D. G. Kelley articulates in his influential 2002 text, *Freedom Dreams*, which he updated in 2022. In the original text, historicizing Black radical struggles for liberation, Kelley wrote, "The map to a new world is in the imagination, in what we see in our third eyes rather than in the desolation that surrounds us."[5] Twenty years later, he added a starkly worded reminder that while a "new world" might be found in the imagination, it necessarily also comes from a critique and a nuanced understanding of what produces the surrounding desolation:

It is not enough to imagine a world without oppression (especially since we don't always recognize the ways we ourselves practice and perpetuate oppression). We must also understand the mechanisms or processes that not only reproduce subjugation and exploitation but make them common sense and render them natural. . . . Freedom dreams are born of fascist nightmares, or better yet, born against fascist nightmares.[6]

Many of the artworks in *Seeing through Stone* lay bare the conditions—the sometimes overlooked ideas, institutions, and ideologies—that enable carceral structures to exist. But these works also refute the permanence and immutability of prisons. Despite the relatively short history of the modern prison, these structures have thrived through the myth that justice and carceral punishment are inseparable. How often do people ask, when confronted by ideas of abolition, "But what will we do with the rapists and murderers?" The mere repetition of this question renders prisons ever more permanent. There is a reinforced perception that prisons have always been—and always will be—the solution to harm. Yet as abolitionists have argued for decades, backed by the centuries of research and data that have accompanied prison building, reform, and expansion, the prison has not brought an end to such violence. Instead, the prison causes inordinate further harms.

Against the persistent inability to see the frailty of carceral logic, the artists and collectives in *Seeing through Stone* question the apparent permanence of prisons. Patricia Gómez and María Jesús González archive the interiors of closed and deactivated prison buildings and abandoned immigrant detention centers in Spain and West Africa. Using a technique from architectural mural preservation, the artists peel off the painted surfaces of the walls of these closed institutions, transforming the structures into ghostly skins— remnants bearing the traces of graffiti, the names, hopes, and protests written on the walls by the people held within them. These walls made into skin bear material witness: prisons close, their walls fall.

Maria Gaspar used jail cell bars claimed from the demolition of the Division I building of the Cook County Department of Corrections in Chicago to create two works: the sculptural work *Invisible Things Are Not Necessarily Not-There (after T.M.)* and the performance work *We Lit the Fire and Trusted the Heat (After Angela Davis)*. To make the first work, Gaspar arranged glass casts of those bars, emphasizing and reclaiming their fragility; in the second, she collaborates with musicians who play the salvaged iron bars, quite literally making music from the rubble of the prison. In this way, both works emphasize and make visible the transitory nature of the entire system. On a molecular level, as iron alloys resonate, they vibrate with motion, temporarily dislodged from their rigid materiality. Artist collective Timesfive (jackie sumell and Moira Murdock) expands on this ability of iron to transform, returning it to

ferrous oxide before transforming it into steel, bronze, titanium, or even a rich blue pigment. Prison bars *could* be Prussian blue paint—there are other ways of being.

Through delicate manipulations of ideas and materials, the artists in the exhibition reveal the cracks and seams of carceral histories and logics. So, too, do the artists begin to draw out what Kelley calls "the map to a new world," found in the collective resistances to oppression that have taken place across centuries. In the multimedia work *At Pelican Falls*, Rebecca Belmore reclaims the history of the Pelican Falls Indian Residential School in Sioux Lookout, Ontario, which operated from 1929 through 1969 as part of the historical dispossession and genocide that can be considered the original carceral system in North America. Belmore references this history to also reflect the deep and ongoing resistance that has transformed these former carceral classrooms into a First Nations–controlled and operated high school.

Other works powerfully engage oppressive racial histories. Two works by Charles Gaines look to the insidious *Dred Scott* decision—in which the US Supreme Court ruled that enslaved people were not citizens of the United States—to chart a changed world. In *Manifestos 4*, Gaines converted the texts of the justices' majority and minority opinions into musical notation, with each letter of the alphabet corresponding to a

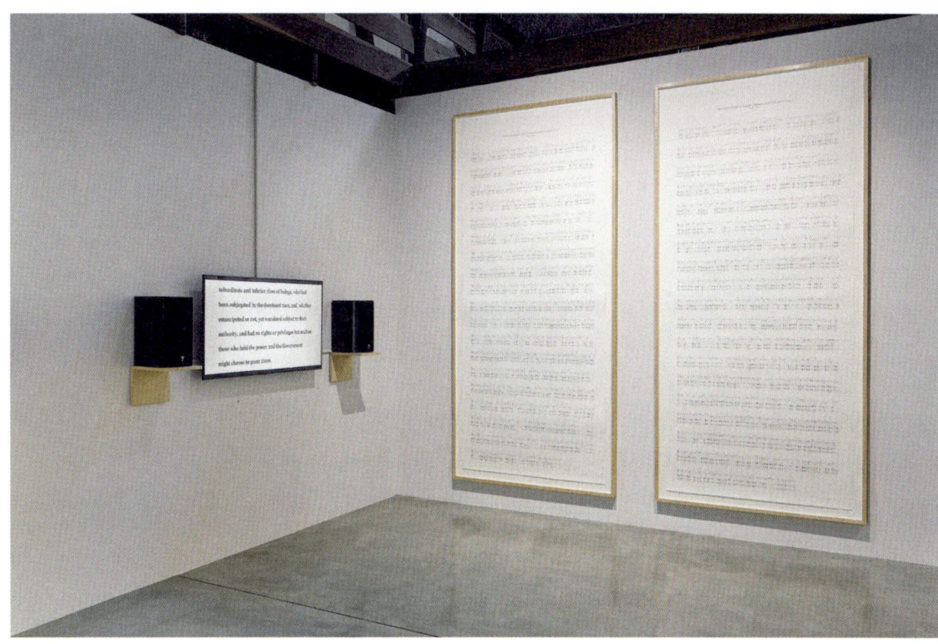

Charles Gaines, *Manifestos 4* (detail), 2020. San Francisco Museum of Modern Art. Purchase through a gift of Amy and David Abrams, Jim DeMare, Sarah and Jason DiLullo, Randi and Bob Fisher, Danielle and David Ganek, Peggy Yeoh Lee, Michael and Jodi Price, Jonas Prince, Lu Zhou, and the International Contemporary Accessions Committee at SFMOMA.

specific note, re-creating the legal arguments as a soaring aural experience. In *Sky Box II*, legal processes and testimonies that led up to the famous decision are similarly translated, or dissipated into a starry night sky. As words dissolve into music in one instance and, in the other, into a celestial sky, the works lay bare the process of how meaning is constructed, and how emotional experiences of music and awe can be fabricated or wielded to justify unrelated ends. Laying bare constructs, revealing how they are assembled, is an important first step in demonstrating that these constructions can also be unbuilt.

In a scathing critique of Brazil's rates of incarceration for Black women, Brazilian scholar and anti-prison activist Denise Carrascosa calls prison "the eye of the sinkhole that marks the limit of humanity—an abyss that one neither wants to nor can behold."[7] Prison orients sensory life, acting as a limit to perception. This is most obvious behind prison walls, where sight, sound, touch, taste, and smell are dulled. Yet none of the artists in *Seeing through Stone* accept these limitations, nor the social relations that support such limited ways of seeing. The expansive world imagined in their artworks is built on cooperation and collectivity rather than individualism, and on mutual thriving rather than self-preservation. It reflects the long, slow work of abolition, reenvisioning and rebuilding social relations and institutions unbound by the multiple ways in which our bodies, minds, and actions have been shaped by the ideas and practices of imprisonment.

Robert Hillary King, for instance, spent thirty-one years in the Louisiana State Penitentiary, twenty-nine of those in solitary confinement. This might seem the very definition of the abyss. Yet it was in prison that King began making *Freelines*, the praline candies included in *Seeing through Stone*. Refusing the social isolation and division that prisons produce, even when locked in a six-by-nine-foot cell, King brought what he calls "the taste of freedom" to the people (including those on death row) with whom he shared the candies.[8] Frank Alejandrez's intricately carved wooden walking sticks, which he gifts to elders in his community, likewise manifest a lesson he learned over his more than two decades of incarceration: that regardless of how carceral institutions try to limit social relations, no one has to walk alone. And in her filmic work, Steffani Jemison poetically draws on historic episodes with Black acrobatic figures to imagine new forms of social dependency and support. In slow, meditative shots, bodies contort and stretch into structures of mutual aid, where freedom is found with, rather than from, one another.

Against the abyss of the prison system, the artworks in *Seeing through Stone* show that abolition involves recalibrating our eyes and reorienting our

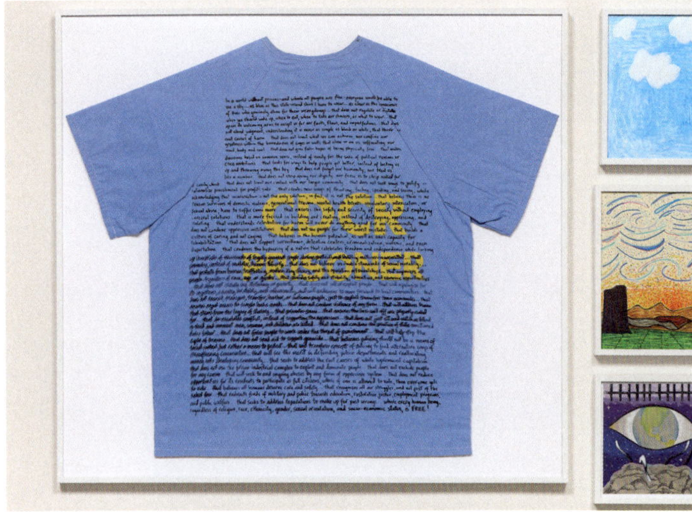
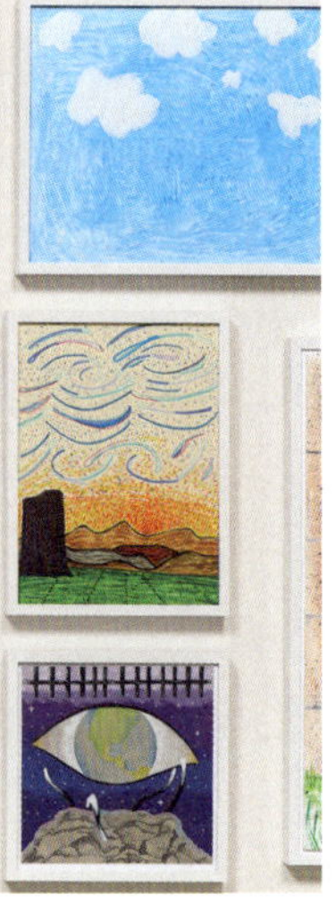
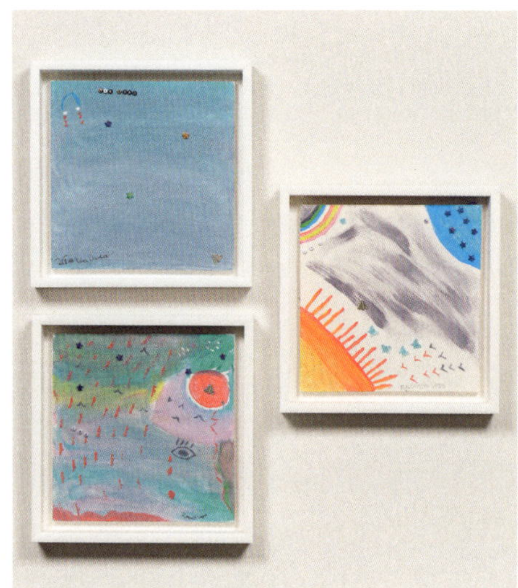

senses to recognize what might seem unfamiliar—reconceiving the world we inhabit through the myriad connections, dependencies, responsibilities, and social relations that carceral institutions sever. To return to Etheridge Knight's poem quoted in the epigraph to this chapter, the one who "sees through stone" does so from "under prison skies," and this paradox lies at the heart of this exhibition.

Another sky, hanging above a world without prisons, comes into view in a collective work created by almost fifty artists who are currently incarcerated in the United States, Brazil, and Australia. While the ability to see the sky can seem fundamental to the human condition, many incarcerated people are denied a view of the sky unmarred by bars and wire for years, if not decades. In recognition of this reality, we asked artists inside carceral institutions how they imagined a sky without prisons. Arrangements of the assorted drawings, paintings, and other works made in response are displayed in each of the three exhibition venues, to form a shared vision of a sky that is no longer artificially divided. For one of these works, Aimee Gana instructed us to use as a canvas the blue prison uniform that she wears daily, musing on what it might mean to wear the sky and embody freedom. Her words were screen-printed on a (counterfeit) California Department of Corrections and Rehabilitation uniform shirt. Mark A.

Cadiz painted a figure joyfully shouting through a gaping hole in a wall, while Christopher "Khalifah" Christensen depicted the back of a figure in a yoga warrior pose while a nearby stone wall dissolves into sky. In a pencil drawing by an unnamed artist, turbulent skies and seas meet at a craggy horizon. The visions are personal, but together they form one sky and one vision of the shared work required to imagine, and to build, a world without prisons.

Resistance is not a solitary action. Solitary confinement is torture. The imagination creates reality. Let us transform our witnessing into collective action and meaningful solidarity.

Multiple artists, *In a world without prisons, everyone would be able to see the sky* (details), 2024. Courtesy of the artists.

1. Etheridge Knight, "He Sees through Stone," in *The Essential Etheridge Knight* (Pittsburgh, PA: University of Pittsburgh Press, 1986).

2. Nicole R. Fleetwood, *Marking Time: Art in the Age of Mass Incarceration* (Cambridge, MA: Harvard University Press, 2020), 15.

3. Fleetwood, *Marking Time*, 14.

4. "Special Rapporteur Says Israel's Unlawful Carceral Practices in the Occupied Palestinian Territory Are Tantamount to International Crimes and Have Turned It into an Open-Air Prison," Office of the United Nations High Commissioner for Human Rights, July 7, 2023, https://www.ohchr.org/en /news/2023/07/special-rapporteur -says-israels-unlawful-carceral -practices-occupied-palestinian.

5. Robin D. G. Kelley, *Freedom Dreams: The Black Radical Imagination* (Boston: Beacon Press, 2002).

6. Robin D. G. Kelley, "Twenty Years of Freedom Dreams," *Boston Review*, August 1, 2022, https://www.bostonreview.net /articles/twenty-years-of-freedom -dreams/. Adapted from the twentieth-anniversary edition of *Freedom Dreams: The Black Radical Imagination*, by Robin D. G. Kelley (Boston: Beacon Press, 2022).

7. Denise Carrascosa, "I'm Not an Animal, I Am a Woman!" *NACLA Report on the Americas* 54, no. 2 (2022): 226–30.

8. Robert Hillary King, interview by Rachel Nelson, December 2023.

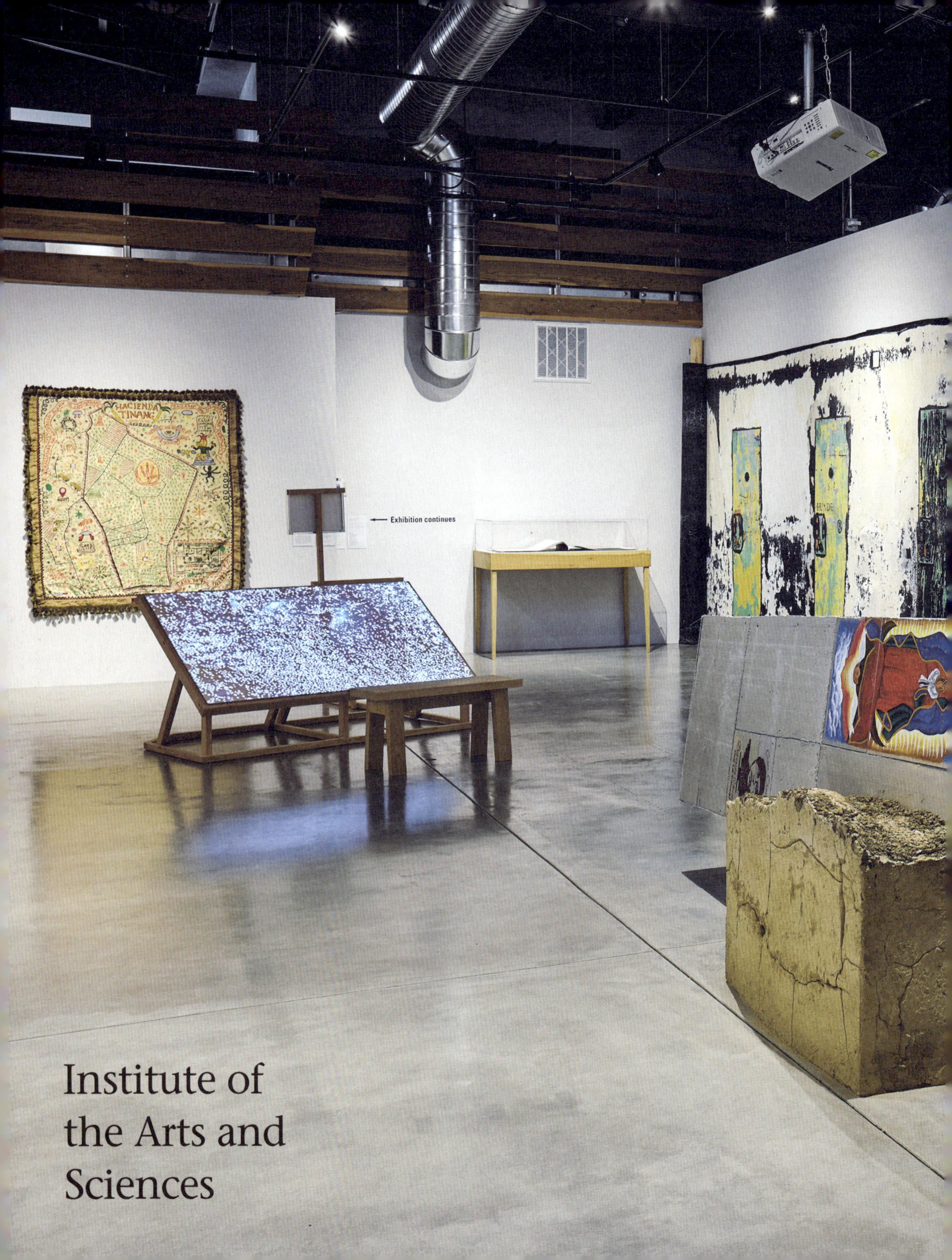

Institute of
the Arts and
Sciences

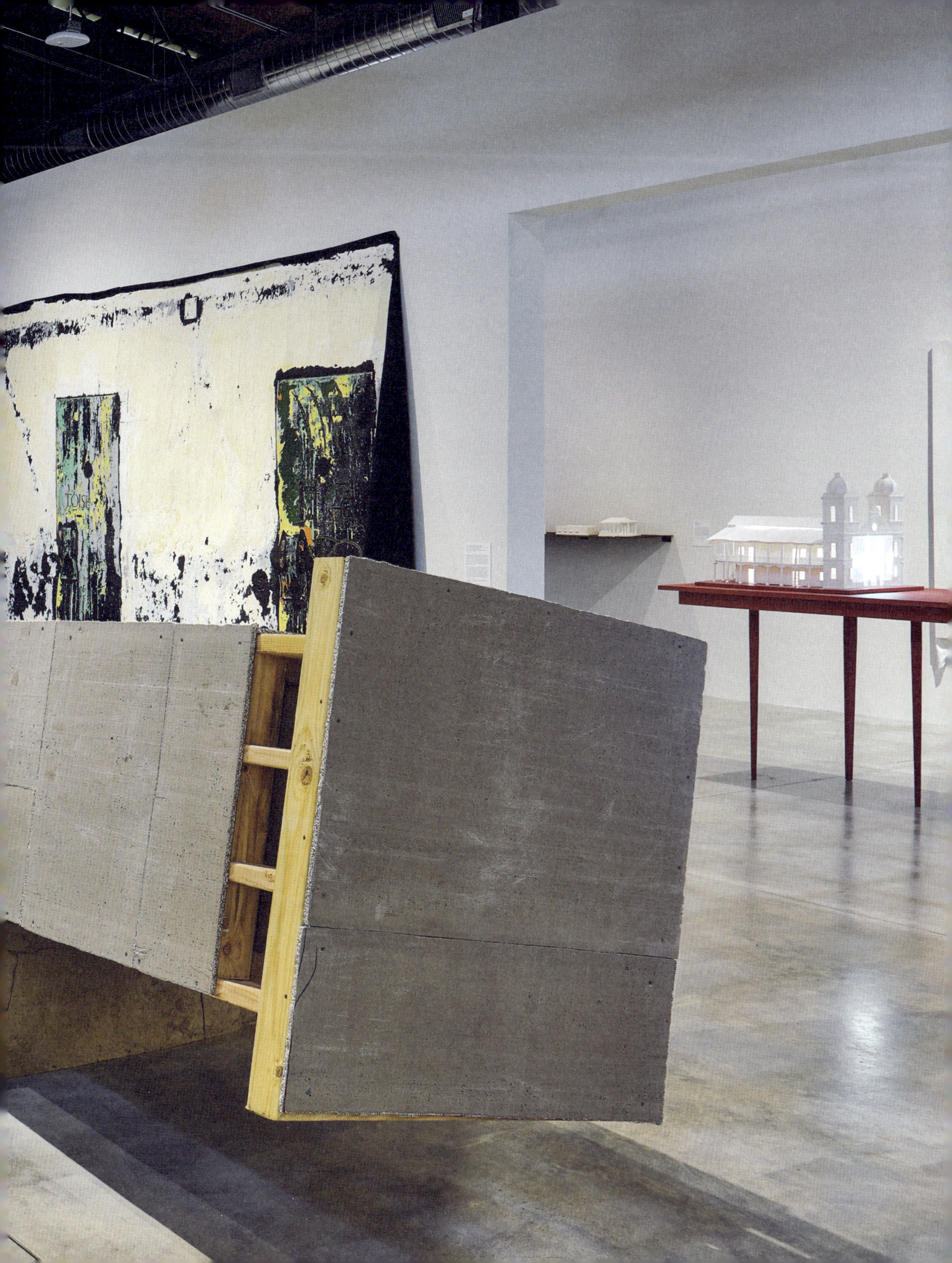

Seeing through Stone

He sees through stone
he has the secret eyes
this old black one
who under prison skies
sits pressed by the sun
against the western wall
his pipe between purple gums

—Etheridge Knight, 1968

Prisons are so ingrained in history and the cultural imagination as to appear inevitable. From current structures of prisons, jails, and immigrant detention centers to past manifestations, such as Native American boarding schools and American chattel slavery, our world is bound together by carceral structures that equate punishment with justice. Yet as long as prisons have existed, alternatives to prison have also flourished. When poet Etheridge Knight (1931–1991) wrote from Indiana State Prison in 1968 of "seeing through stone," he evoked the secret eyes of those able to see beyond the realities of prison to a world otherwise.

The over eighty artists and collectives in *Seeing Through Stone* see otherwise. Sharing a capacity for radical sight, they include currently and formerly incarcerated artists alongside those without that lived experience from different sociopolitical contexts around the globe. Their projects include supporting creative networks in Guantanamo, educating youth in Rio de Janeiro, and organizing landless farmers in the Philippines, as well as more poetic and conceptual projects engaging an aesthetics of abolition. Their work brings into view a world where people seek safety with, rather than from, one another; where medicine grows from prison manure and land is cultivated for food, not capital; where blue finally means sky.

In sixteen newly commissioned projects, alongside other works of video, painting, sculpture, installation, sound, and performance, across three exhibition sites, *Seeing Through Stone* provides a model of hope in practice. The exhibition is a celebration of the expanding constellation of abolition: the organizing, dreaming, worldmaking, and creative activism around the globe that offers ways to see—and live—differently.

Seeing Through Stone is a collaboration between the Institute of the Arts and Sciences at University of California, Santa Cruz, San José Museum of Art, and Santa Cruz Barrios Unidos, and works are on view at all three sites.

The exhibition is co-curated by Gina Dent, Lauren Schell Dickens, and Rachel Nelson, as part of Visualizing Abolition, an ongoing series exploring justice, prisons, and art, with exhibitions co-organized by the Institute of the Arts and Sciences and San José Museum of Art.

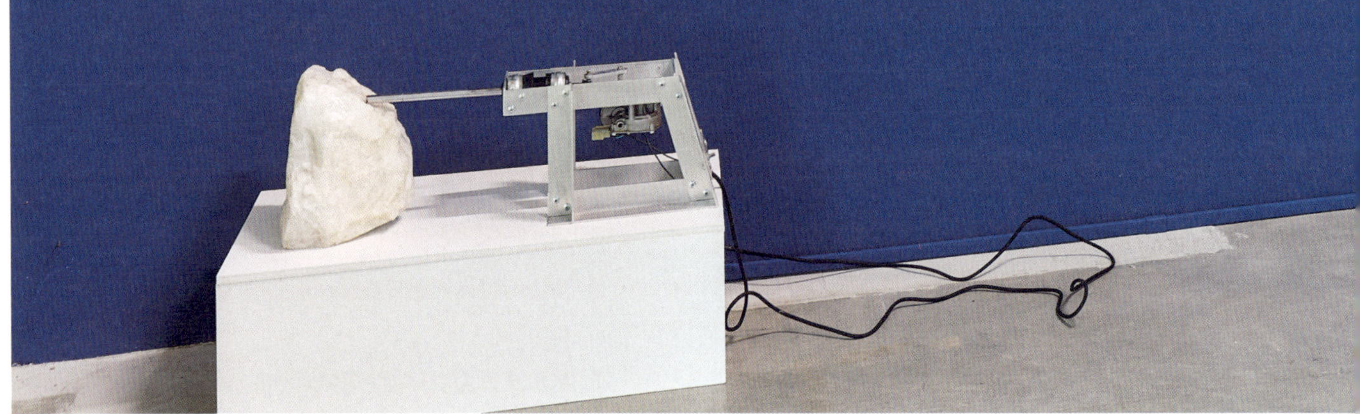

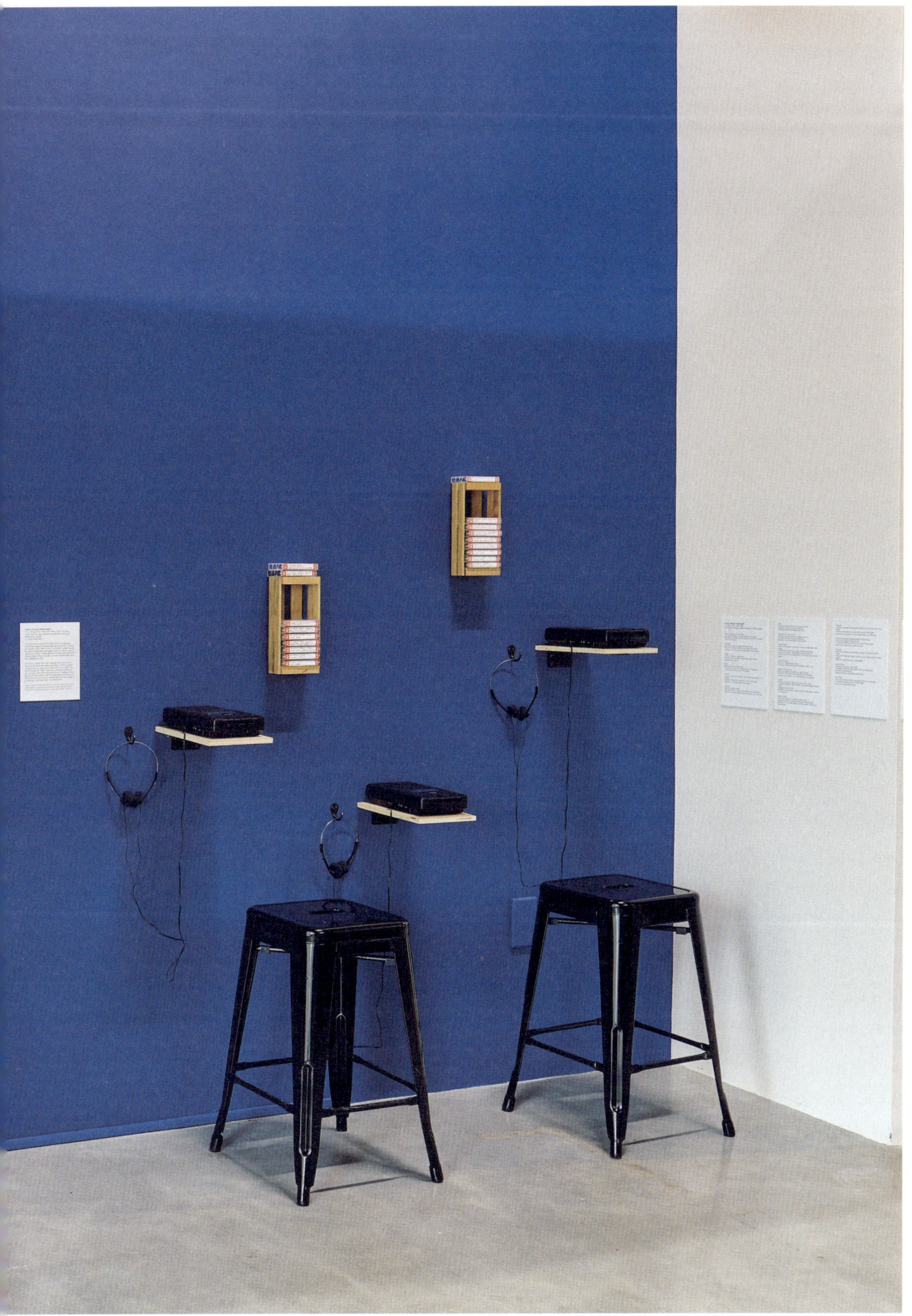

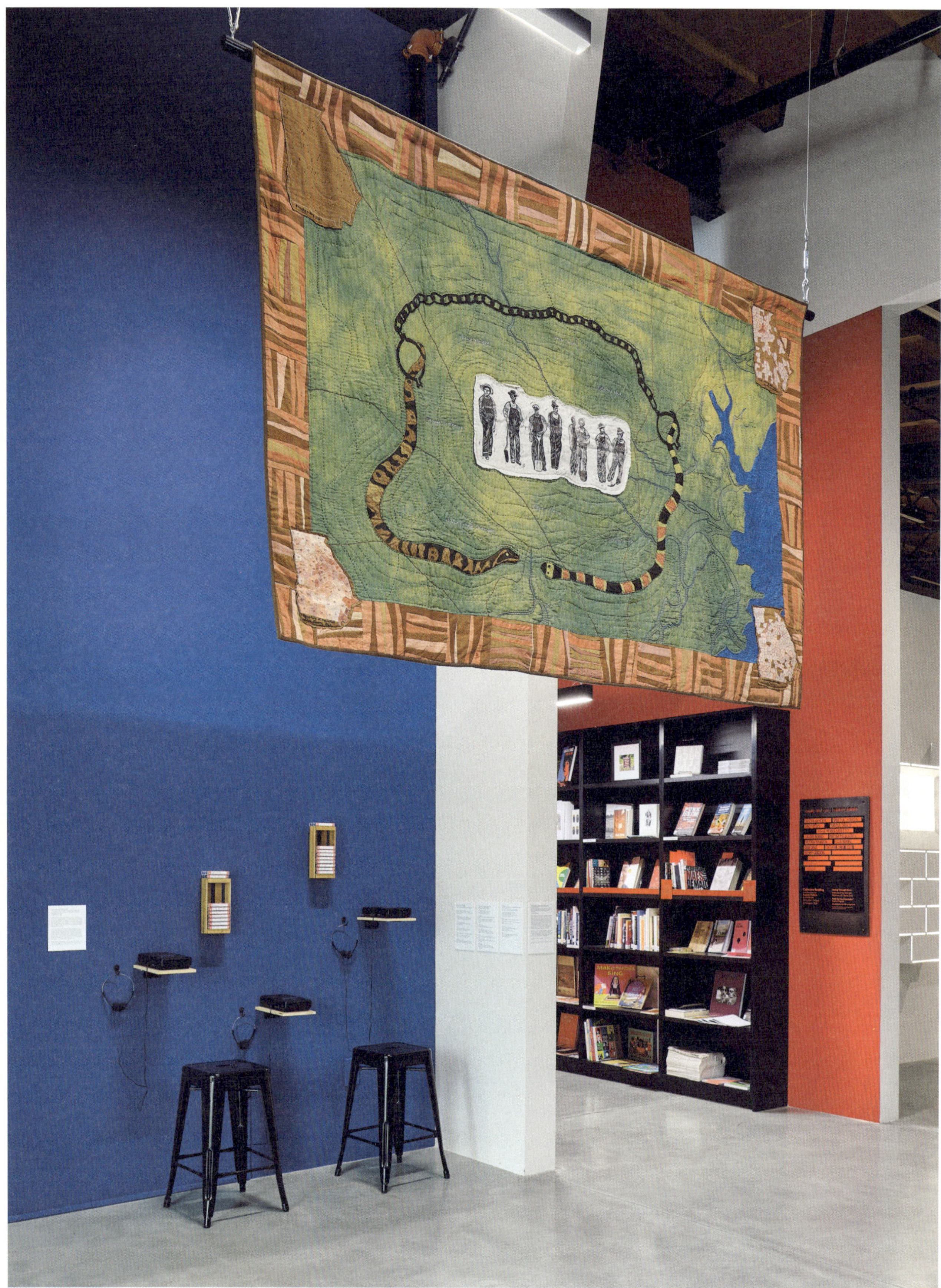

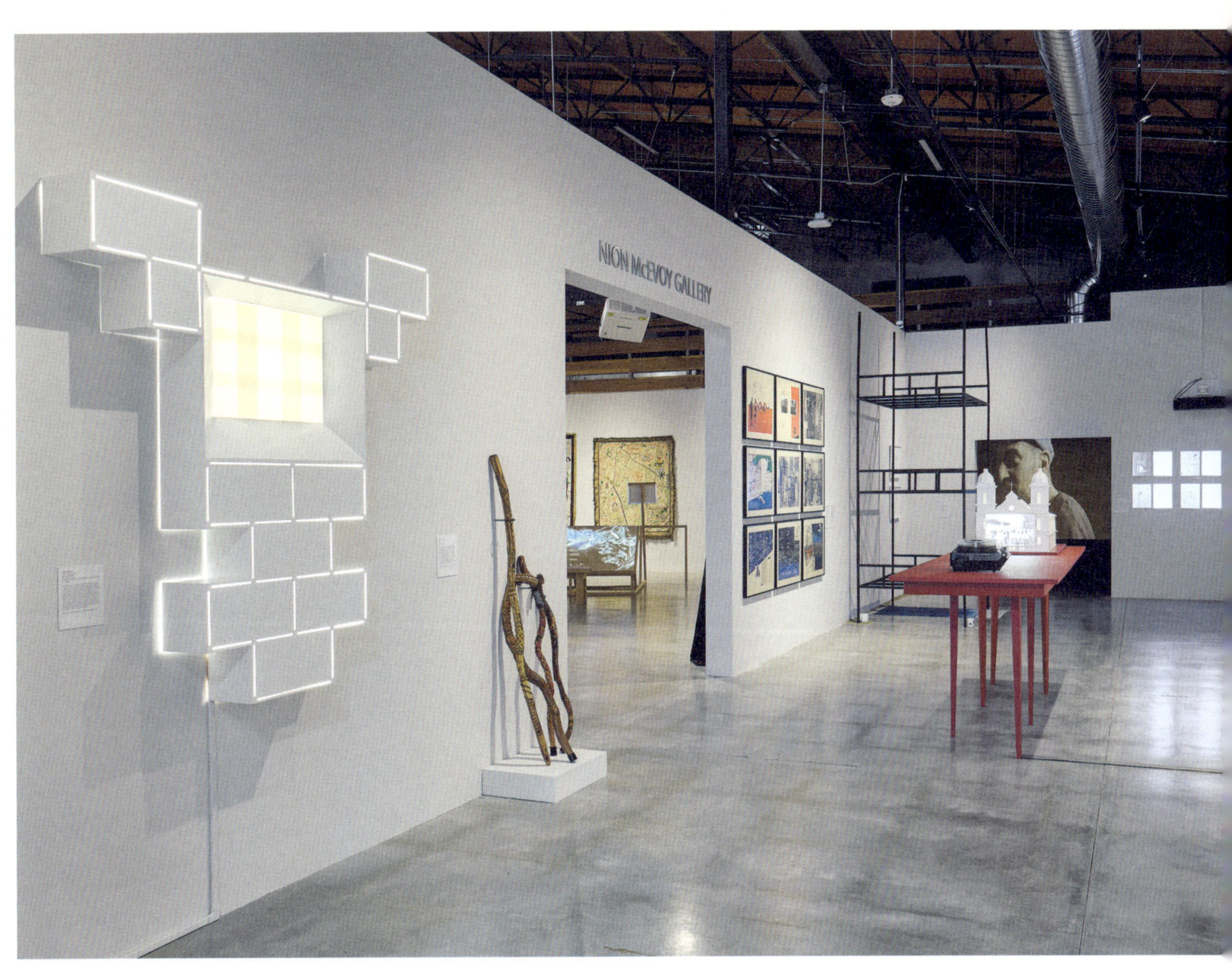

NION McEVOY GALLERY

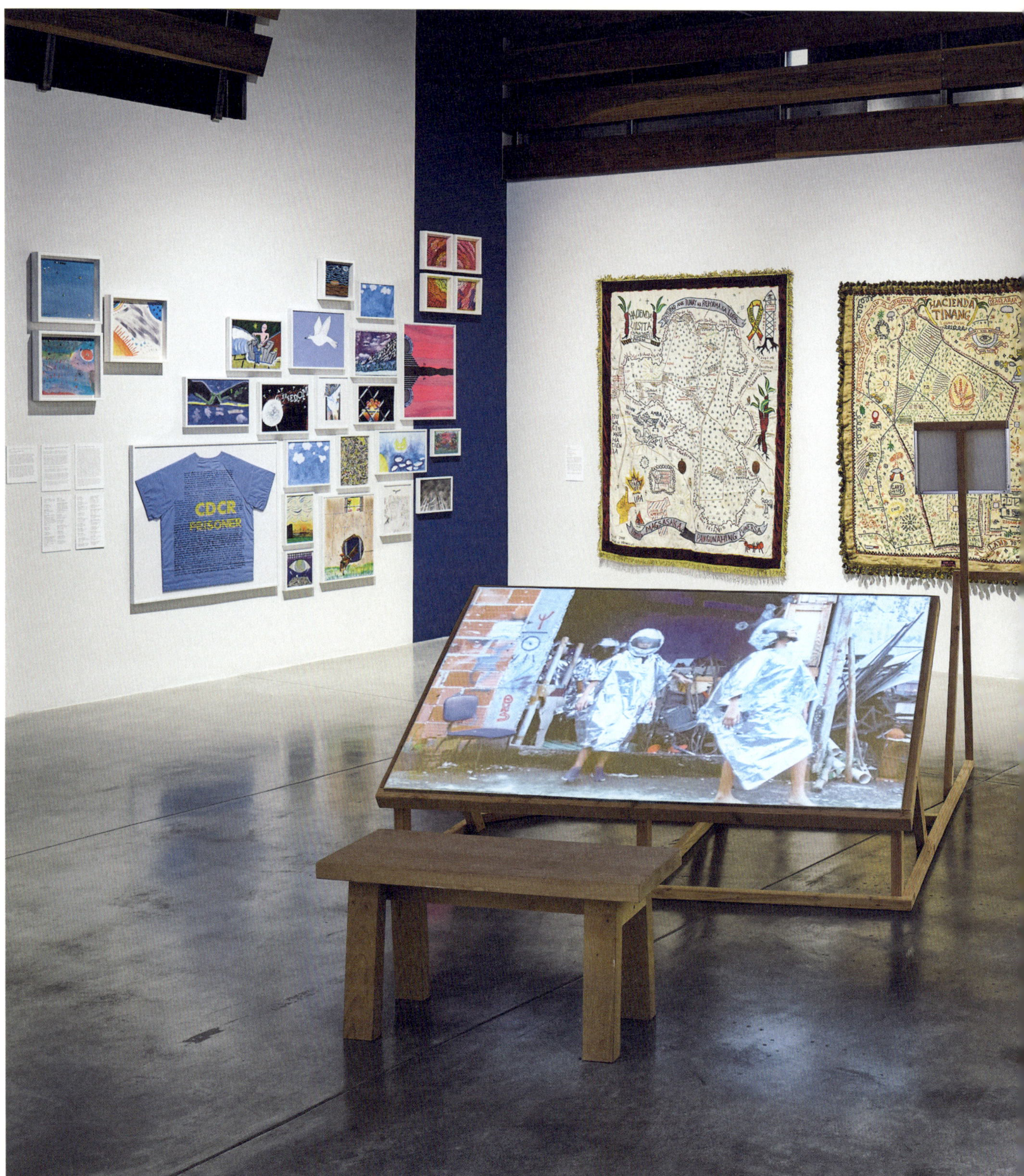

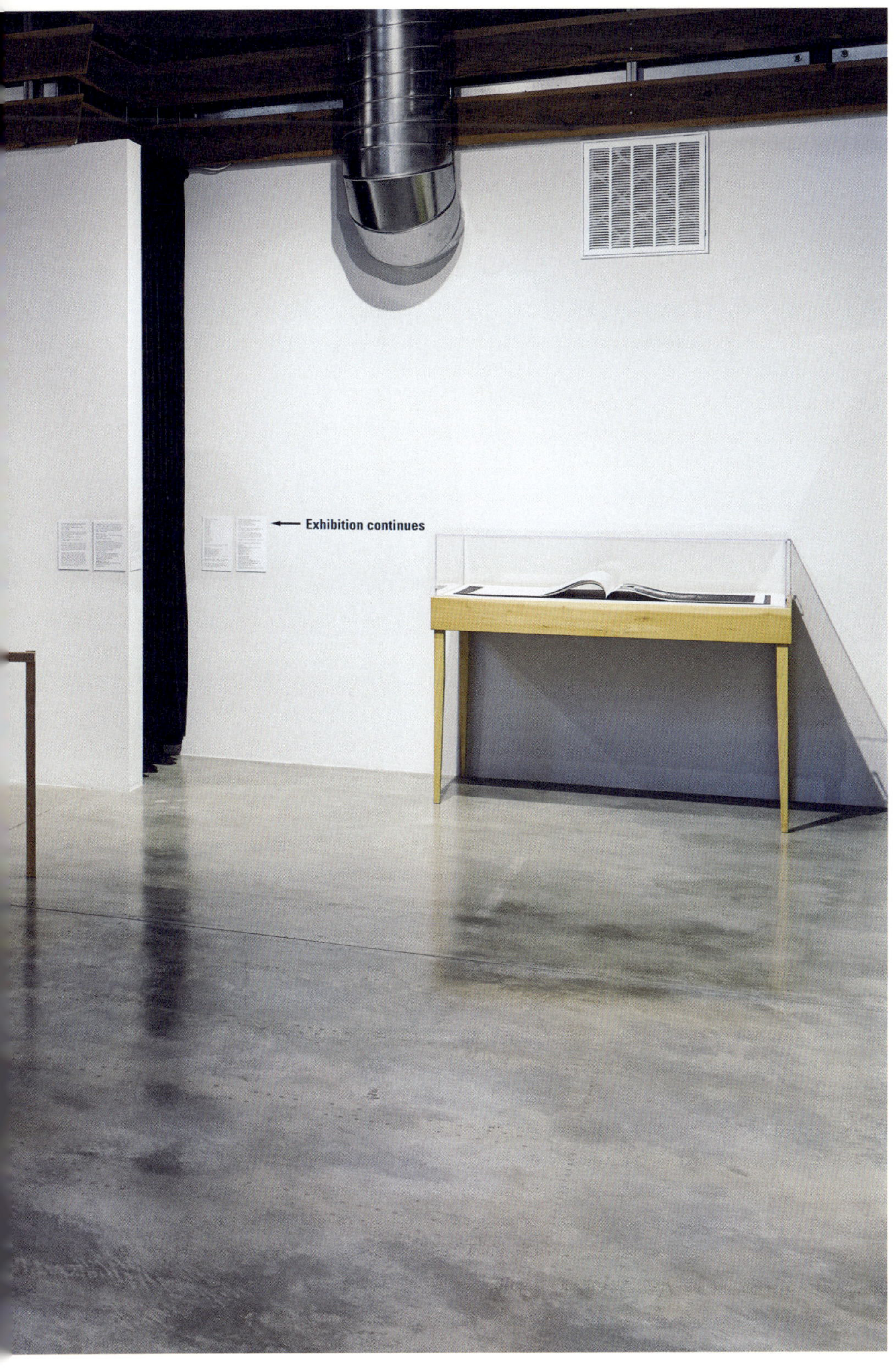
← Exhibition continues

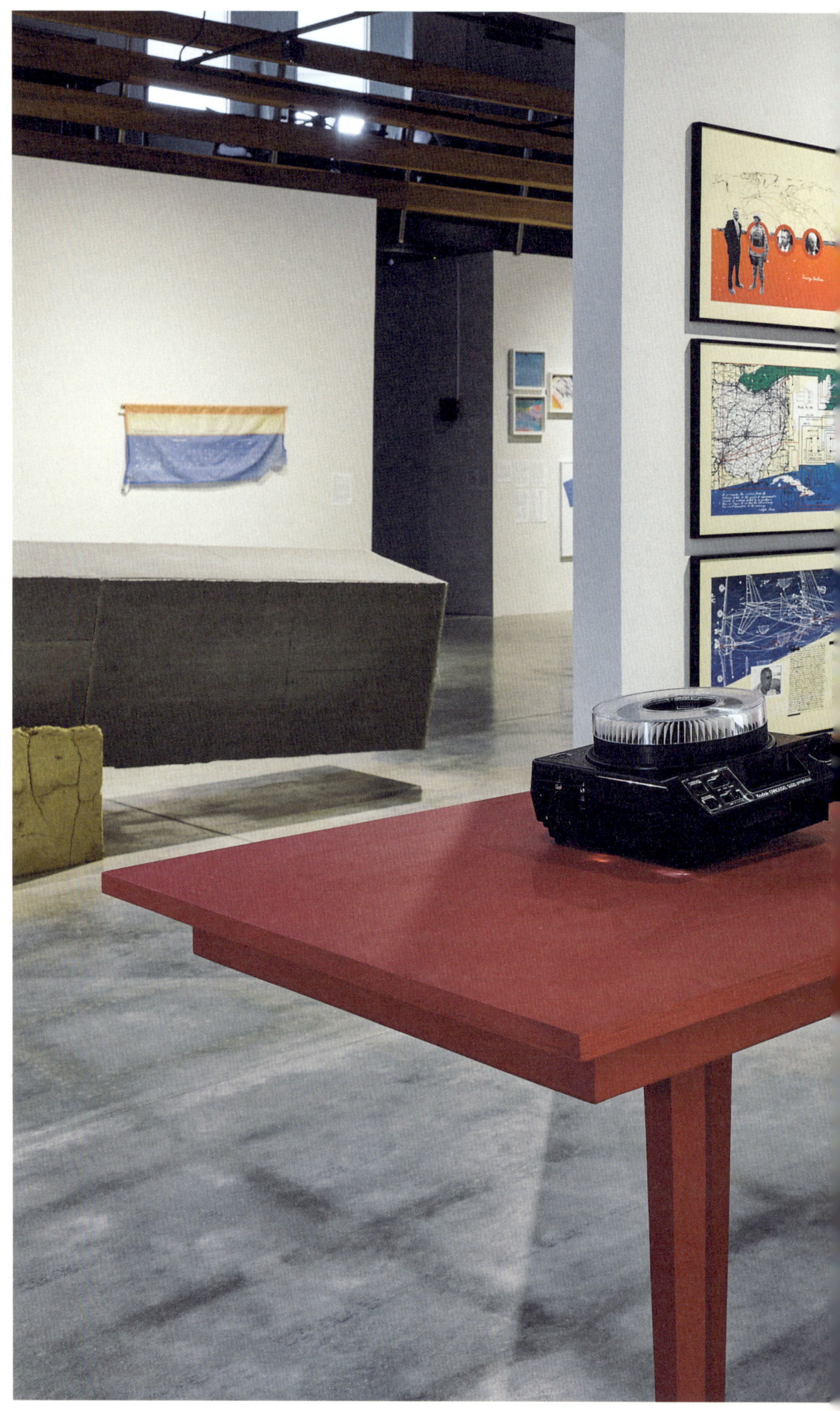

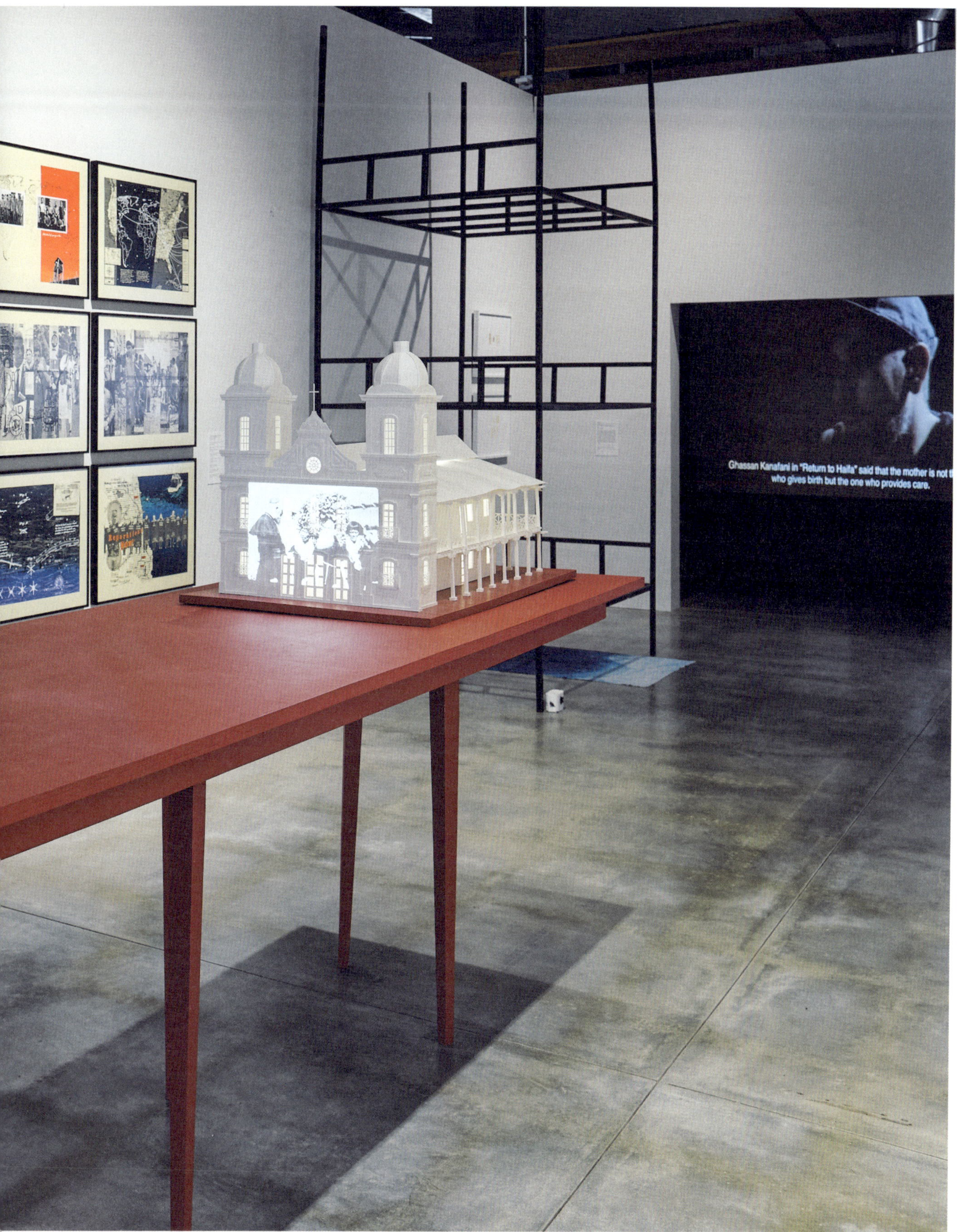
Ghassan Kanafani in "Return to Haifa" said that the mother is not the one who gives birth but the one who provides care.

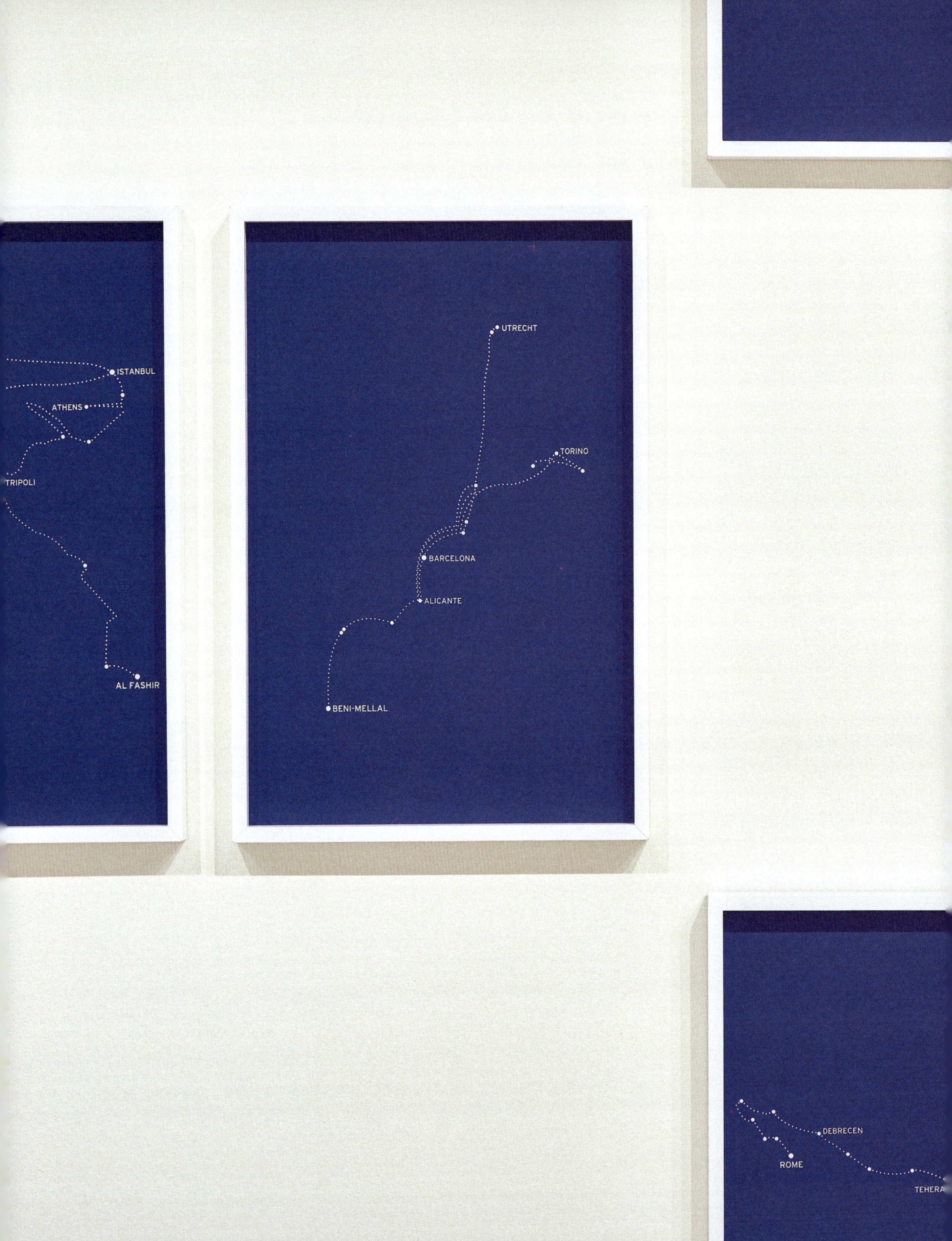
UTRECHT
ISTANBUL
ATHENS
TRIPOLI
TORINO
AL FASHIR
BARCELONA
ALICANTE
BENI-MELLAL
DEBRECEN
ROME
TEHERA

Plates

Frank Alejandrez
Walking with Love, 2023–24
Wood
Four sticks: approx. 40 × 1½ × 1½ in., each

Walking sticks have historical and cultural significance spanning centuries and continents, and they often function as symbols of authority. In *Walking with Love*, intricately hand-carved wooden walking sticks decorated with bears, hummingbirds, and snakes draw on this history of power and authority, with a significant twist. Instead of the walking sticks bestowing authority on an individual, they give significance to the lessons Frank Alejandrez learned in the decades he spent in an eleven-and-a-half by seven-and-a-half-foot security housing unit at Pelican Bay State Prison in Crescent City, California. During the enforced isolation of that time, and with the support he received both when incarcerated and in the years following his release, the importance of the community and mutual aid became paramount in the artist's practice. As Alejandrez explains, "I want to destigmatize our shared—and human—need for help and support. The walking sticks, which I often make as gifts for elders in the community, are symbolic of the fact that no one needs to walk alone. We all can walk together and support each other along the way."

Walking with Love reflects the commitment found throughout Alejandrez's expansive creative practice, which spans painting, drawing, and installation and casts art making as an act of love and community building. Central to Alejandrez's artworks are the practices of nonviolence and compassion, which the artist sees as foundational to creating a world free of prisons.

Frank Alejandrez, born 1965 in Fresno, California, is currently artist in residence at the Institute of the Arts and Sciences. He lives in Santa Cruz, California.

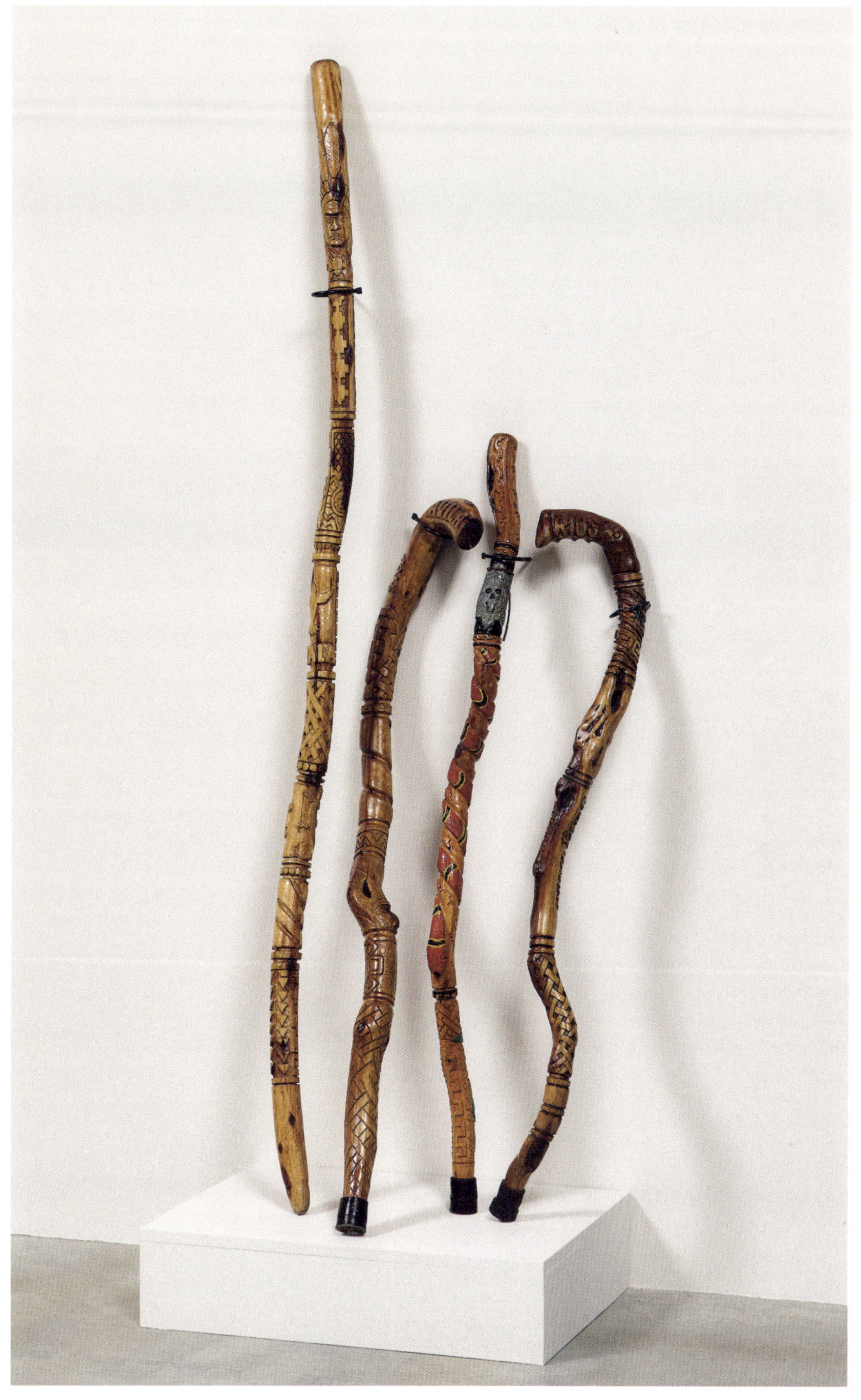

Juan E. Arredondo "Noodles," Robert E. Barber, Albert Bell, Darwin Billingsley, C. J. Black, Mark A. Cadiz aka Rev. M. Seishin, Ben Chandler, Christopher "Khalifah" Christensen, Joseph Dole, Vitória Daiane Emídio dos Santos, Darrell W. Fair, Flávia Ferreira dos Santos, Aimee Gana, Roquelina Gomes de Souza, Jessica Marie Hann, Huicho Herrera, J. Huynh, Jeffrey A. Isom, Donnie Wayne Ivy, Michael Jones, Just Me Expressions, Juan Luna, Poipi Mabo-Harrison (Meriam, Munbarra, Poorooma, Kokomini), Erick MacieL, Bryan Matheson, Nathaniel McCray #R63745, Jessie Milo, Brad "Trust None" Odell, JOHN ORTEGA, Robert Ortiz, Mesro Dhu Rafa'a, George Red, Tiffanie Sedgwick (Noogar), Ronnie Shelton, Gwenda Skeen (Nunckle, Kuku-Thaypan), Kyeemah Skeen (Nunckle, Kuku-Thaypan), Smiley, Harold "Ace" Smith, O. Smith the Artivist, Mark A. Stanley aka Stan-Bey, Ronald Steele, Luis Trevino, L. T2023, Unknown, Ernesto Valle, and Love'ly ocean Williams

In a world without prisons, everyone would be able to see the sky, 2024

Various media

Dimensions variable

Being able to see and experience the sky can seem like a basic human right. Yet many incarcerated people are denied access to an unencumbered view of the sky for years, if not decades. For *Seeing through Stone*, incarcerated artists from around the world were invited to respond to the following prompt: "In a world without prisons—and where all people are free—everyone would be able to see the sky. What do you imagine the sky in a world without prisons would look like?"

The drawings, paintings, and other works made in response are varied meditations on freedom. Artist Aimee Gana engaged the blue of the prison uniform that she wears daily, musing about what it might mean to wear the sky—and to embody freedom. In *My Son*, Nathaniel McCray painted a young man leaping in a wide expanse of blue. In George Red's work, a reversal is performed: a hand reaches out from a hole in a prison wall. The hole reveals a deep blue, suggesting that the wall might contain the sky. Mark A. Cadiz painted a figure joyfully shouting through a gaping hole in a wall, while Christopher "Khalifah" Christensen's faceless figure is shown from behind, engaged in a yoga warrior pose, as a nearby stone wall dissolves into blue. In a pencil drawing by an unnamed artist, turbulent skies and seas meet along a craggy horizon.

As of this catalog's publication date, more artwork contributions were still in transit, delayed by bureaucracy and red tape and the many strategies by which people on the inside are made to disappear. These visions are individual, but together they form a collective sky that continues to grow—and a vision for the shared work required to imagine, and create, a world without prisons.

Contributions came from artists imprisoned in California, Illinois, Brazil, and Australia.

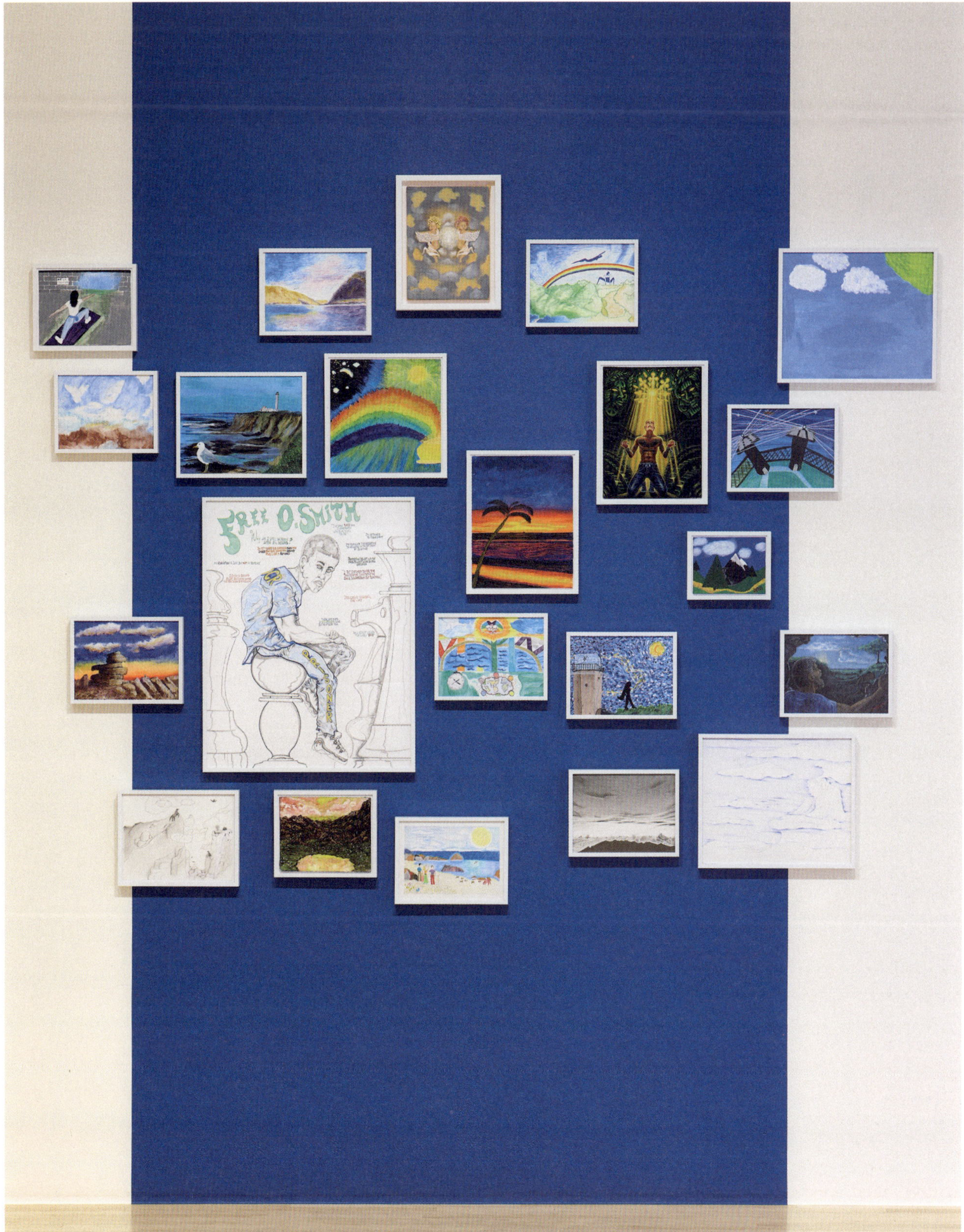

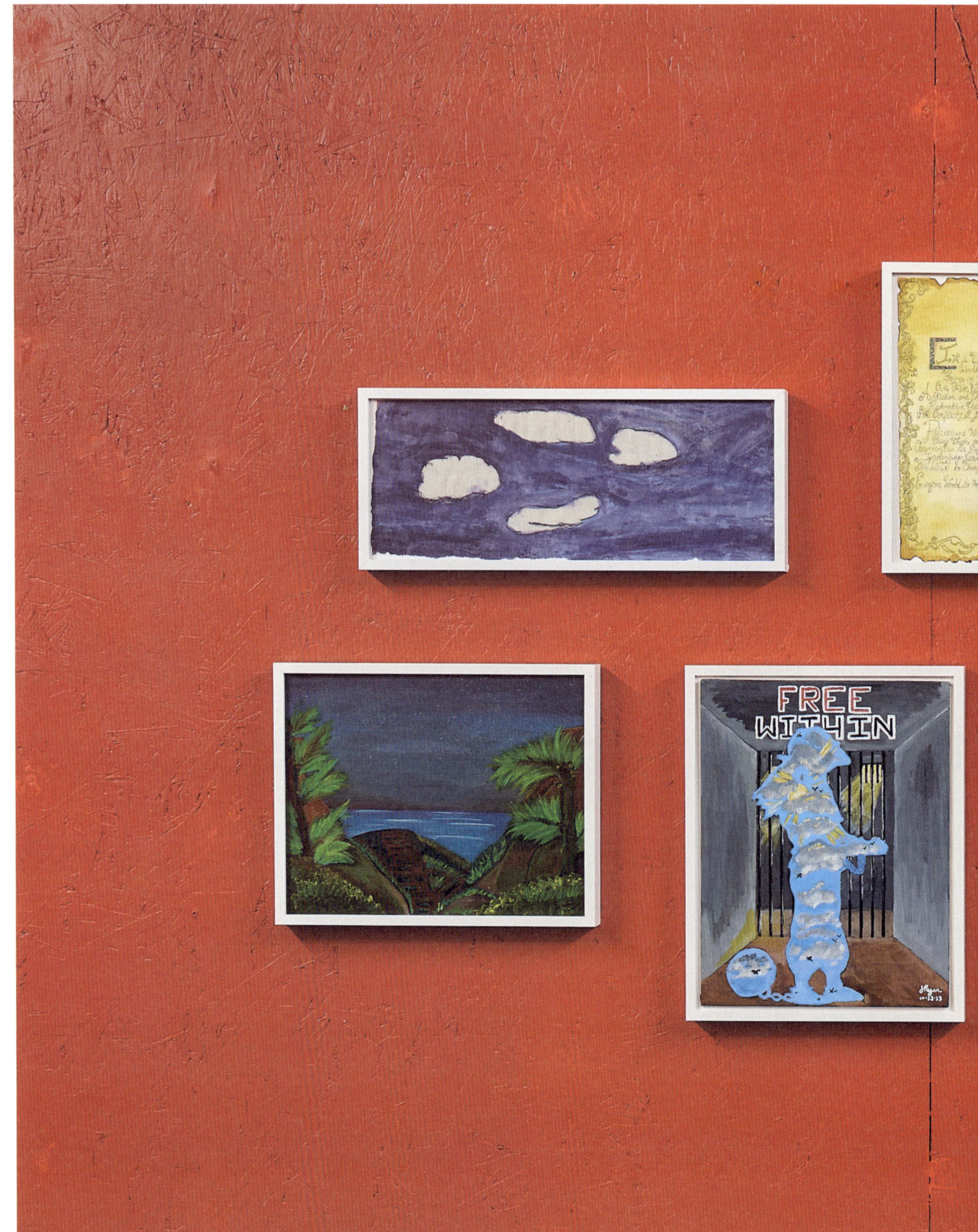
FREE
WITHIN

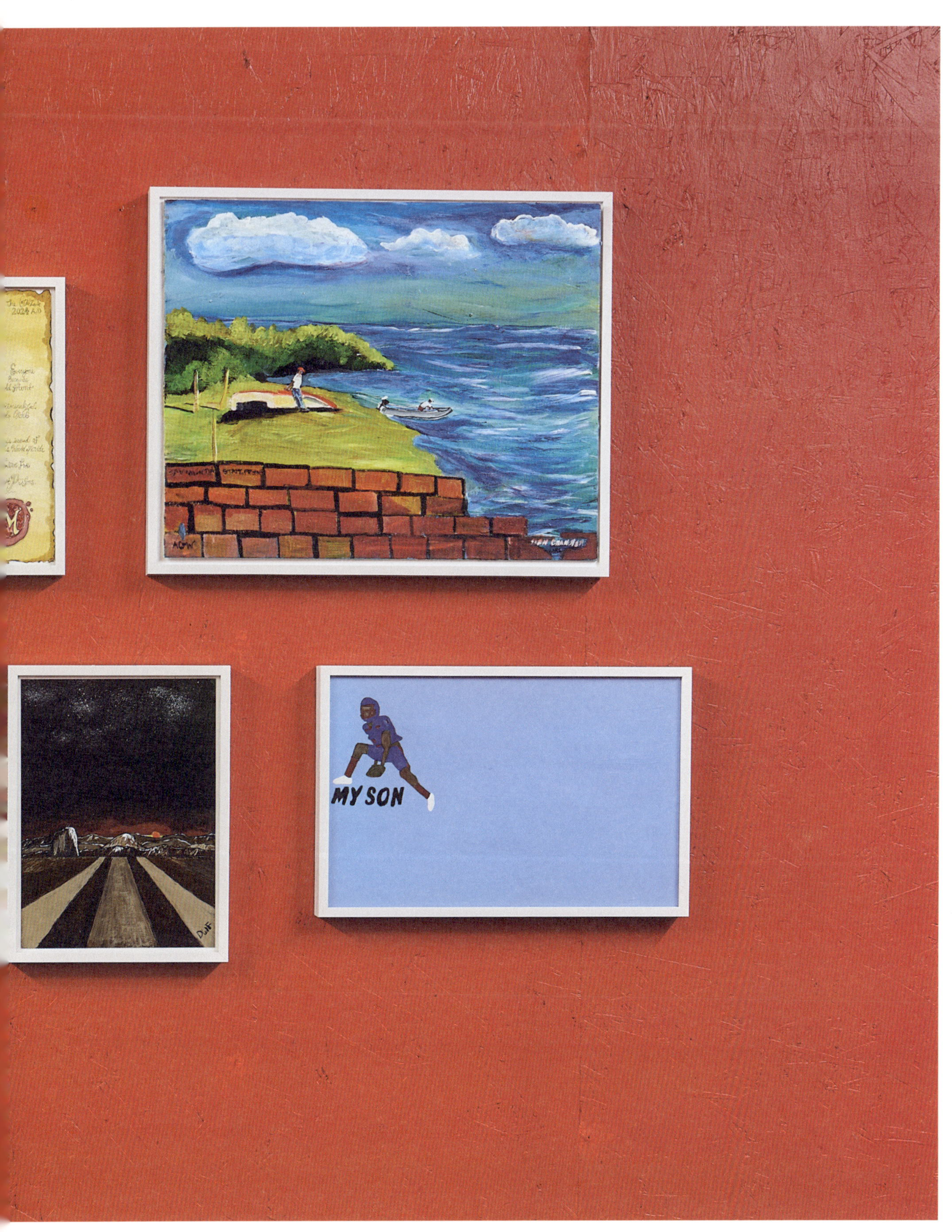
MY SON

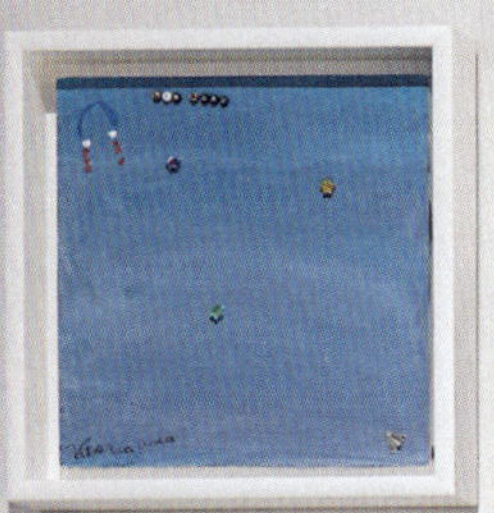
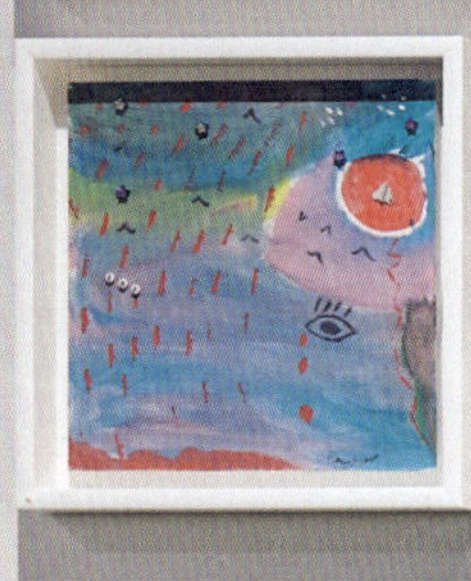
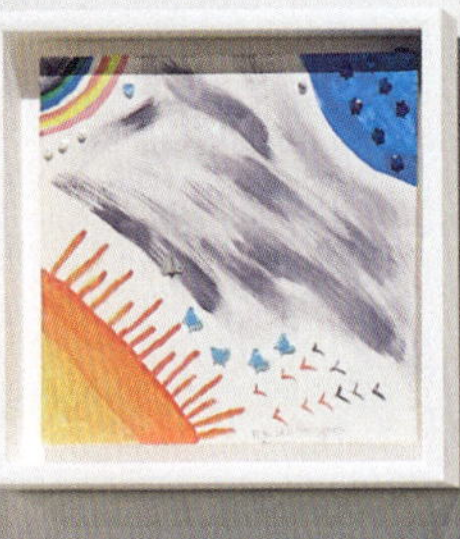
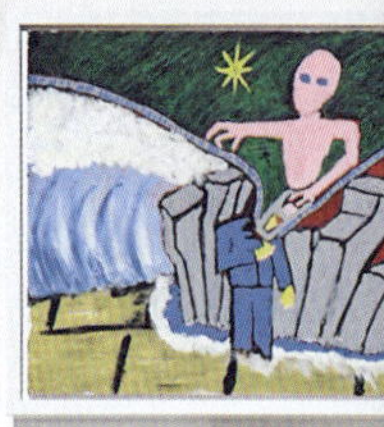
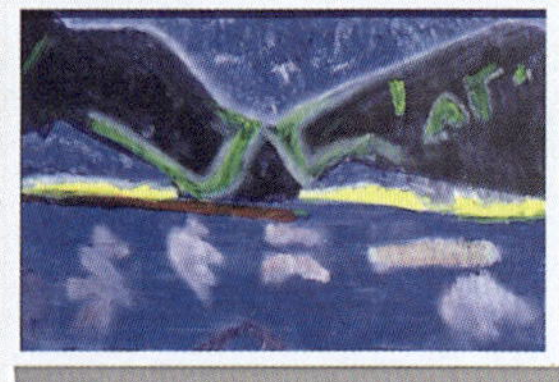
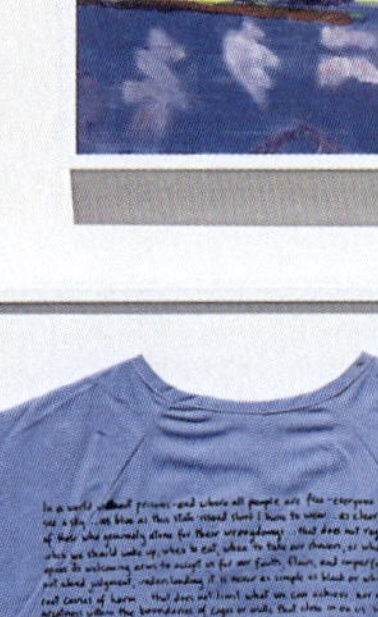

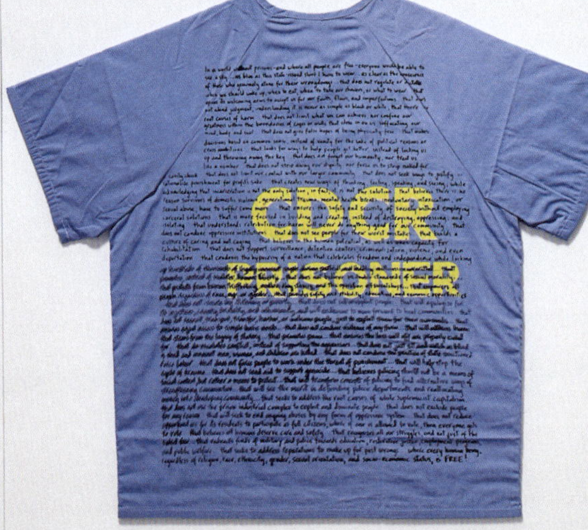

CDCR
PRISONER

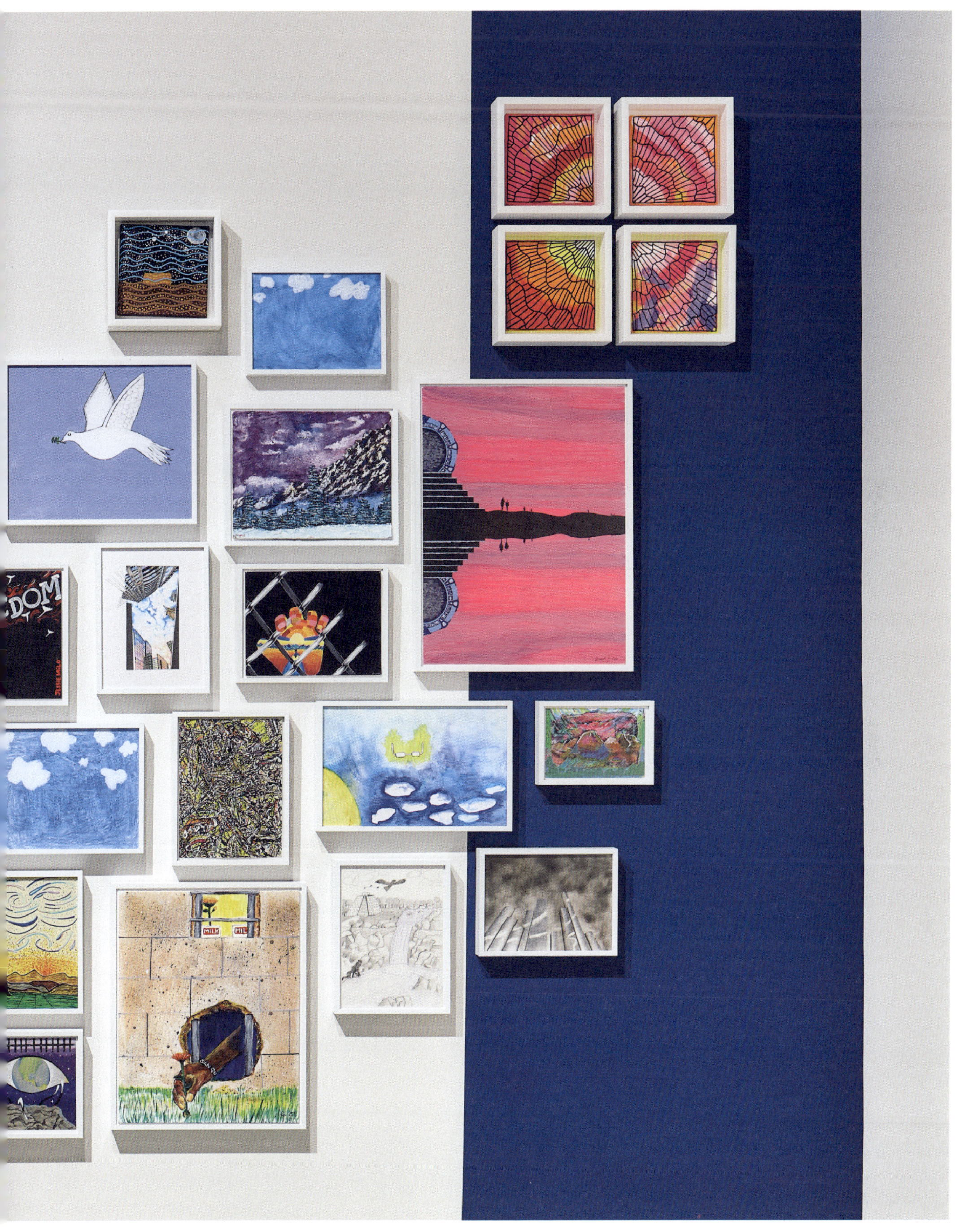

Sadie Barnette
West Oakland 2065, 2024
Archival pigment print and rhinestones
13 × 13 in.

An Oakland, California, street sign for Martin Luther
King Jr. Way stands on a rocky beach that gives way
to an azure sea. Sadie Barnette created the image to
depict a future washed of prisons, where legacies
of freedom fighters remain, signposts in a history of
oppression that we have overcome. The photograph
is dotted with rhinestones, a material intervention that
the artist uses often to punctuate moments of everyday life with luminescence and love.

Barnette's multimedia practice frequently explores
her family history—her father, Rodney Barnette,
founded the Compton chapter of the Black Panther
Party—which mirrors a collective history of repression
and resistance in the United States. For her video *Family Business* (2023), a prior commission for Visualizing
Abolition, Sadie Barnette drew from family photographs, home movies, and familiar domestic settings
to animate an alternate history of Black America, one
shaped not only by state-sanctioned terror but also by
quotidian love, celebration, and the fullness of human
relationships.

Sadie Barnette is an artist born 1984, in Oakland,
California, where she currently lives and works.

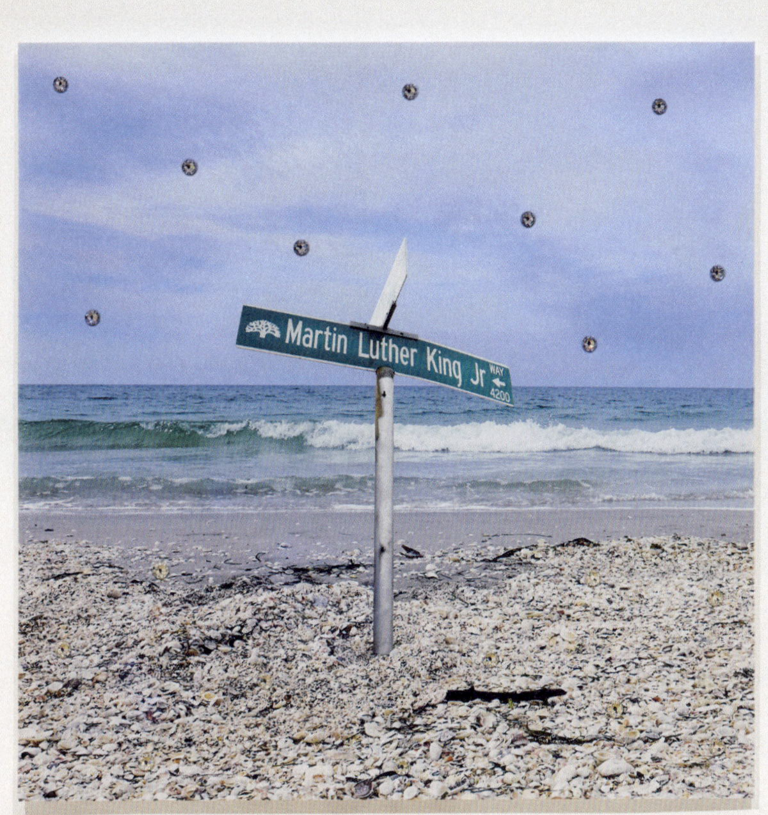

Martin Luther King Jr
WAY
4200

Rebecca Belmore
At Pelican Falls, 2017
Sculpture, video, wall text, and photograph
77 × 264 × 175 in., overall

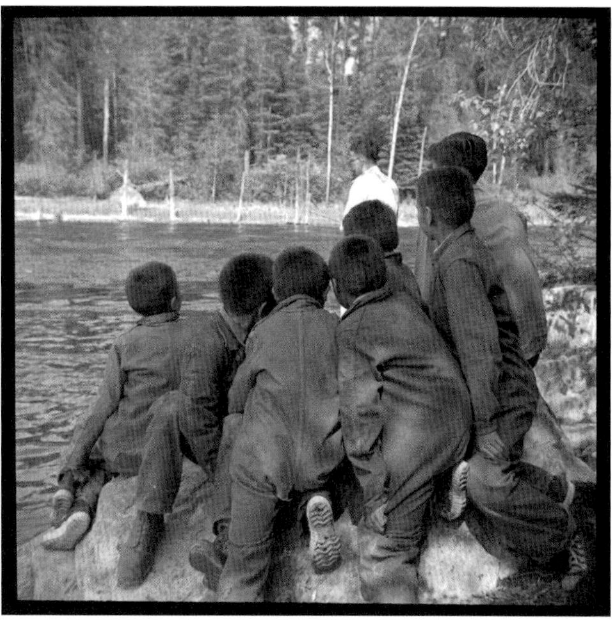

John Macfie, *Students of the Anglican Residential School at Pelican
Falls Near Sioux Lookout, Watching
a Fisherman,* ca. 1955. Archives of
Ontario, C 330-8-0-0-5.

A photograph from 1955 is the point of departure for *At Pelican Falls.* In the black-and-white image, boys wearing Pelican Falls Indian Residential School uniforms sit on a rock, their backs to the camera, watching a white man fishing in the river. Located in Sioux Lookout, Ontario, Canada, near Belmore's hometown, the residential school operated from 1929 through 1969, during which time thousands of children were taken from their families and exposed to physical and psychological abuse.

A refusal to drown in this history spreads across the floor in front of the image. Indigo denim, the material from which the residential school uniforms were made, twists into a turbulent river. A uniformed figure emerges from the river rapids, a phantasmic inversion of the still photograph. The video playing alongside the sculpture shows this figure given flesh: a child bursts out of the water and then slips back under the surface on a loop. The repeated moment of cleansing, the washing off of the violent past, is a reminder that the Pelican Falls Indian Residential School no longer exists; it was torn down in 1978. Where carceral classrooms once stood is now a First Nations–controlled and operated school, Pelican Falls First Nations High School, which offers educational services to students from twenty-four First Nation communities within the Northern Nishnawbe Education Council and the

Nishnawbe Aski Nation. On a nearby wall, a phrase from a short story written by the artist's sister, Florene Belmore, reminds us of the power of collective healing, as a single, lonesome loon wail carried over the water "gives way to a chorus of call and response. 'I am here.' 'Where are you?' 'I am here.'"

Since the 1990s, Rebecca Belmore's performances, installations, photographs, videos, and sculptures have engaged the tensions between representation and the political and social realities experienced by First Nations communities. With works that delve into crucial issues including water and land rights, violence by the state and police, gendered violence, houselessness, and displacement, Belmore mines the potential of art to effect social change.

Rebecca Belmore, RCA, DFA, born 1960, is a Canadian Anishinaabe interdisciplinary artist. She is Ojibwe and a member of Obishikokaang (Lac Seul First Nation). Belmore currently lives in Vancouver, British Columbia.

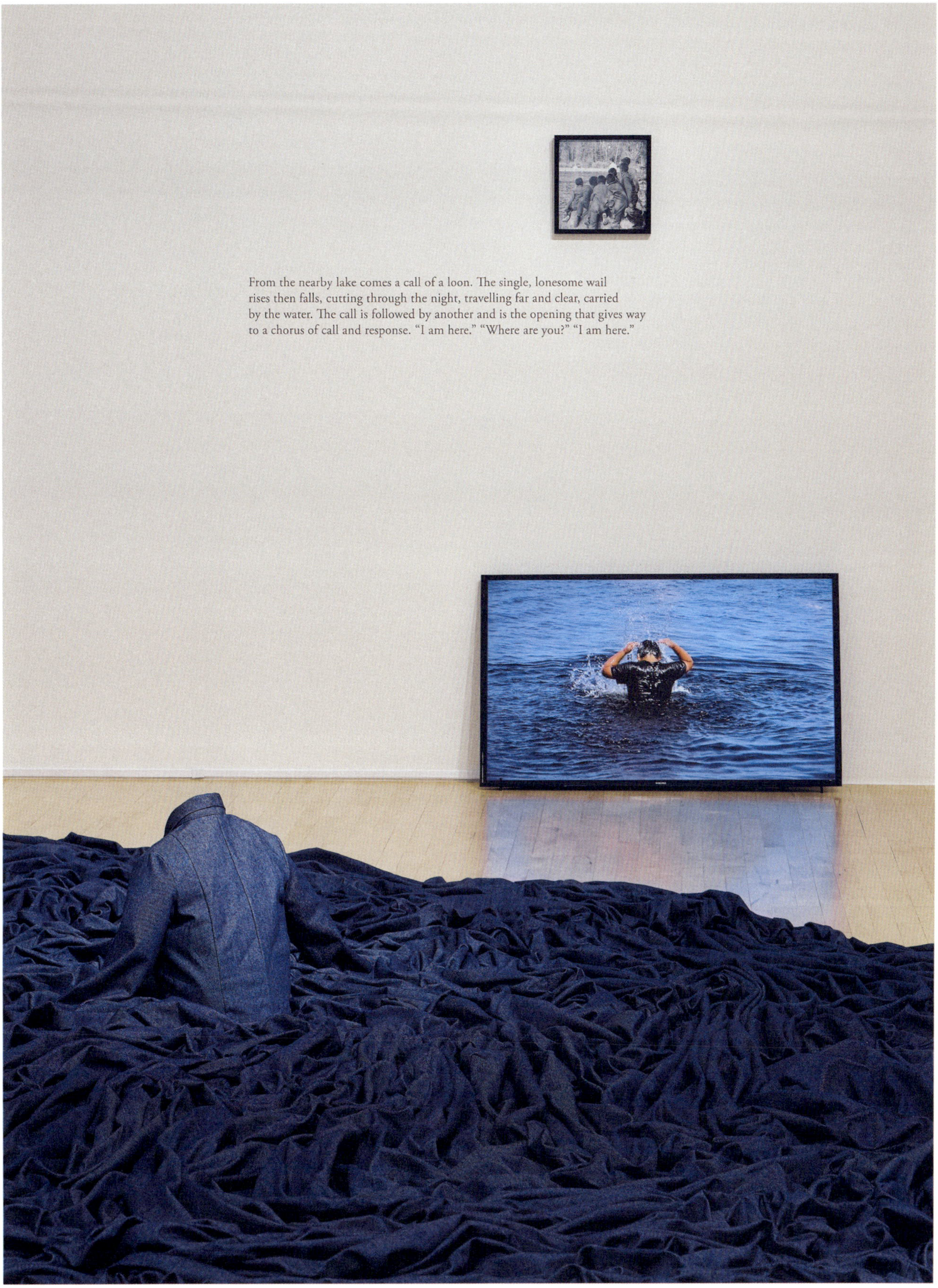

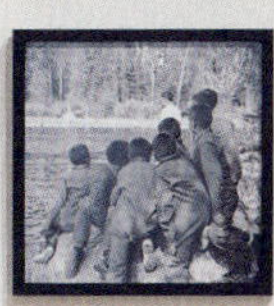

From the nearby lake comes a call of a loon. The single, lonesome wail
rises then falls, cutting through the night, travelling far and clear, carried
by the water. The call is followed by another and is the opening that gives way
to a chorus of call and response. "I am here." "Where are you?" "I am here."

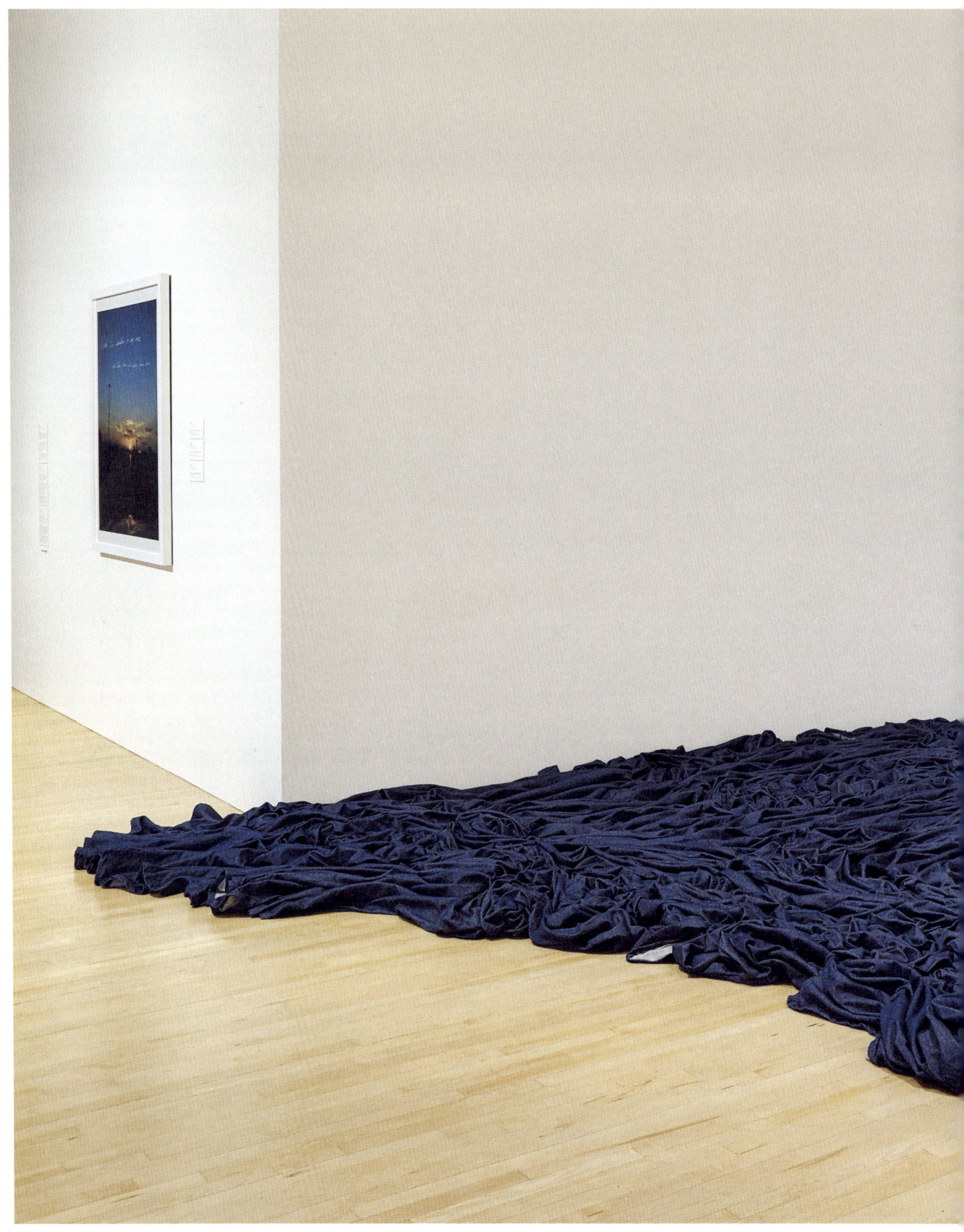

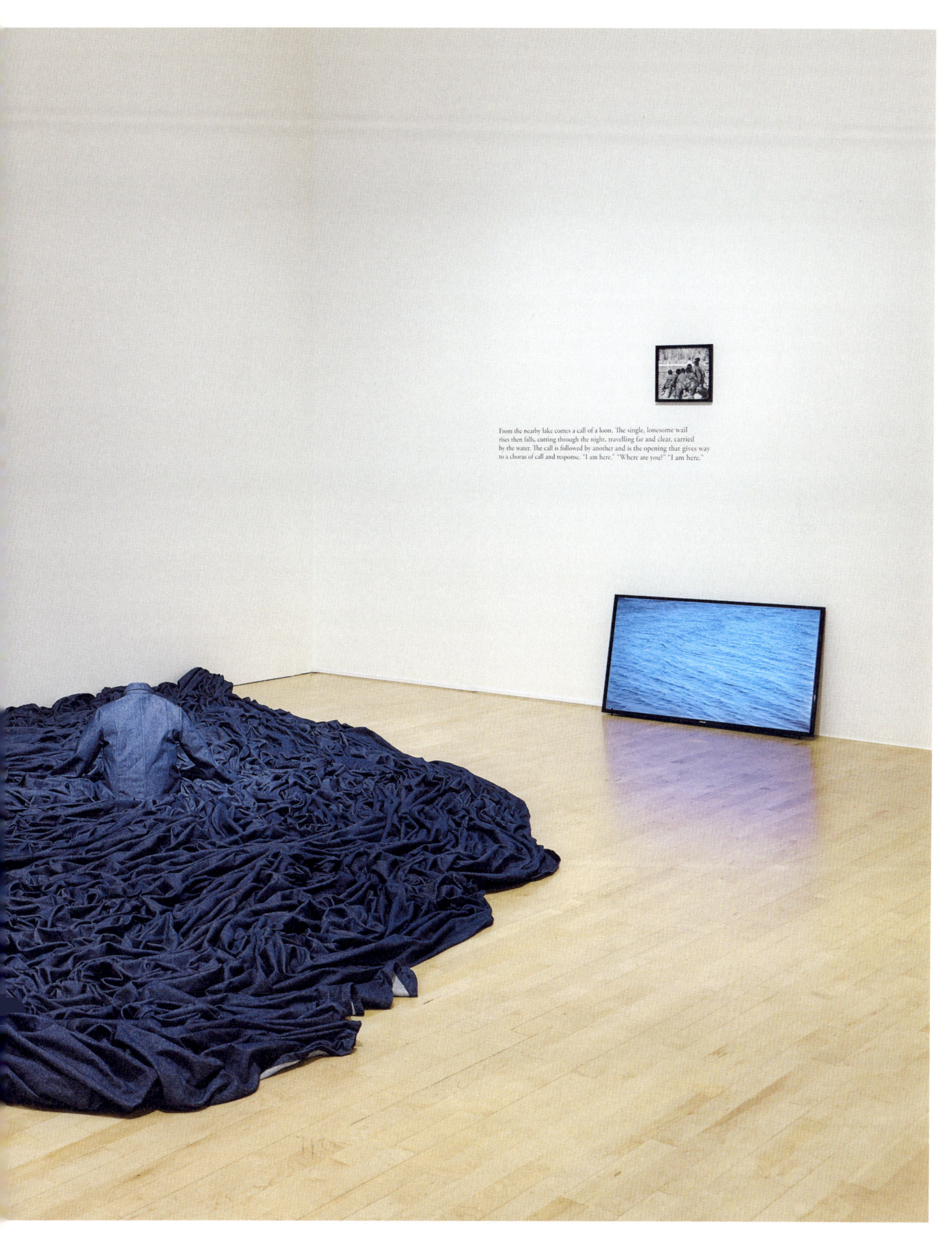

From the nearby lake comes a call of a loon. The single, lonesome wail rises then falls, cutting through the night, travelling far and clear, carried by the water. The call is followed by another and is the opening that gives way to a chorus of call and response. "I am here." "Where are you?" "I am here."

Imani Jacqueline Brown
*The holes in the earth mirror the holes in our souls
(and from them we can grow trees)*, 2023
Media installation with soundscape "Enbas" by Les Cenelles
218 × 127½ × 152 in., overall

Poetically traversing the extractive history of Louisiana—from settler colonialism to slavery to prisons, and including the fossil fuel industry—*The holes in the earth mirror the holes in our souls (and from them we can grow trees)* creatively choreographs these intersecting systems and their ecological impacts.

Taking the form of an immersive video installation, *The holes in the earth* consists of two video projections and an accompanying audio track. The first projection, on a curved screen, merges satellite imagery of the oil and gas infrastructure in the Louisiana wetlands with photographs and video recorded from propeller planes and from canoes traveling through the region. Archival documents punctuate the images, tracing the harsh continuum of extraction that destroys people and the lands they inhabit through the same racialized logics.

The other projection provides a poignant counterpoint. On a concave dome hanging from the ceiling, an animation has transformed satellite imagery documenting the oil and gas infrastructure and the prisons and carceral institutions that permeate and invade Louisiana's wetlands. The network of pipelines, canals, wells, prisons, and jails has been removed from its geographical context and reimagined to form vast constellations across a night sky, charting the history of extraction in the stars.

Uniting the images of the oil and gas industry made celestial with the video that more explicitly maps the industry's ecological, racialized effects is a soundscape created by Les Cenelles, a Louisiana-based Creole string quartet. Sung in French Creole, Yoruba, and Indigenous languages, the result is a lyrical summoning of past and present modes of bodies living in relation—humans and other life forms, lands, and waters—outside the logics of extraction.

The holes in the earth is part of a larger body of work by Imani Jacqueline Brown reflecting her commitment to art as activism. A research fellow with the London-based organization Forensic Architecture as well as an independent artist, she disseminates her work internationally through art installations, public actions, reports, and testimony delivered to courts and organs of the United Nations.

Imani Jacqueline Brown, born 1988, is an artist, activist, and researcher from New Orleans. She currently lives in London.

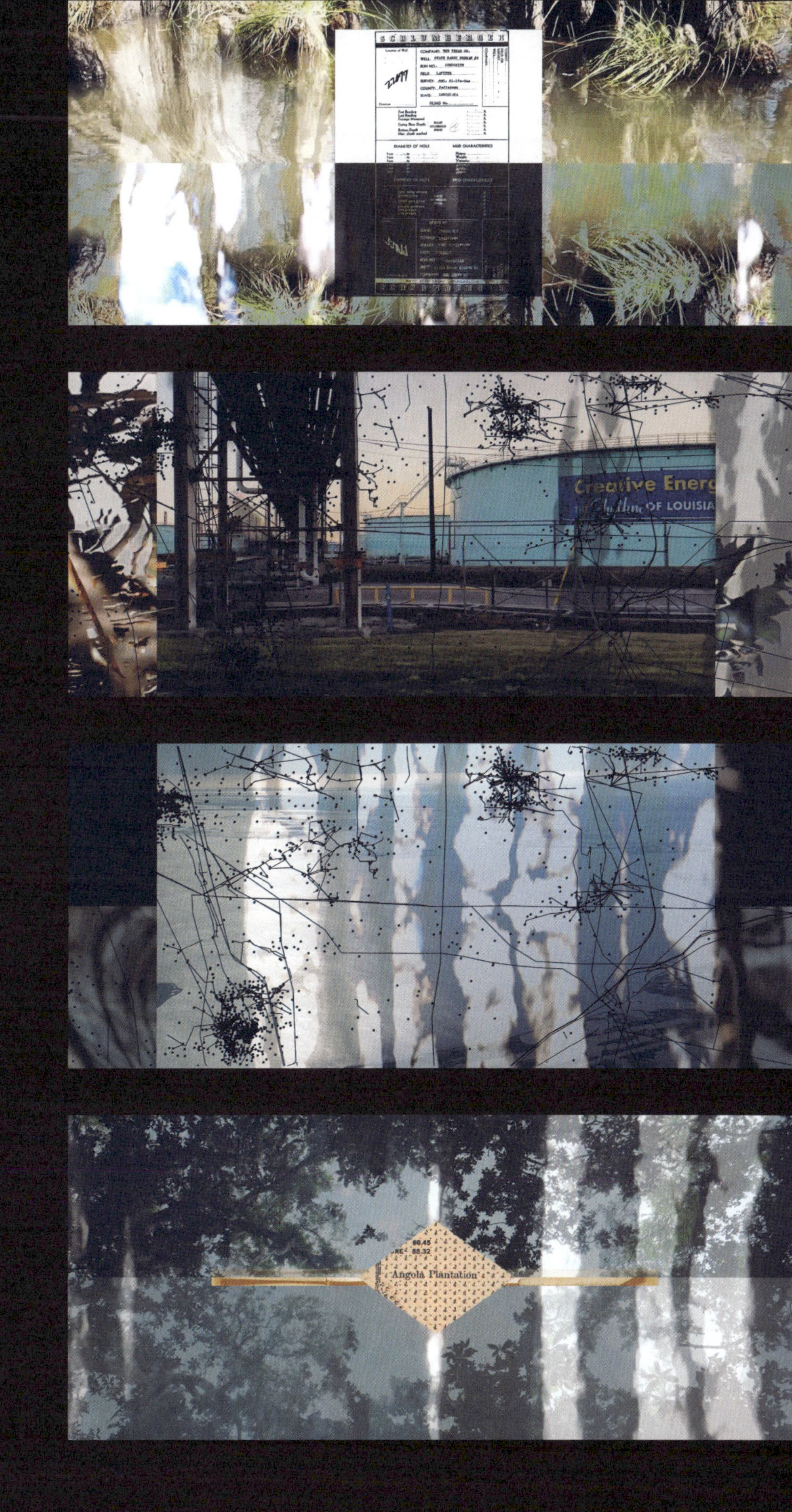
Creative Energy
The Rhythm OF LOUISIA
60.45
55.32
Angola Plantation

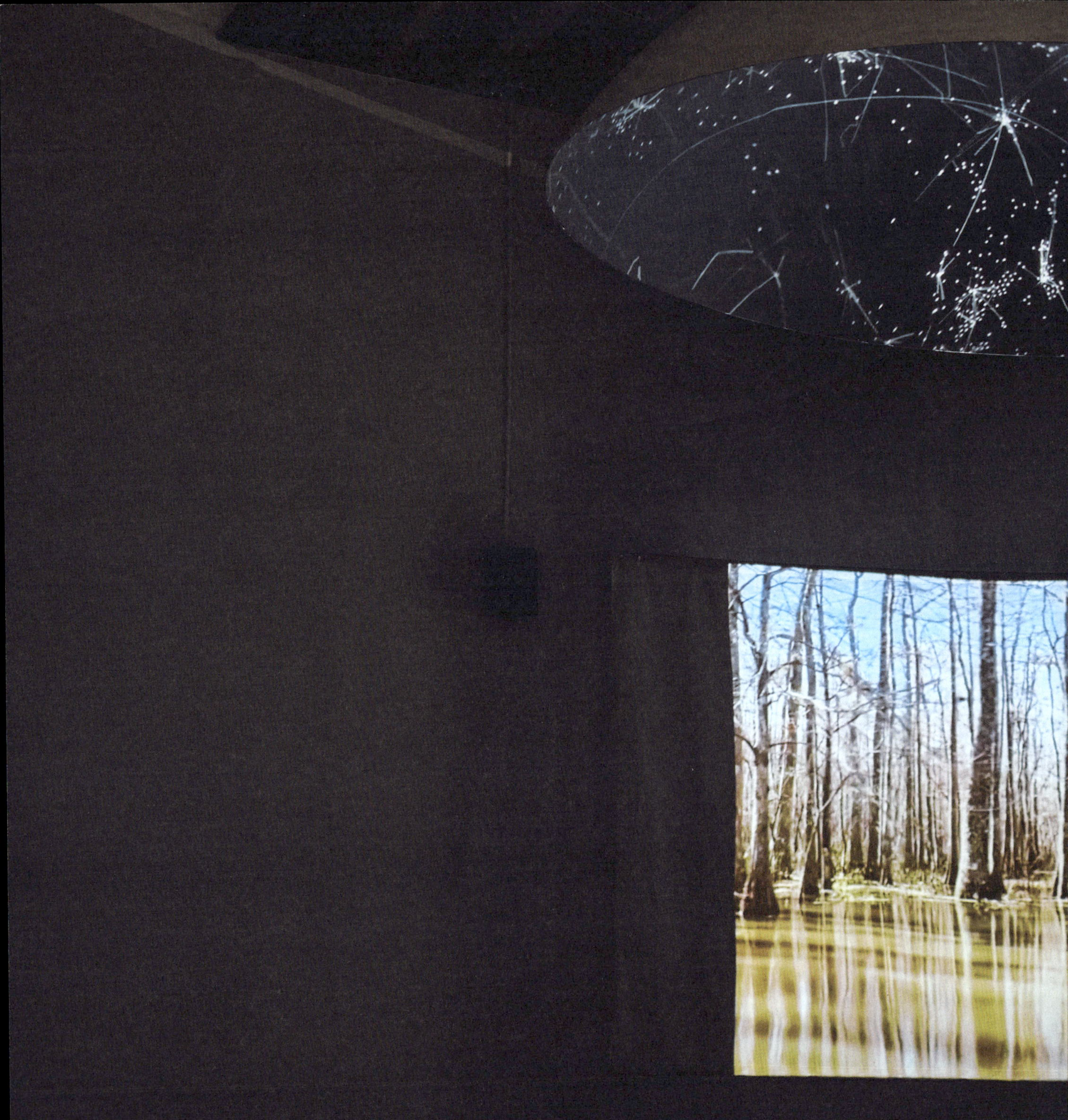

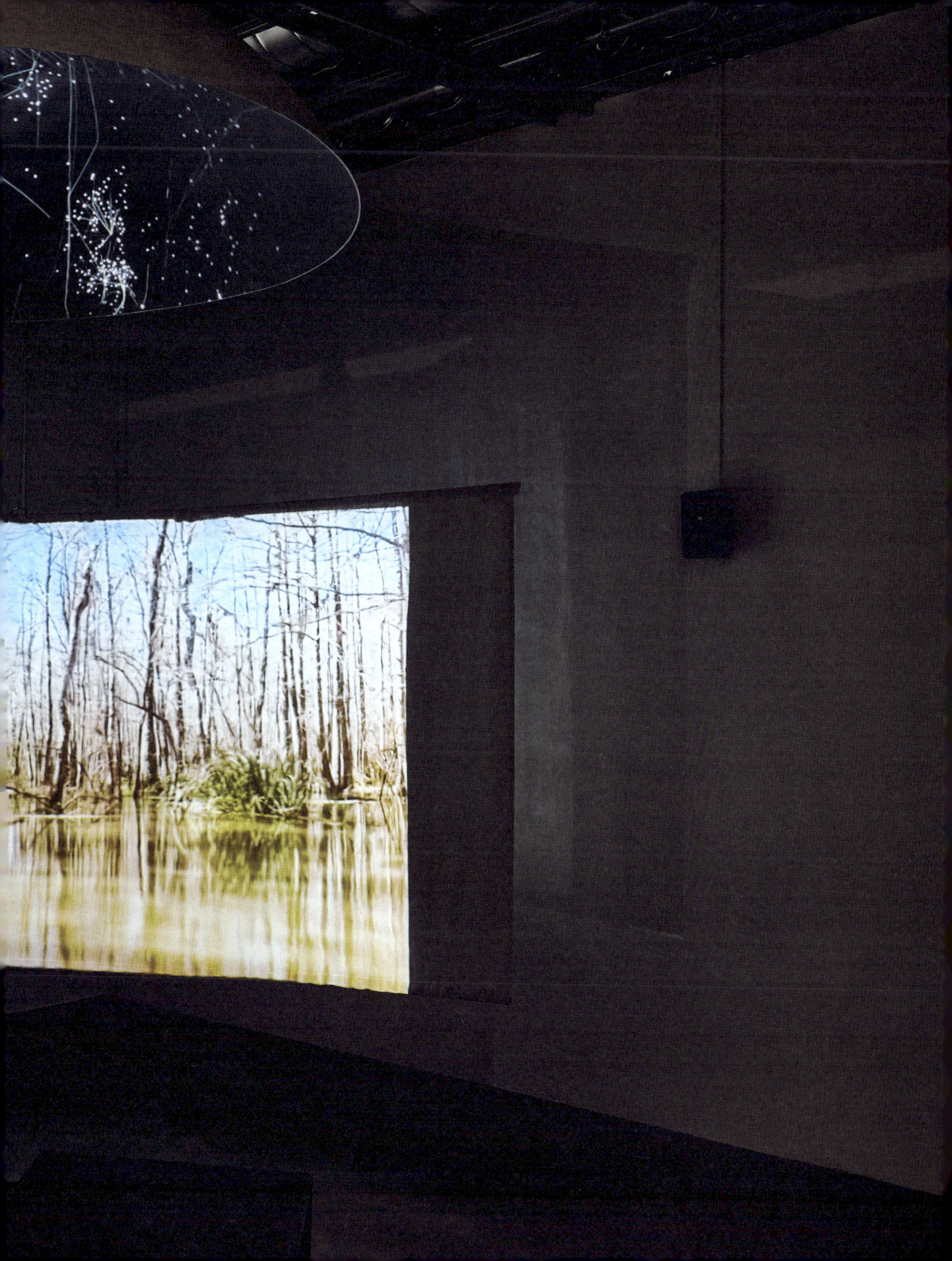

Sharon Daniel
Reasonable Doubt(s), 2024
Three-channel film and sound
71:06 minutes

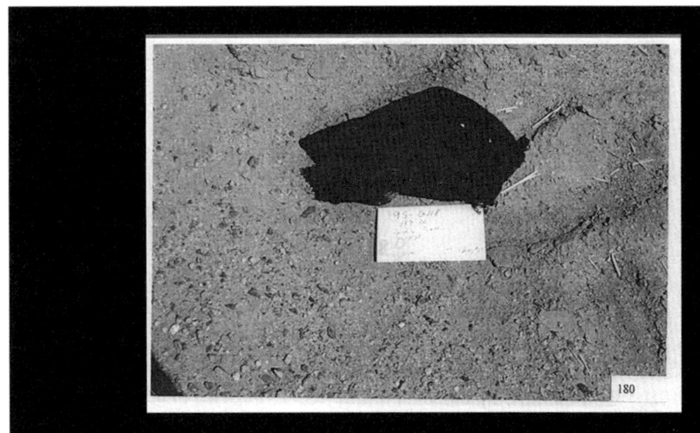

The United States has not only the highest incarceration rate in the world but also unprecedented rates of false conviction. Documenting the forms of official misconduct and legal abuse that lead to wrongful convictions, *Reasonable Doubt(s)* exposes the intrinsic issues in the nation's criminal legal system that lead to these injustices—and the fatal flaws of a structure that has made racist and unjust arrests and prosecutions so ordinary. Linking the stories of six Black exonerees and defendants, the project both uncovers the racism and structures of injustice that feed the criminal legal system and reveals what could be the basis for the system's demise.

Reasonable Doubt(s) is part of a series of media projects by Sharon Daniel that tracks social and economic injustices across a spectrum of public institutions, including the criminal legal system, the public health system, and the public education system. The series documents and analyzes testimony and evidence to show how state institutions, social structures, and economic conditions connect in a causal chain, from inequality in health care and education to racial and economic discrimination in the legal system.

Sharon Daniel, born 1954, lives in San Francisco and is a professor of film and digital media at the University of California, Santa Cruz.

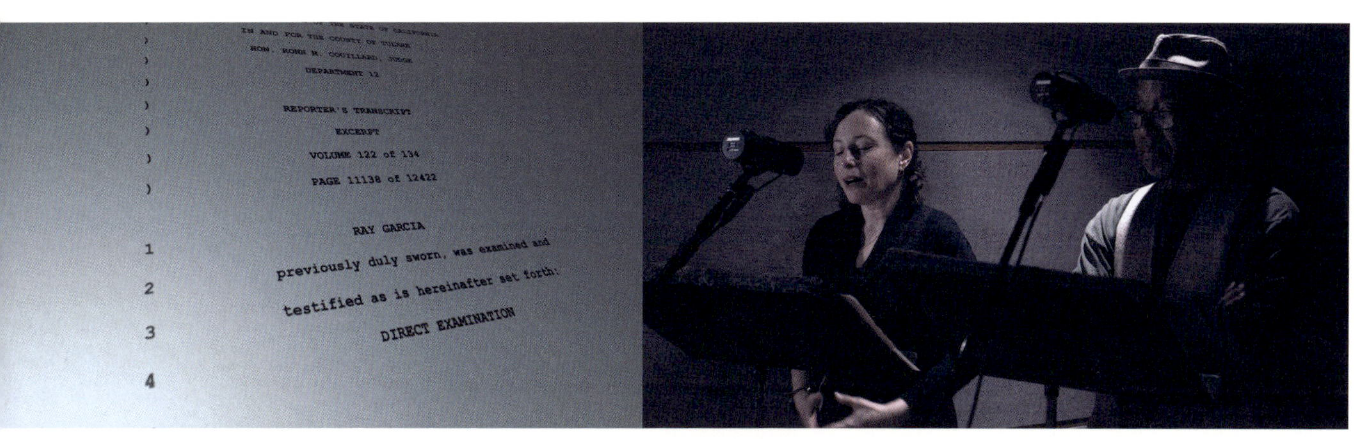
IN AND FOR THE COUNTY OF TULARE
HON. ROBB M. COUILLARD, JUDGE
DEPARTMENT 12
REPORTER'S TRANSCRIPT
EXCERPT
VOLUME 122 of 134
PAGE 11138 of 12422
RAY GARCIA
previously duly sworn, was examined and
testified as is hereinafter set forth:
DIRECT EXAMINATION

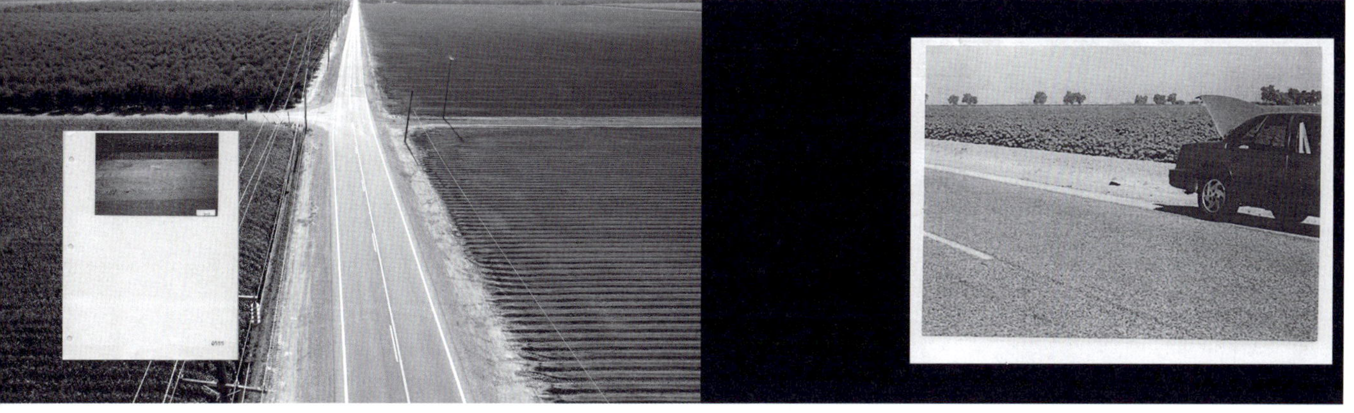

Cian Dayrit

Agrev Algorithm, 2022
Tapestry
70⅞ × 74¾ in.

Monuments of Great Divide, 2019
In collaboration with Felman Bagalso
Wood and metal
Three sculptures: approx. 7 × 14 × 3 in., each

Feudal Fields, 2018
Mixed media and embroidery on fabric
72 × 60 in.

Feudal Fields II: Tinang, 2024
Mixed media and embroidery on fabric
72 × 60 in.

Selection of counter-maps with plantation,
2017–ongoing
In collaboration with Abby Bucad, Alvin Dimarucut, Annabelle Magana, Christine Olado, Dagohoy P. Magaway, Ernie P. Baratas, Fermiza and Arnold, Florinda Callena, Israel M. Axelino, Jef Alipo-on and Jaspe Mallo, Joebert S., Johny B. Dalapan, Manuel A. Garubat, Melche G. Balbiran, MJ Avics, Pedro, Peter, Rafael Pallanan, Ranel Manggatawan, Raymond Pimentel, Rhoy Cabudoy, Roselyn B. Catampungan, Salik Maguindanao, Sarah Jane T., Steven G., Virginia B. Jinang and Mimi Sawoud, and Von Patlunag
Reproductions of drawings
Thirty documents: approx. 8½ × 12 in., each

During the three-hundred-year-long Spanish colonial period in the Philippines (1565–1898), opulent tapestry maps were carried from one region to the next as an exercise of colonial control; the maps were used to claim state ownership of the land, indenturing farmers to feudal landowners. Though the Comprehensive Agrarian Reform Program of 1988 was supposed to redistribute private and public agricultural lands key to the survival of many peasant communities, a compromised legal system fed by US interests opened so many loopholes that the law was effectively suspended. Against such struggles, the legally recognized yet still landless agrarian reform beneficiaries have been asserting their rights by planting food crops instead of cash crops, and by using and reclaiming land for health and sustenance instead of capital.

Cian Dayrit takes up this history through a series of tapestries and other artworks charting the contemporary manifestations of dispossession. *Feudal Fields*, Dayrit's earliest tapestry, maps the massacre of farmers protesting on the sugarcane estate at Hacienda Luisita in Tarlac province in 2004. The tapestry *Agrev Algorithim* resembles a geographic map but is actually a timeline, plotting different land and economic policies alongside movements of resistance and solidarity from throughout Filipino history. These tapestries are embedded with medallions bearing inscriptions in

Latin (at times mistranslated by Google) and QR codes linked to a working archive of literature, images, and media on the agrarian struggle. His latest artwork, *Feudal Fields II: Tinang*, centers on protests that took place in June 2022 at Hacienda Tinang, also in the province of Tarlac. Artists, writers, and activists joined farmers in an act of collective land cultivation known as *bungkalan*, a form of protest in which cash crops are uprooted and replaced with food crops. This led to the arrest of some ninety activists, including the artist.

In these and other works, Dayrit charts a revolution in progress, with different frameworks of knowledge production and power stitched into maps and timelines. *Monuments of Great Divide* comprises intimate wooden sculptures of distinct plantation walls, including small, intricate renderings of a tarp wall, one made of cinder blocks, and a bamboo barricade. Dayrit worked with craftspeople in Paete, a town known for its carving of traditional religious objects and icons, to make these sculptures, highlighting the carceral logic of walls and fences as reliant on the corruption of belief systems in which protection has become oppression.

Since 2017, Dayrit has facilitated counter-mapping workshops with landless agrarian communities across the Philippines, inviting participants to draw maps of where they live, work, worship, and organize, reclaiming land for everyday life and exposing geographies

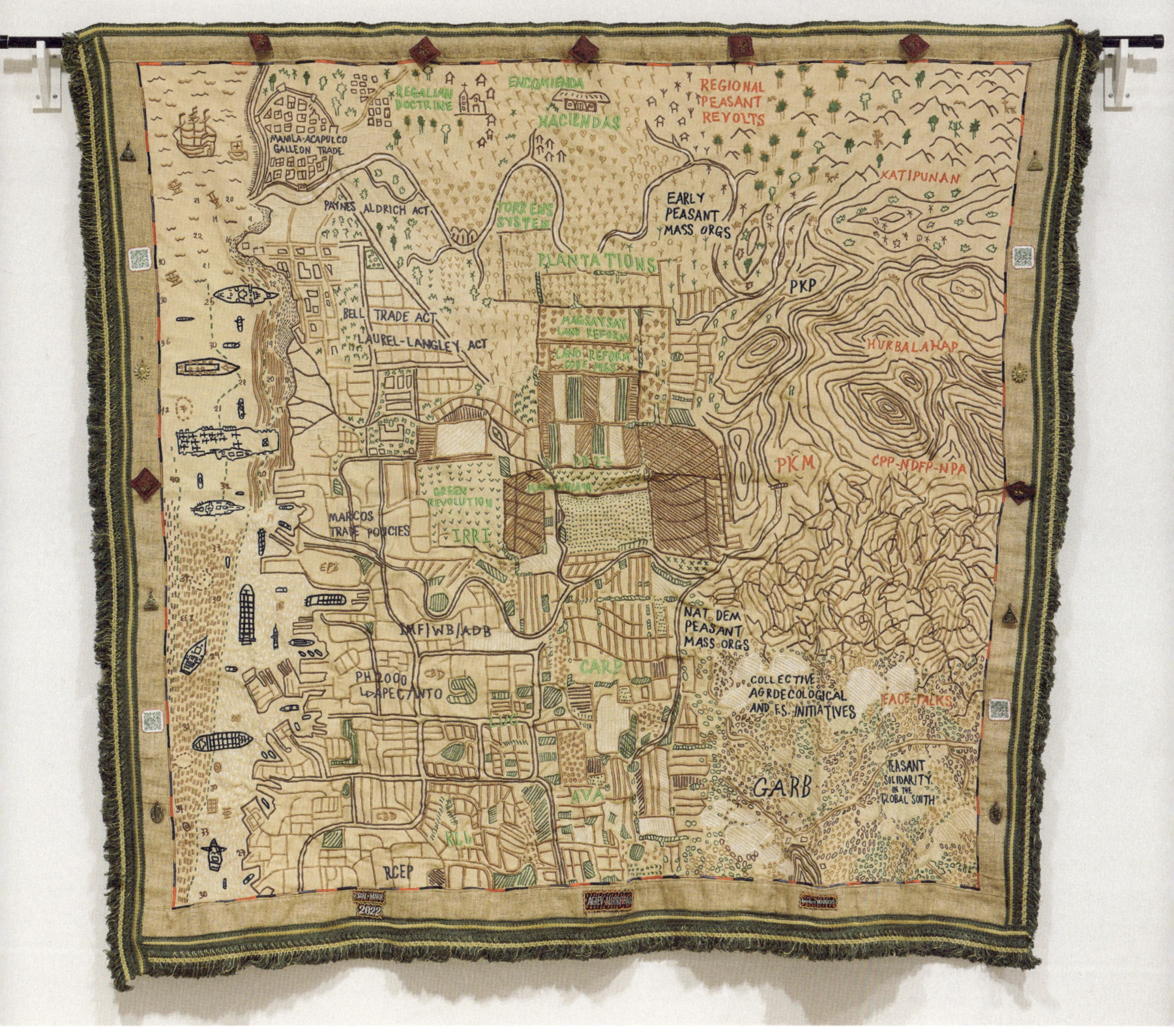

of control. Written in community, these maps are evidence of alternative relationships to land, unbound by inherited colonially imposed borders. The workshops are ongoing, with a selection of maps included in the exhibition.

Cian Dayrit, born 1989 in Manila, Philippines, is a founding member of SAKA (Artist Alliance for Genuine Agrarian Reform and Rural Development).

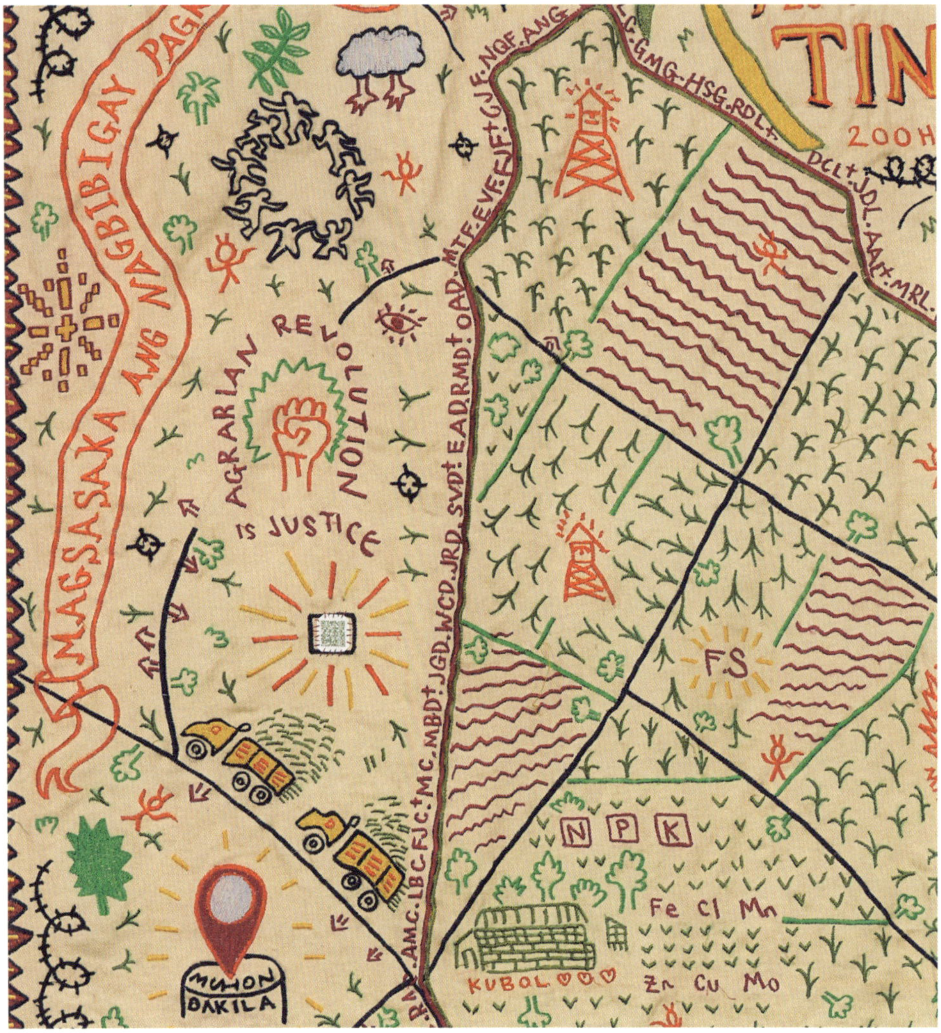

MAGSASAKA ANG NAGBIBIGAY PAG...
AGRARIAN REVOLUTION IS JUSTICE
MUHON DAKILA
TIN
200 H
...CD.JRD.SVD†:EADRMD†:OAD:MTF:EVF:EJF†:GJF:NGF.ANG
...G.GMG.HSG.RDL†:DCL†:JDL.AAt.MRL.
...RA.AMC.LBC.FJC†MC.MBD†:JGD.WCD.JRD.SVD†:EADRM
NPK
FS
KUBOL
Fe Cl Mn
Zn Cu Mo

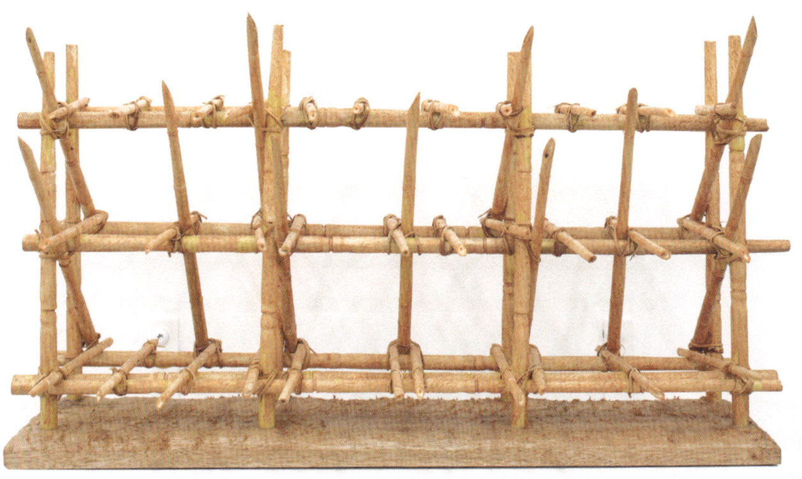

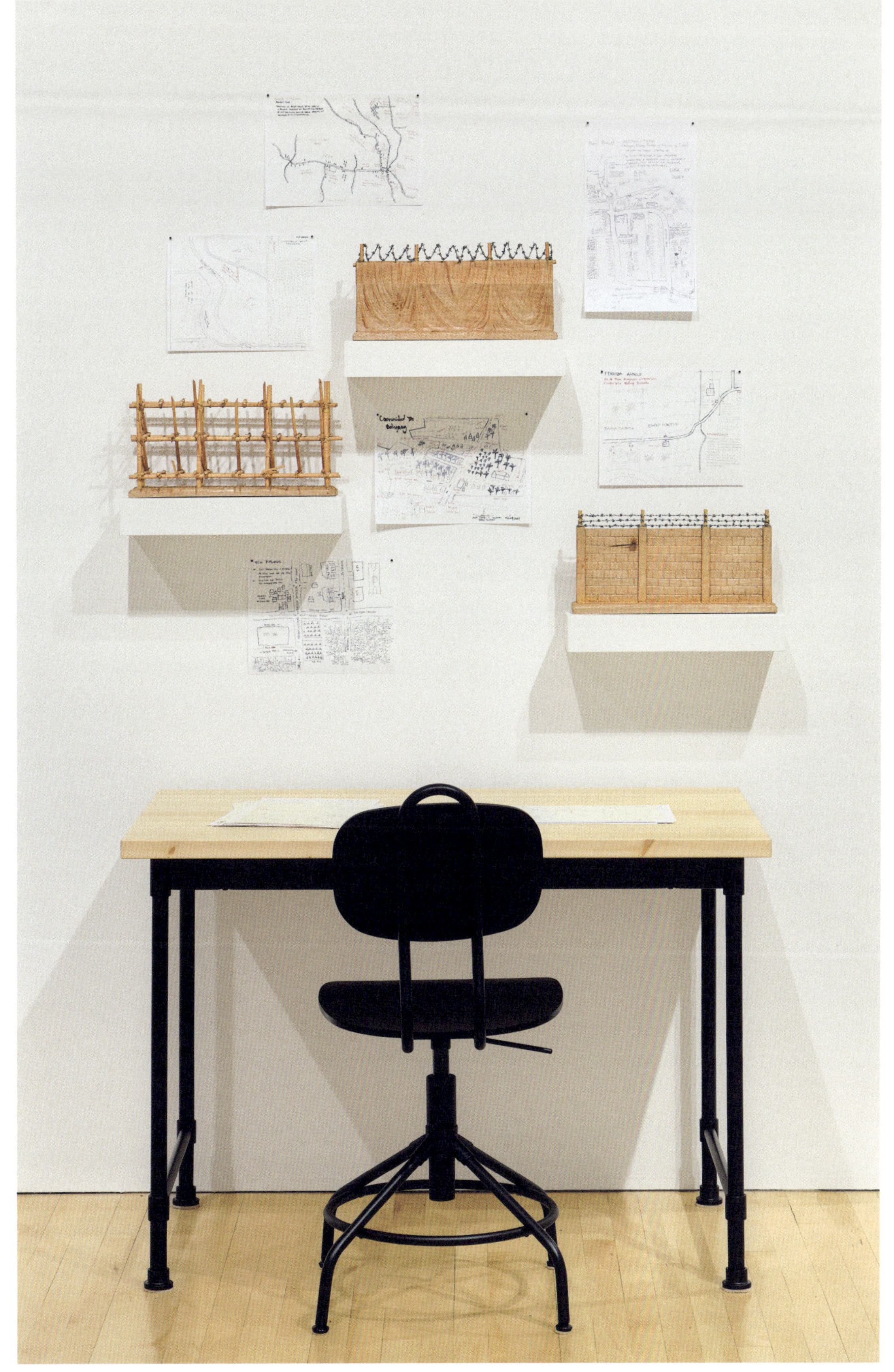

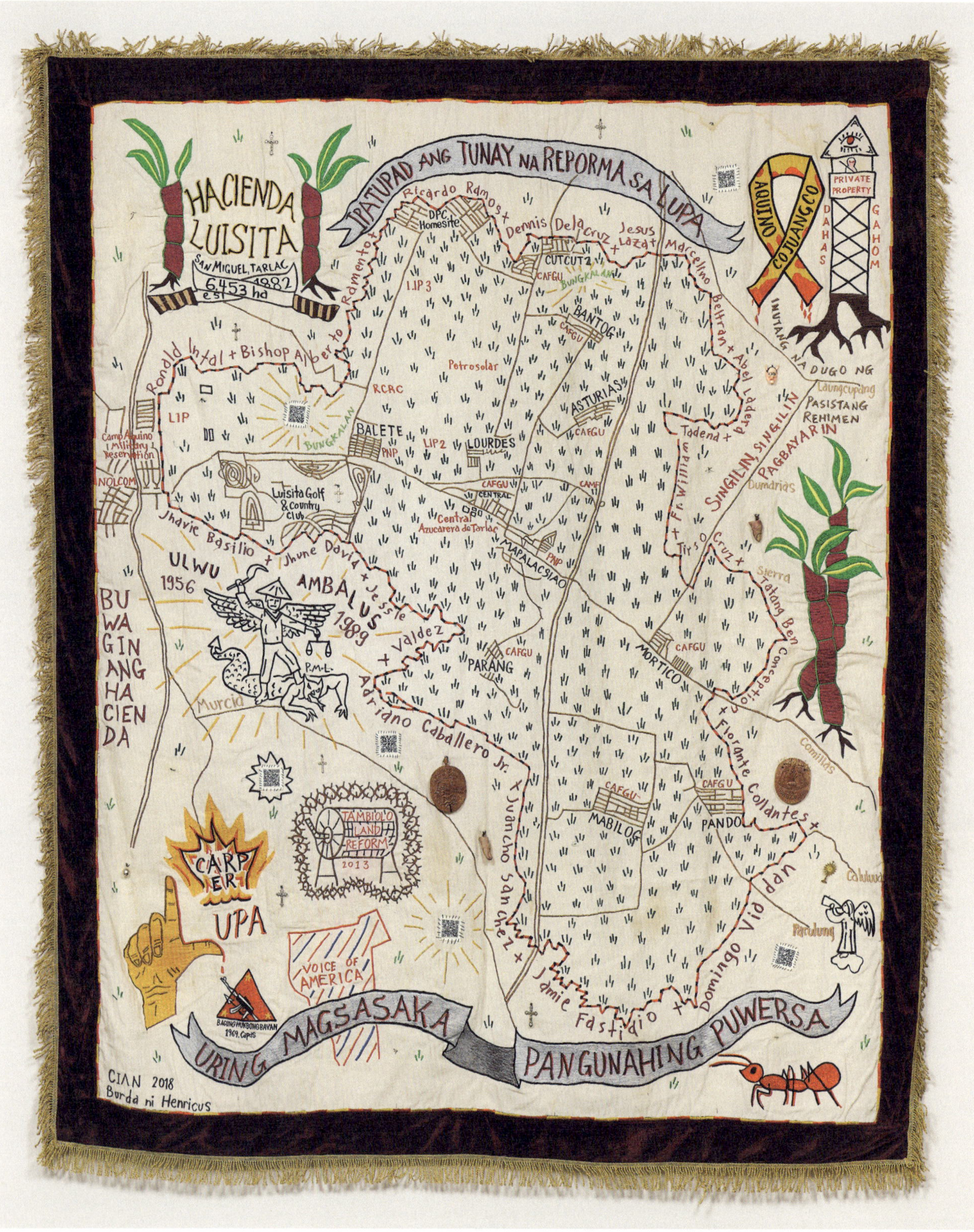

Feudal Fields, 2018

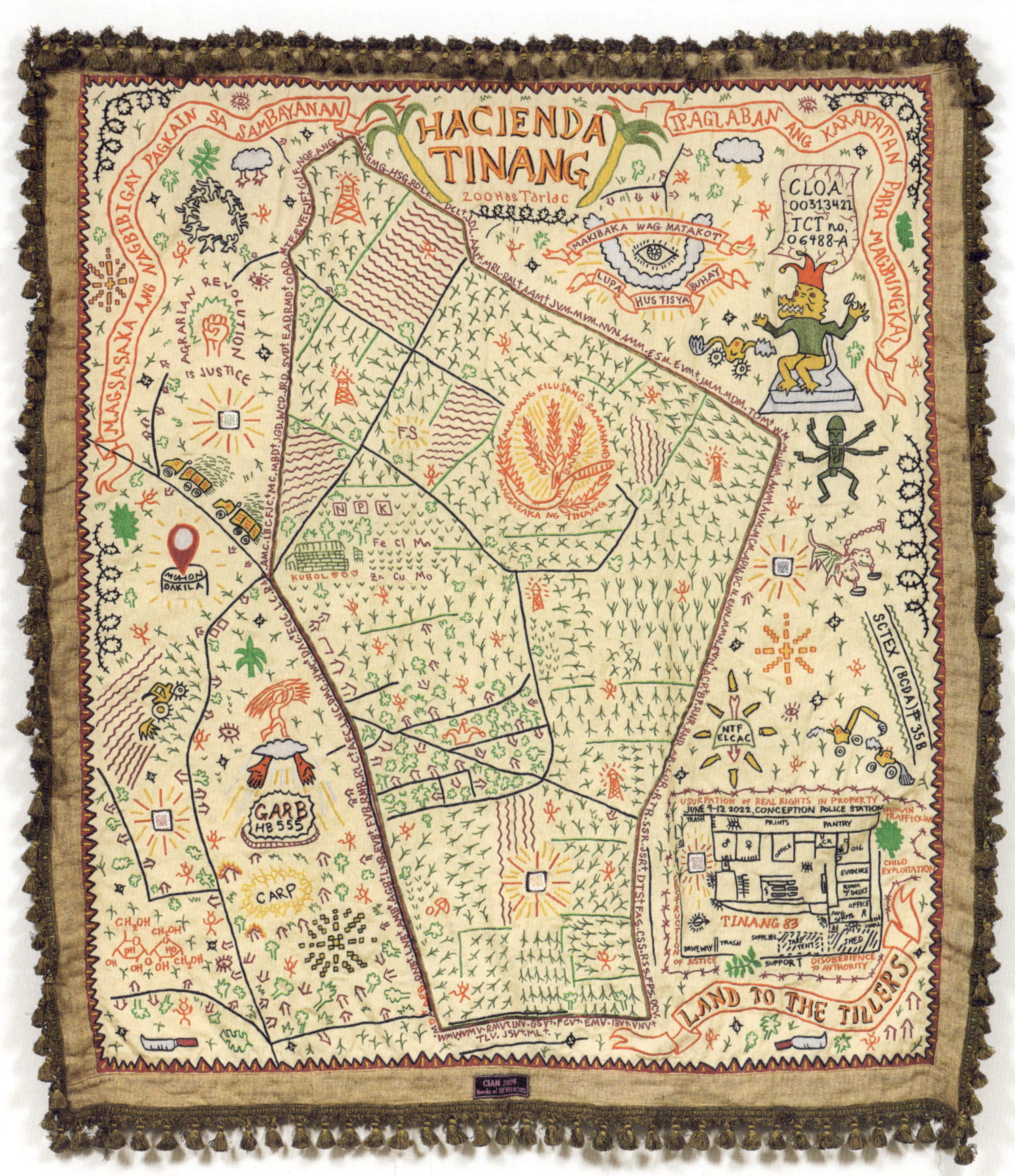

Feudal Fields II: Tinang, 2024

Caleb Duarte with Santa Cruz Barrios Unidos
Tres Terrenos, 2024
Wood, concrete, soil, and paint
Three towers: 144 × 32 × 32 in., each

Each of the three venues for *Seeing through Stone* is anchored by a prison surveillance tower. Over the course of the exhibition, these towers are transformed into beacons of freedom through collaborative community actions manifesting the care work and world-building done by Santa Cruz Barrios Unidos (SCBU). SCBU is a community center where art and life are blended, providing culturally driven and spiritually informed services to youth and adults while working to end incarceration. Run by formerly incarcerated and system-impacted individuals and serving as an autonomous space within the city of Santa Cruz, SCBU educates the public on the harms of prisons and carceral society. The center functions outside of carceral logics, offering community services including a food pantry, reentry resources, open mic poetry nights, after-school programs, a recording studio, and more, to create a space of belonging—a home—for those who have been marginalized in society.

Tres Terrenos emerged from a series of workshops artist Caleb Duarte undertook at SCBU as part of the center's everyday community-building practices. In each iteration of *Tres Terrenos*, compressed dirt at the base of the guard tower-turned-lighthouse provides grounding and support for the imposing structure. Over days and weeks, the tower's concrete walls are enlivened by colorful paintings created by workshop participants. These images, many of which draw from the Chicano Movement, evoke the long history of struggle, embodying relationships and beliefs that contradict structures of surveillance and control.

Caleb Duarte, born 1977 in El Paso, Texas, currently lives and works in Fresno, California.

Santa Cruz Barrios Unidos was founded in 1977 by Nane Alejandrez to promote multicultural social justice, nonviolence, and economic equity through cultural healing, civic leadership, and community development.

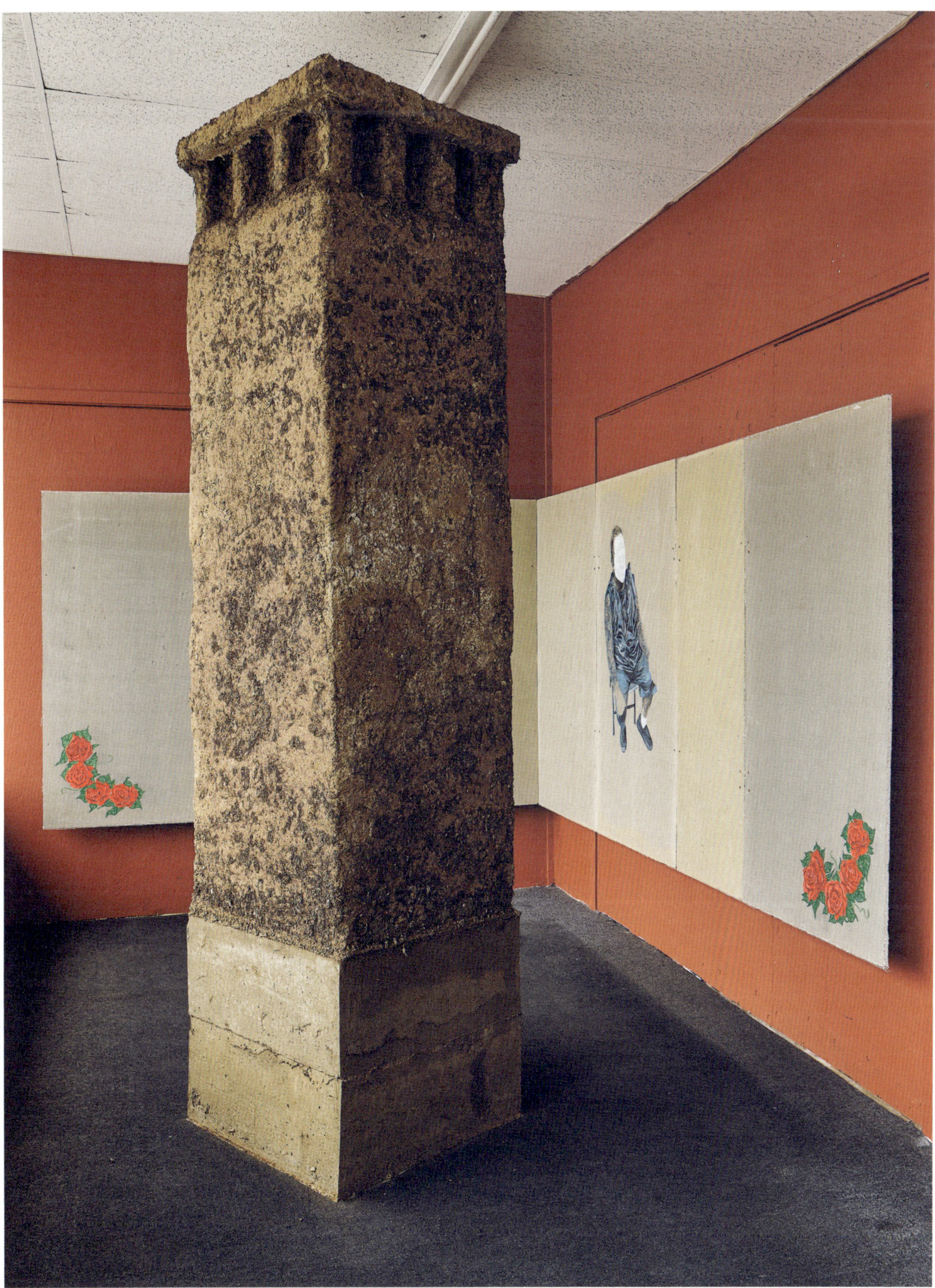

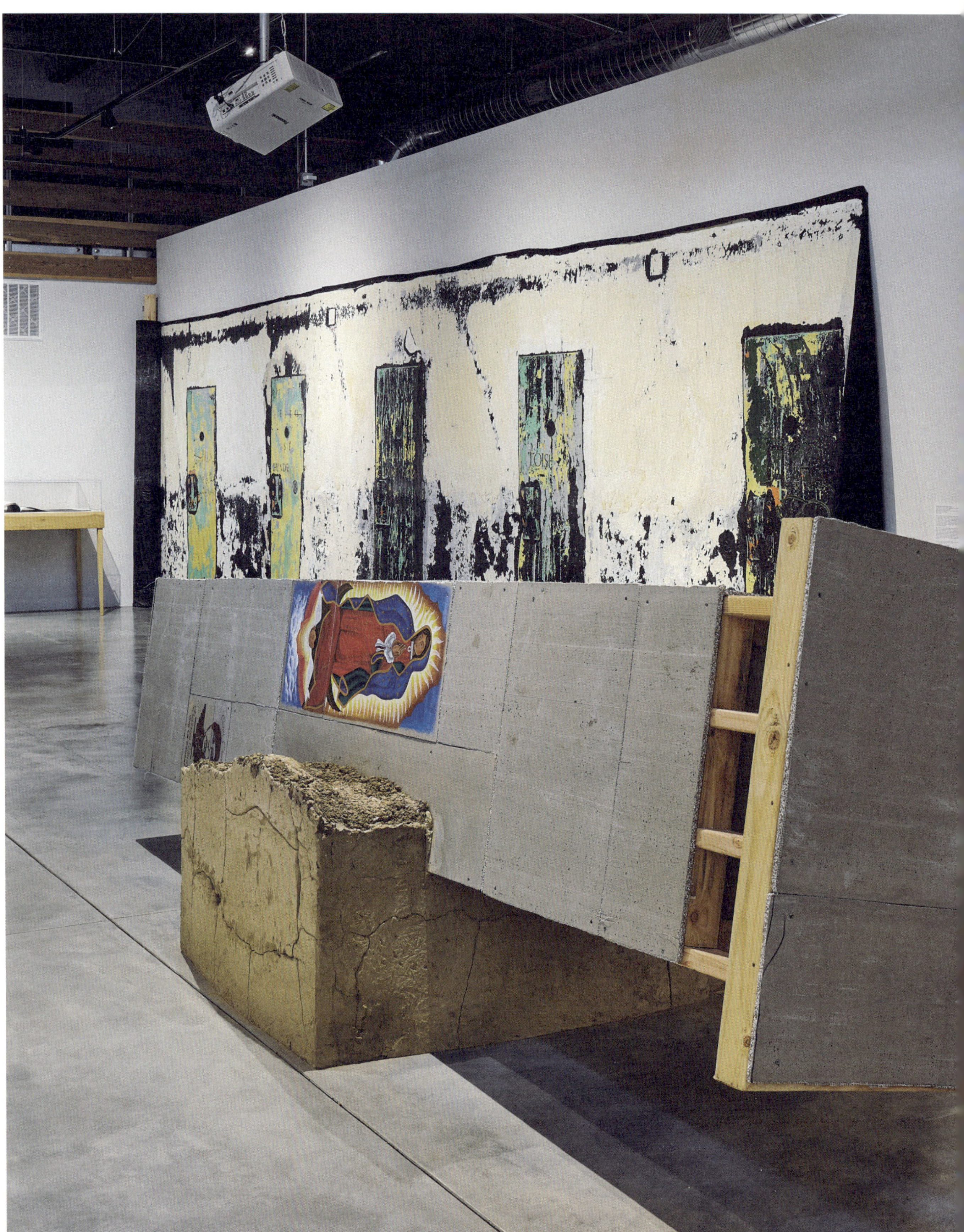

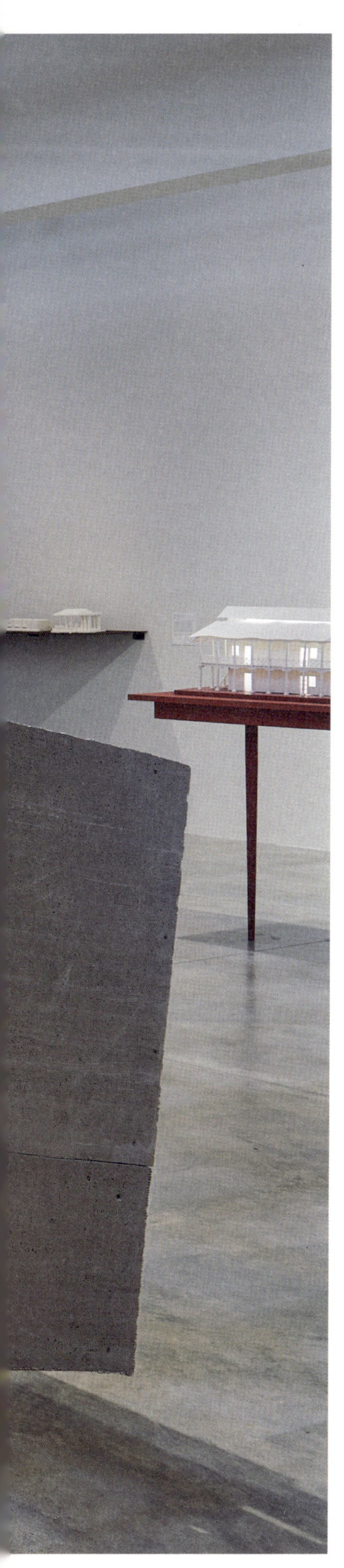

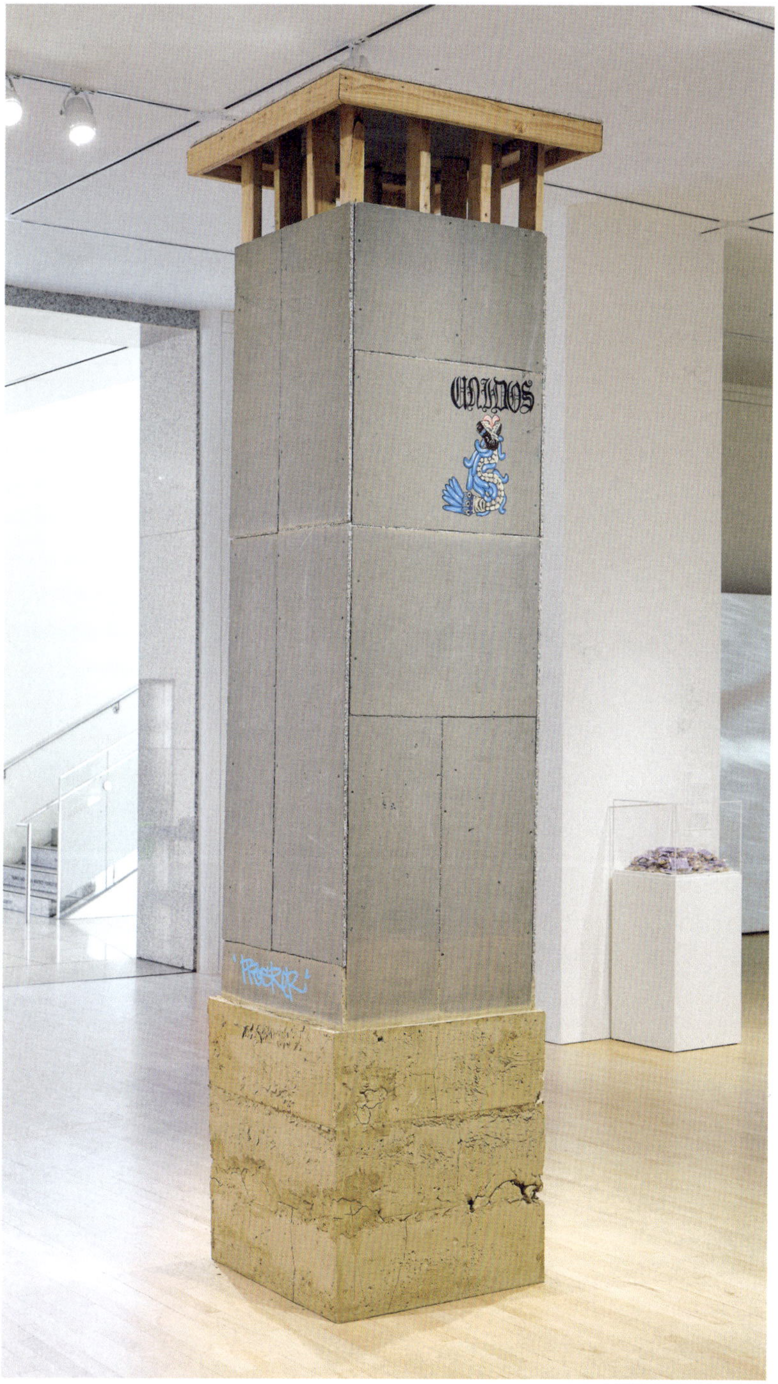

Explode! Platform (Cláudio Bueno and João Simões)
Passagem, 2024
Installation of books, paint, metal sheets, videos, and public program
Dimensions variable

For *Passagem*, Explode! Platform transformed the small library of the Institute of the Arts and Sciences (IAS) into an area of study, translation, and performance as part of an ongoing dialogue between artists, activists, and scholars in Brazil and the Visualizing Abolition program at the University of California, Santa Cruz.

In 2023, Explode! Platform launched this transnational dialogue with a dinner at Casa do Povo [House of the People], a historic cultural center in São Paulo run by the Coletivo de Diálogo e Diversidade de Táticas [Collective for Dialogue and Tactical Diversity]. Explode!, the Coletivo, and members of the Visualizing Abolition team were joined by a group of forty people involved in the abolitionist debate in Brazil. The resulting discussion touched on shared and distinct issues around prisons, the movement for abolition across geographies, the problems of translation and the reductiveness that can result, and the potential for international solidarity.

Videos of testimonies from the Casa do Povo dinner are included in *Passagem*, the architectural enactment and continuation of this discussion. The library at the IAS is housed in a corridor off the gallery's main lobby, which ends at a door marked "Staff Only." As a result, the participatory artwork operates in the physical ambiguity of a place of circulation, in which movement and confinement are blurred. Within this ambiguous space, Explode! has added books in Portuguese about prisons and abolition in the context of Brazil to the existing collection of texts about the same subjects in the United States. Walls have been transformed into a repository for ideas about abolition as a border-crossing movement, with visitors invited to contribute. These interventions manifest the difficult work that is required for transnational solidarities to flourish, and highlight the untranslatability, nuance, and opacity of concepts produced in geopolitically specific contexts. However, the space is also an escape route—leading to an emergency exit—and thus a provocation to overcome the social, political, and spatial obstacles that limit our ability to imagine, fabulate, and create radically free worlds.

Explode! Platform, founded 2014, operates at the intersections of art, pedagogy, and social justice. Led by artists, researchers, and curators **Cláudio Bueno and João Simões** and a national and international network of collaborators, Explode! facilitates presentations, performances, and immersive interventions in different spaces and formats that emphasize coexistence, listening, debate, and experimentation.

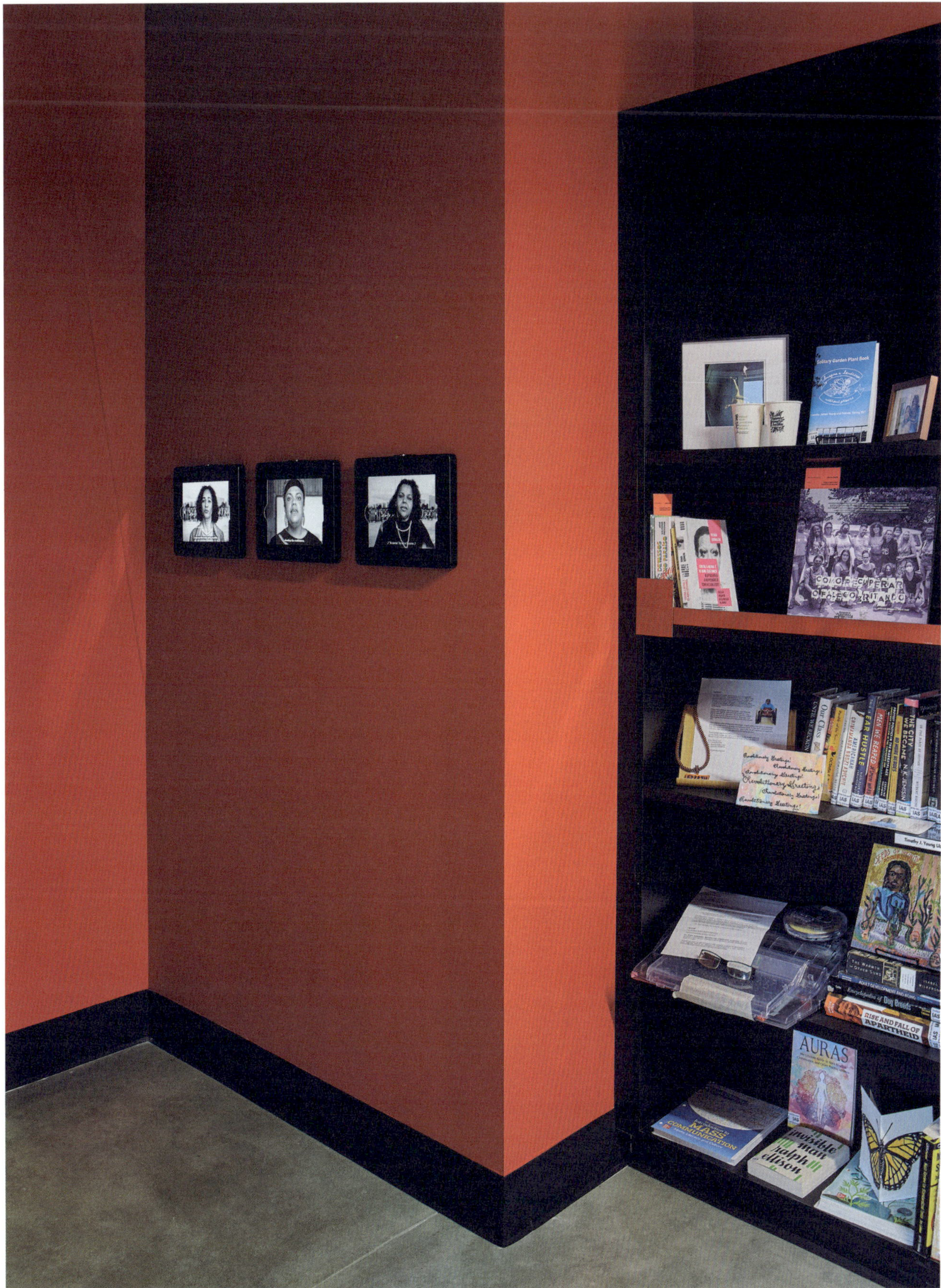

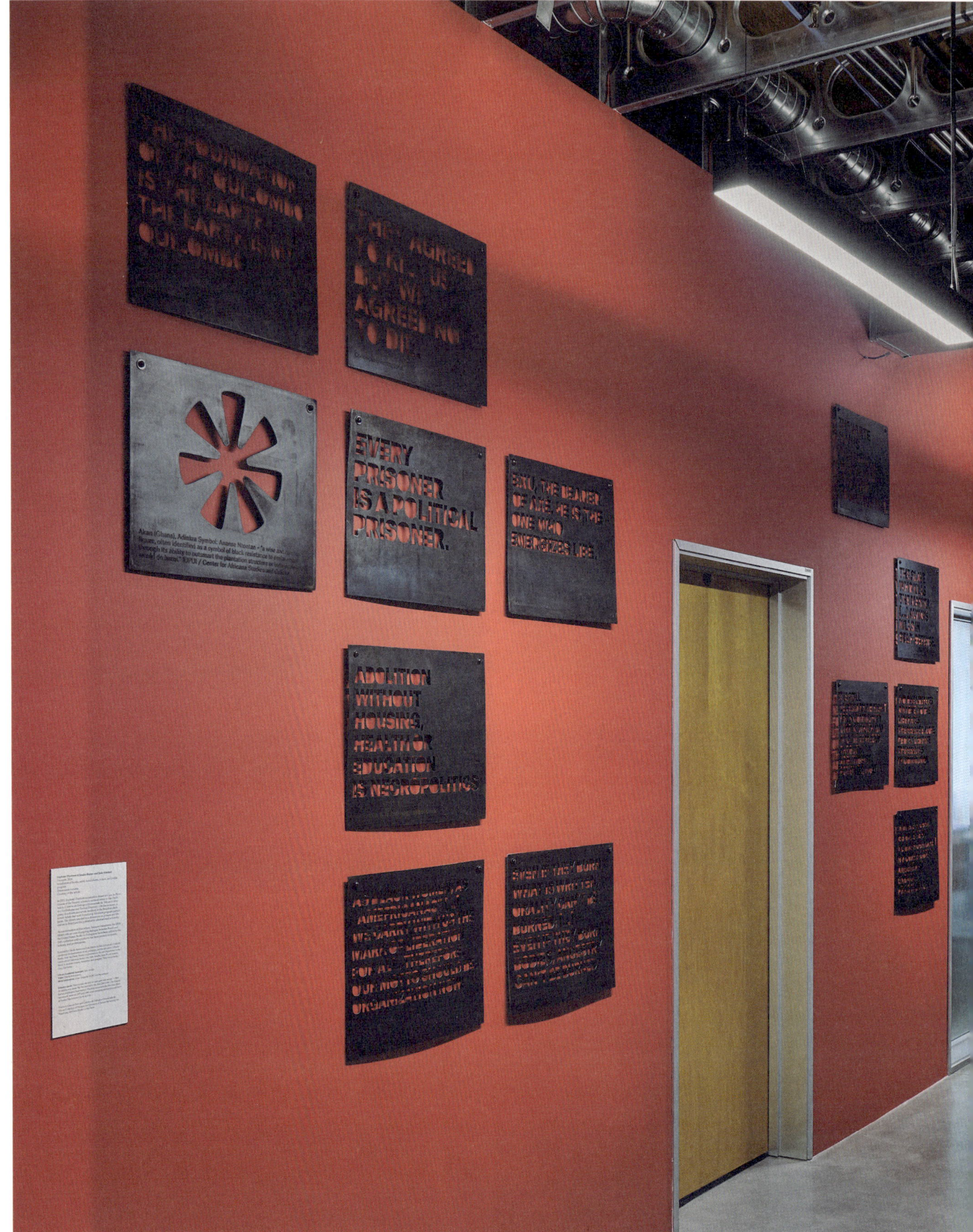
EVERY PRISONER IS A POLITICAL PRISONER.
ADOLITION WITHOUT HOUSING, HEALTH OR EDUCATION IS NECROPOLITICS

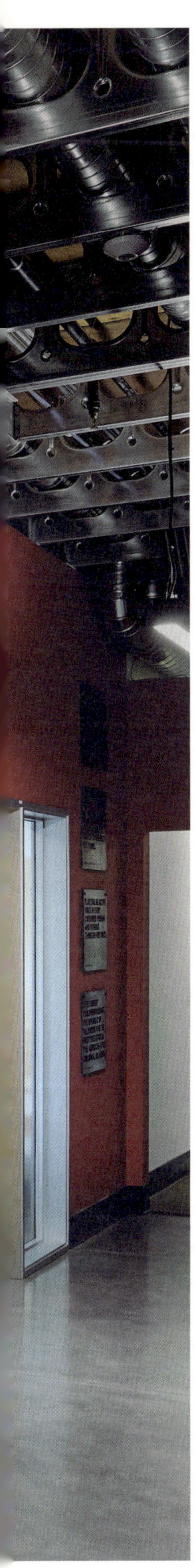

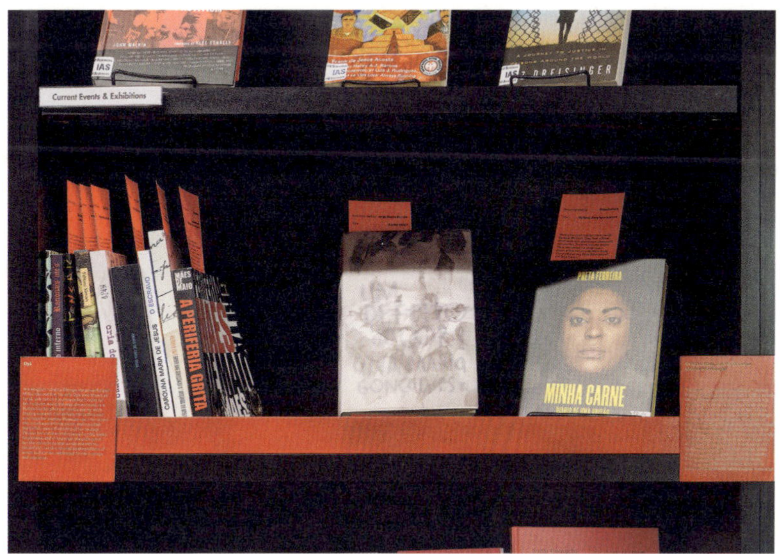

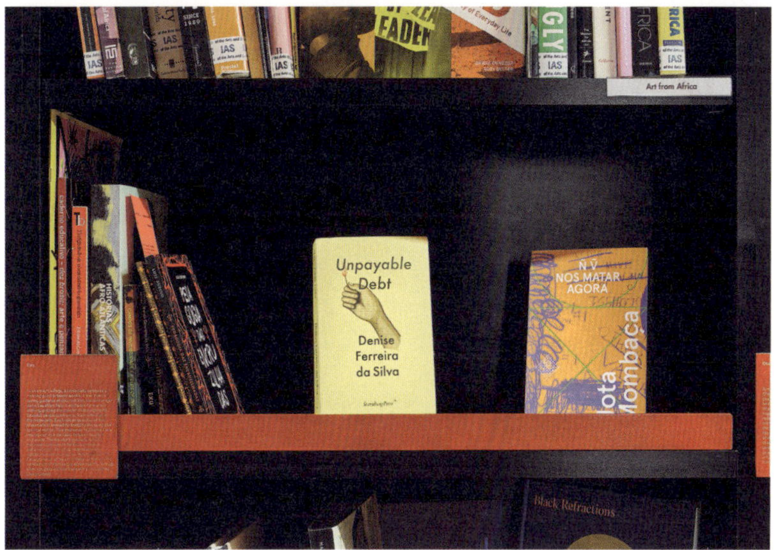

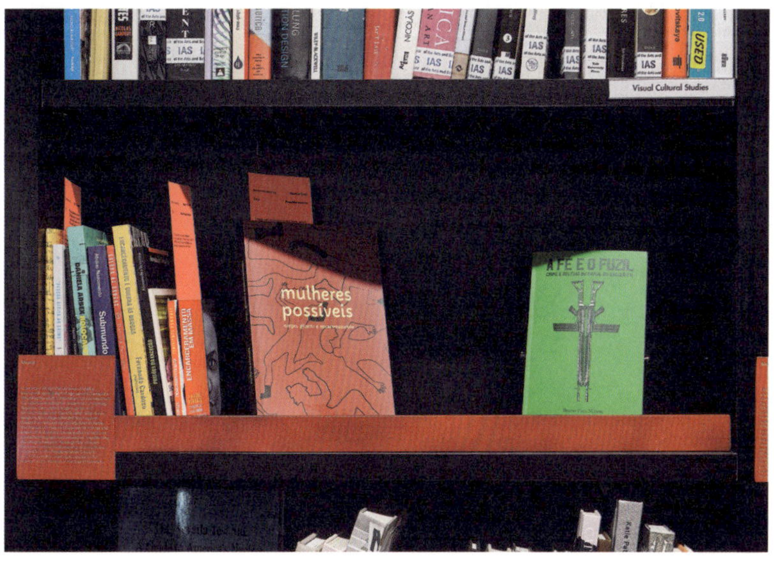

**Forensic Architecture Investigation Unit
at Al-Haq**
Platform for Gaza, 2024–ongoing
Online database and trackpad

For *Platform for Gaza*, the Forensic Architecture Investigation (FAI) Unit at Al-Haq is employing OSINT (open source intelligence) tools to scrape social media and satellite analysis, in order to harvest all available visual evidence to track the ongoing assault on Gaza and the Palestinian people.

Al-Haq was established in 1979 as the first Palestinian human rights organization and one of the first of its kind in the Middle East. Since its inception in 2020, the FAI Unit has worked in service of Al-Haq's mission to protect and promote Palestinian rights and liberation while cultivating a new understanding of how this tradition of monitoring and documentation can function in Palestine, where human rights defenders are themselves living under occupation and apartheid, regularly subjected to both digital and physical violence from Israeli occupying forces.

Since October 2023, for the first time since its establishment, Al-Haq has had almost no direct access to the ground in Gaza. Field researchers have been forcibly expelled from their homes, along with their families and the rest of the population of northern Gaza. As the Israeli occupation has blocked access to Gaza, including by cutting off mobile networks and internet access during its colossal assault on Palestinians in the strip, *Platform for Gaza* represents the FAI Unit's

work to continue to record conditions on the ground and bring them into public view.

The **Forensic Architecture Investigation Unit at Al-Haq** was established in Ramallah, Palestine, in 2020 as a collaboration between Al-Haq and Forensic Architecture, a London-based research agency.

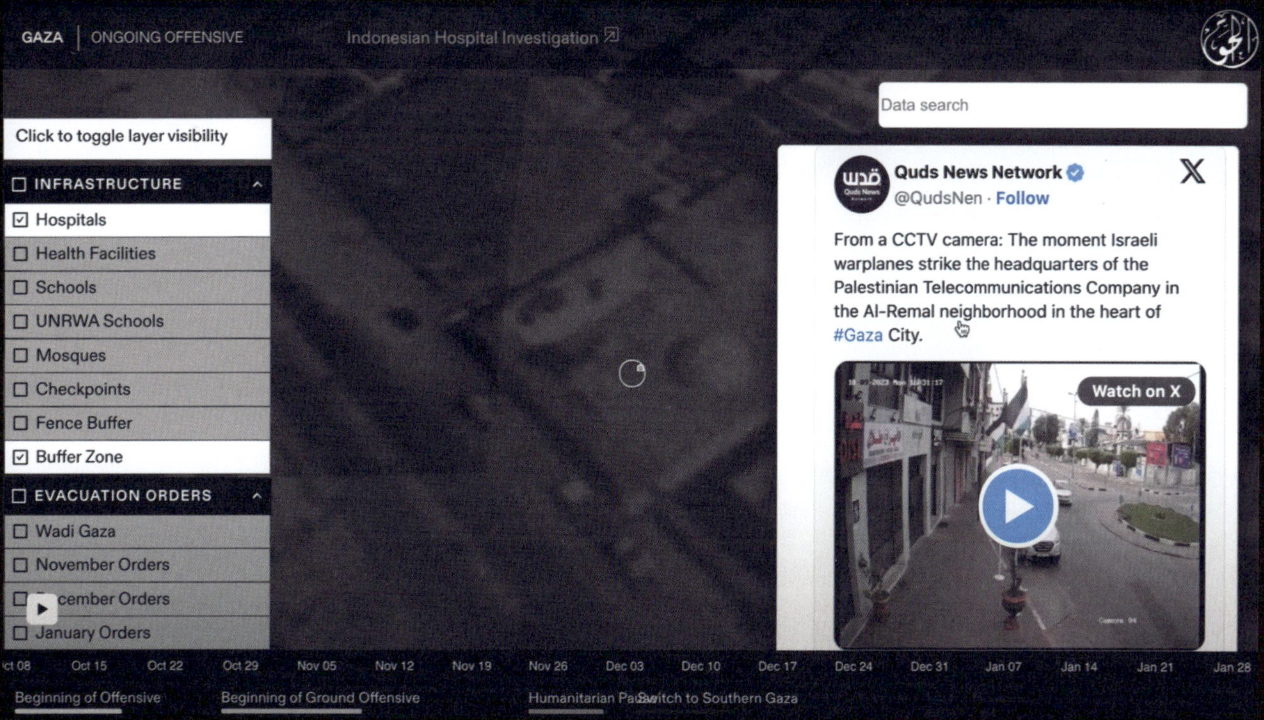

GAZA | ONGOING OFFENSIVE

Indonesian Hospital Investigation

Click to toggle layer visibility

INFRASTRUCTURE
☐ Hospitals
☐ Health Facilities
☐ Schools
☐ UNRWA Schools
☐ Mosques
☐ Checkpoints
☐ Fence Buffer
☑ Buffer Zone

EVACUATION ORDERS
☐ Wadi Gaza
☐ November Orders
☐ December Orders
☐ January Orders

Oct 08   Oct 15   Oct 22   Oct 29   Nov 05   Nov 12   Nov 19   Nov 26   Dec 03   Dec 10   Dec 17   Dec 24   Dec 31   Jan 07   Jan 14   Jan 21   Jan 28

Beginning of Offensive   Beginning of Ground Offensive   Humanitarian Pause   Switch to Southern Gaza

Data search

Quds News Network
@QudsNen · Follow

From a CCTV camera: The moment Israeli
warplanes strike the headquarters of the
Palestinian Telecommunications Company in
the Al-Remal neighborhood in the heart of
#Gaza City.

Watch on X

The Freedom Theatre
Your Time Is Not Your Time, 2024
Single-channel film and sound
34 minutes

Your Time Is Not Your Time centers on a discussion between members of The Freedom Theatre in the Jenin refugee camp. The conversation, which took place while Jenin was under siege, is organized around three words: "time," "space," and "liberation." Members share the lost meaning of time—the impossibility of relying on plans or scheduling appointments. One of the members states that time does not exist for them except as personal moments in which they notice they are still alive—for example, after surviving a raid. Another member mentions the crisis wrought by the sheer repetition of violent events, which cause them to relive past traumas through similarity with recent attacks or torture episodes. Individual feelings and reflections mark a collective experience of trauma in which every aspect of one's routine is deeply repressed. "*Who* is time?" they ask, and they answer: "The occupation." In this restrained space of living genocide, the members of The Freedom Theatre reflect on what liberation would mean if Palestinians were free.

The Freedom Theatre [مسرح الحرية] is a Palestinian community-based theater and cultural center located in the Jenin refugee camp in the northern part of the West Bank. Established in 2006, The Freedom Theatre promotes artistic expression as an integrated part of the quest for justice, equality, and freedom. Operating with the belief that, for the oppressed, the arts have always been a powerful tool for liberation, the organization offers programming that includes theater workshops, professional theater productions, and courses in film, photography, creative writing, and theater. The Freedom Theatre is an integral part of the cultural resistance movement in Palestine, generating a vision of a free society.

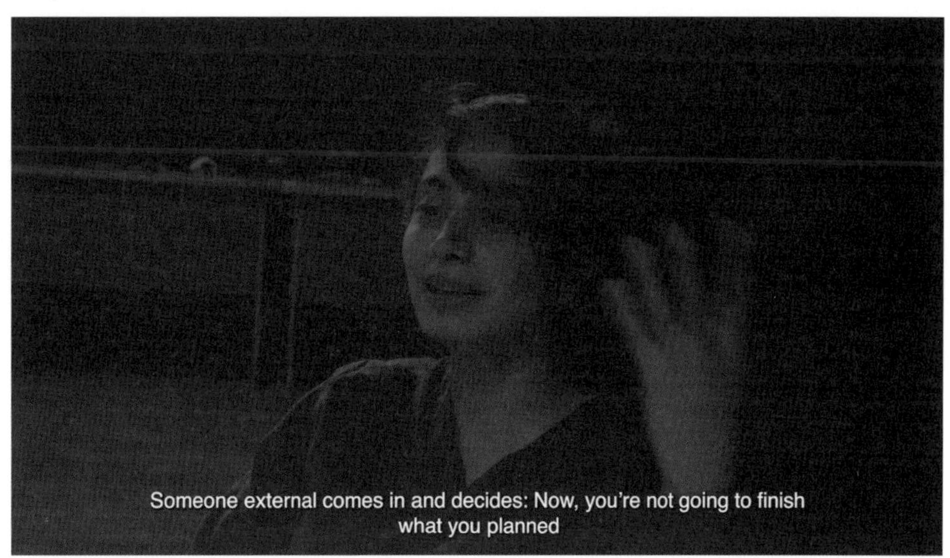
Someone external comes in and decides: Now, you're not going to finish
what you planned

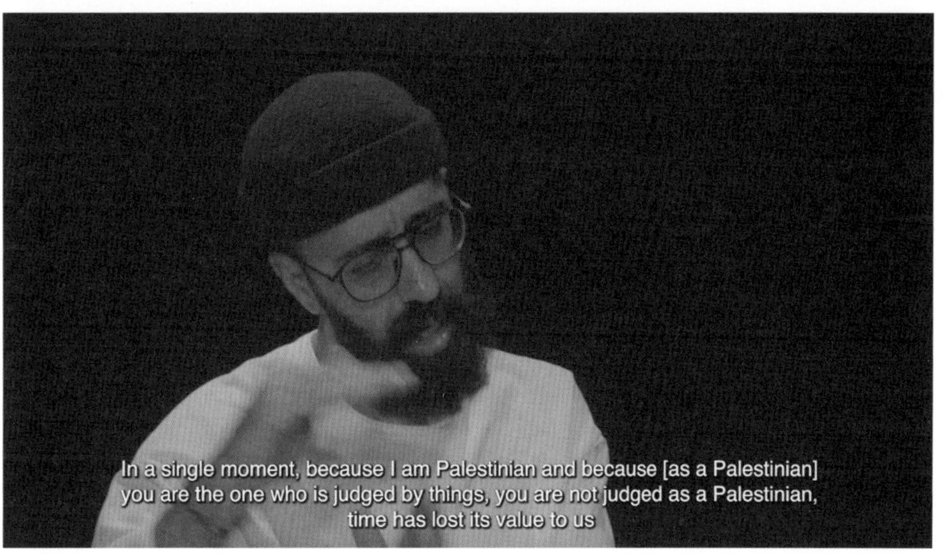
In a single moment, because I am Palestinian and because [as a Palestinian]
you are the one who is judged by things, you are not judged as a Palestinian,
time has lost its value to us

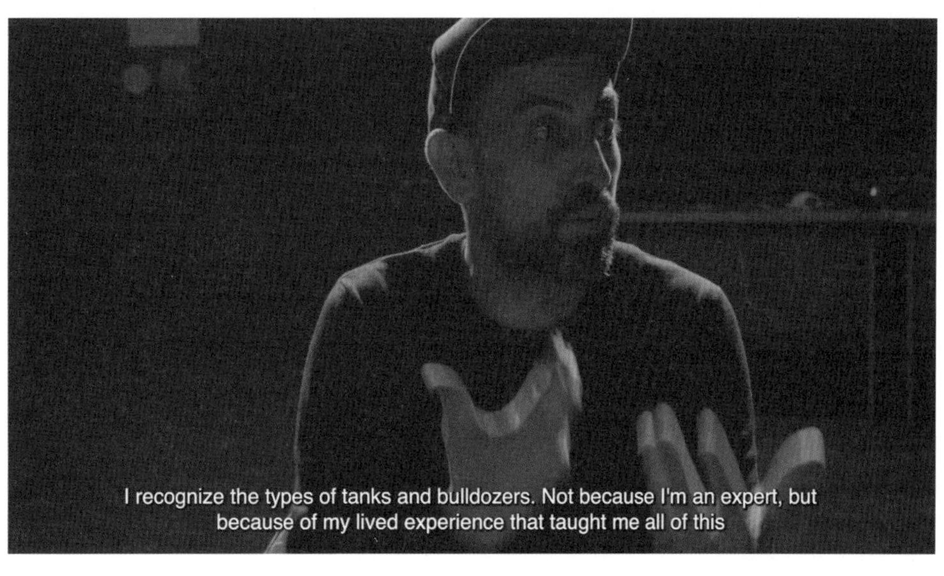
I recognize the types of tanks and bulldozers. Not because I'm an expert, but
because of my lived experience that taught me all of this

Frente 3 de Fevereiro
Ancestral Intelligence, 2023–24
Three-channel video and sound
49:44 minutes

Frente 3 de Fevereiro is a collective founded in 2004 following the murder of Flávio Ferreira Sant'Ana, a Black dentist, by São Paulo military police. Based in São Paulo, the group merges direct action and aesthetics, moving between image, music, performance, and literature to expose and denounce the brutality faced by Black people in Brazil while working to create a new reality.

For *Ancestral Intelligence*, Frente 3 de Fevereiro uses voice cloning and deepfake artificial intelligence technologies to reanimate the movements, gestures, and speech patterns of Dona Maurinete Lima (1942–2018), the collective's founder. AI is deployed as a counter-technology, reembodying and resurrecting Lima, a Black feminist liberation leader, in order to bring ancestral wisdom to current and future struggles.

In addition to the animation, the video installation includes sound files and images of the collective and its radical interventions and world-building efforts against state violence and racism. The protests and collective actions combine with the words of the resurrected Dona Maurinete Lima, creating a vision of the revolutionary possibilities of generational struggle. For this work's second edition—a commission for the *Seeing through Stone* exhibition—the collective included three new chapters showing its research in Haiti, Colombia, and the United States. The chapters map oppressive technologies that impact Black populations across these locations, connecting the Brazilian context to other countries in the Americas.

Frente 3 de Fevereiro was formed in 2004 in São Paulo, Brazil.

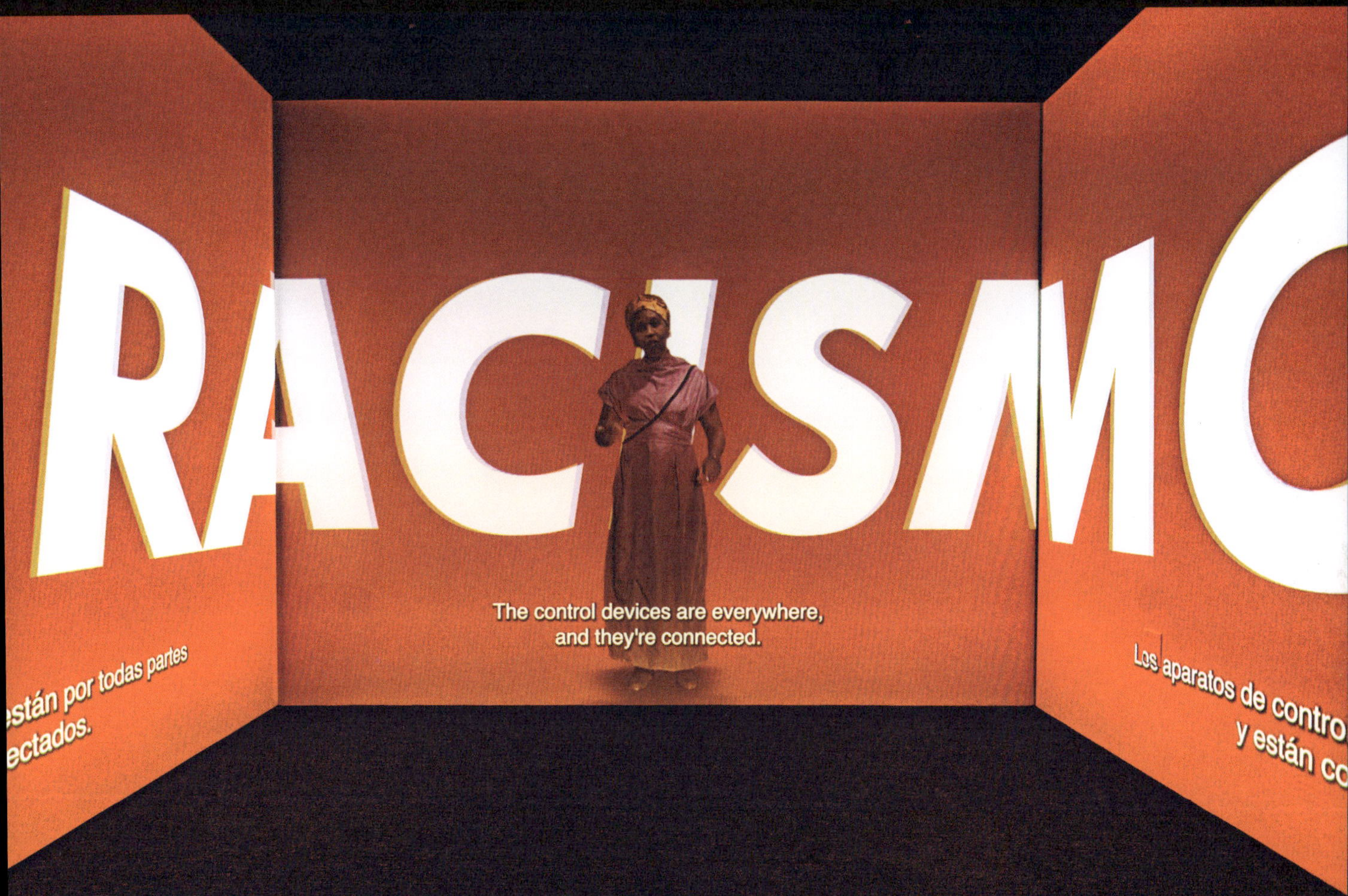

RACISMO
The control devices are everywhere,
and they're connected.
están por todas partes
ectados.
Los aparatos de contro
y están co

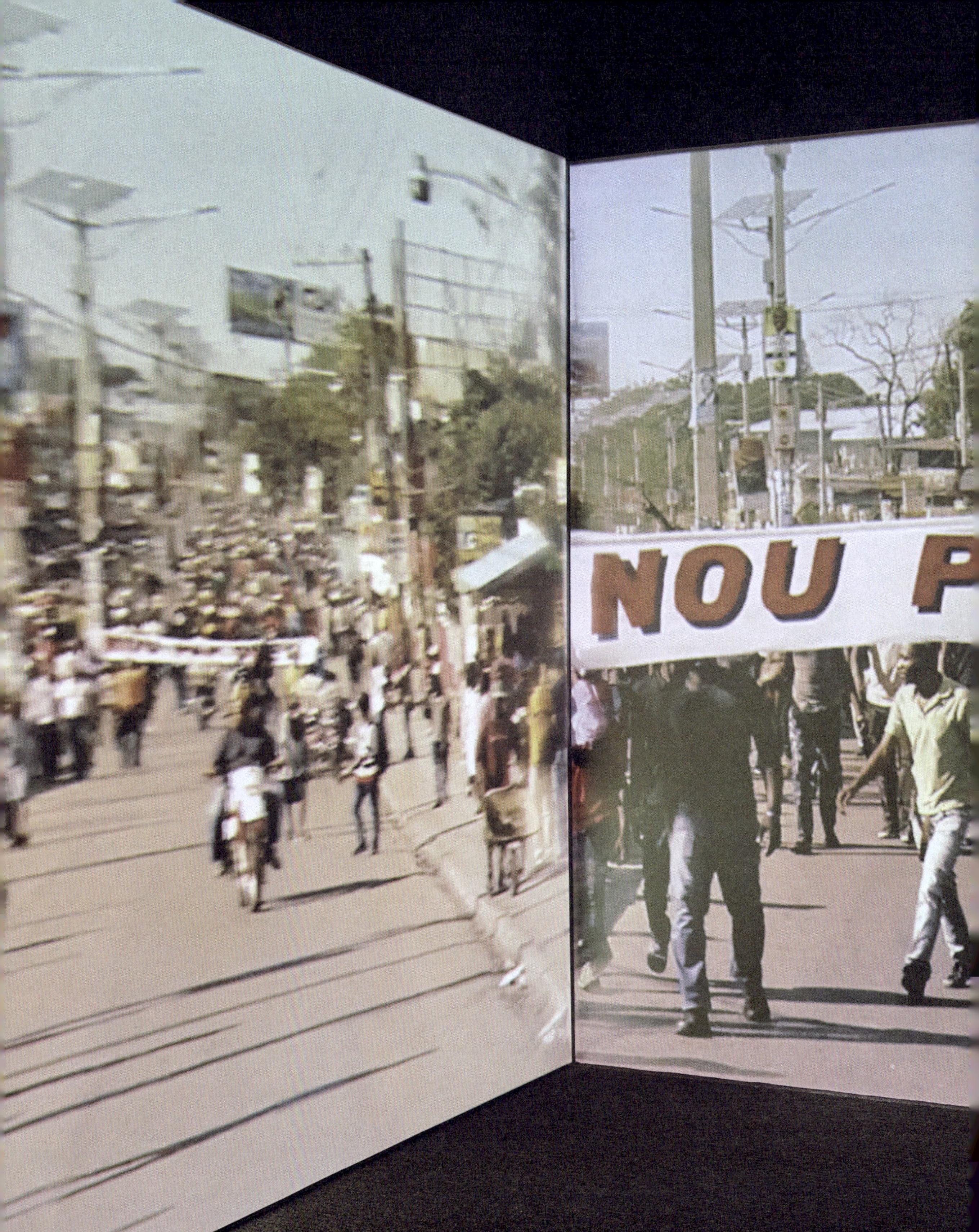
NOU P

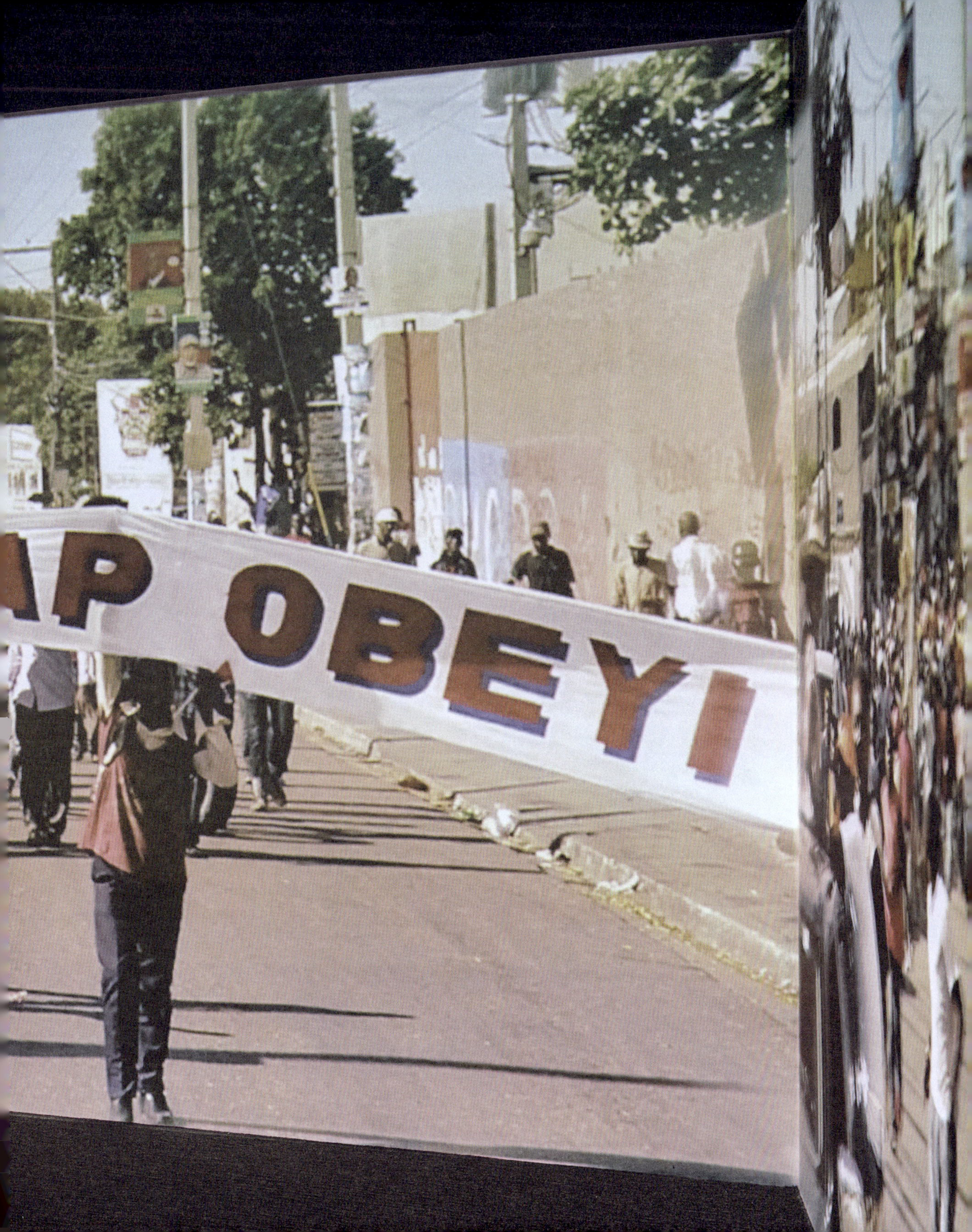
AP OBEYI

Charles Gaines
Manifestos 4, 2020
Four graphite drawings on paper, two monitors, four speakers, and hanging speaker shelves
116¾ × 300 × 12 in., overall

Sky Box II, 2020
Acrylic, digital print, aluminum, polyester film, and LED lights
144 × 288 in.

The *Dred Scott* decision serves as the basis for Charles Gaines' *Sky Box II* and *Manifestos 4*. In this legal case, first tried in 1847 and decided on March 6, 1857, the US Supreme Court ruled 7–2 that enslaved people were not citizens of the United States and, therefore, could not expect any protection from the federal government or courts. The opinion also stated that Congress had no authority to ban slavery from a federal territory.

In *Manifestos 4*, the 1857 texts of Chief Justice Roger Taney's majority opinion and Justice Benjamin Robbins Curtis' minority opinion have been systematically converted into musical notation, with each letter of the alphabet corresponding to a specific note. The notation is then used to realize a musical composition for sextet, shown as a hand-drawn score, alongside soaring audio of it being performed and videos of the scrolling judicial texts.

The legal processes and testimonies surrounding the *Dred Scott* decision form a wall of words in *Sky Box II*. In an upper row, scans of the handwritten court papers show transcribed conversations between lawyers, witnesses, and judges from the initial 1847 trial. A lower row features their typed translation. Highlighting the arguments and trials leading up to the famous decision, rather than the decision itself, *Sky Box II* brings focus to the inner workings of the legal system and the process of constructing meaning through interpreting human bodies and skin.

More than a place for study of the legal processes of discrimination, *Sky Box II* also offers a space for contemplation of what could emerge out of this history of racism and oppression. The texts become illegible as the lights begin to fade in the exhibition space, with the words slowly giving way to a starry sky. Tens of thousands of holes have been laser-cut into the work's surface and lit from within, dissolving the textual and racial logic of the US legal system into stars. Enveloped by the expansive night sky, black and luminous beyond perception, we must grapple with the limits of our own beliefs, and consider how to extend our own imaginations of what is possible.

"I'm not using this to liberate the world," Gaines says. "My thoughts are more abstract than that. But if we engage in this construction of meaning in a way that I try and emphasize in my work, then maybe the cultural discourse will shift and change."[1]

Charles Gaines, born 1944 in Charleston, South Carolina, lives and works in Los Angeles.

1. Charles Gaines, "Why Is a Bird a Bird, and I'm Not?," SFMOMA, video, 6:06 minutes, accessed April 10, 2024, https://www.sfmoma .org/watch/charles-gaines-why-is-a-bird-a-bird-and-im-not/.

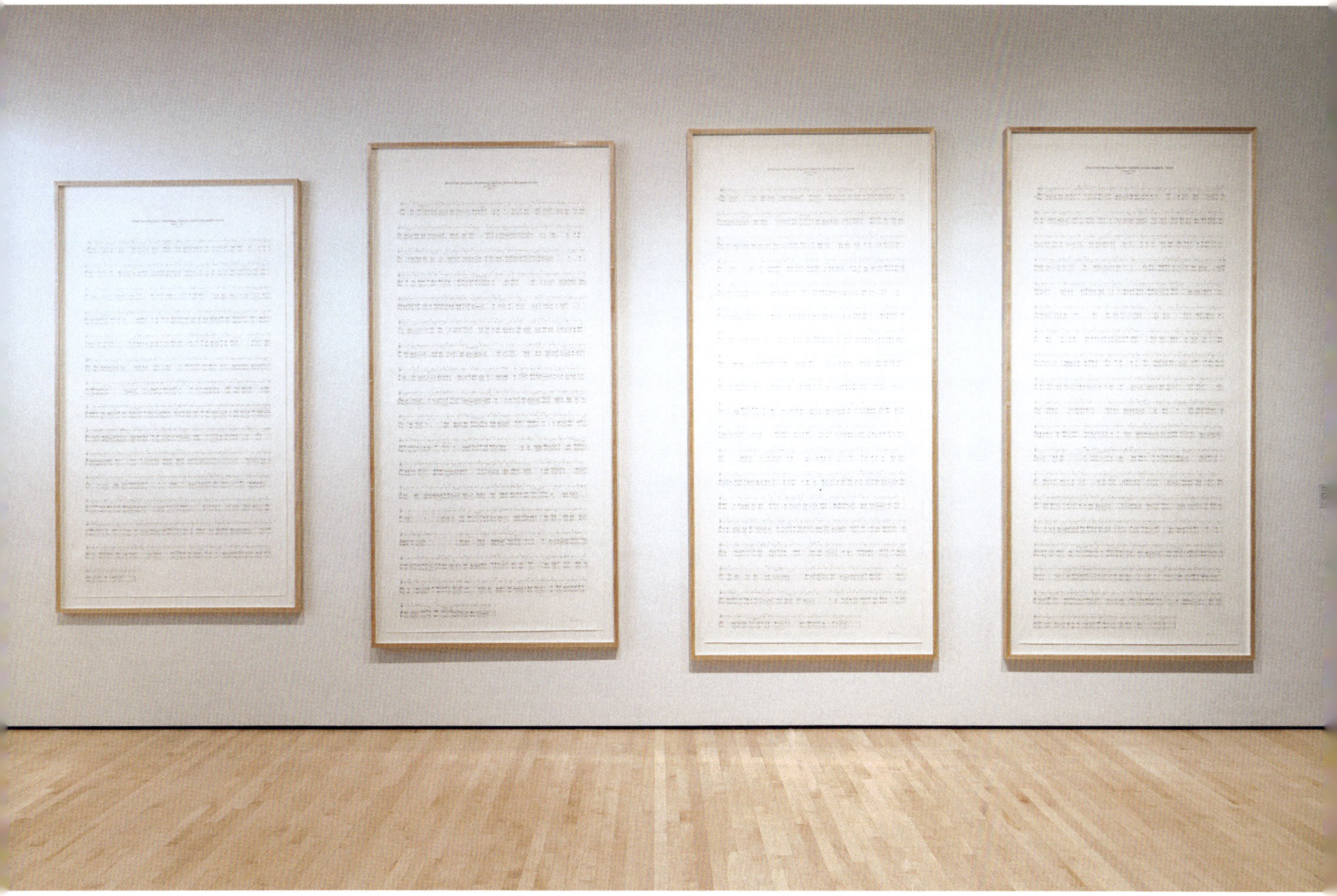

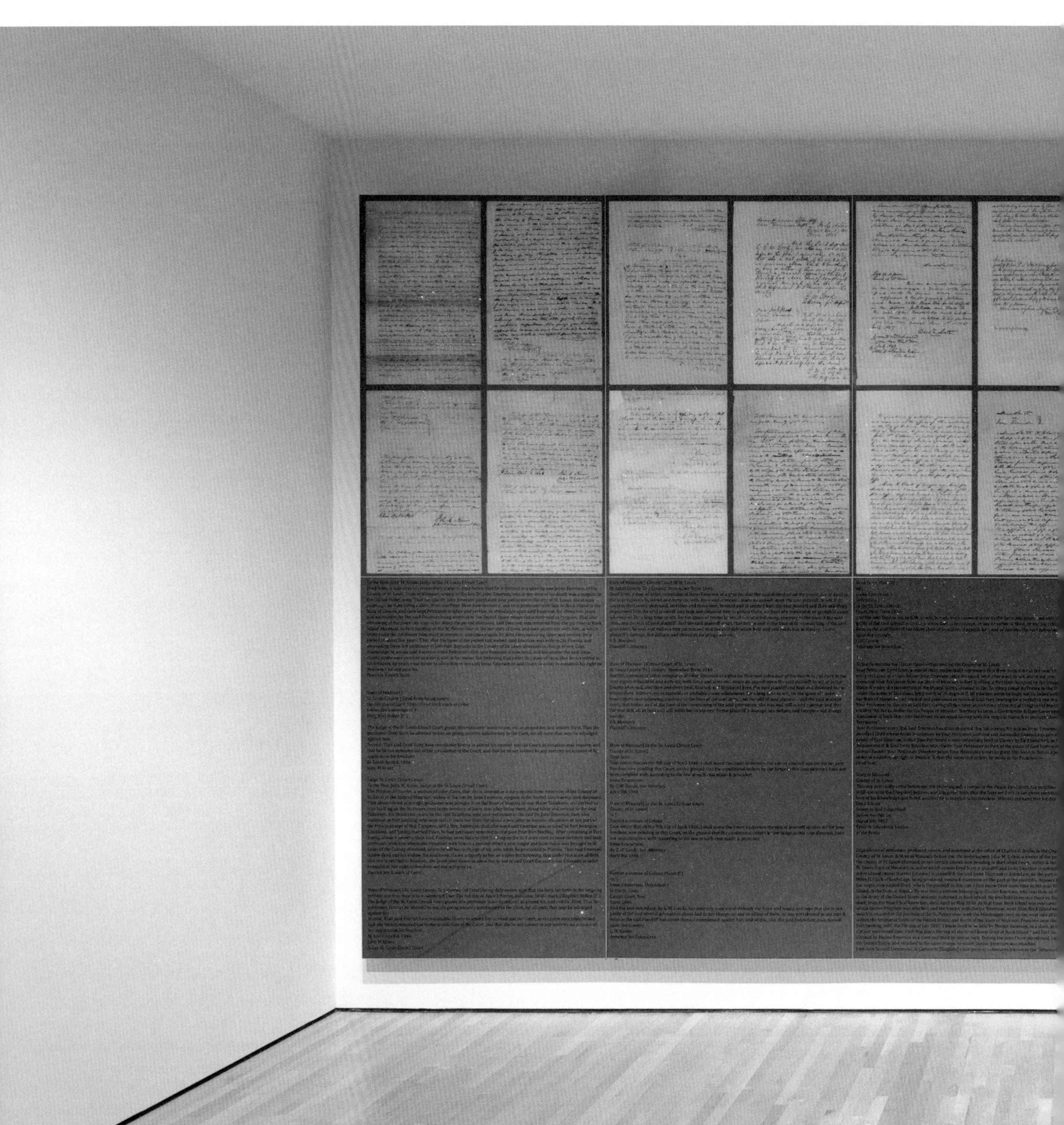

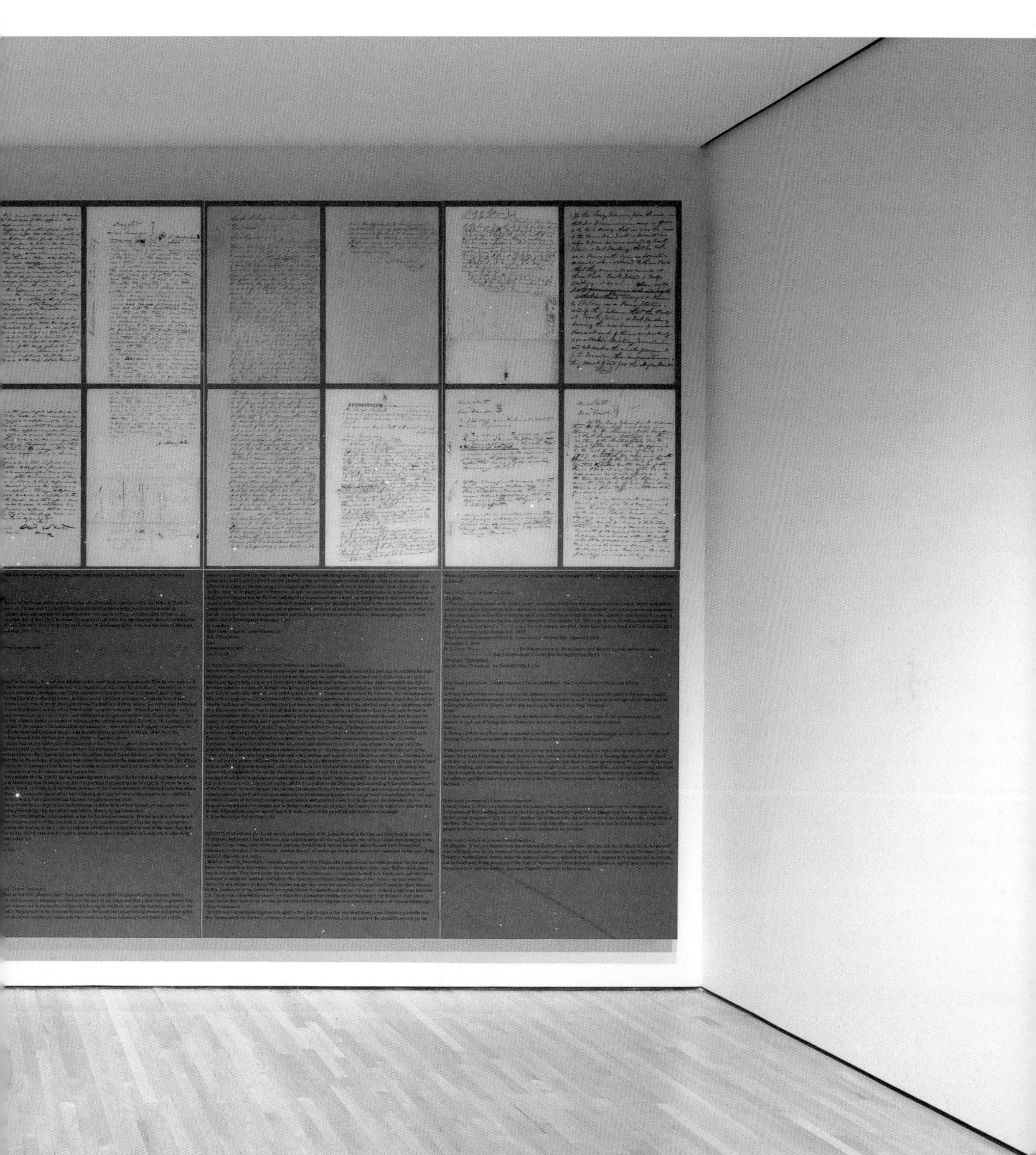

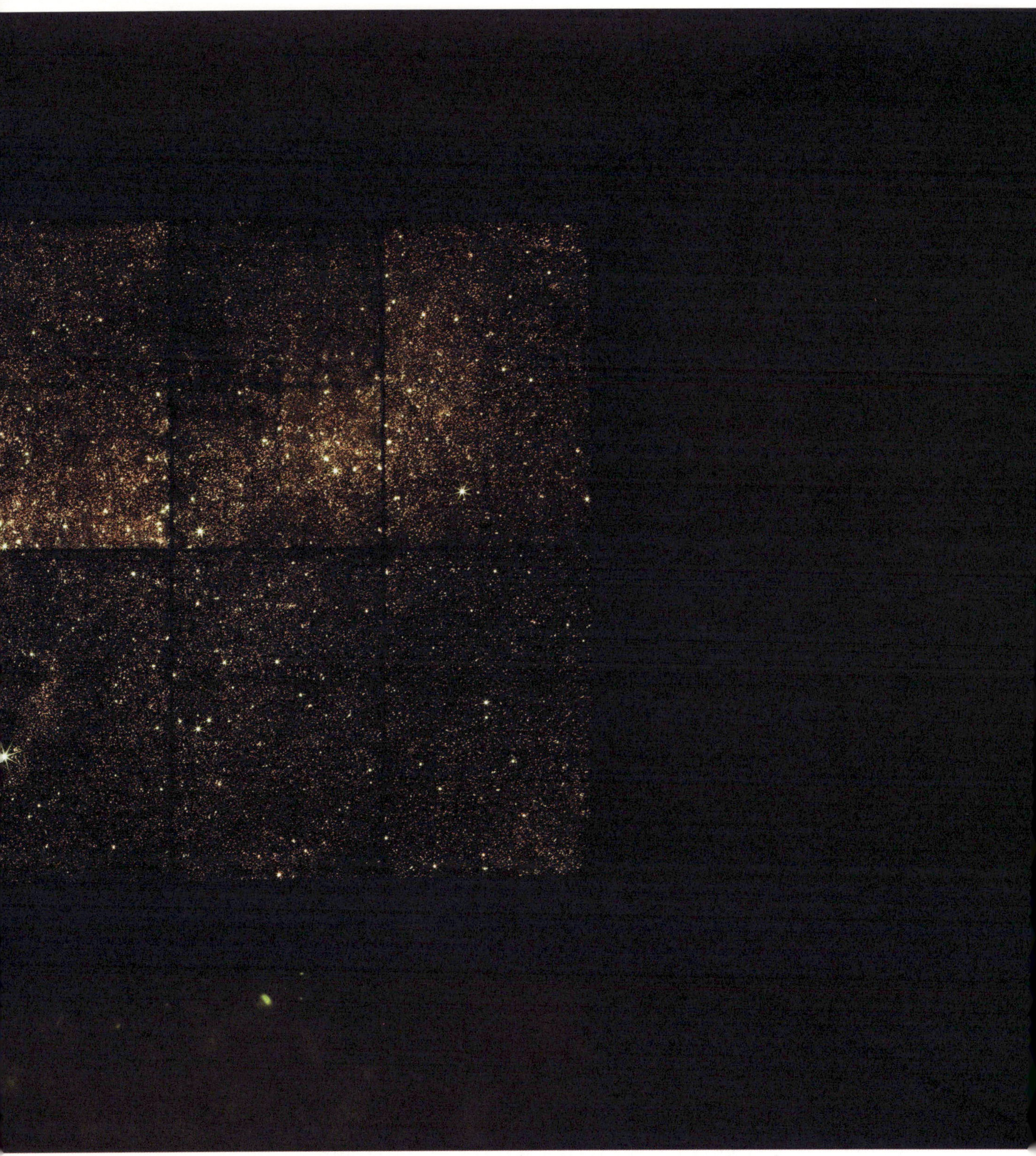

Guillermo Galindo

Llantambores, 2015
PVC pipes, immigrant tire inner tubes, wood, cloth booties, and border barbed wire
35½ × 53 × 17 in.

Caravan Variation Flag, 2015
Acrylic on beacon flag used by humanitarian aid group Water Stations, sewn on linen backing
30 × 47 in.

Voices Flag / Bandera de voces, 2017
Acrylic on beacon flags used by humanitarian aid group Water Stations
21½ × 47 in.

Ojo / Eye, 2015
Bicycle wheel, wood, steel, and amplifier
32¼ × 11¼ × 51¼ in.

Guillermo Galindo's charged objects and instruments are made of discarded materials and personal items found in the desert along the US-Mexico border. The drum-like *Llantambores* is fashioned from inner tire skins used as innertubes to cross the Rio Grande in Texas, found carpet booties used by immigrants to hide their footsteps in the sand, and torn barbed wire fencing. *Ojo*, meanwhile, is made from a bicycle wheel that the Border Patrol ran over to prevent its use. Galindo has refashioned it into an antenna for a theremin, an instrument that produces sound when one interferes with its electromagnetic field. The instrument's inventor, Leon Theremin, developed the technology into an electronic motion sensing alarm system implemented in Alcatraz and other US prisons.

Galindo activates these "sonic objects" in rituals, in which he believes traces of the energy carried by the objects—their history of hope, desperation, and escape—transfer into the bodies of those listening. Experimental scores, printed and sewn into weathered and discarded flags once used by humanitarian aid groups to mark the presence of water tanks placed in the Calexico desert, suggest new ways of listening. It is the sonic vibrations, the microgestures that materially resonate and are amplified, that transform residues of surveillance and escape into new ways of connecting bodies and resonating together.

Guillermo Galindo, born 1960 in Mexico City, is an experimental composer, sonic architect, and visual and performance artist who currently teaches at the California College of the Arts, in San Francisco.

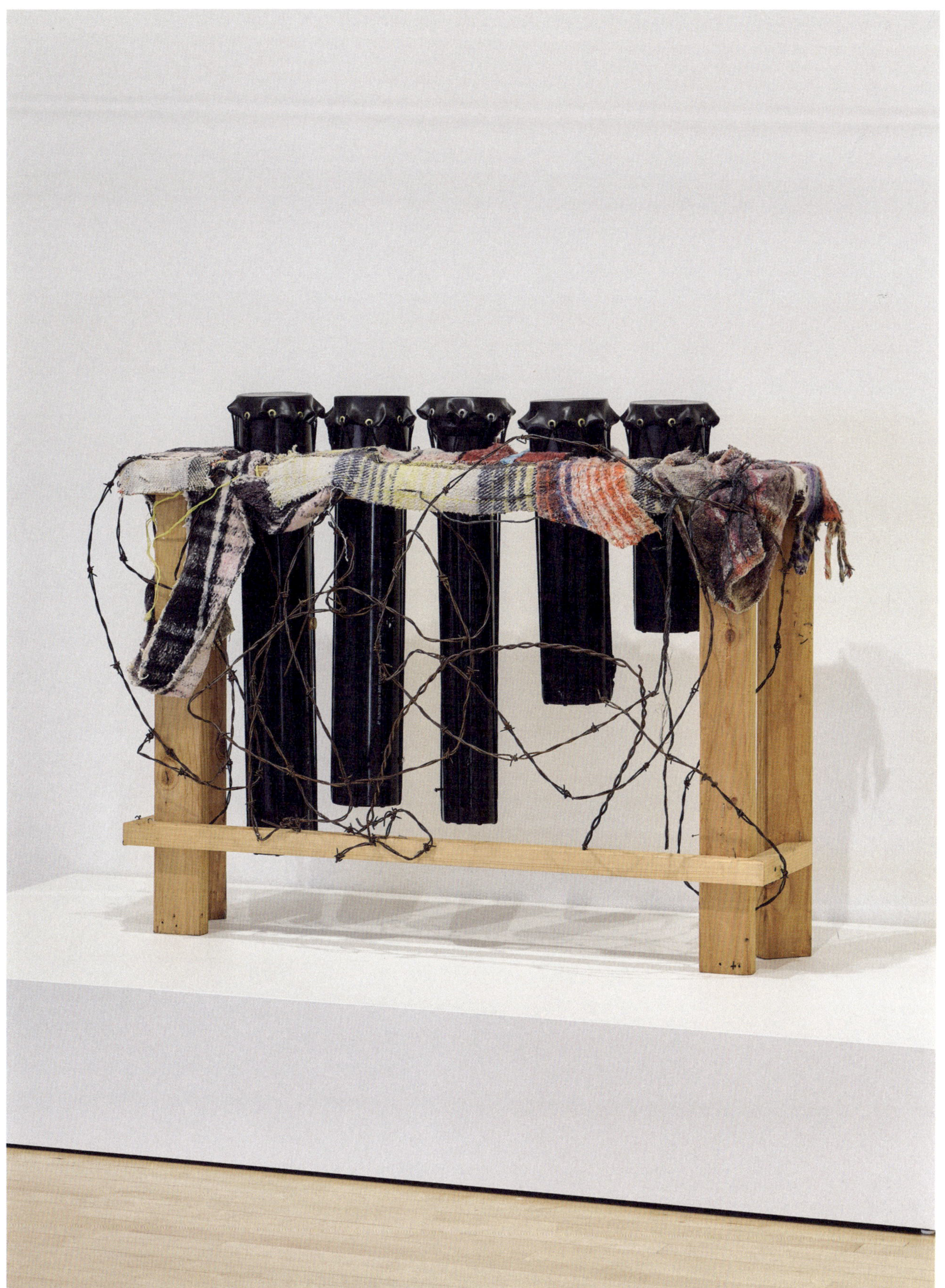

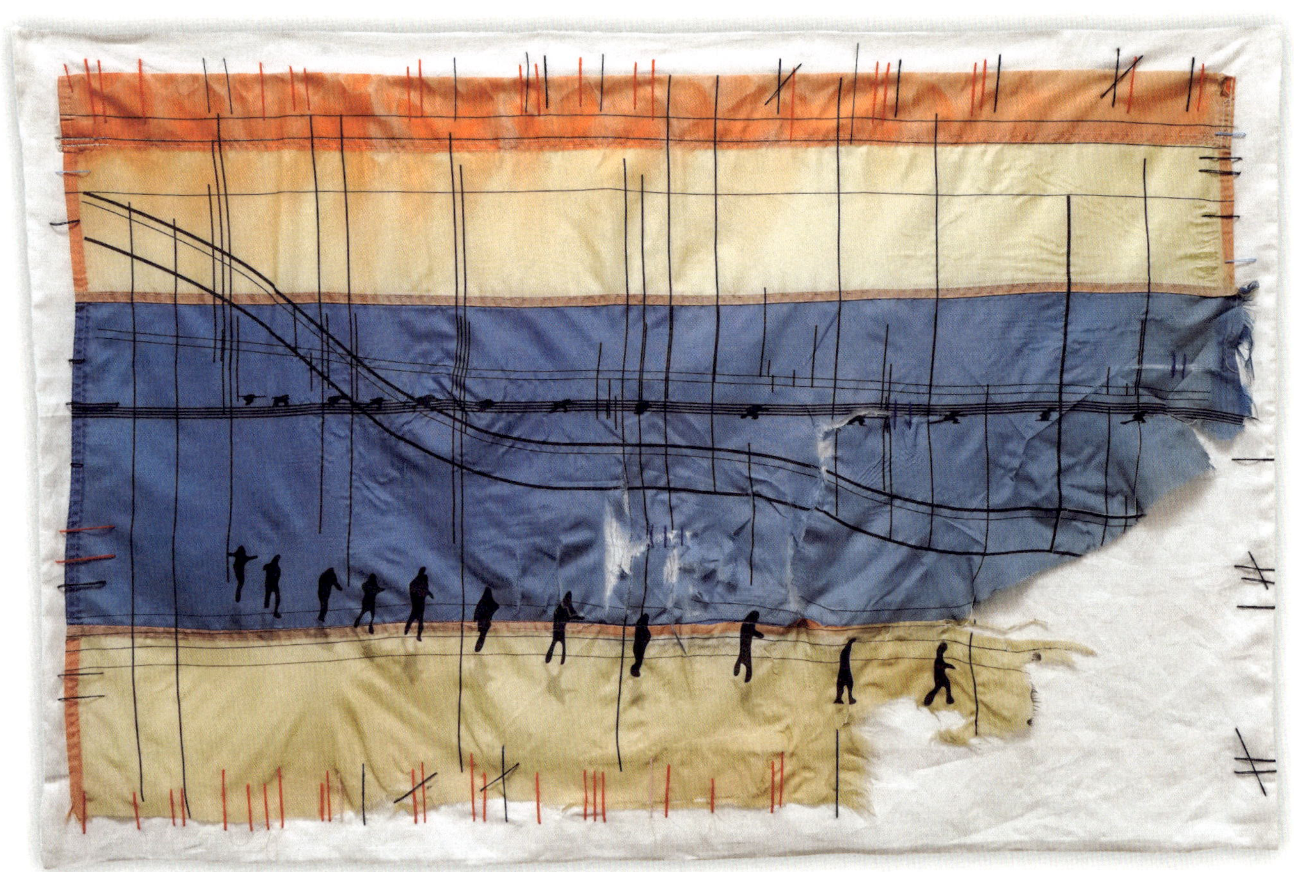

Caravan Variation Flag, 2015

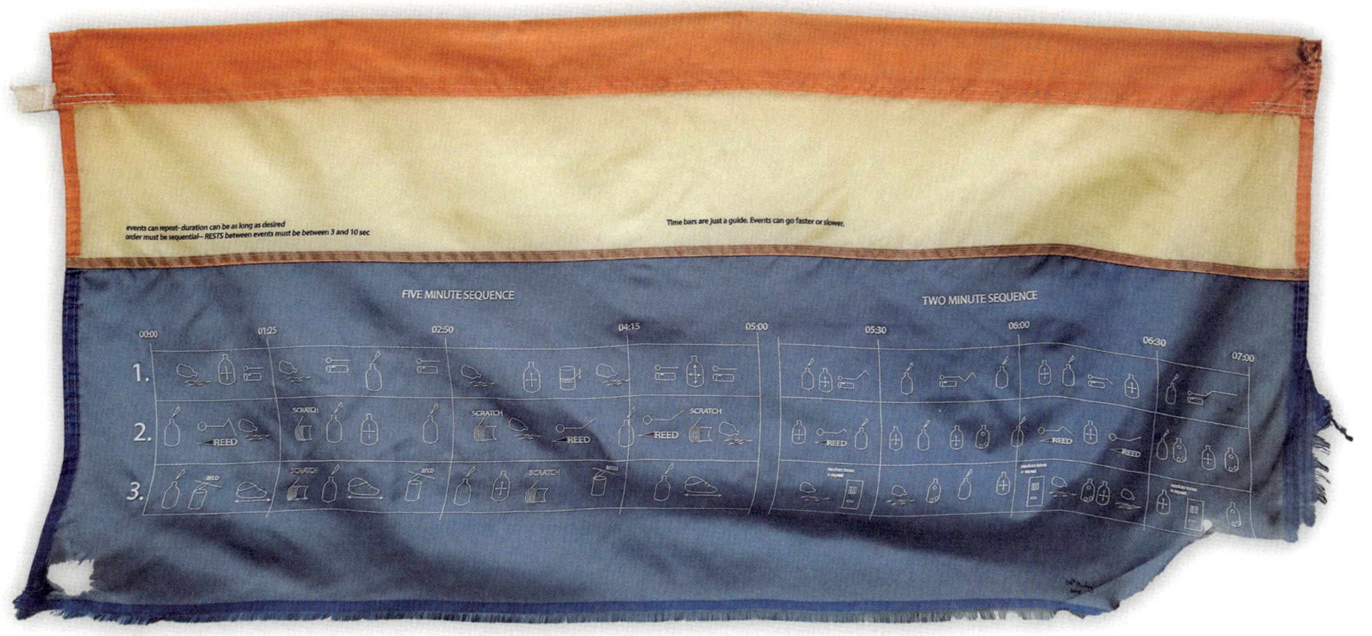

Voices Flag / Bandera de voces, 2017

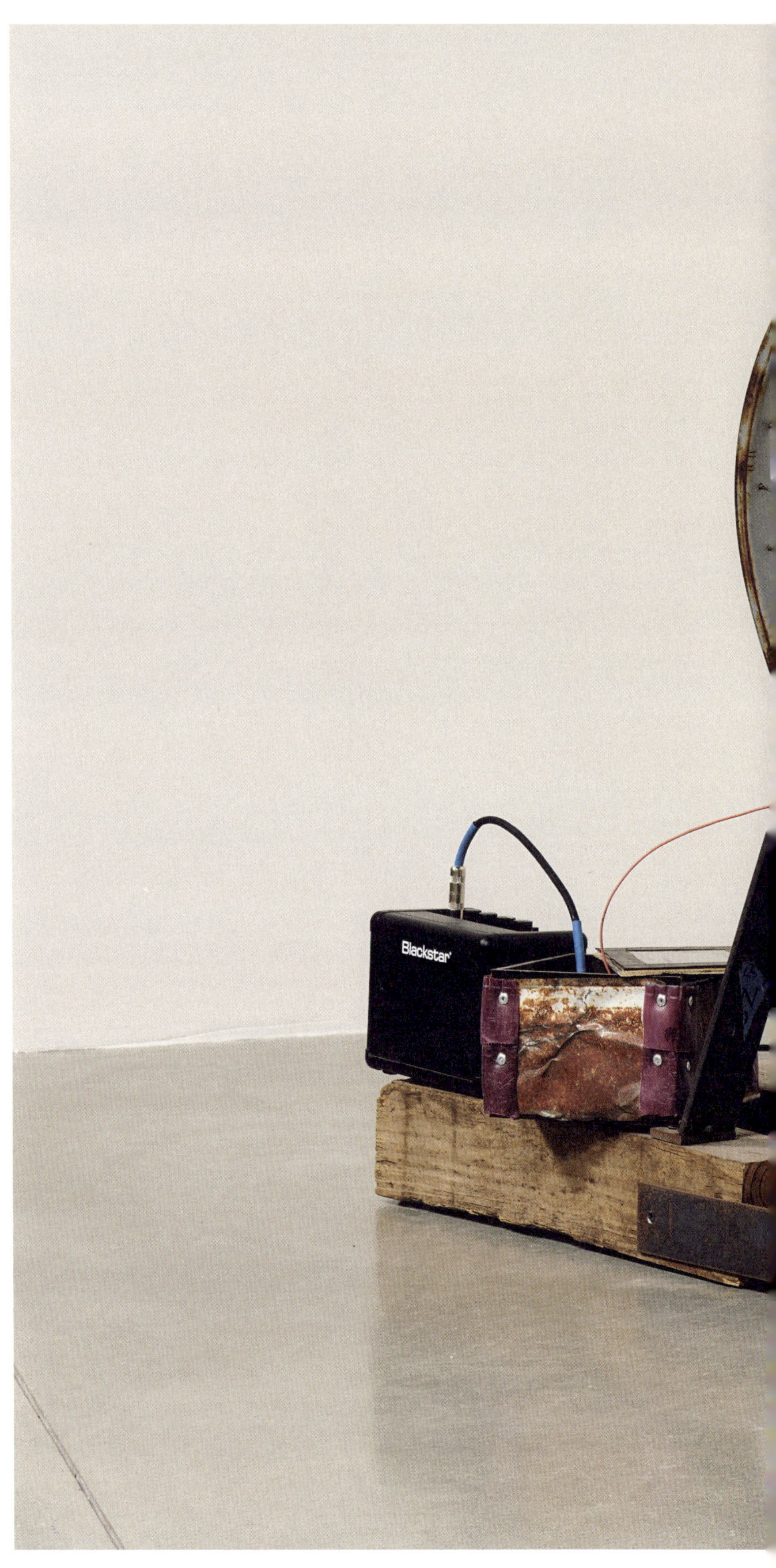

Ojo / Eye, 2015

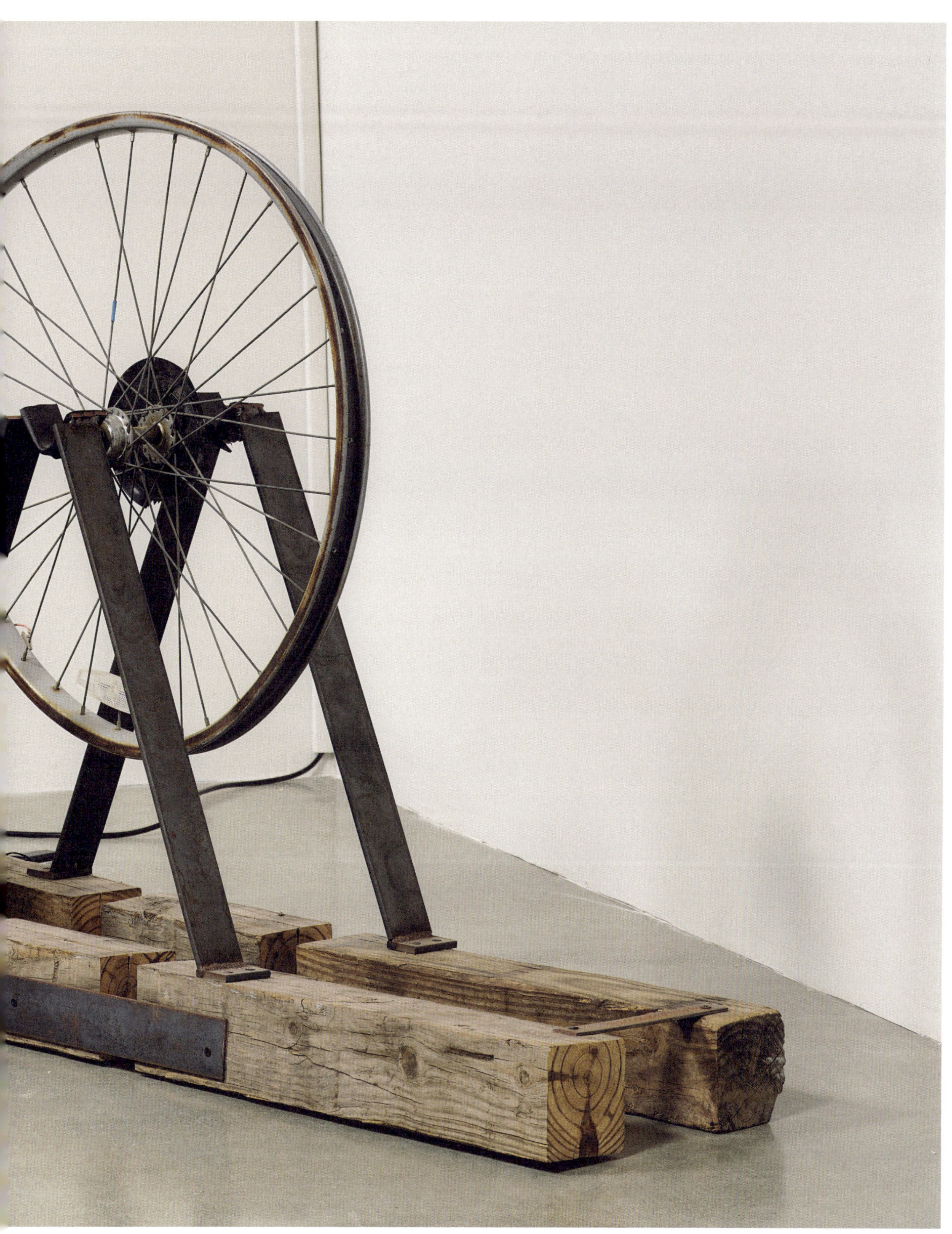

Maria Gaspar
Invisible Things Are Not Necessarily Not-There
(after T.M.), 2023
Twenty-three glass casts
12 × 144 × 72 in., overall

Cloud Out (Evanesce), 2023
Archival inkjet print with oil pastel on paper
41 × 75 in.

Cloud Out (Suspend), 2023
Archival inkjet print with oil pastel on paper
41 × 75 in.

Maria Gaspar created the twenty-three glass casts of jail cell bars and bricks featured in *Invisible Things Are Not Necessarily Not-There (after T.M.)* using construction debris salvaged after the demolition of the Division I building of Chicago's Cook County Department of Corrections, the largest single-site jail in the United States. The delicate glass sculptures carry the history of the impenetrable iron bars and bricks they emerge from, materials that had harshly structured—and contained—the lives of innumerable people since the jail wing was built in 1926. Rendered in glass, however, this history is made fragile and translucent. Bars can now be broken, and bricks are also windows.

Cloud Out (Evanesce) and *Cloud Out (Suspend)* feature large-scale images of the same carceral facility obscured by ethereal skyscapes painted in pastels. In one image, the top of the Cook County Jail Division I building is murky, as if enveloped by fog. Clouds roll over and off its concrete surface, and the immense wall that surrounds it vanishes into mist. In the other image, the building and wall have disappeared almost entirely into cumulus clouds. In both images, the jail fades from the landscape, overtaken by sky.

Across these works, Gaspar has performed aesthetic acts of alchemy. Material that was made to confine is reimagined into that which can create a new, more just society. The clouds and glass debris offer an outline of a future yet to come, with the eventual—and, in Gaspar's poetic vision, inevitable—erasure of carceral geographies.

Maria Gaspar, born 1980, lives and works in Chicago.

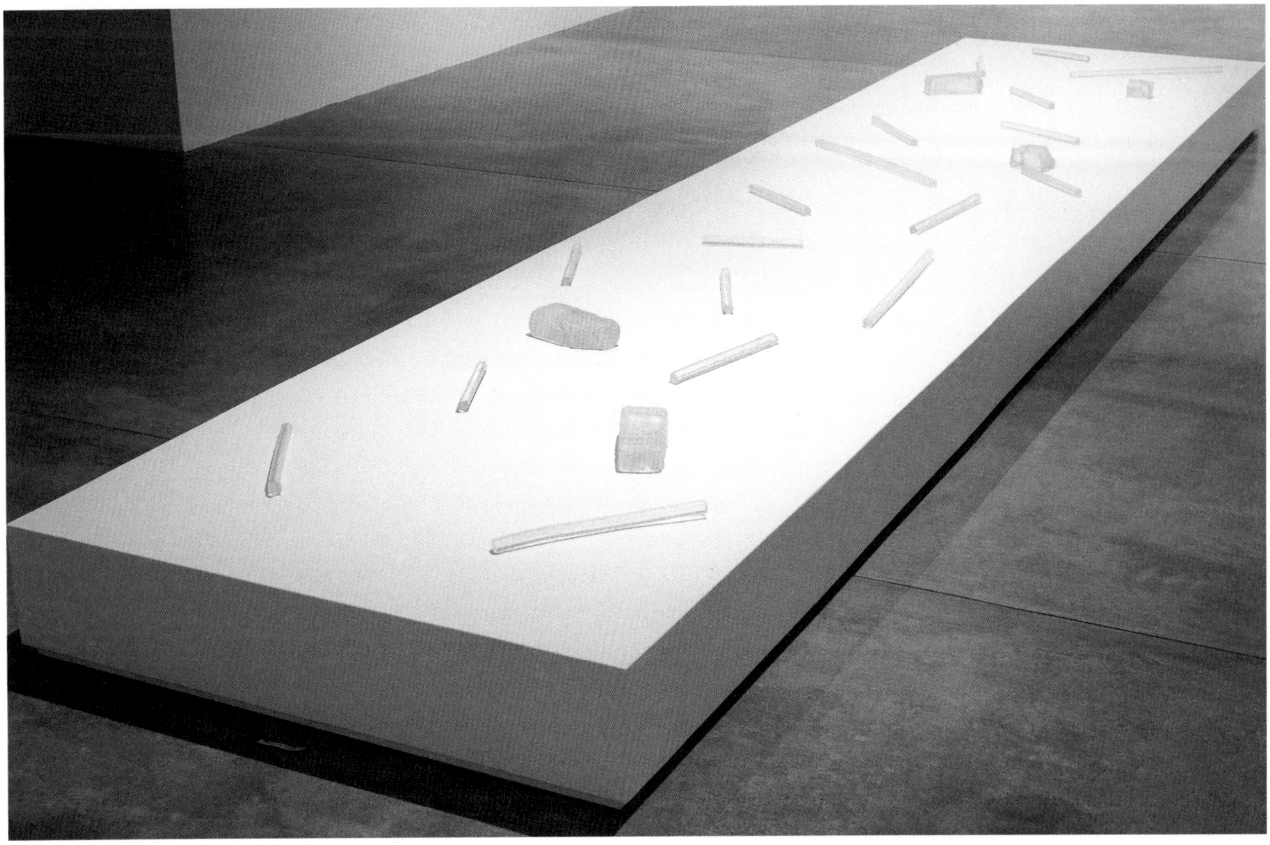

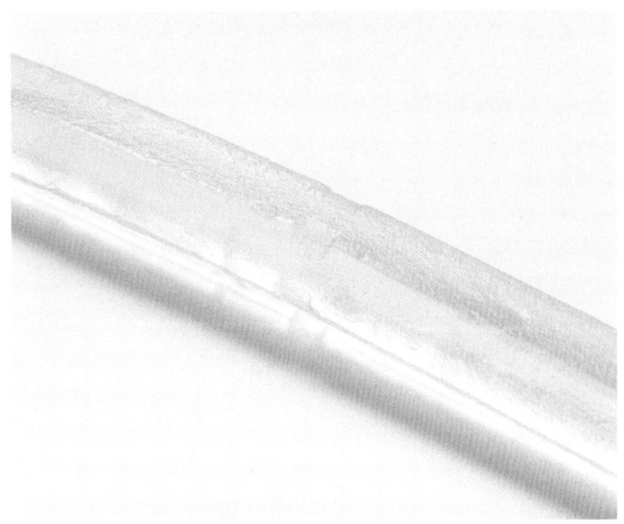
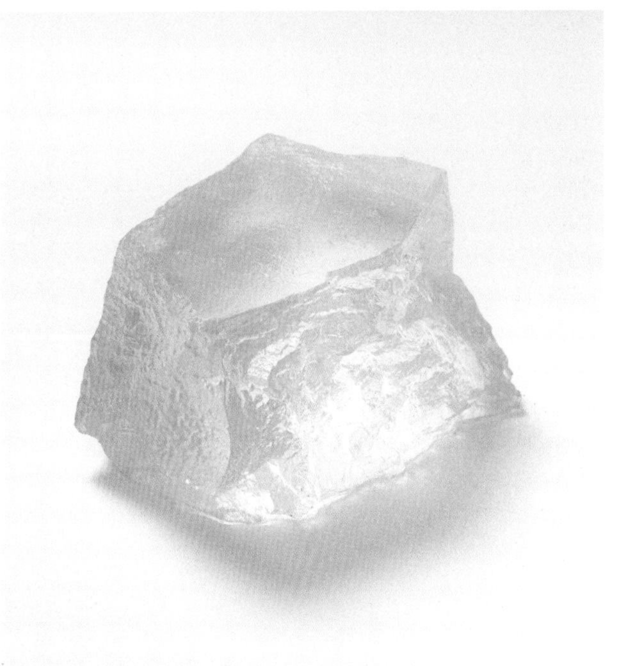

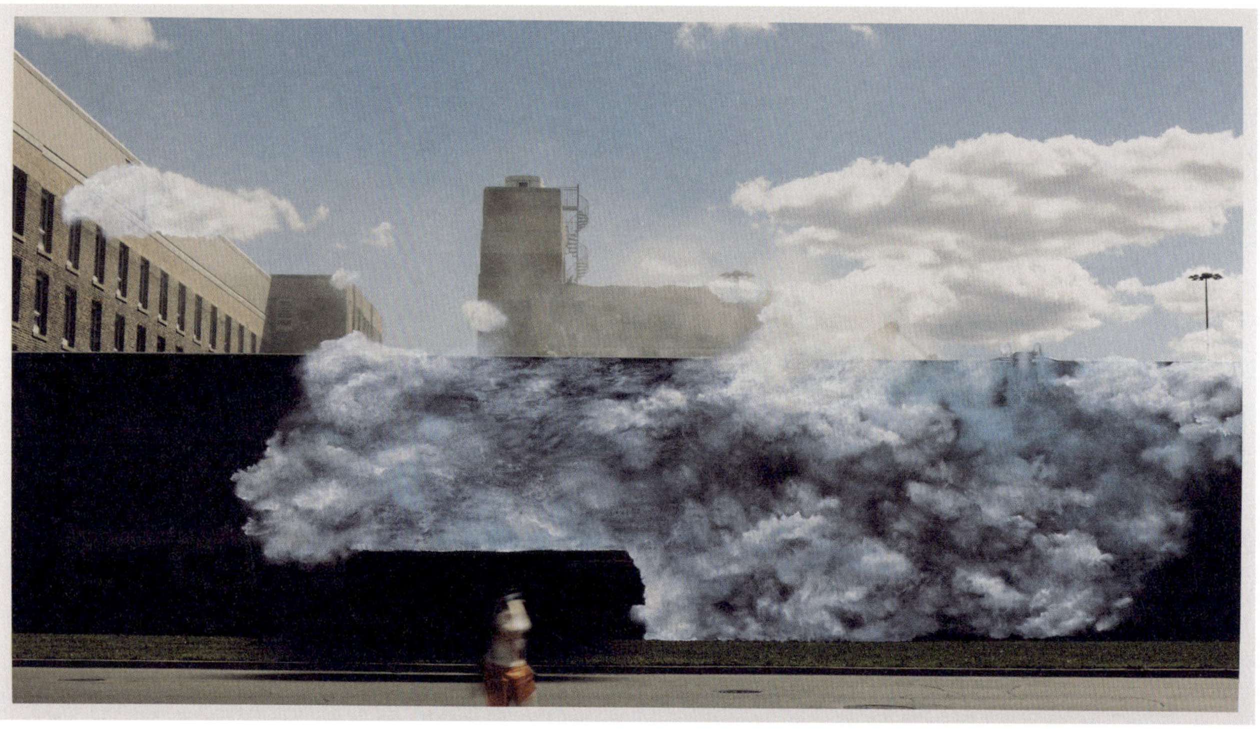

Cloud Out (Evanesce), 2023

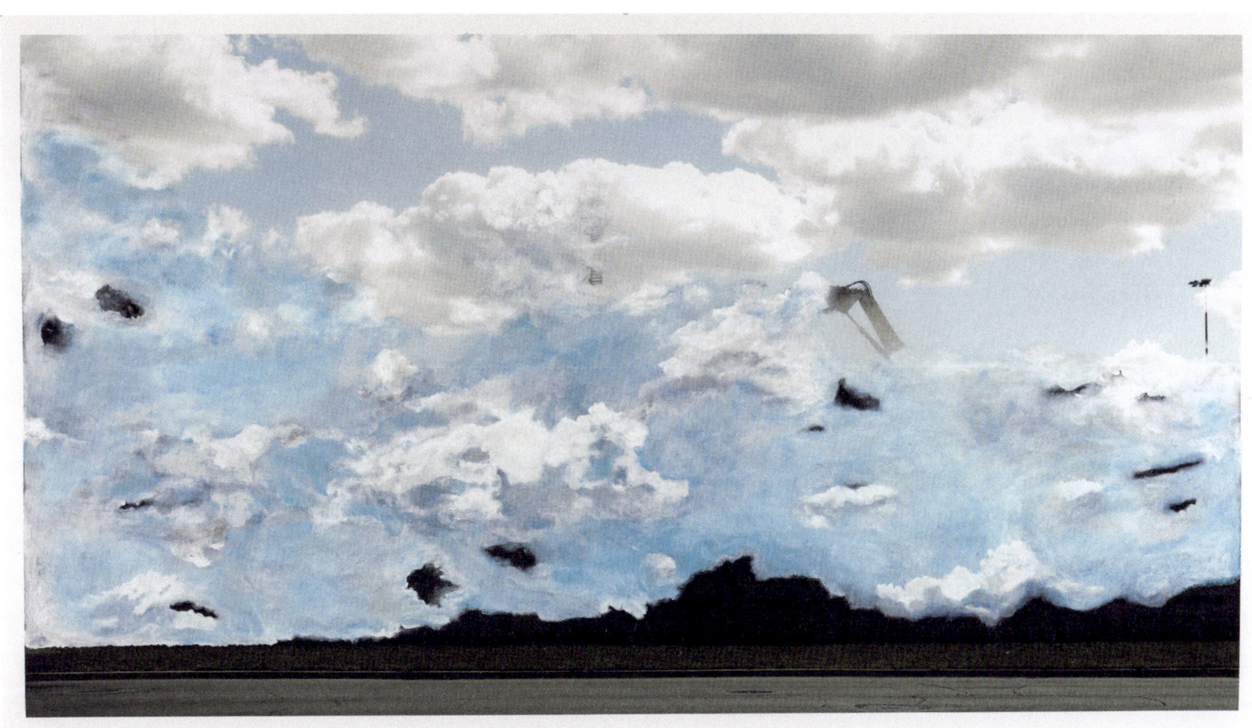

Cloud Out (Suspend), 2023

Gabriela Golder
Cartas/Letters, 2018
Four-channel video installation with sound
Four videos: approx. 15 minutes, each

Child-size chairs neatly arranged in front of monitors create a space reminiscent of a schoolroom. Videos of children between the ages of eight and twelve years populate this space of learning. These children read letters from or to people held in Argentinian prisons or placed in exile during the National Reorganization Process, the military dictatorship that ruled Argentina with support from the United States between 1976 and 1983. The letters offer testimony to the family relations and communications that take place through prison walls; they are written to children, from children, to parents, from parents, or to or from other family members. In jarring juxtaposition, a childish voice reads the letter of a father begging for the release of "a daughter, taken without cause."

The video presents the letters chronologically, delineating the passage of time: a child who was four when their mother was arrested is five, then six, as the years accumulate. The letters contain words of advice about how to survive. They speak of hope for change, for freedom, but also to the mounting years of disappointment, desperation, and waiting. These intimate communiqués, spoken in the voices of children, resonate through the simulated schoolroom, raising questions about the generational trauma inscribed by the histories of incarceration.

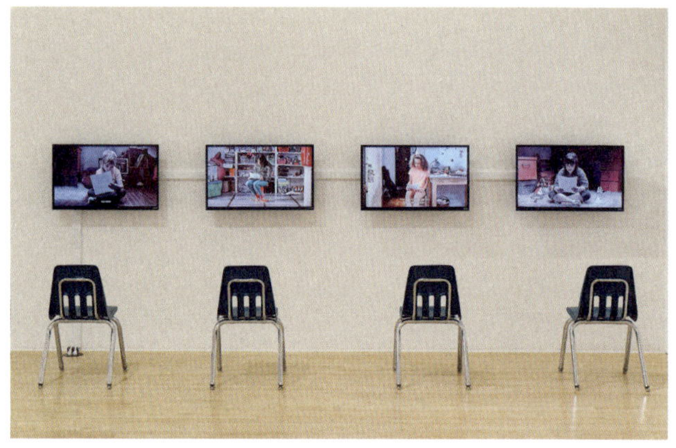

Gabriela Golder, born 1971, lives and works in Buenos Aires, Argentina.

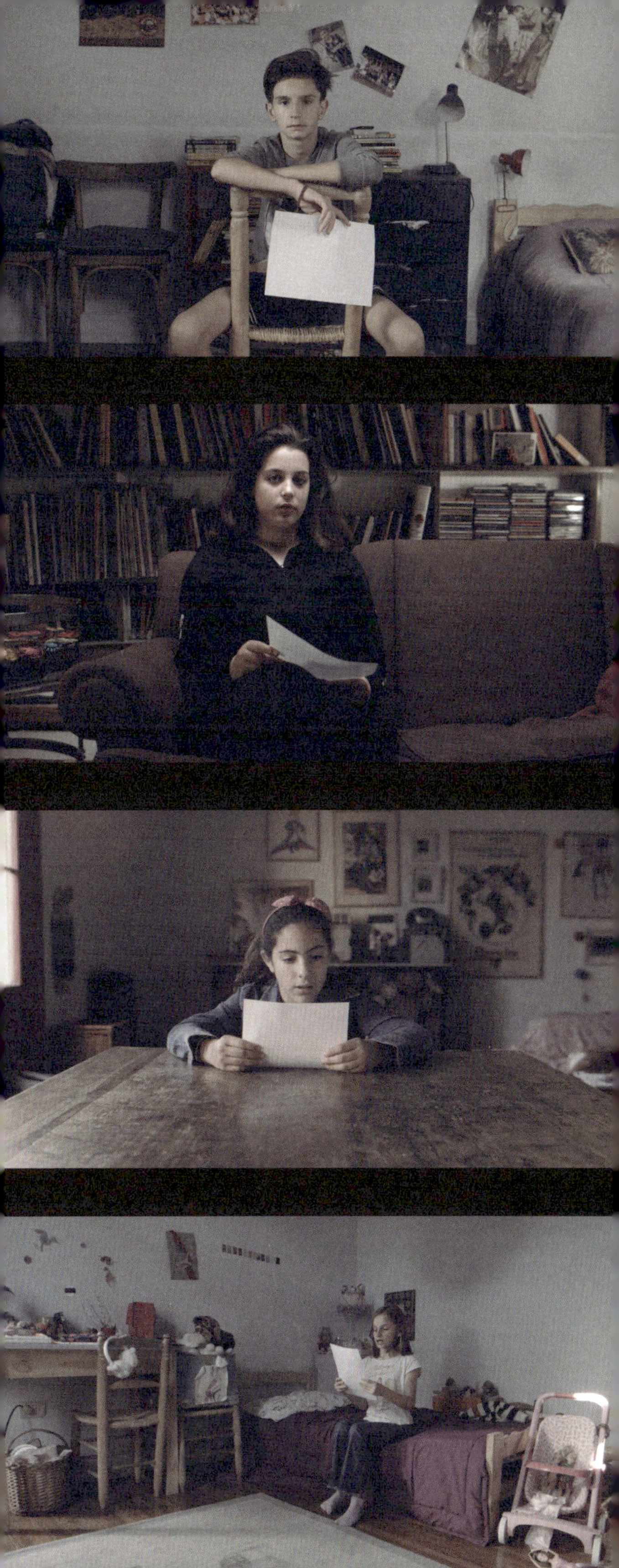

À tous les clandestins, from the series "À tous les clandestins," 2019

Poster

65 × 43¼ in.

Celda 3-1 and *3-2*, from the series "Centro de Retención de Migrantes de Nouadhibou (Mauritania)," 2015–16

Mural detachments on black canvas

59 × 181 in., each

Las 7 puertas, from the series "Tiempo Muerto, Proyecto para Sección Abierta (Cárcel de Palma de Mallorca)," 2011–13

Mural detachment on black canvas and photographic book

Canvas: 108 × 660 in.; book: 19¾ × 26⅜ in.

Deteriorating, once-white walls are scrawled with names, written hopes and protests, and drawings of figures and boats. These are the testimonies of people held in the now-closed migrant detention center in Nouadhibou, Mauritania. The Spanish government established the center in 2006 in what used to be a school, as part of a larger border control policy designed to prevent migrants from leaving the West African coast of Mauritania for the Canary Islands.

For *À tous les clandestins*, Patricia Gómez and María Jesús González traveled to different points along the West African migration route, documenting both the graffitied interiors and exteriors of closed and deactivated prisons, psychiatric hospitals, and detention centers. The oversize posters combine their photographic documentation with excerpts of written testimonies transcribed from the walls. "I've been in Nouadhibou for 3 months, sleeping with the fleas, eating disgusting meals and when you get out the police catch you / I've made the trip 4 times," reads one inscription. "I wish freedom to all those who are in this prison," reads another.

To make their wall detachments, the artists employed a modified version of the "strappo" technique used in architectural mural preservation, in which a canvas is glued to a wall and then removed, peeling off the painted surface so that it can be transferred in its entirety to a second canvas. The transcribed words are anchored by the physicality of the scratched markings. While many are by anonymous prisoners passing through the system, *Las 7 puertas* records the imprints made in the iron doors of the now-closed Palma de Mallorca prison in Spain (it was replaced by the Centro Penitenciário de Palma de Mallorca). The doors bear the epigraphs of the last seven prisoners held within that institution.

These works archive the humanity and lives of those the institutions contained. They also serve as material witness to the impermanence of the prisons themselves. Prisons close, their walls fall. As archaeological remnants, these walls are evidence of historical cruelty, but this does not determine the future. Perhaps we will preserve the walls as reminders of a dark history. Or perhaps we will just tear them down.

María Jesús González and Patricia Gómez, born 1978, have been collaborating since 2002. They live and work in Valencia, Spain.

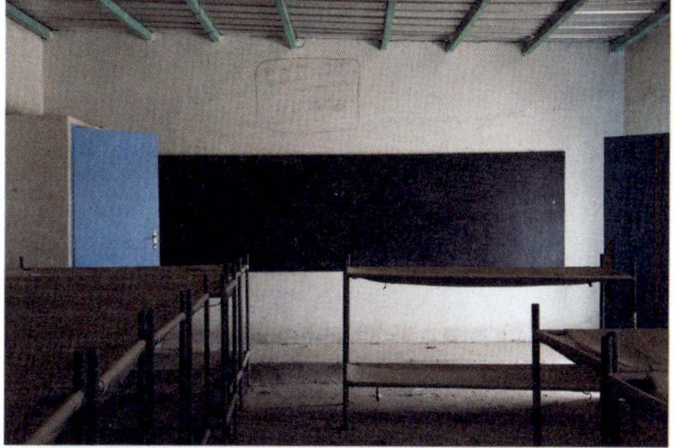

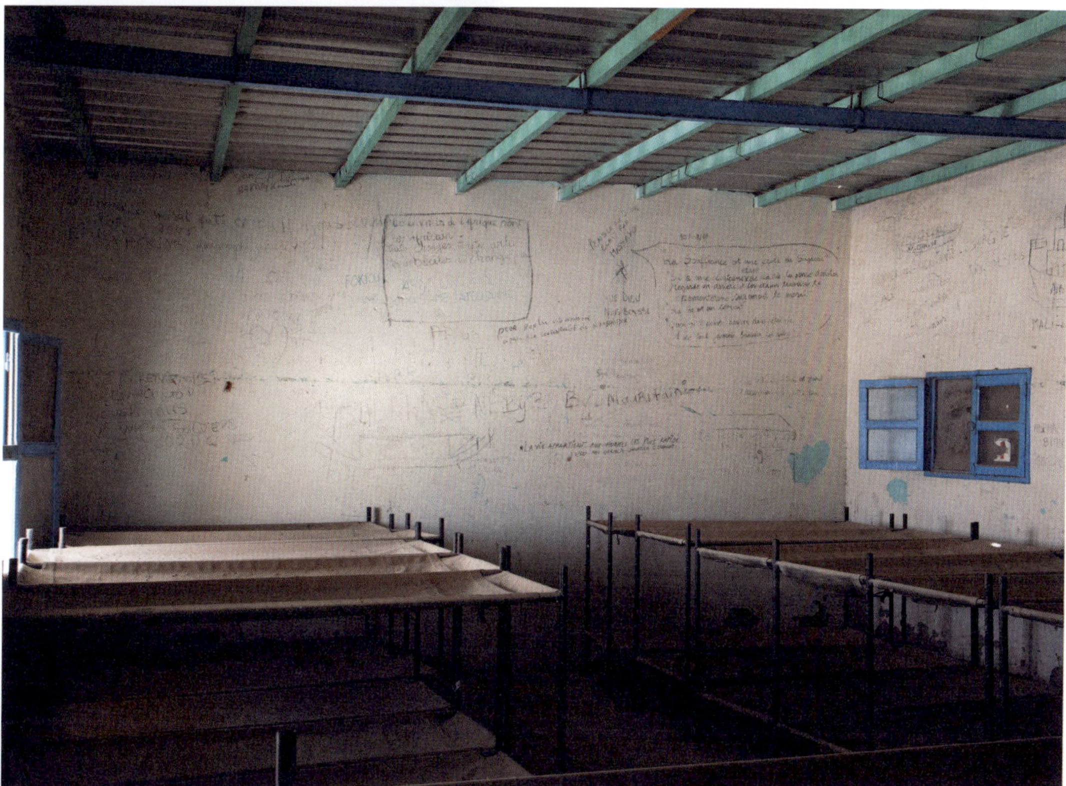

Celda 3

El que tiene ojos, déjales ver a nuestra gente morir por falta de conocimiento. Pero un día el mundo será redimido / No nos rendimos nunca / Rendirse no es africano / Dedicado a todos los clandestinos / Que Dios nos ayude y cumpla nuestro deseo sobre las pateras / Crees que la inmigración ilegal se acabará?

Esto nunca lo olvidaré en mi vida. He estado 3 meses en Nouadhibou, acostándome con las pulgas, comiendo una comida asquerosa y cuando llegas a salir, la policía te coge / Yo he hecho 4 veces el viaje.

Nosotros los clandestinos no buscamos mujeres, solo buscamos 2080 para pagar a los que están en la orilla. Porque la mujer es dinero. Chef: de cladeste gorselin-Congo-KAV / Clandestinos, no os desaniméis. África + Europa = la Vida. LA VIDA: Definición= Voluntad-Inteligencia-Esfuerzo. Profesor: Gorselin-Congo.

Los enemigos de África son los africanos. Todo cambia todo evoluciona. Solo los imbéciles no cambian.

Para entrar rápido en España, pasa por la Cruz Roja de Nouadhibou / La vida pertenece a los hombres más rápidos. Gorselin-Sanzele (Congoleño).

Pensamiento del día, escrito por Massayo. 10/08/06. "El sufrimiento es una escuela de sabiduría". "Si en cierta etapa de la vida te sientes derrotado, mira atrás, y las etapas atravesadas seguramente te levantarán la moral". "La vida es un combate". "Pase lo que pase en la vida, no puedes bajar jamás los brazos".

Que Dios nos bendiga / La casa de Dios no es un lugar para lamentarse, confía en Dios.

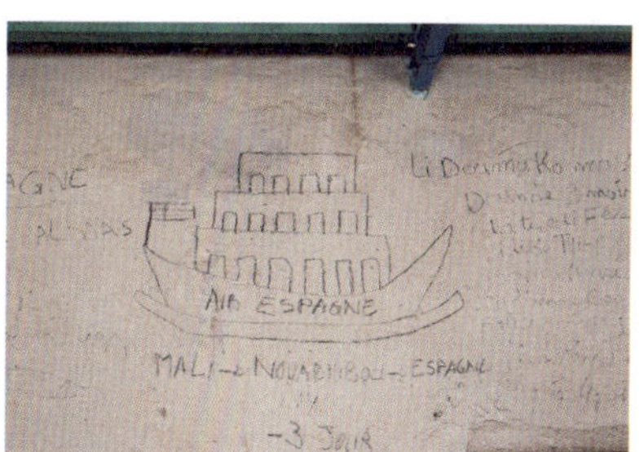

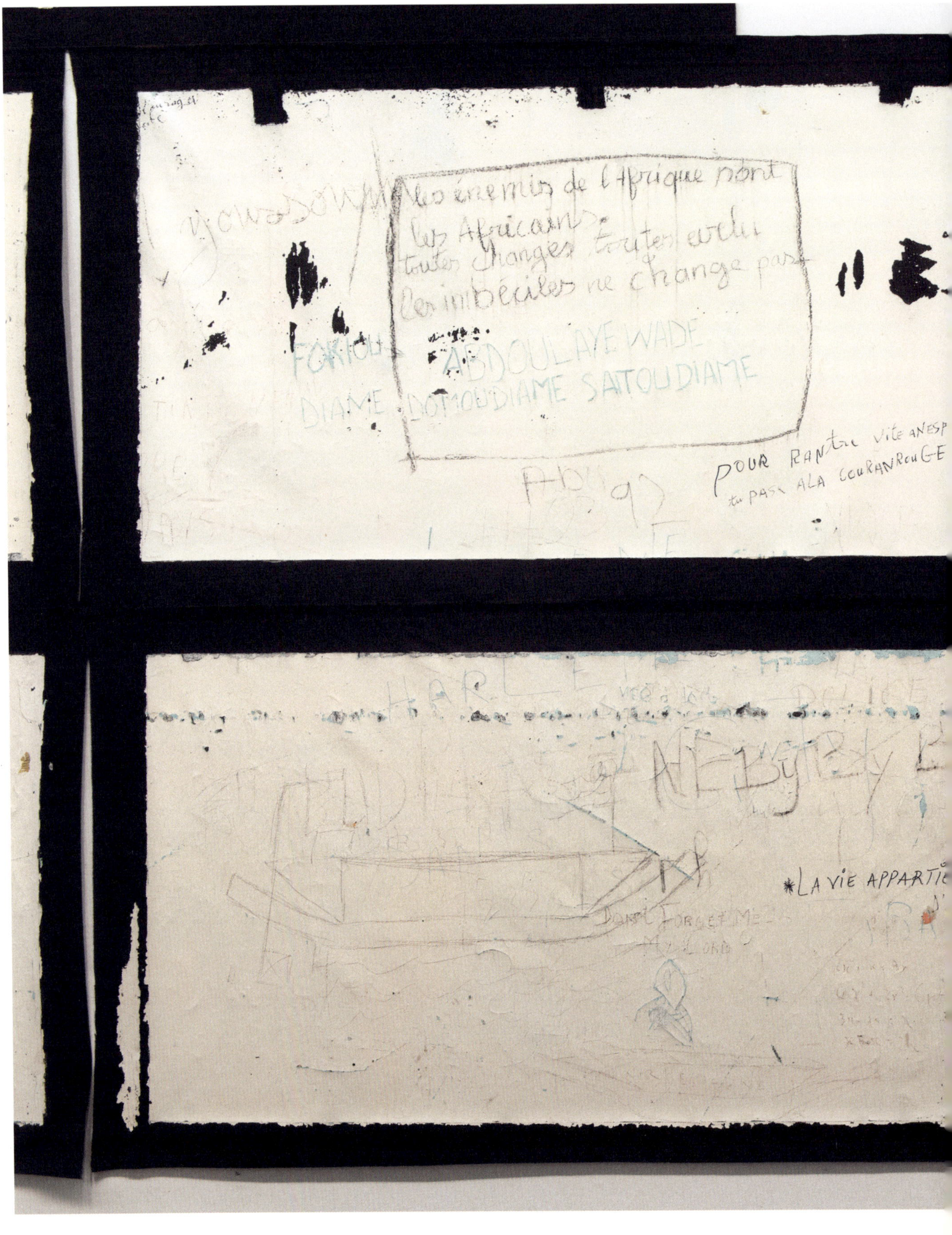

les énemis de l'Afrique sont
les Africains
toutes changes toutes evolu
les imbéciles ne change pas

ABDOULAYE WADE

FORIOU DIAME DOMOU DIAME SAITOU DIAME

POUR RANTRE VITE ANESP
tu PASS ALA COURANROUGE

LA VIE APPARTIE

DON'T FORGET ME MY LORD

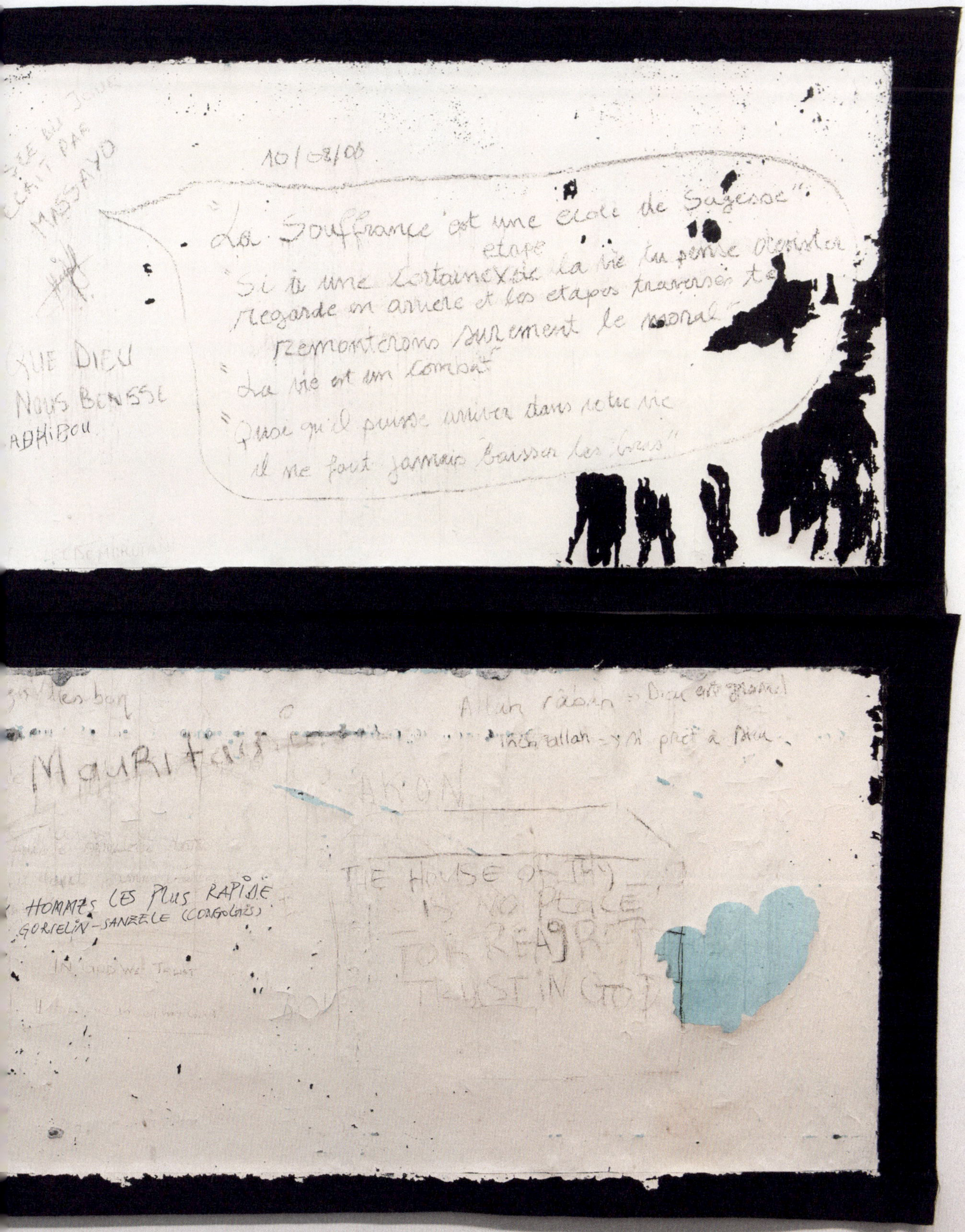

QUE DIEU
NOUS BENSSE
ADHIBOU

10/08/06

"La Souffrance est une école de Sagesse"
étape
"Si à une certaine vie la vie tu pense craquer
regarde en arrière et les étapes traversées te
remontrons sûrement le moral"
"La vie est un combat"
"Quoi qu'il puisse arriver dans notre vie
il ne faut jamais baisser les bras"

Allah râbar = Dieu est grand
Inch'allah = si prêt à Dieu

Mauritius

HOMMES LES PLUS RAPIDE
GORSELIN-SANZELE (CONGOLAIS)

IN GOD WE TRUST

THE HOUSE OF THY
IS NO PLACE
FOR BEAR
TRUST IN GOD

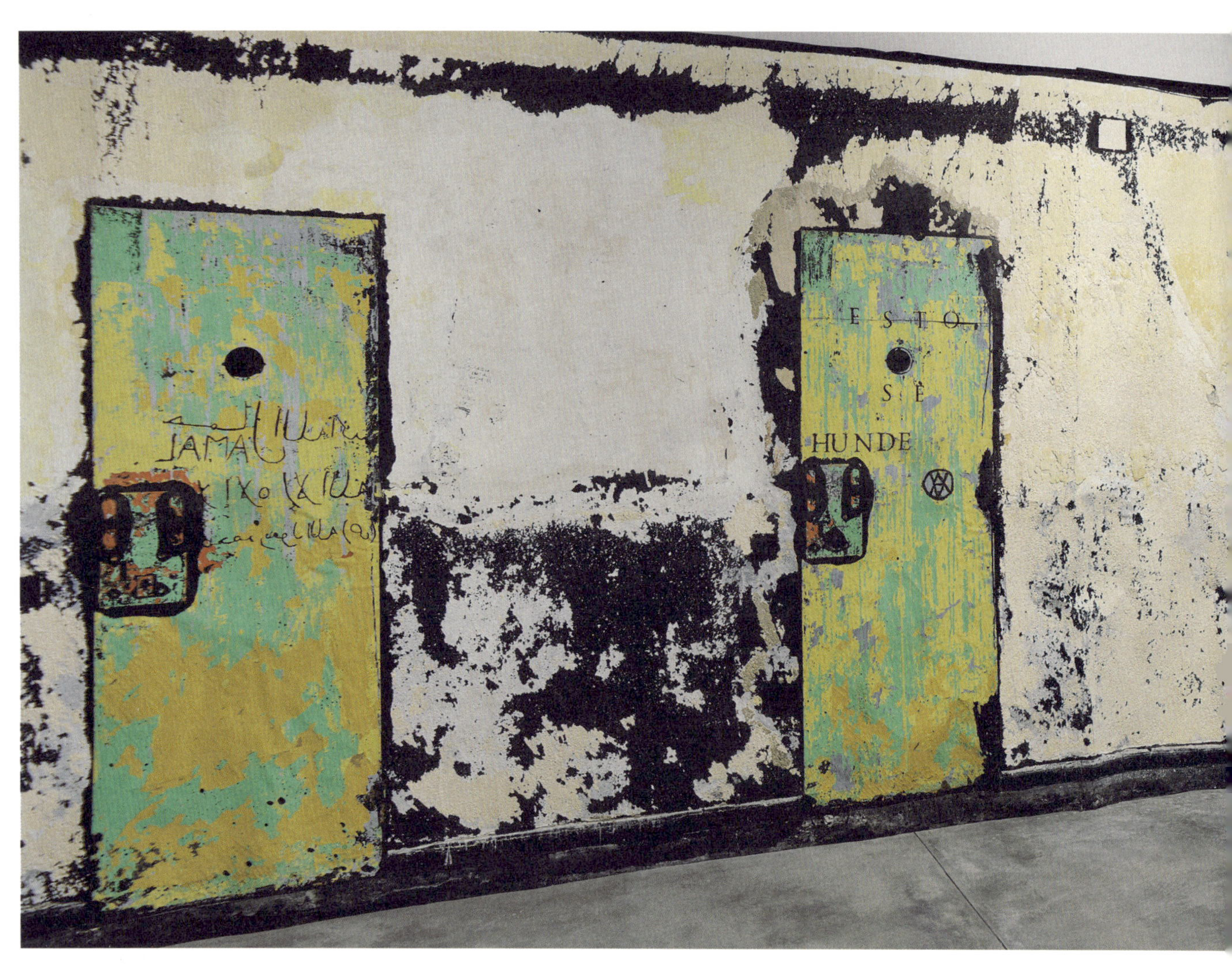

Las 7 puertas, 2011–13

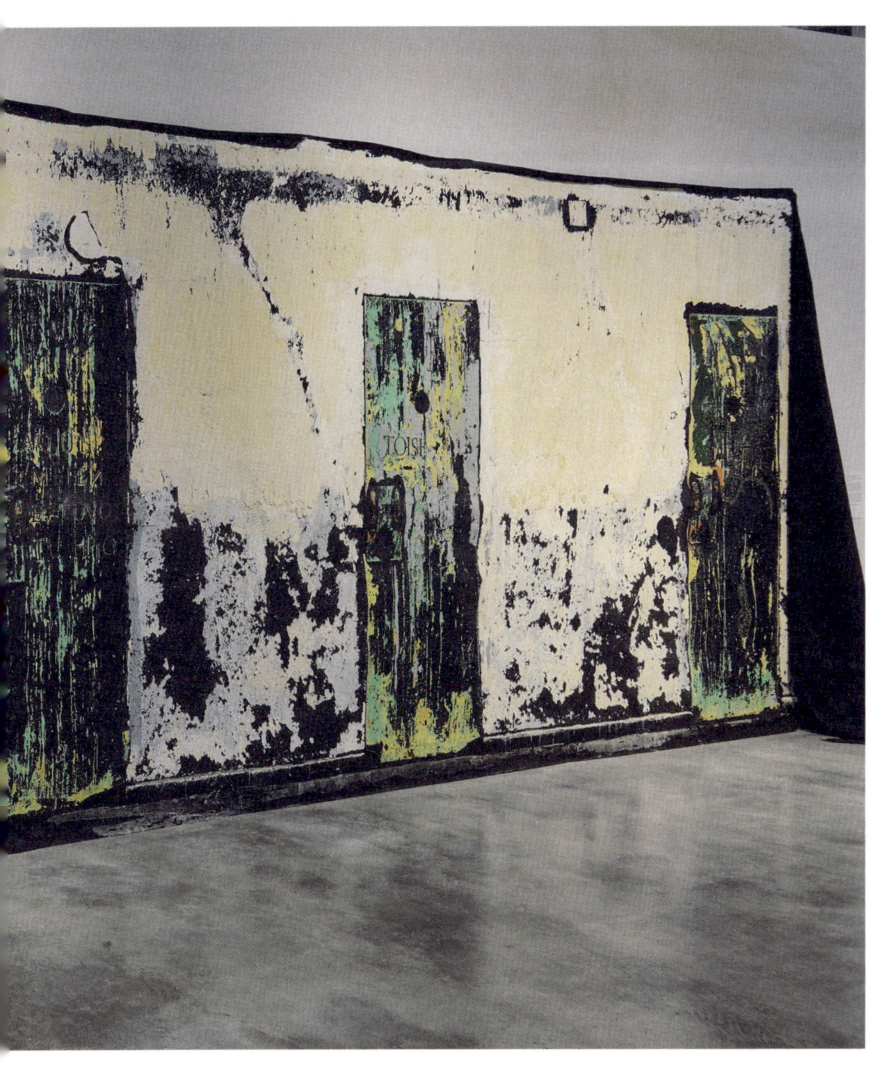

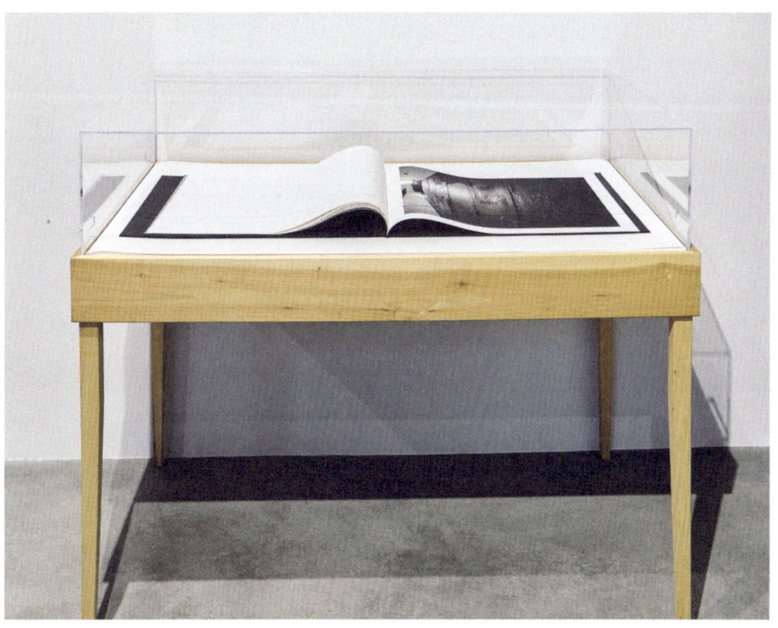

Shilpa Gupta
Untitled (There Is No Border Here), 2005–06
Wall drawing with self-adhesive tape
118 × 118 in.

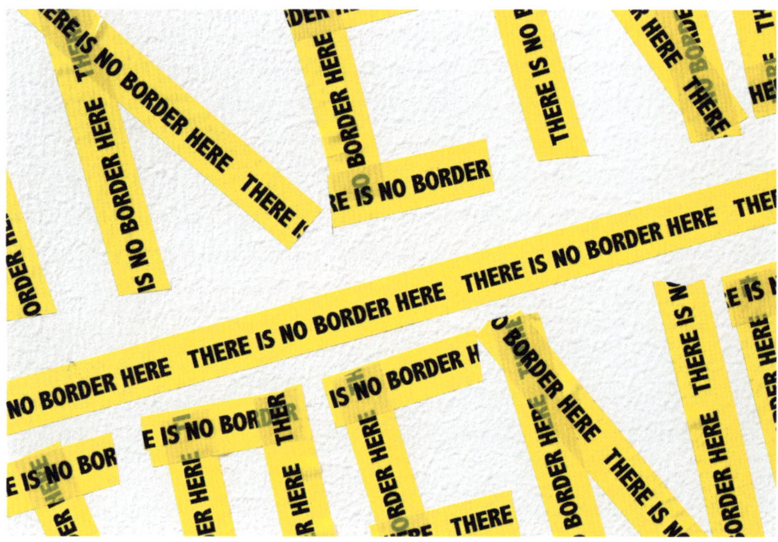

Flags, like maps and anthems, are symbols that structure and define nation-states. They reinforce drawn borders, many of which, like the contested line separating Shilpa Gupta's home country of India from Bangladesh and Pakistan, are maintained through violence and surveillance. Yet such divisions are hardly natural or eternal, and *Untitled (There Is No Border Here)* is a direct, poetic refusal of such separation. Using yellow police tape (printed with the repeating titular phrase "There is no border here"), Gupta outlines a waving flag covered in lyrical verse describing repeated attempts and failures at dividing the sky:

> I tried very hard to cut the sky in half, one for my lover and one for me. But the sky kept moving and clouds from his territory came into mine. I tried pushing it away, with both my hands, harder and harder but the sky kept moving and clouds from my territory went into his. I brought a sofa and placed it in the middle, but the clouds kept floating over it. I built a wall in the middle but the sky started to flow through it. I dug a trench, and then it rained and the sky made clouds over the trench. I tried very hard to cut . . .

The final phrase begins to repeat the first sentence, suggesting a cycle of repetition, but it is abruptly unfinished, creating an opening for the viewer/reader/listener to complete it differently, breaking the cycle of oppression. Borders cannot limit imagination or human connection by restricting mobility. Walls will inevitably fail.

Having grown up in India at a time when the media landscape was growing exponentially, Gupta makes work that questions who is speaking for whom, and embraces poetry as representing the multitude of voices that are drowned out by those in power. Collective agency and communal listening are core to her practice.

Shilpa Gupta, born 1976, lives and works in Mumbai, India.

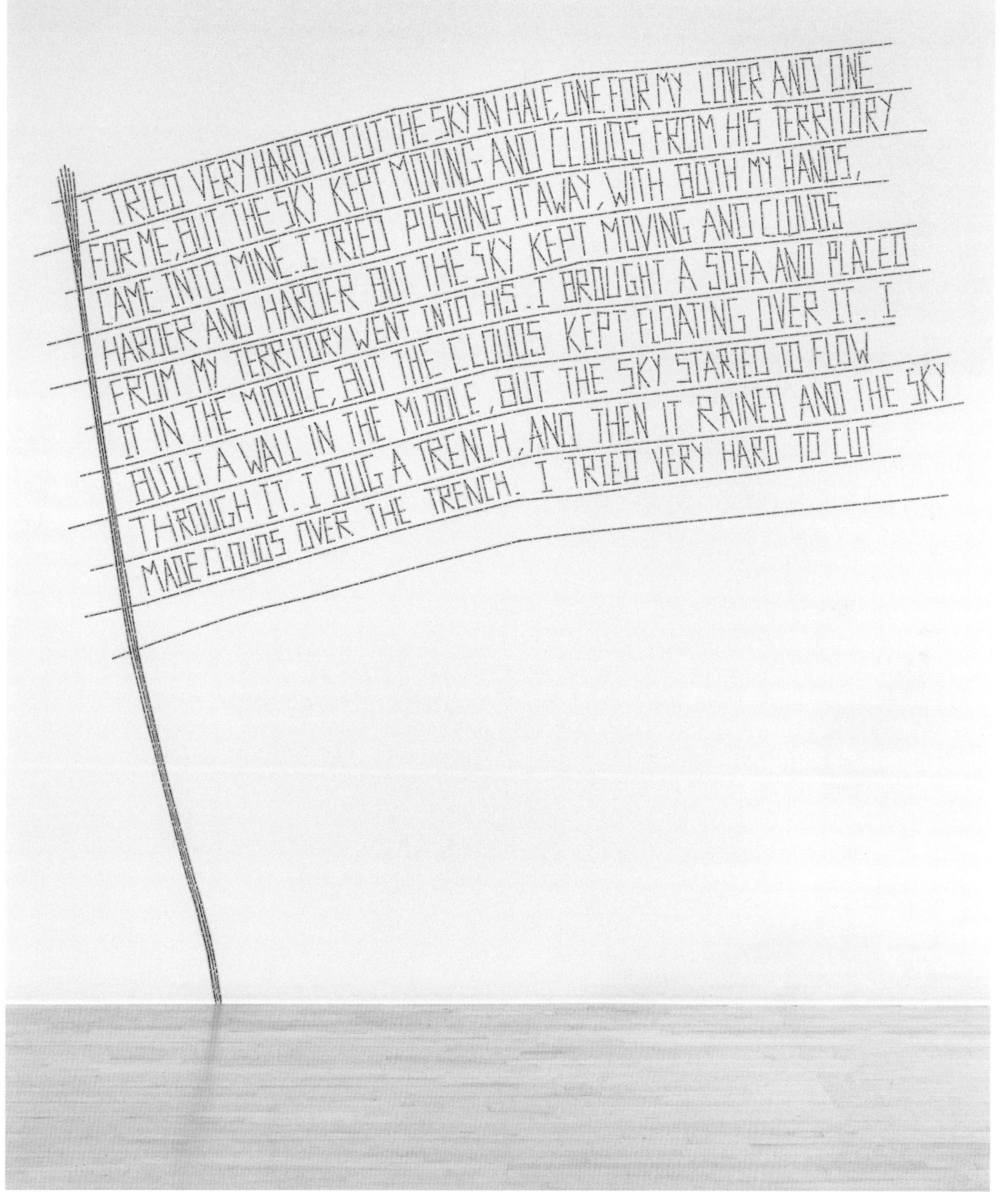

I TRIED VERY HARD TO CUT THE SKY IN HALF, ONE FOR MY LOVER AND ONE
FOR ME, BUT THE SKY KEPT MOVING AND CLOUDS FROM HIS TERRITORY
CAME INTO MINE. I TRIED PUSHING IT AWAY, WITH BOTH MY HANDS,
HARDER AND HARDER BUT THE SKY KEPT MOVING AND CLOUDS
FROM MY TERRITORY WENT INTO HIS. I BROUGHT A SOFA AND PLACED
IT IN THE MIDDLE, BUT THE CLOUDS KEPT FLOATING OVER IT. I
BUILT A WALL IN THE MIDDLE, BUT THE SKY STARTED TO FLOW
THROUGH IT. I DUG A TRENCH, AND THEN IT RAINED AND THE SKY
MADE CLOUDS OVER THE TRENCH. I TRIED VERY HARD TO CUT

Sky Hopinka
*I held the ancestor in my arms and took them far away
from here*, 2022
Inkjet print with hand-scratched text
40 × 40 in.

Sunflower Siege Engine, 2022
HD video, 16 mm to HD video, stereo, color
12:23 minutes

The logic of wandering, a mode and method of making that resists depictions of Native American experience shaped by colonial mandates, runs throughout Sky Hopinka's visually striking and linguistically rich experimental practice. He has called his work "ethnopoetic," describing its foundations in biography along with its poetic expansion outward, teasing out legacies of both oppression and Native resistance, illuminating continuities between past and present, the known and the unknowable. *I held the ancestor in my arms and took them far away from here* shows an interstitial stretch of highway leading toward the setting sun. Hand-scratched into the blue sky of the photograph are words of caretaking and escape, a moving away in time and space from carcerality.

Hopinka's video *Sunflower Siege Engine*, a prior commission for Visualizing Abolition, reflects on the carceral origins and nature of the reservation system. In it, moments of resistance are collapsed and woven together. Imagery of the reclaimed Cahokia Mounds, the site of an ancient trading city, is combined with footage from the 1969 occupation of Alcatraz, a nineteen-month-long protest during which a group of Native Americans and their supporters reclaimed the San Francisco Bay island and former federal penitentiary. Describing similarities between the prison and an Indian reservation, protest leader Richard Oakes called out the transformative potential in recognizing Alcatraz as "Indian land" instead of as a carceral landscape. Oakes' words combine with Hopinka's vibrant, kaleidoscopic imagery to express an Indigenous worldview, one that is not beholden to current systems of oppression but rather suggests another path—always present, though not always recognized—in the ongoing and restless struggle for freedom.

Sky Hopinka, born 1984, is a member of the Ho-Chunk Nation/Pechanga Band of Luiseño Indians.

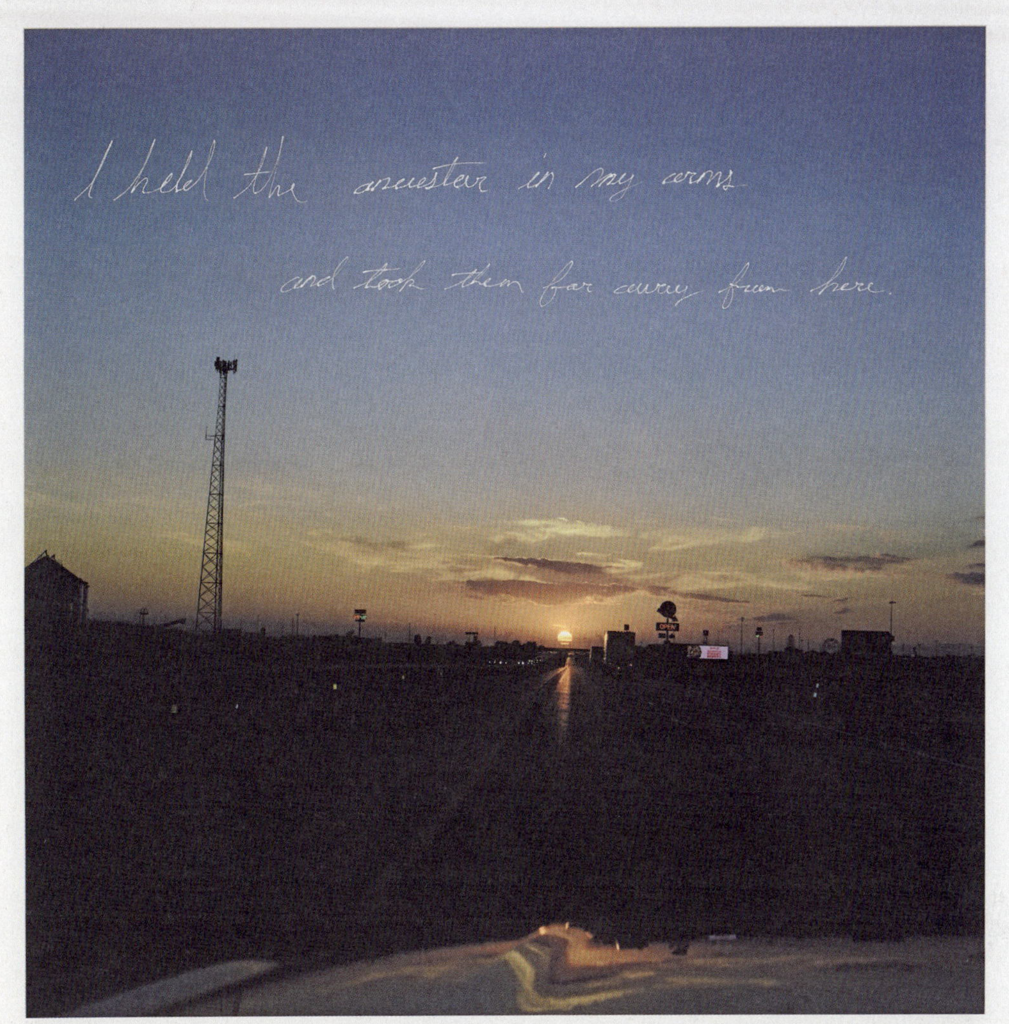
I held the ancestor in my arms.
and took them far away from here.

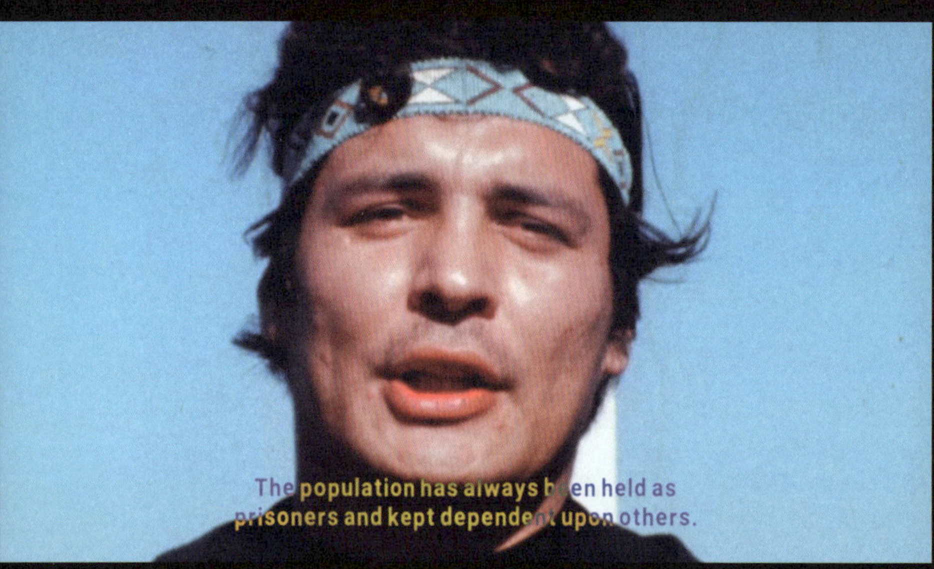

I held an ancestor in my arms and we spoke of dust.
The population has always been held as prisoners and kept dependent upon others.
...further, it would be fitting and symbolic that ships from all over the world, entering the Golden Gate, would first see Indian Land, and thus be reminded of the true history of this nation.

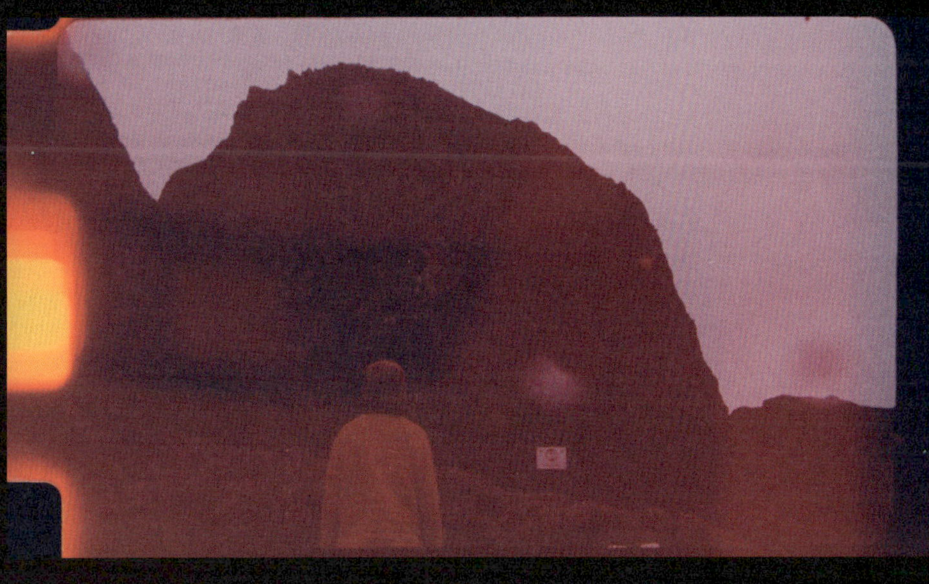

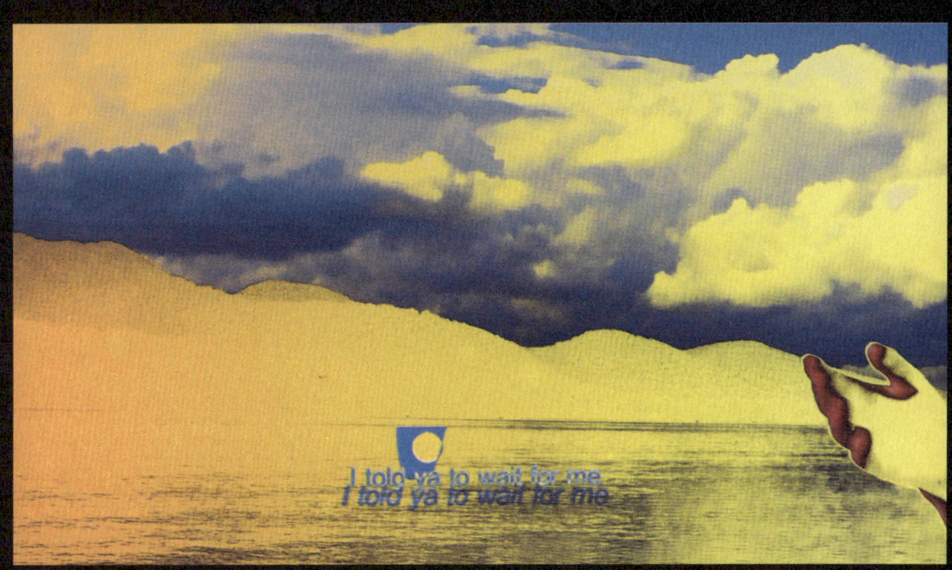
I told ya to wait for me

There's no right way to be indin, just a whole lot of wrong ways.

I told ya to wait for me...

Ashley Hunt
And Water Brings Tomorrow, 2024
Single-channel film and sound
38 minutes

Imagine that prisons have already been abolished, washed away by a persistent deluge of people organizing.

And Water Brings Tomorrow moves fluidly through shuttered prisons in the United States, including prisons transformed into a youth sports center, an art center, a community farm, a distillery, and a prison tourism site, as well as one left in ruin. The film follows campaigns and community efforts to shut down more carceral facilities, charting the practical, visionary, ecological, and emotional work required to replace them with anti-carceral communities and economies of care. For example, members of Californians United for a Responsible Budget, a statewide coalition campaigning to close ten prisons across California by 2025, are shown lobbying legislators, organizing to bring together prison closure campaigns from across the country, strategizing, and providing care for one another.

The work is set within landscapes fast transformed by an environment demanding to be reckoned with. Layered among the footage of closed prisons and organizing are images of water—falling from the sky, puddled in streets, rising in floods, or streaming as waterfalls. Aerial footage records water encroaching on a prison constructed on an industrially drained lakebed, swelling against the built environment. Accompanying these saturated scenes is a poetic narration, drawn from writings by and interviews with people reckoning with the emotional and psychological labor necessary to create an abolitionist future in the face of wrongs that can never be erased, regardless of the victories of liberation and movement work. The spoken words are a reminder that even the flood of struggle for liberation cannot wash away the past. As prisons are made into history, losses and harms must be addressed, and cultural and social attachments to violent and oppressive systems must be released.

And Water Brings Tomorrow is the last in a trilogy of films by Ashley Hunt, which also includes *Ashes, Ashes* (2020) and *Double Time* (2021). Each starts with the closure of a prison and moves on to question what will grow in its place. Funded by the Art for Justice Fund and Visualizing Abolition, *And Water Brings Tomorrow* was made in part as an organizing resource to facilitate conversation, public education, coalition building, campaign momentum, and visibility for the work being done by system-impacted people, organizers, and communities in places where prisons are contested or where aspects of the prison-industrial complex remain or are finding a foothold.

Ashley Hunt, born 1970, lives and works in Los Angeles.

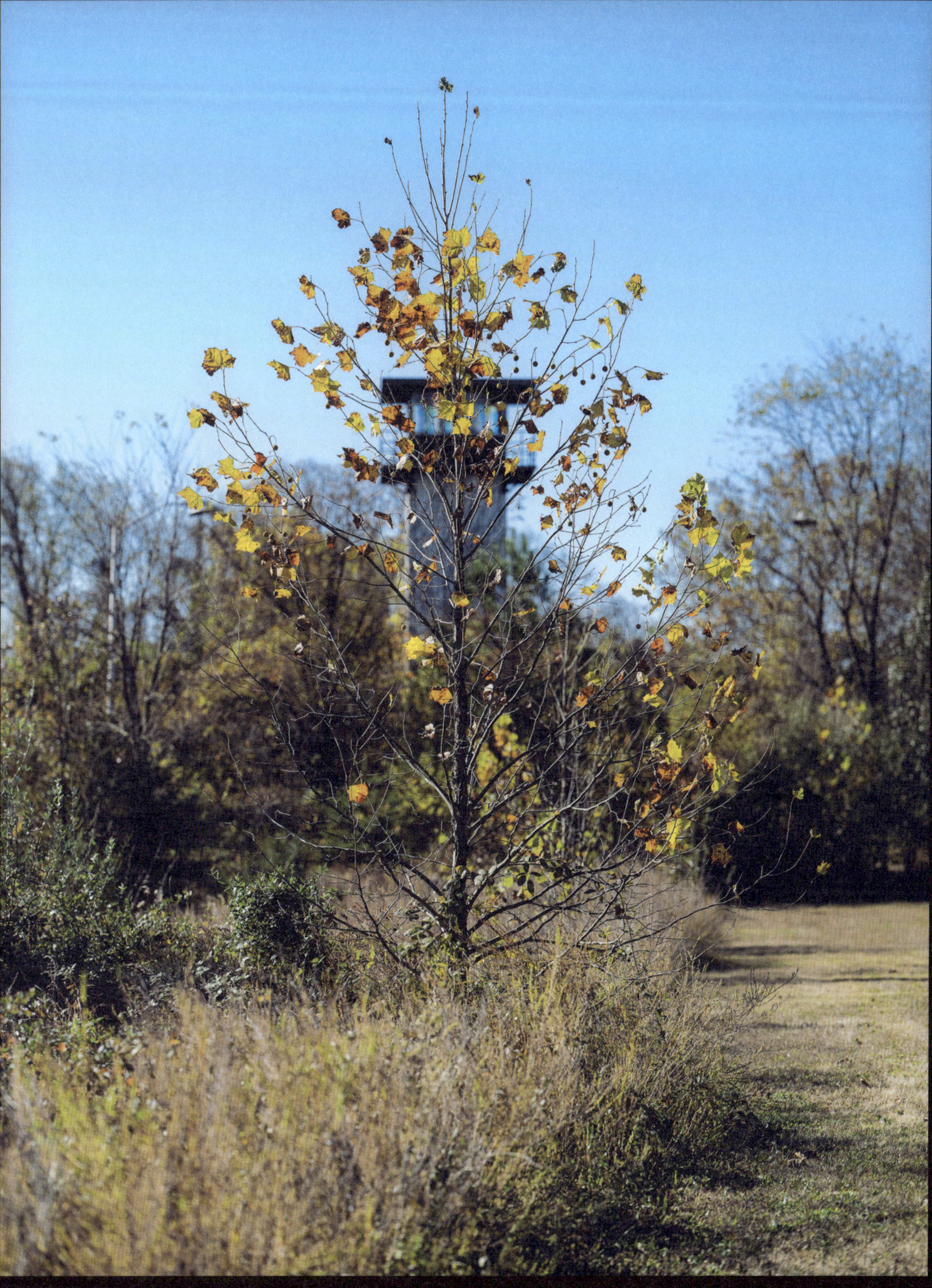

Steffani Jemison
In Succession (2019), 2019
Black-and-white HD video with sound
18:19 minutes

In Succession is loosely based on several episodes reported in newspapers in the early twentieth century, in which Black men carried out acrobatic feats of physical and architectural transgression. In 1900, for example, the *New York Times* reported that six Black men in Middlesex County Jail, New Jersey, formed a human pyramid, cut a hole in the ceiling, and successfully escaped. In another episode, a group of Black men made national news by forming a human pyramid to save a white woman from the second story of a burning building. In a news item, an acrobatic Black man burgled upper-floor apartments of white families on the Upper East Side of Manhattan, aiming to steal gems from the rich to provide food to the poor in Harlem.

In her split-screen video, Steffani Jemison uses contemporary imagery of highly disciplined movement practices. Several men in white-collar dress sustain acrobatic poses, with the slow-panning camera focusing on fragments of their entangled bodies: reaching and clasped hands, torsos, feet, entwined shadows. In a negation of gravity and reorientation of "progress," the split-screen images are turned on their side, obfuscating notions of an upward trajectory, instead foregrounding contact, mutual support, and meditative focus. How can bodies become means, supports, to stand on and be stood upon at the same time? How do bodies become architecture to find freedom *with* rather than freedom *from* one another? Occasional whispers of cooperative labor are heard against the hum of passing traffic.

Steffani Jemison, born 1981 in Berkeley, California, lives and works in New York.

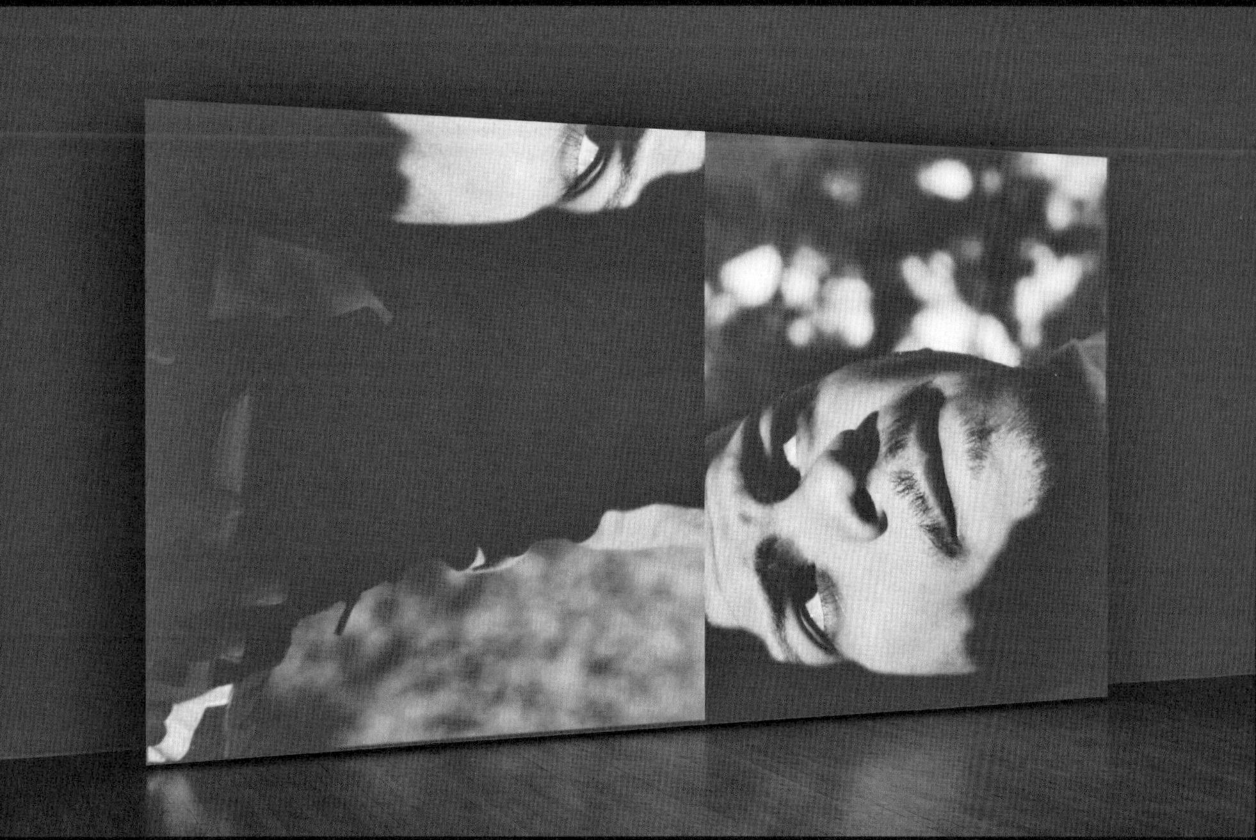

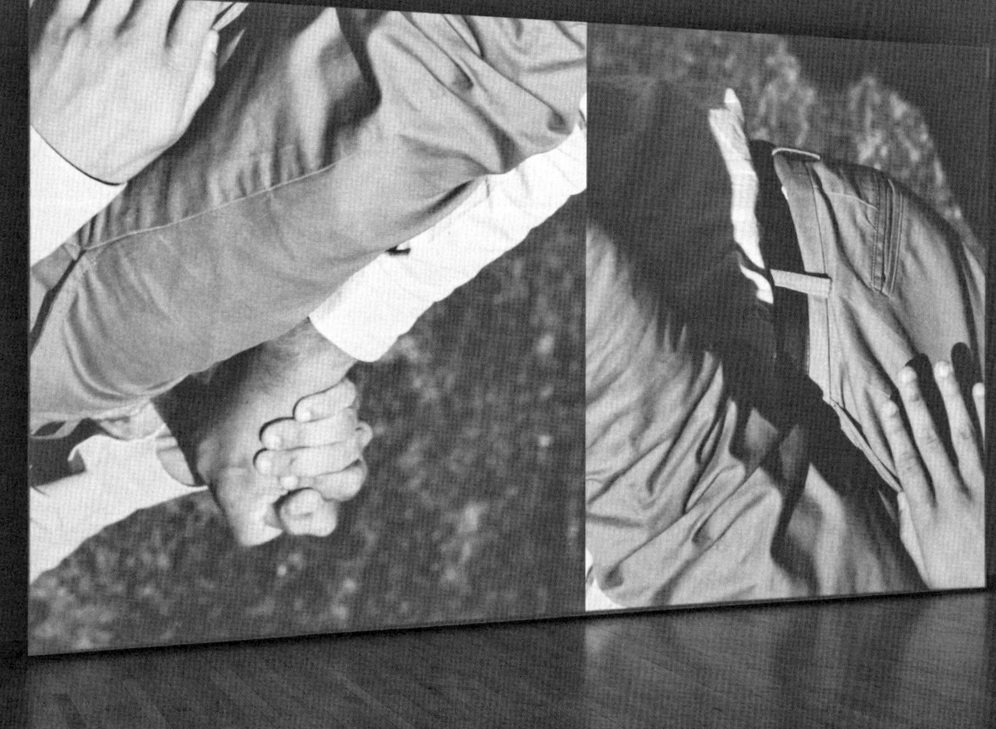

Sofia Karim
Memories of Keraniganj Jail, 2019
3D-printed models
Nine models: approx. 6 × 9 × 6 in., each

Diptychs, 2023
Projections on paper with text
12 × 19 in., each

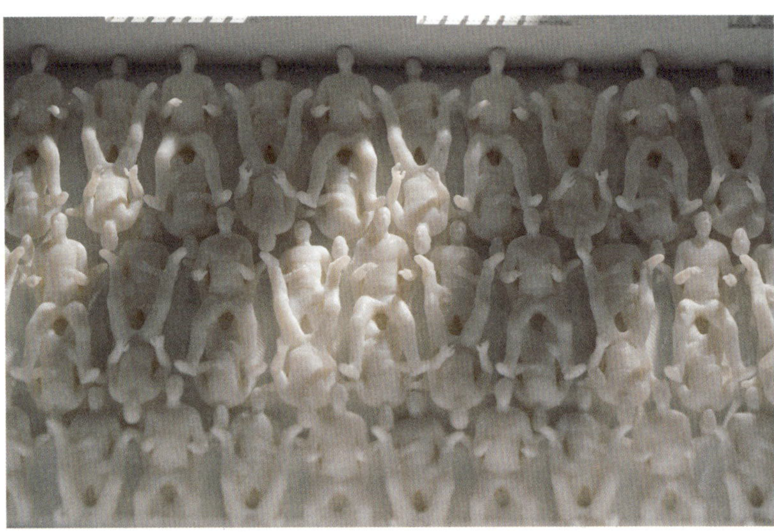

Memories of Keraniganj Jail materializes the recollections of Sofia Karim's uncle, the photographer and activist Shahidul Alam, of the time he spent as a political prisoner in Bangladesh. Karim, an architect, has created small 3D-printed models based on Alam's descriptions of the jail. The models show, for instance, the *amdani* [intake] cell, in which individuals are made to lie, according to Alam, like "packed sardines." Another model shows the prison hospital, where Alam described two rows of prisoners lying on the floor along the central aisle. These are models of oppression, revealing what Karim has called an "architecture of disappearance." However, the modeled memories also reveal that which exceeds this architecture. Tiny details—like the shelves Alam improvised in his cell to serve as bird feeders or the people he played music with as guards sat and listened—point to the creative relationships and modes of care that exist even within the built environment of repression.

Karim further explores architecture as both a means of confinement and a language of struggle and resistance in *Diptychs*, a work created from correspondence with Professor G. N. Saibaba, a political prisoner in India, who in 2017 was sentenced to life for his alleged Maoist links. While corresponding with Saibaba, Karim noticed that the way she made drawings for her architectural day job began to change. Details of precisely rendered joists, support beams, and concealed connections took on new, poetic meaning in relation to Saibaba's descriptions of his architectural confinement. *Diptychs* pairs these delicate, colorful drawings with printed excerpts from the letters. A rendering of a window reveal detail, for example, is paired with text that reads, "You stand on the other side of the opaque fiberglass window; words fail me, as though I have forgotten our language of love and intimacy." A drawing of a picture window corner junction corresponds with the text "It's poetry stupid. It's stupendous poetry. It doesn't need weapons to smelt break the iron heels of history."

Viewers see only black-and-white projections of these drawings. In correspondence with Karim, Saibaba lamented the lack of color in prison, and in response, Karim mailed her colorful abolitionist architectures to him and his fellow prisoners. What remains on the outside are ghosts of images, haunting the built environment, incomplete until the prison walls come down.

Sofia Karim, born 1976, is a London-based architect and activist.

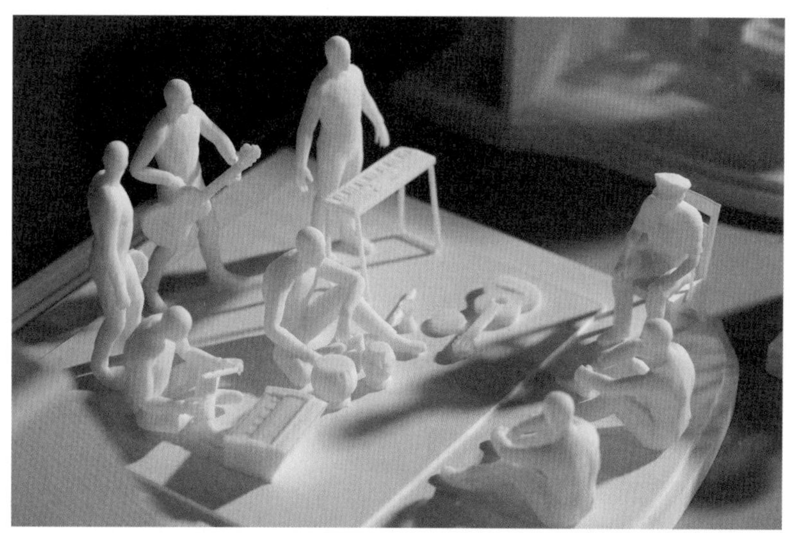

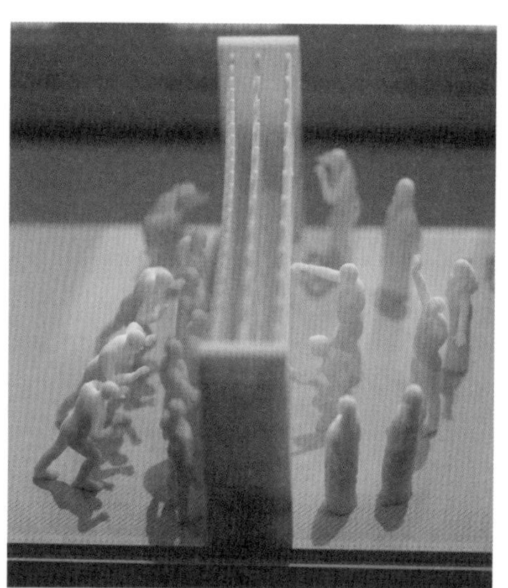

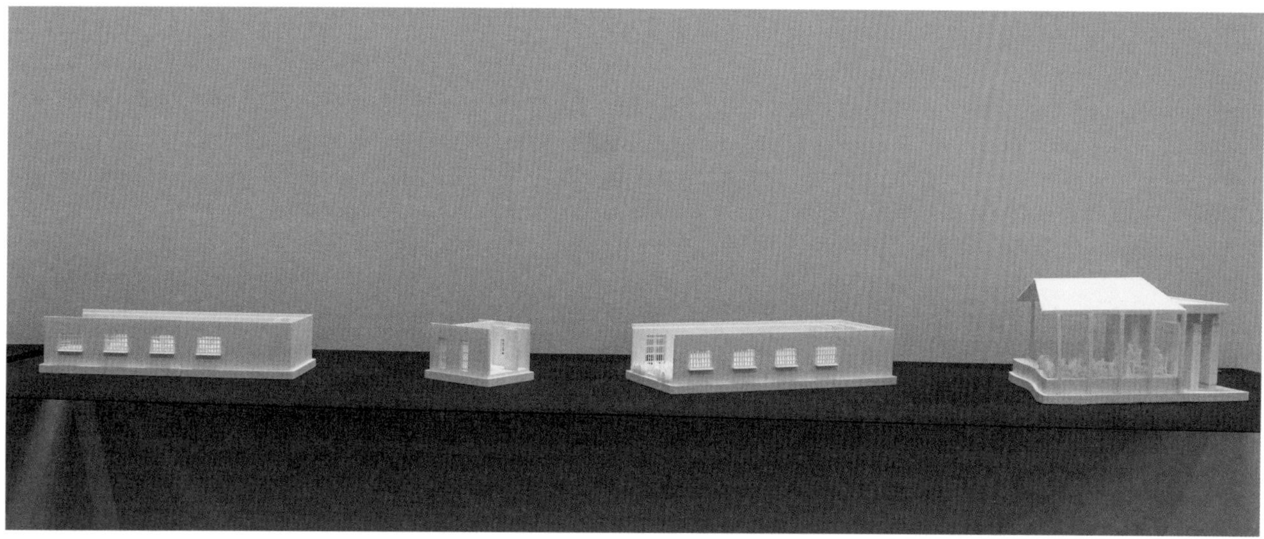

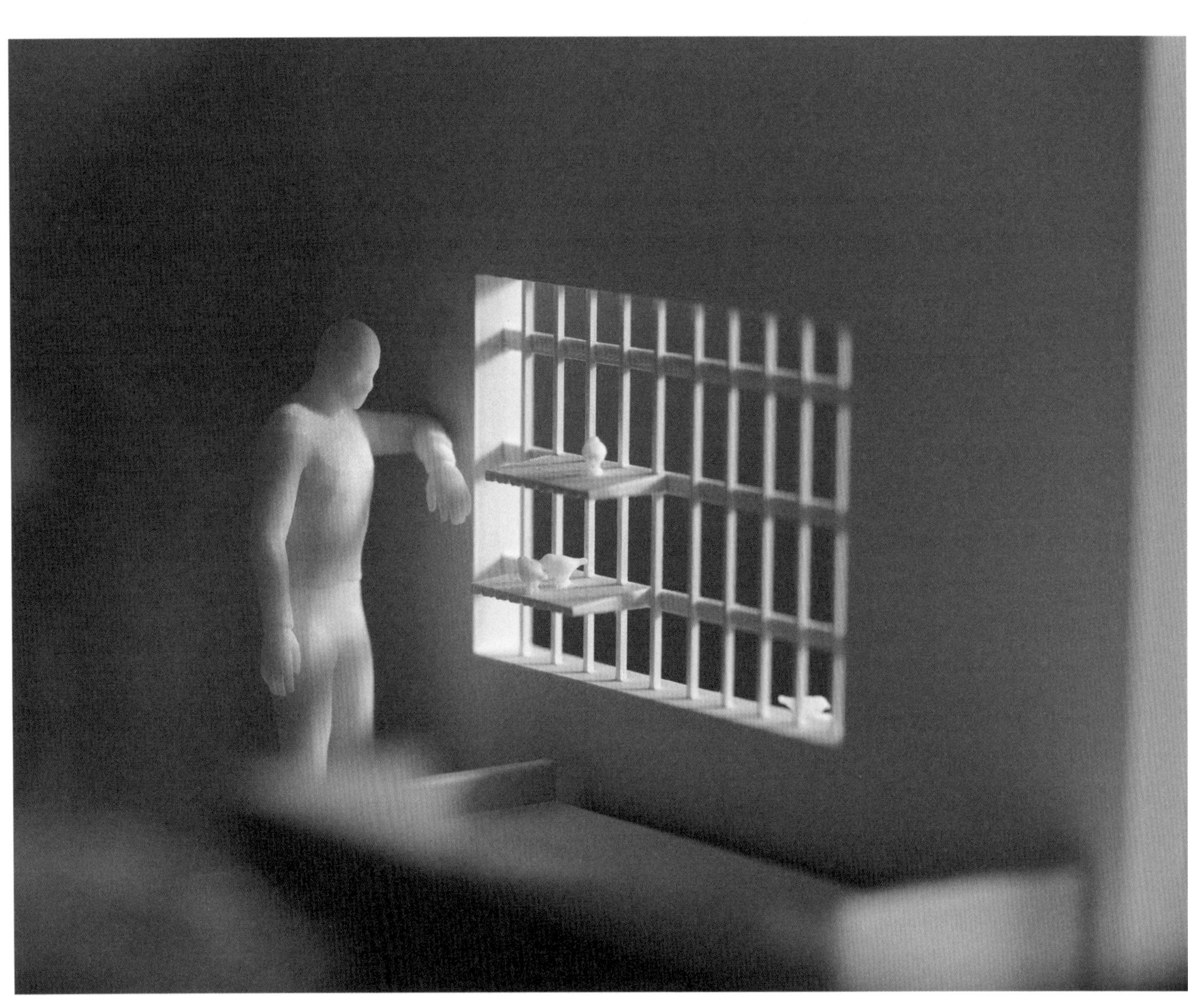

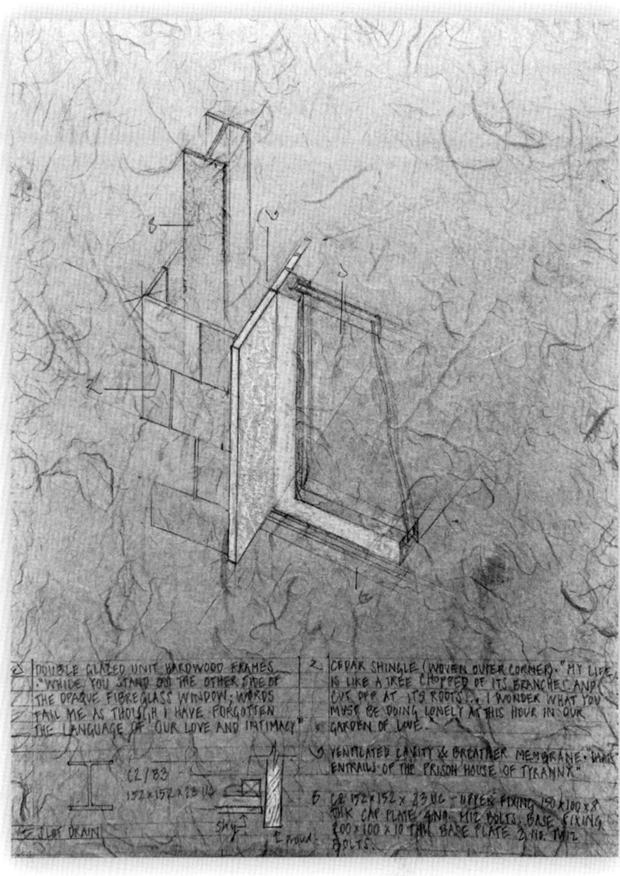

while you
stand on the other side of the opaque
fibreglass window; words fail me, as though
I have forgotten our language of love and intimacy,

G.N. Saibaba

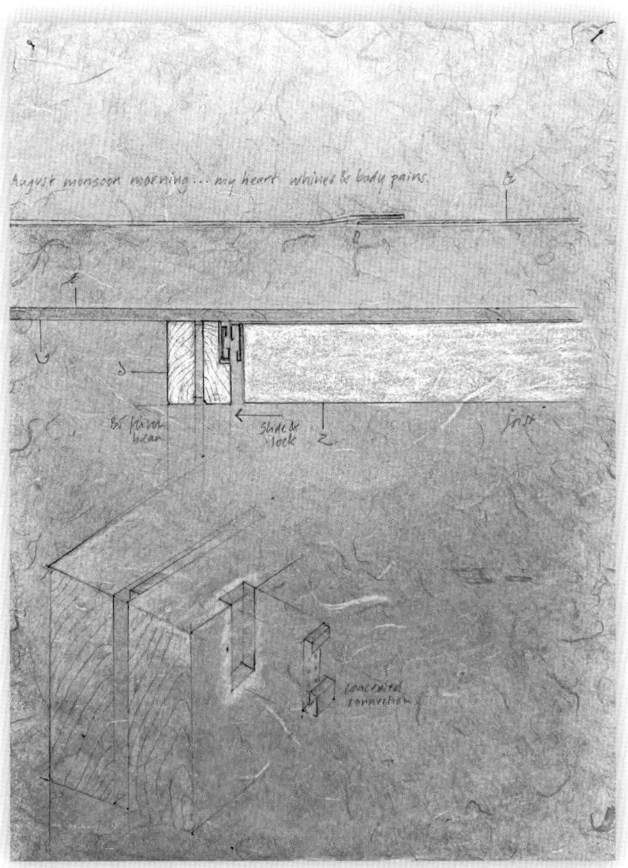

...In the Maximum Security
Prison of the nation on this cloudy
August monsoon morning, I think of the pain
of the people and their everyday struggles
for life and death amidst the shooting pain
in my left hand, twirling aches in my shrunken legs
and exploding pain in my grisly gut.

G.N. Saibaba

Bouchra Khalili
The Constellation Series, 2011
Eight silkscreen prints on paper, mounted on aluminum and framed
24 × 16 in., each

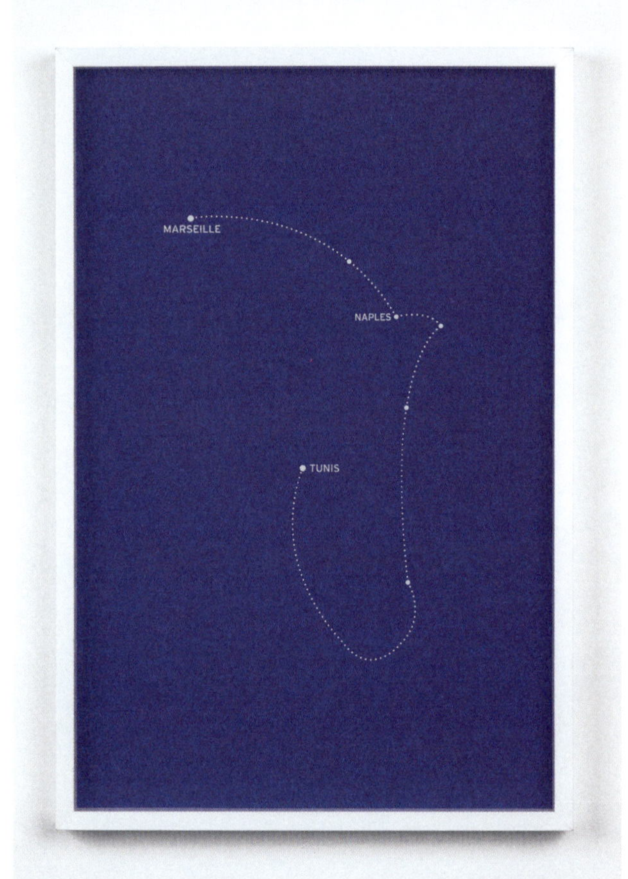

Each of the eight drawings comprising *The Constellation Series* depicts the journey of an individual forced by political and economic constraints to cross borders illegally in the Mediterranean Basin. Some routes are linear—dotted lines connecting Rome, Debrecen, Tehran, and Jalal-Abad—while others double back or make detours. In the drawings, these treacherous roads and sea passages have been transcribed from geographic maps onto stars, forming constellations. Sky and sea blur, erasing boundaries, echoing the centuries-old practice of sailors navigating by the stars.

Bouchra Khalili, born 1975, is a Moroccan French artist who lives and works in Berlin and Oslo.

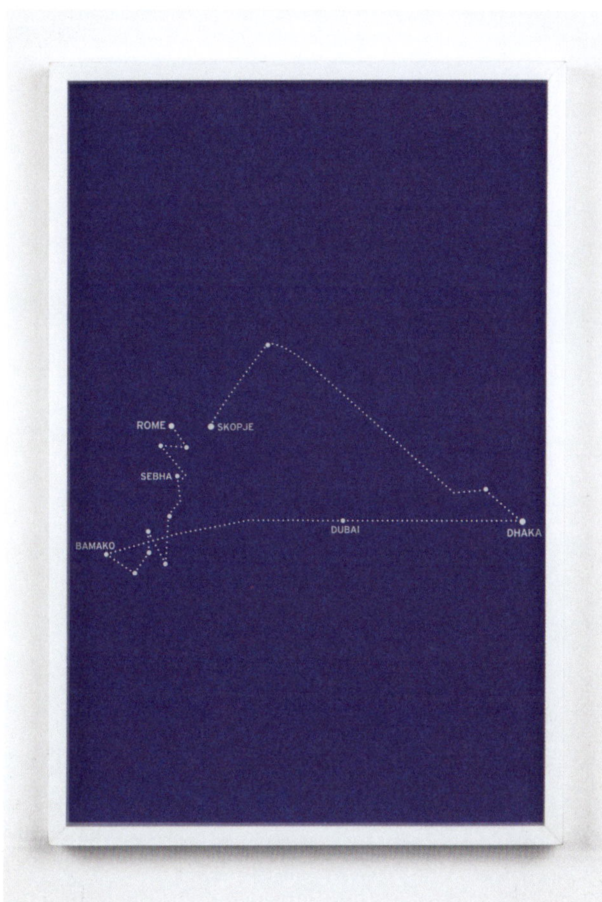

ROME
SKOPJE
SEBHA
BAMAKO
DUBAI
DHAKA

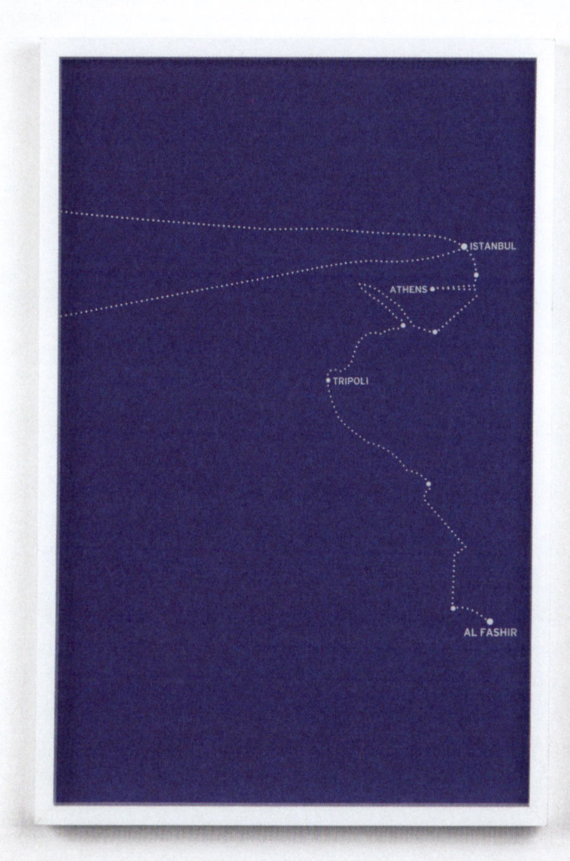

ISTANBUL
ATHENS
TRIPOLI
AL FASHIR

Robert Hillary King
Freelines, 1962/2024
Pralines and labels
4½ × 3¾ in., each

Pralines are a sweet New Orleans treat, creamy and fudgy, made by caramelizing pecans in a mixture of brown sugar, granulated sugar, cream, and butter. While Robert Hillary King was incarcerated in the Louisiana State Penitentiary, known as Angola, he learned to make the candies from a fellow prisoner in the prison kitchen. He began making pralines in his cell to give to other prisoners, calling them *Freelines*.

As King explains, the candies tasted like freedom: "When you're in prison like that, you have to come up with ideas to do the thing that your space and your environment restrict you from doing—that you are not allowed to do. . . . You're in a hopeless situation, but in a hopeless situation you still could envision hope."

Since his release from prison, King has continued to make *Freelines*, using them to spread the word about prisons and injustice, and to carry on the pursuit of freedom.

Robert Hillary King, born 1974 in New Orleans, was the first freed member of the Angola Three, who were held at the Louisiana State Penitentiary for decades in solitary confinement. After his release, King helped lead the campaign for the freedom of his comrades. He was imprisoned in the Louisiana State Penitentiary for thirty-one years, twenty-nine of which he spent in solitary confinement, and was released on February 8, 2001.

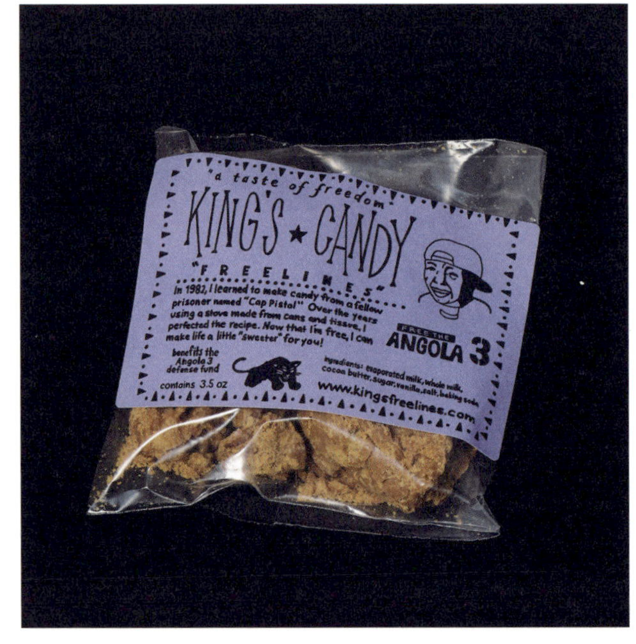

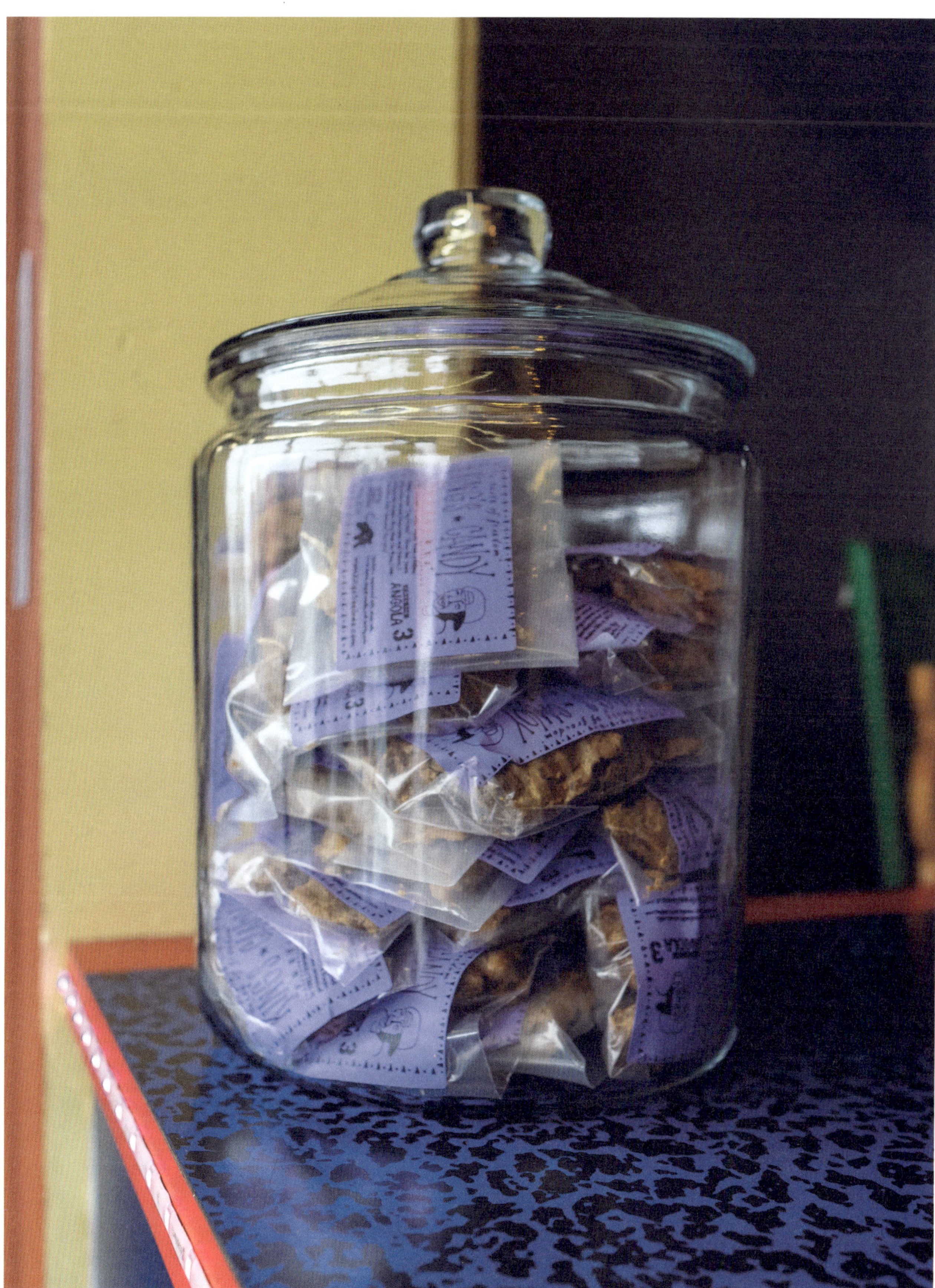

Carlos Motta
The Capuchin Order, 2023
Paper architectural model, slide projector, 35 mm slides, and table
25 × 36 × 25¾ in.

A hybrid sculpture made from paper and cardboard depicts the Casa Arana, an infamous building in La Chorrera, Amazonas, Colombia, merged with the facade of a colonial Catholic church. The Casa Arana was built at the turn of the twentieth century for rubber production by the Peruvian Amazon Company. It was also the unofficial headquarters of the "Putumayo genocide" in the Amazon, during which tens of thousands of Indigenous people were enslaved and forced to collect rubber between 1879 and 1912. During that time, over thirty thousand Indigenous people were killed or died from mistreatment, and tens of thousands of others died from resulting epidemics. Following a public outcry, the Casa Arana was shut down, and the building was given to Capuchin missionaries as a residential boarding school, which forcibly housed the Indigenous children who had survived the genocide only to be taken from their families. The school has had an immense impact on the region, resulting in the disuse of Indigenous languages, the truncated transmission of cultural knowledge, and the establishment of Christianity as an institutionalized religion.

The architectural splicing in *The Capuchin Order* shows this transformation from slave quarters to residential school, reconstructing an extended carceral history that speaks to the roles captivity and forced labor played in destroying communities and cultures even before the rise of the modern prison. Projected on the surface of the sculpture are 35 mm slide photographs taken by the missionaries, an unwitting archive of resistance.

Carlos Motta, born 1978 in Colombia, currently lives in New York.

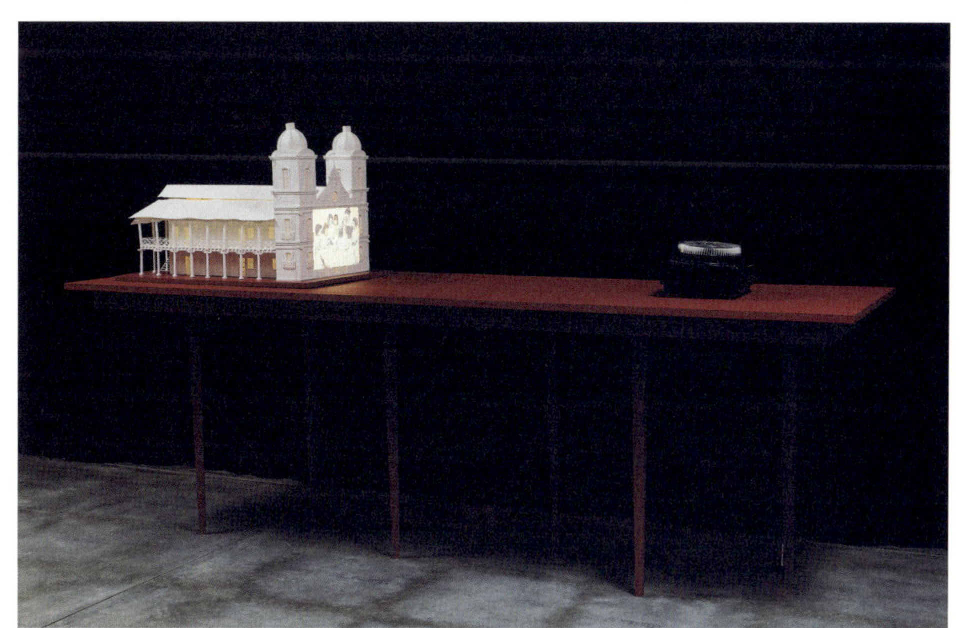

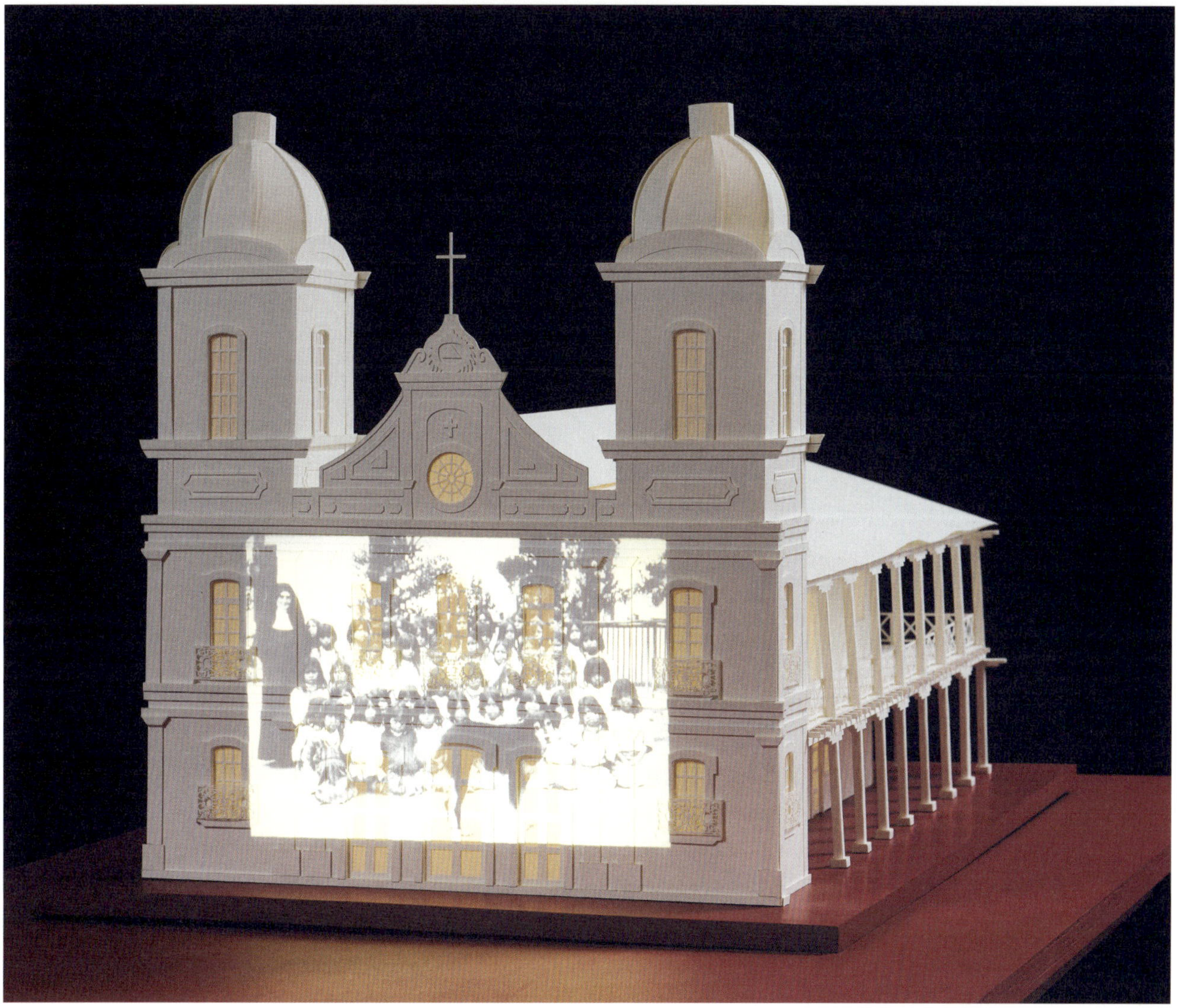

Mulheres Possíveis

Lines to cross walls, 2024

In collaboration with Ana Paula, Ângela, Anísia, Caline, Caren, Cilceli, Cristiane, D., Dagma, Daniela, Eliane, Erica Fernanda, Fátima, Fernanda, Gislaine, Grazielle, Hilda, Hortência, Ingrid, Juliana, Juliana Fernanda, Juliet, Kamila, Lea, Lourdes, Maria Carmim, Maria Edivânia, Maria Gabriela, Marlyn Elizabeth, Mercedes, Miriam, Monica, Nady, Naftali, Paola, Renata, Samara, Sarah, Scheine, Shandelies, Silvia Alejandra, Suellen, Tabatha, Tanaka, Tanira, Tatiane, Thayane, Tubarão, and Uthopom

Vinyl sticker

112 × 118 in.

Livro de atividades, 2020/24

In collaboration with Bárbara Esmenia, Fábia Karklin, Maré de Matos, Olga Torres, and Olivia Niculitcheff

Pedagogical consultant: João Innecco

Book

6¾ × 9½ in.

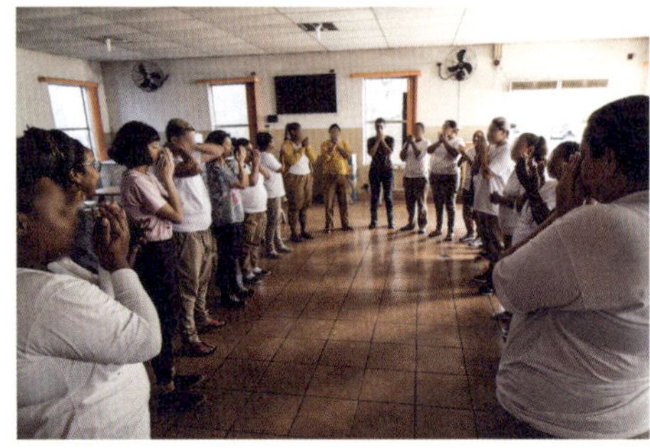

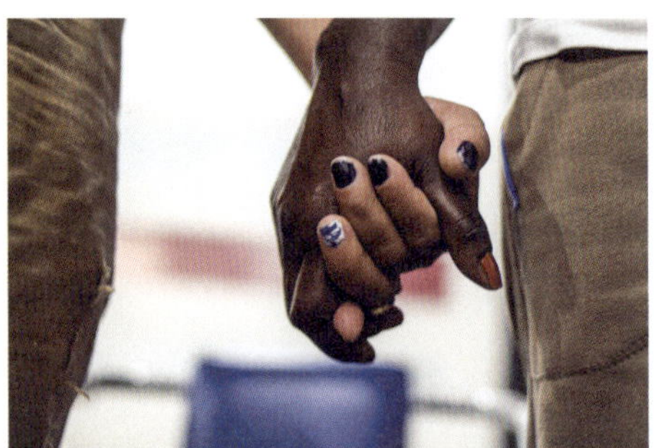

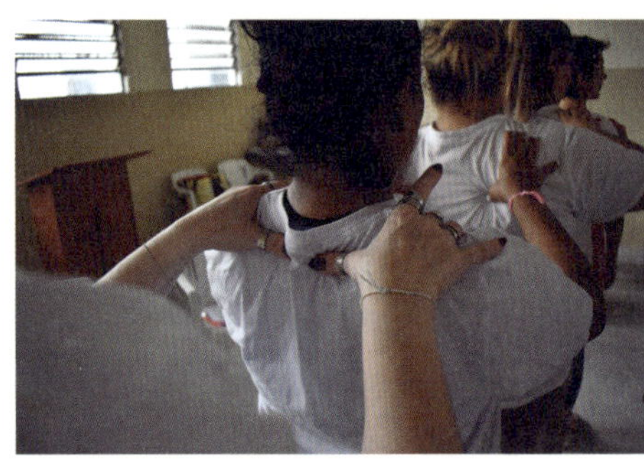

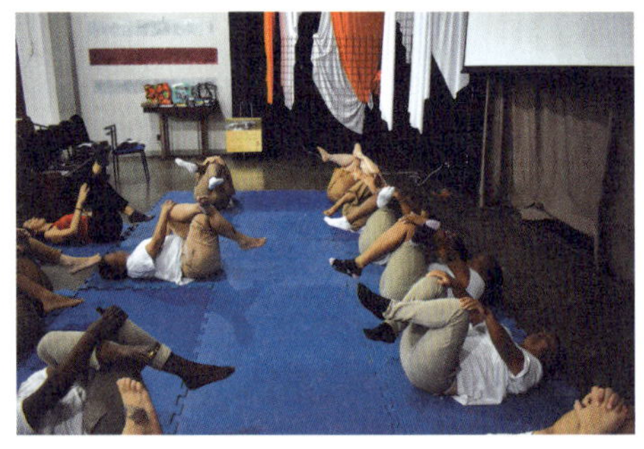

The collective Mulheres Possíveis has worked in collaboration with incarcerated women at São Paulo's Penitenciária Feminina da Capital [Women's Penitentiary of the Capital, or PFC] since 2016. In 2020, due to the COVID-19 pandemic, the collective's in-person activities at the penitentiary were suspended. To continue their artistic and pedagogical work, Mulheres Possíveis created the *Livro de atividades* [*Activity Book*] and distributed two thousand copies to prisoners in the PFC and in the Franco da Rocha Penitentiary. The book offers a series of propositions designed to encourage poetic reflection on the body, gender, and incarceration; the activities seek to create spaces for self-care, sharing, and reflection on the world as it is and as we want it to be.

For *Seeing through Stone*, Mulheres Possíveis has translated *Livro de atividades* into English for distribution to people held in women's facilities in the United States, creating community across national borders and through the walls of prisons. Images and texts drawn from the collective's collaboration with people held in the PFC also adorn the windows of the Institute of the Arts and Sciences.

Mulheres Possíveis is a São Paulo, Brazil–based collective led by artists Beatriz Cruz, Leticia Olivares, Sandra Ximenez, and Vânia Medeiros.

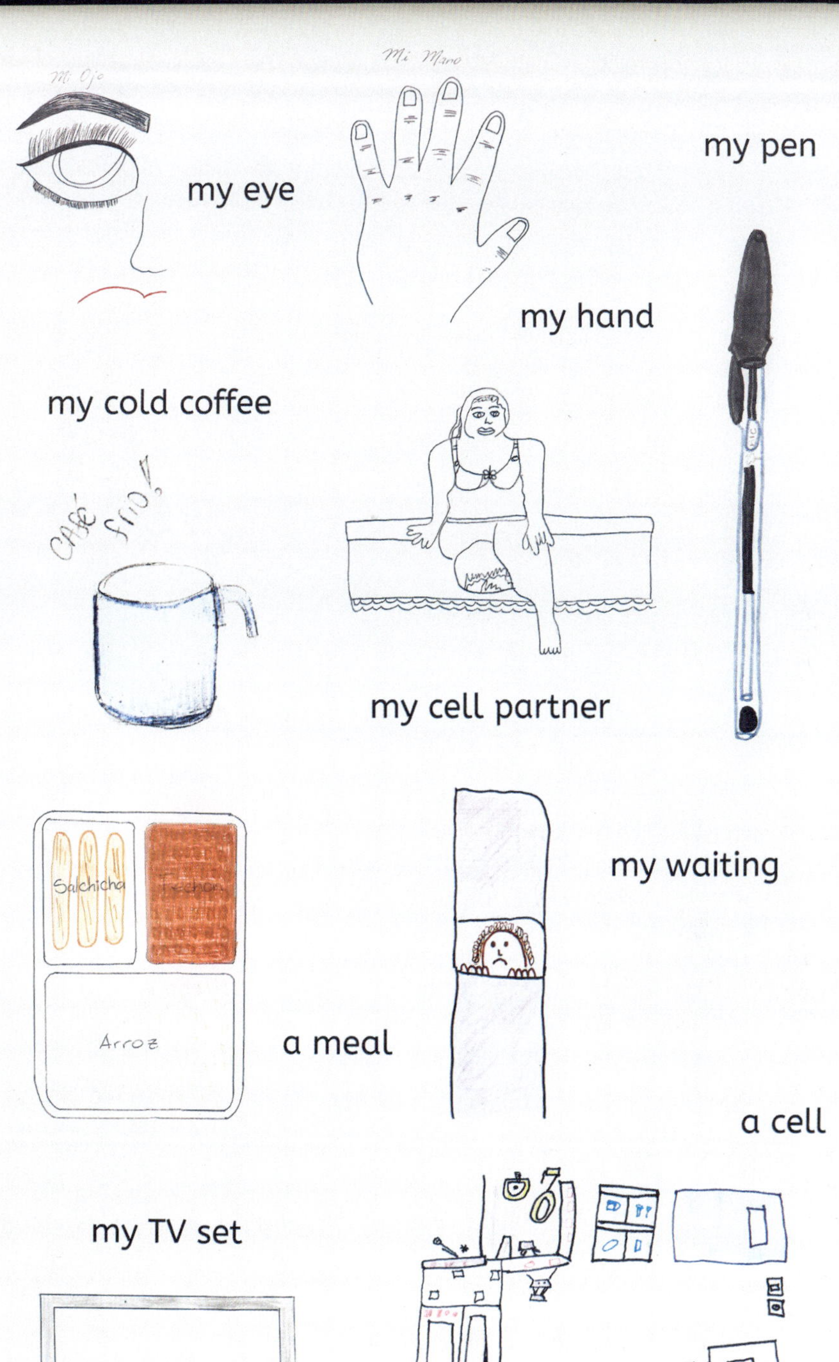
Mi Ojo
my eye
Mi Mano
my hand
my pen
my cold coffee
Café frío!
my cell partner
my waiting
Salchicha
Frijol
Arroz
a meal
a cell
my TV set
PHILCO
Lo que mas me gusta es la T.V.

Gabriela Mureb
Machine #4: Stone (Crank), 2017
Engine, stone, and aluminum
13¾ × 29½ × 9⅞ in.

A simple motorized rod pounds against a rock, continuously and rhythmically, in *Machine #4: Stone (Crank)*. Over time, the rod will bore a hole into the stone. Eventually, this hole will alter the stone's weight, perhaps causing it to topple. Foregrounding the physical experiences of continuity, rhythm, and repetition, Gabriela Mureb draws the viewer into a temporality of steady time and perseverance. The work is inspired by the popular Brazilian proverb "Soft water on hard stone hits until it bores a hole," a saying that speaks of patience and transformation.

In the context of *Seeing through Stone*, Mureb's futile machine is a poetic image of the eventual pulverization of stone into dust. First one stone falls, and then the whole wall comes down.

Gabriela Mureb, born 1985 in Niterói, Brazil, currently lives and works in Rio de Janeiro.

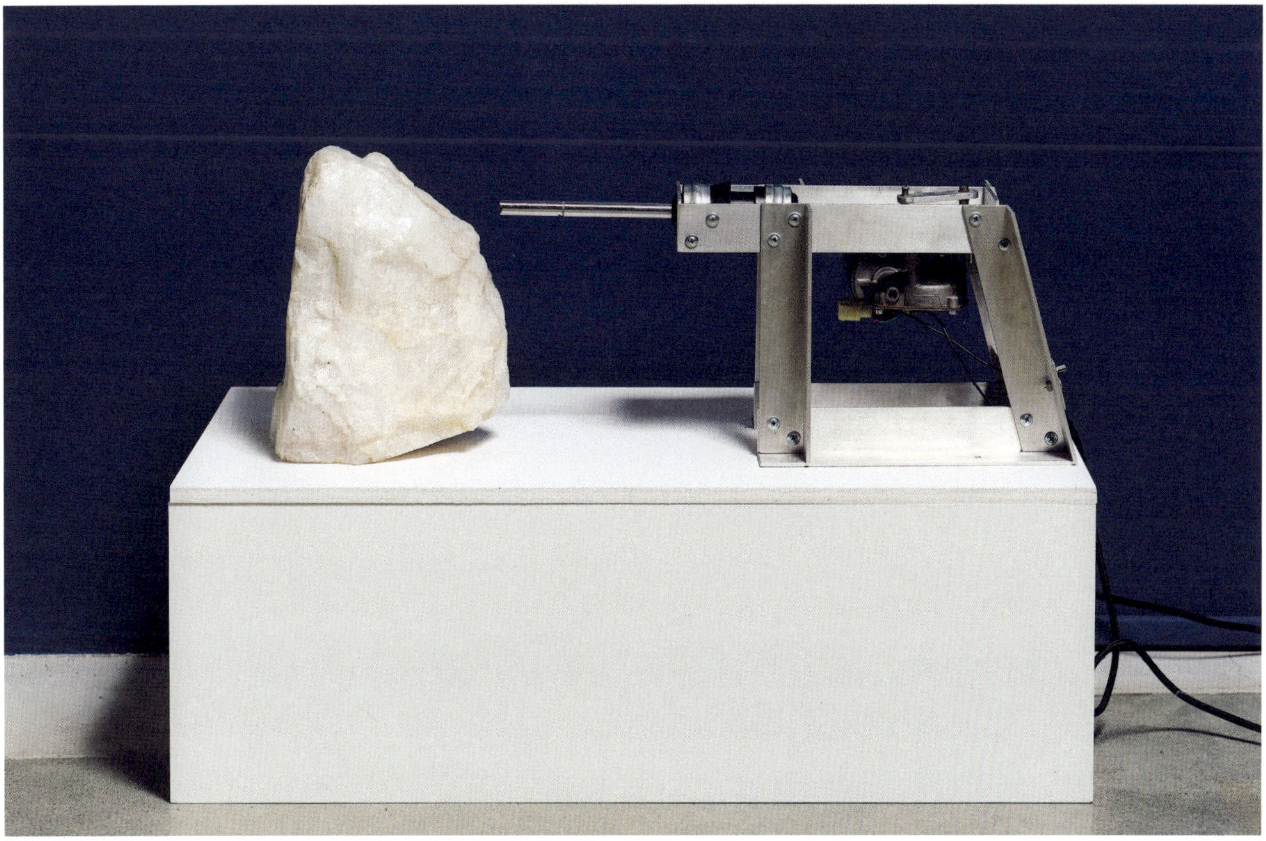

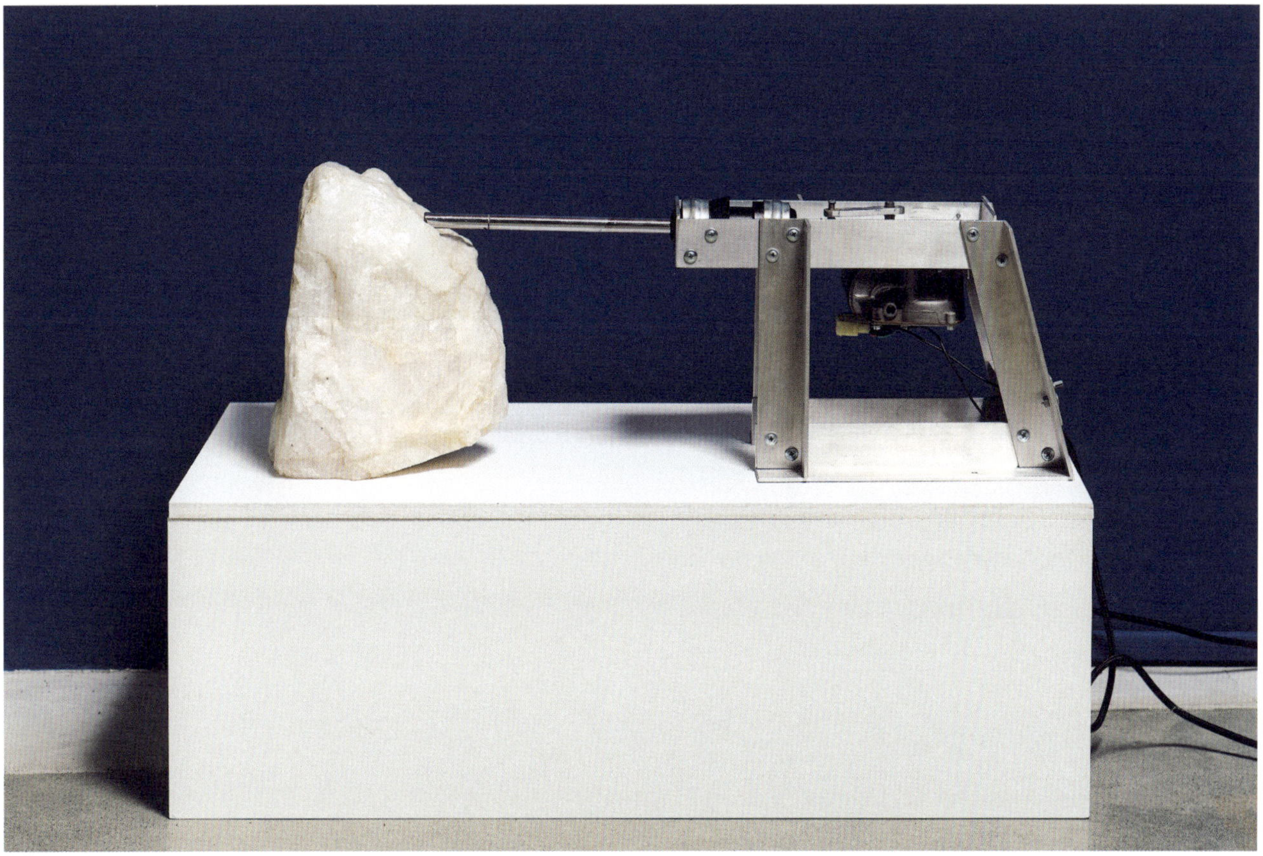

Hương Ngô
And the State of Emergency Is Also Always a State of Emergence, 2017–ongoing
Installation with black poster paper, black gaffer's tape, cyanotypes, sand, plaster, studio refuse, and framed archival pigment prints
132 × 72 × 48 in., overall

Hương Ngô's multimedia art practice materially enacts what the artist calls "refugee epistemologies," expanding concepts of time and knowledge held by those who have experienced generational, geographical, or ecological rupture.

For *And the State of Emergency Is Also Always a State of Emergence*, Ngô made a six-by-four-by-eleven-foot bunk bed frame, similar to those found in crowded rooms of jails, detention centers, and prisons across the globe, out of reinforced paper. This precarious architectural sculpture is based on the stories told by Ngô's siblings about her family's nearly two-year-long stay, when they were children, in a Hong Kong detention center. It adheres to the architectural dimensions noted in official reports about the treatment of Vietnamese refugees in those centers, for whom "life . . . consists of a home that is half of a four by six foot cubicle."[1] Around the paper bed frame, which stands on an uneven rectangle of sand, unpainted plaster models of canned food are stacked, and cyanotypes, arranged in a row, record the fleeting imprints of waves. Titled after a quote by postcolonial literary scholar Homi Bhabha,[2] the artwork renders the carceral space of the detention center as slippery and unstable as memory.

Hương Ngô, born 1979 in Hong Kong, lives in Santa Barbara, California.

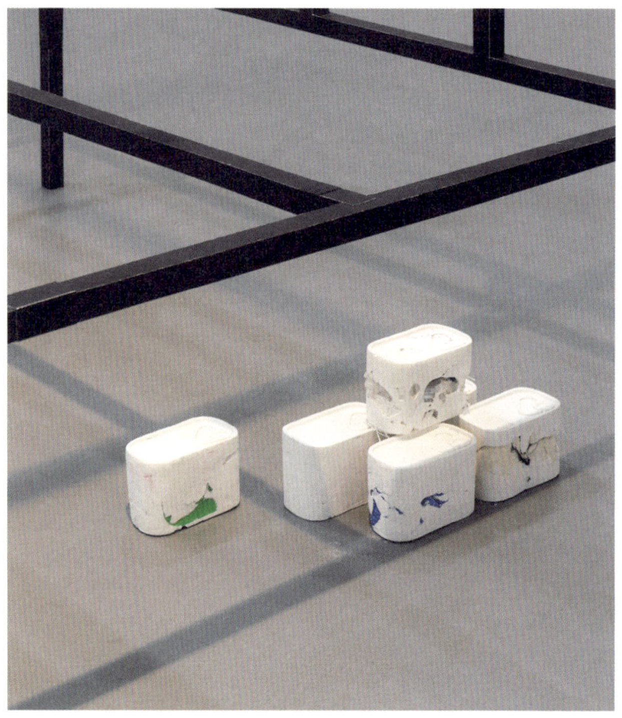

1. Donald Larson, *The Hong Kong Refugee Crisis: Suggestions for U.S. Policy Makers* (Washington, DC: Heritage Foundation, 1989).

2. "The state of emergency is also always a state of emergence." Homi Bhabha, foreword to *Black Skin, White Masks*, by Frantz Fanon (London: Pluto Press, 1986).

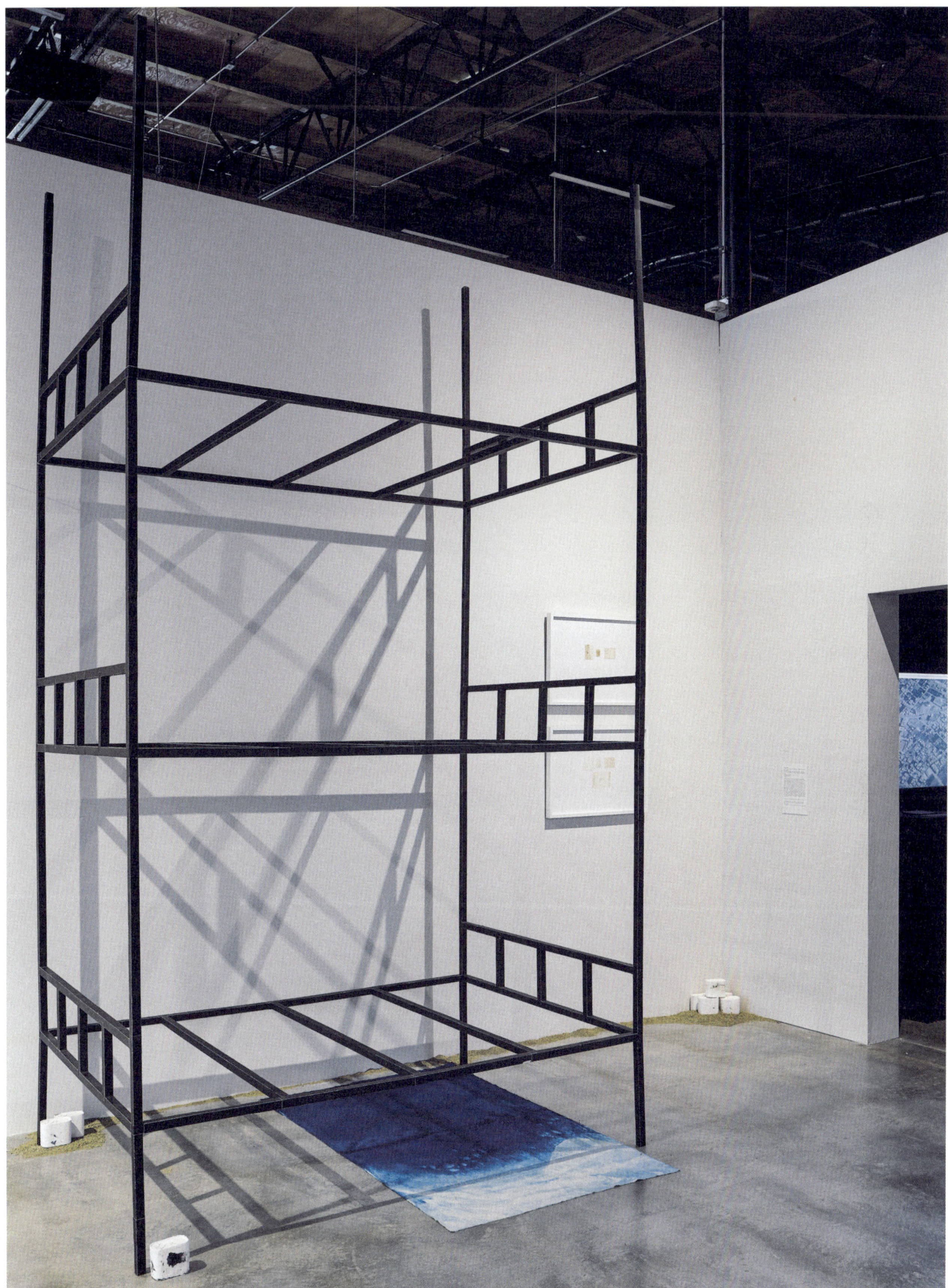

O grupo inteiro (Carol Tonetti, Cláudio Bueno, Ligia Nobre, and Vitor Cesar) with Vanessa Soares and Lorran Dias
Liberdade Zero (Freedom Zero), 2024

In collaboration with Centro de Estudos e Ações Solidárias da Maré and Complexo de Favelas da Maré

Video installation, poster, and charcoal drawing

Video: 13:54 minutes; poster: 36 × 24 in.; drawing: 13 × 18 in.

Mars is a rock—cold, empty, almost airless, dead. Yet it's heaven in a way. We can see it in the night sky, a whole other world, but too nearby, too close within the reach of the people who've made such a hell of life here on Earth.
—Octavia E. Butler, *Parable of the Sower*

Children have to let their imaginations run wild. It's not nice to stay at home in forty-degree heat. Freedom is a right. Anyone who hasn't experienced it is missing out. People who have never been out to try new food, a new place.
—Samuel, eleven years old, student at CEASM

In the dark, I'm invisible. I'm Black when the light comes on.
—Student at CEASM

Liberdade Zero (Freedom Zero) is a video installation addressing notions of justice, punishment, freedom, and abolition from the perspective of children ten to twelve years of age who live in the Complexo de Favelas da Maré [Maré Favela Complex], the largest complex of favelas in Rio de Janeiro, and study at the Centro de Estudos e Ações Solidárias da Maré [Center for Studies and Solidarity Actions of Maré, or CEASM]. Over the course of three months, the children participated in a series of bodily, spatial, and imaginative exercises, led by educator and choreographer Vanessa Soares in collaboration with O grupo inteiro and Lorran Dias. The exercises were designed to bring the children into relationship with places, times, and people outside of their immediate surroundings but that inhabit their imaginations.

In the video installation, which records these exercises, children shimmer in silver helmets and cloaks as chalk drawings become a trip to the moon. Like planets, the children whirl and spin, creating what one child calls "the world of the imagination." Mirrors left by astronauts on the moon refract this imaginative world, where memories of a military occupation of Maré in advance of the 2014 World Cup and of Astronauta, the nickname of the person who ran Maré before being imprisoned, become fantastical. Octavia Butler turns words into worlds. A child's fingers rub a

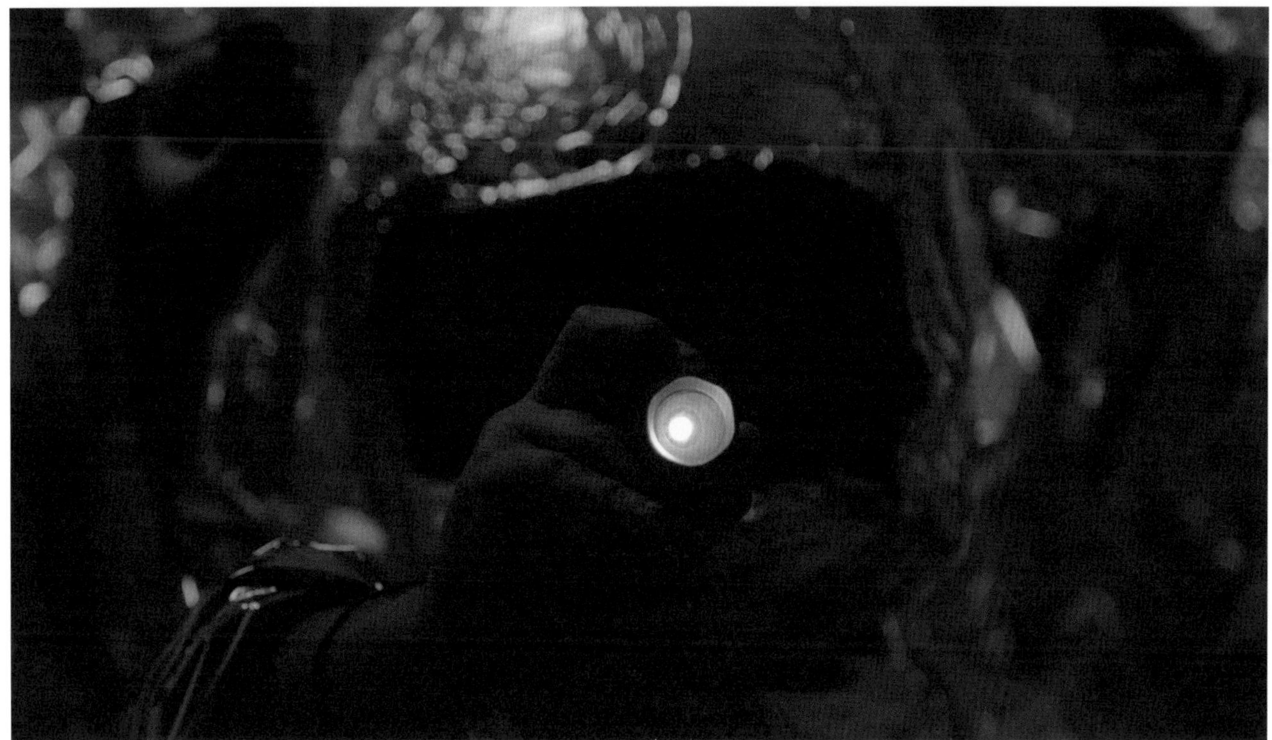

mirror and it becomes the sky. Freedom, the children explain, is being able to play.

Liberdade Zero features images captured by the Rio de Janeiro–based TV Coragem team, drawings made by CEASM students, audio recordings, and text excerpts. The exercises with the children were developed within the concept-practice-pedagogy of *Zombaria*, an embodied mode of learning developed by Soares.

O grupo inteiro was founded in 2014 in São Paulo, Brazil, by Carol Tonetti, Cláudio Bueno, Ligia Nobre, and Vitor Cesar. *Liberdade Zero (Freedom Zero)* was created in partnership with Vanessa Soares, Lorran Dias, Centro de Estudos e Ações Solidárias da Maré, and Complexo de Favelas da Maré.

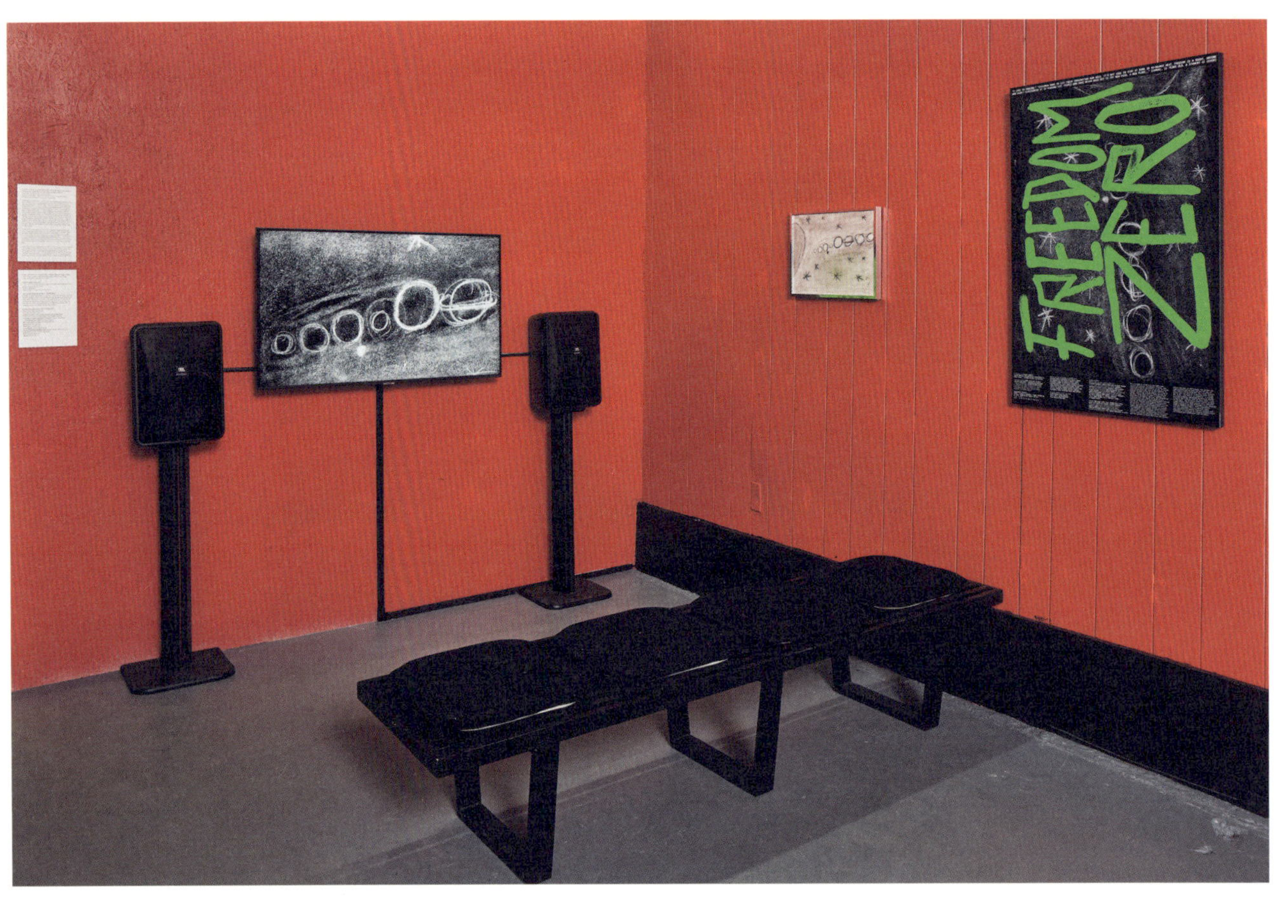

FREEDOM
ZERO

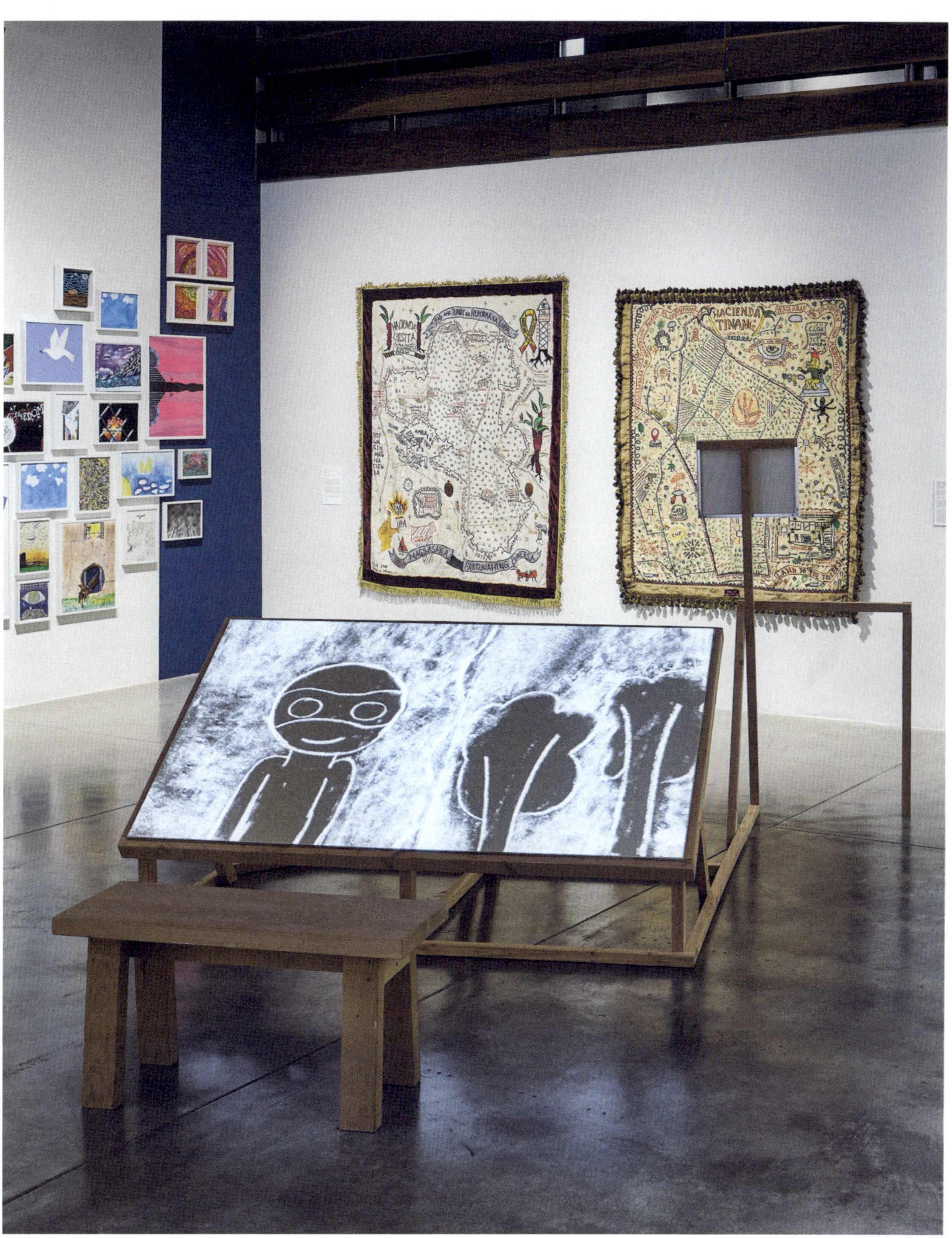

Samora Abayomi Pinderhughes
Listening Station (excerpt), from *The Healing Project*,
2016–ongoing
Audiocassettes

Listening Station is part of *The Healing Project*, an ongoing, community-engaged project that uses music, film, and people's stories, told in their own voices, to reveal the damage caused by carceral institutions and suggest alternative ways to protect, heal, and support each other outside of these oppressive systems. At the core of the project is a library of audio interviews. Since 2011, Samora Abayomi Pinderhughes has recorded more than one hundred people who have been harmed by the system as they share their healing processes, working with dozens of artistic collaborators to translate their stories into music and video.

In *Listening Station*, conversations recorded on audiocassettes offer an intimate experience of listening to people who are currently incarcerated speak about their experiences, with their voices set against original compositions created in response to the stories being told. Pinderhughes, a musician by training, sets the spoken testimonies against musical soundscapes: "I wanted to force us all to listen to folks more closely and hear the musicality of their voices—their tones, their rhythms, the spaces and pauses between their words, the ways their voices change as they reflect and speak."[1] The personal testimonials of those affected by incarceration, policing, violence, and detention reveal the realities of the prison-industrial complex. They also communicate the journeys people—collectively and individually—undergo to heal from structural violence. In addition to spotlighting the violence of present-day structures, the audio recordings illuminate the profound possibilities that exist for collective recovery and the end of carceral systems, propelling a necessary revolution built on self- and collective care.

Samora Abayomi Pinderhughes, born 1991 in the San Francisco Bay Area, lives and works in New York. He is a composer, pianist, vocalist, and multidisciplinary artist who uses music to examine sociopolitical issues.

1. Samora Pinderhughes, "Samora Pinderhughes: *The Healing Project*," Yerba Buena Center for the Arts, March 8, 2022, https://ybca .org/samora-pinderhughes-the -healing-project/.

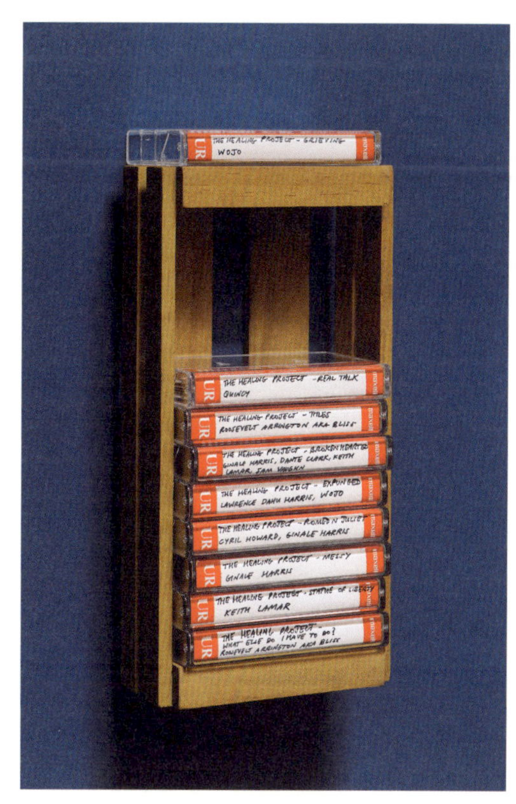
THE HEALING PROJECT - GRIEVING
WOJO
THE HEALING PROJECT - REAL TALK
QUINCY
THE HEALING PROJECT - TITLES
ROOSEVELT ARRINGTON AKA BLISS
THE HEALING PROJECT - BROKEN HEARTED
GINALE HARRIS, DANTE CLARK, KEITH
LAMAR, SAM VAUGHN
THE HEALING PROJECT - EXPUNGED
LAWRENCE DAHU HARRIS, WOJO
THE HEALING PROJECT - ROMEO N JULIET
CYRIL HOWARD, GINALE HARRIS
THE HEALING PROJECT - MESSY
GINALE HARRIS
THE HEALING PROJECT - STATUE OF LIBERTY
KEITH LAMAR
THE HEALING PROJECT -
WHAT ELSE DO I HAVE TO DO?
ROOSEVELT ARRINGTON AKA BLISS

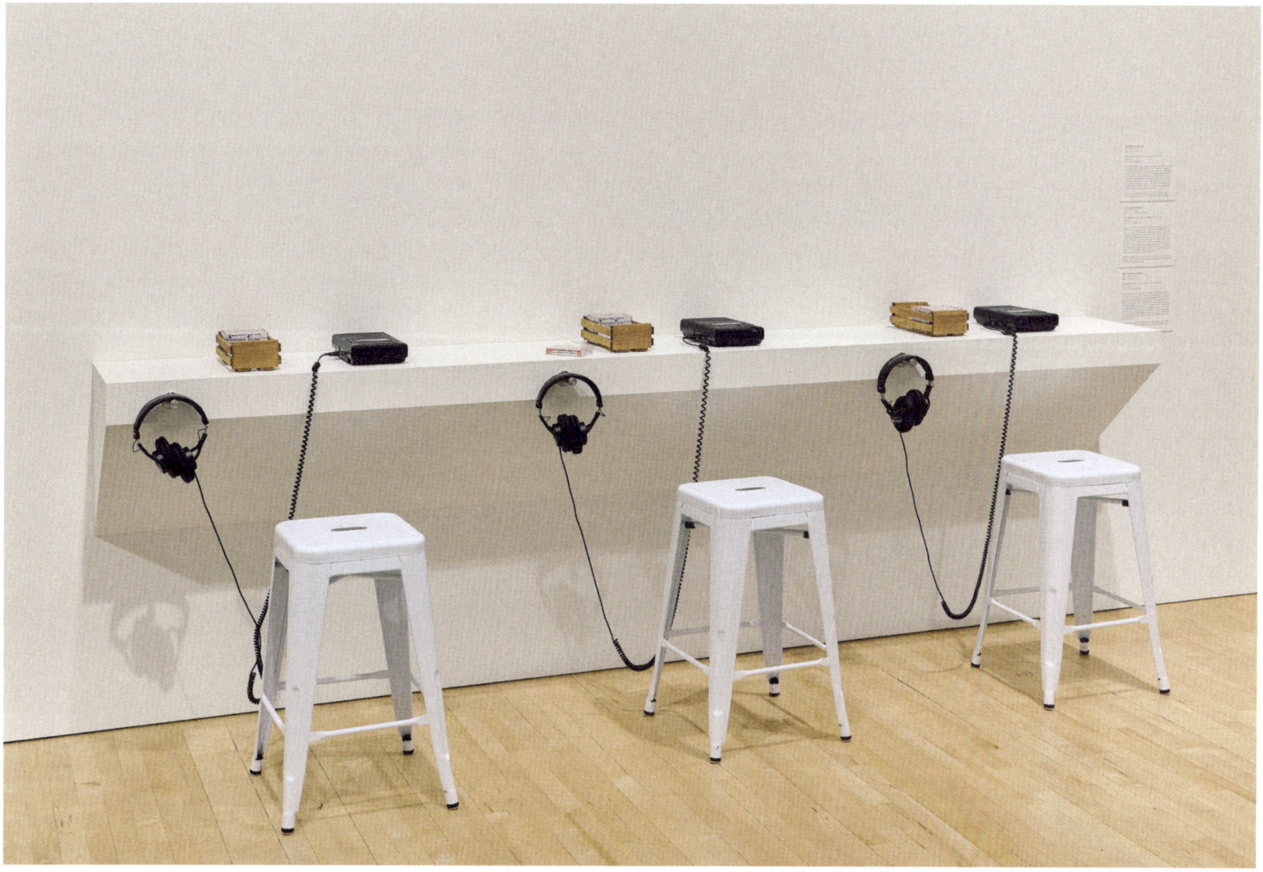

Sherrill Roland
Forecast, 2023
Steel and LED light box
66½ × 67 × 8 in.

In *Forecast*, a glow outlines the structure of a window
embedded within the cinder blocks of a prison cell. The
perspective is from within the confines of the cell, with
the window reflecting a constrained rectangle of sky.
Drawing on the months the artist spent in prison for a
crime for which he was later exonerated, *Forecast* works
within the haunting nuances of carceral aesthetics to
illuminate the invisible costs, damages, and burdens
of incarceration. Positioned just out of reach, the inop-
erable window functions as an architectural reminder
of life in the so-called free world, outside of prison
walls. While the sculpture poetically encapsulates the
longing for freedom of the body and the spirit experienced by the physically constrained, the glowing light
that manages to slip through the bars draws the eye
toward hope.

Sherrill Roland, born 1984, lives and works in
Raleigh, North Carolina.

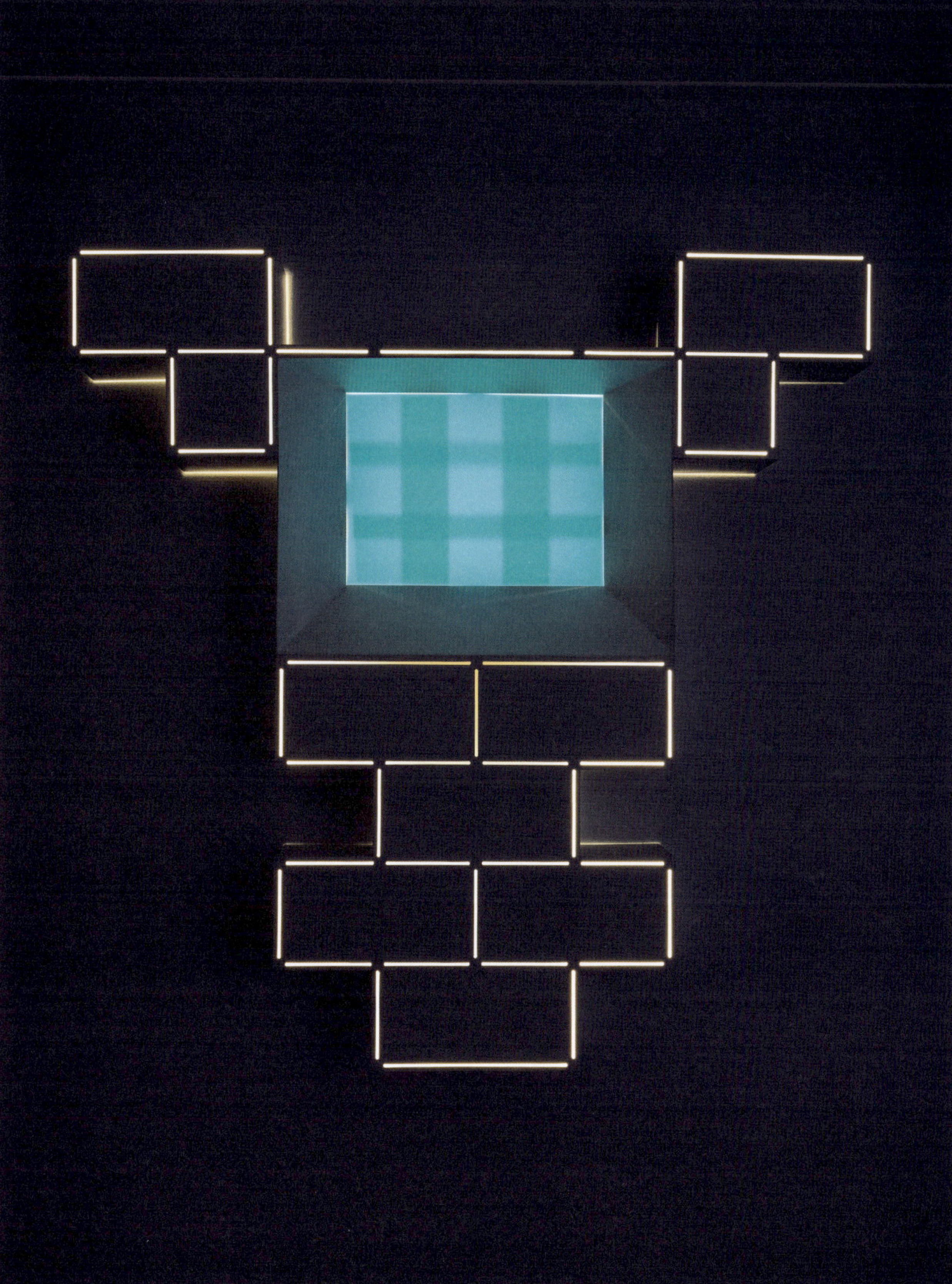

Sable Elyse Smith
Landscape V, 2020
Neon
37 × 178 in.

Neon takes a nearly imperceptible toll on the human experience. It grates on one's eyes. Its subtle buzzing is often not noticeable until it is silenced. The harsh glow touches and impacts an area much larger than what it physically occupies, and its electricity-sucking transformers drain power that might have been used for other purposes. *Landscape V* is one of a series of text-based neon works in which Sable Elyse Smith addresses the small, quotidian ways in which the carceral state impacts the human body. Light and color draw on histories of landscape painting, the sublime, lingering legacies of manifest destiny, and questions about control and dominion. In *Landscape V*, the poetic white text hovers over a blue line, suggestive of the horizon and a possible beyond. Yet the piece is riddled with tensions, between sublime light and neon light, language and silence, white and black, infinite and human-scaled time. We are left with a linguistic elision in the written text, where blue no longer refers to police and "finally means sky."

Smith's artworks focus on the multifocal, multi-sensorial experience of the carceral system and its destruction. Her practice examines the complex language and emotional landscapes embedded in systems of surveillance and structures of constraint, and the often invisible ways in which these systems and structures shape our minds and bodies. Smith connects her "Landscape" neons to the painted mural backdrops she encountered in visiting rooms over decades of visiting her father in California prisons. The painted scenes of tropical beaches and sunsets, meant to serve as cheerier backdrops for photographs capturing family visits, suggest false escapes and captive landscapes —flickering neon in place of warm sunlight.

Sable Elyse Smith, born 1986 in Los Angeles, is a visual artist, writer, and educator currently living and working in New York.

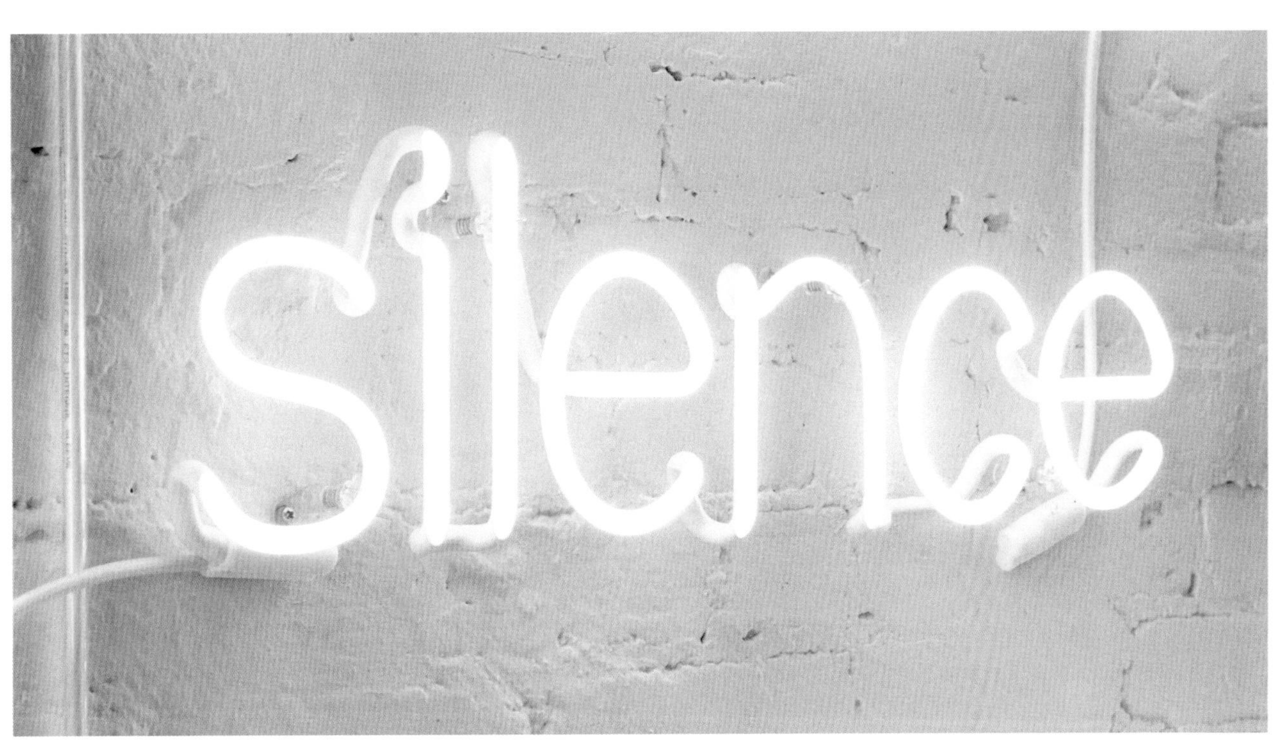
silence

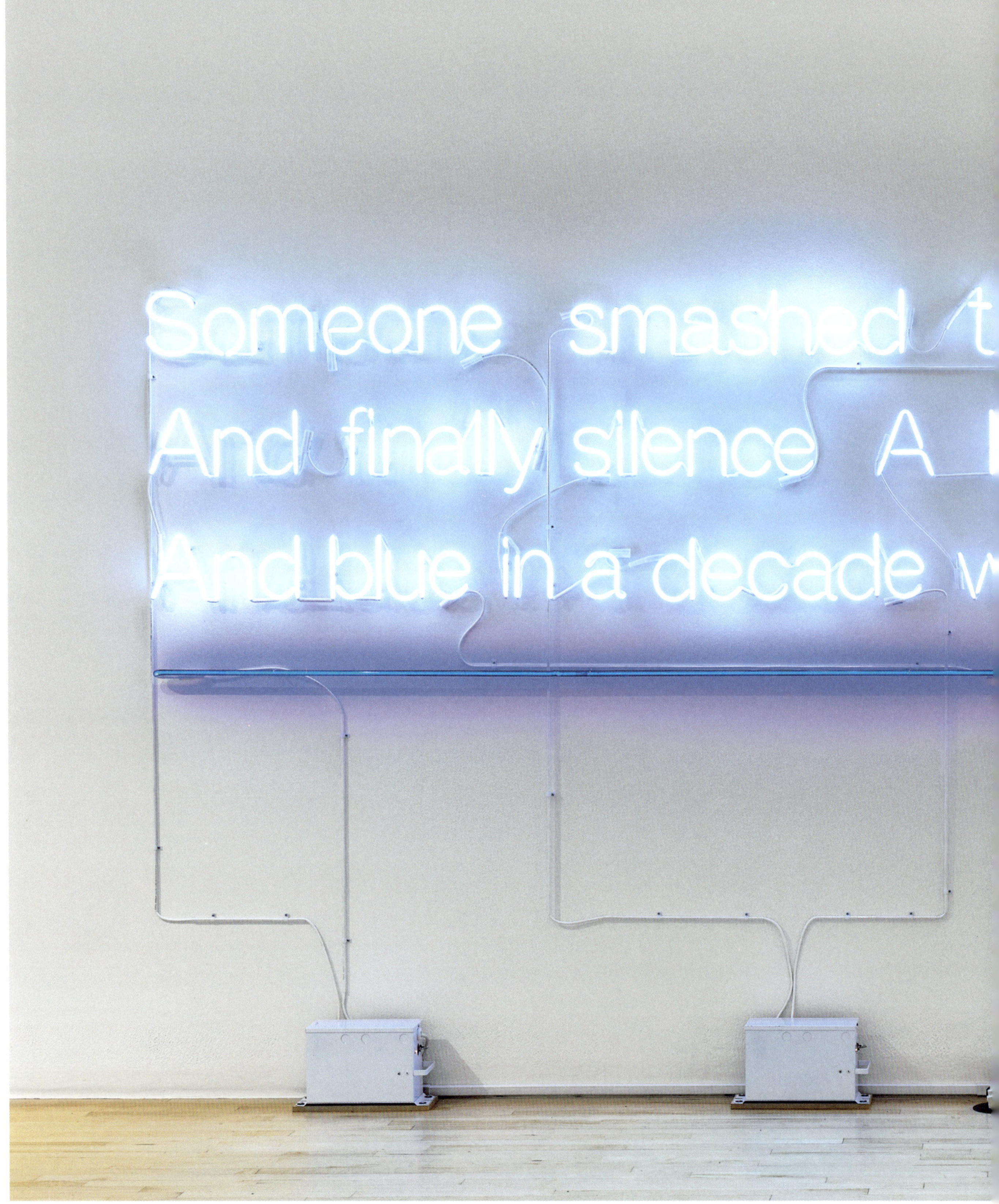

Someone smashed t
And finally silence   A
And blue in a decade w

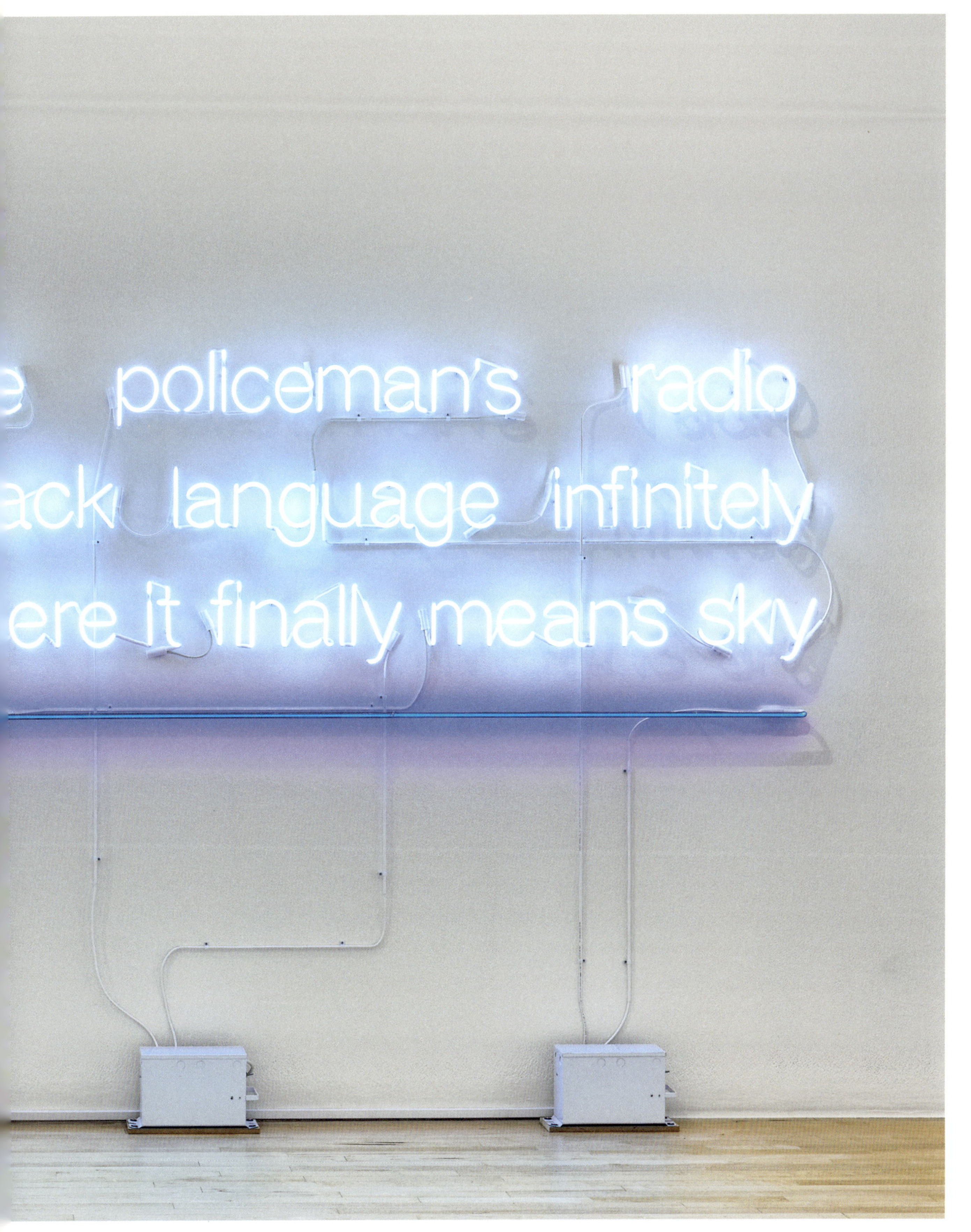

e   policeman's   radio
ack language infinitely
ere it finally means sky

jackie sumell
The Abolitionist's Apothecart, 2021–ongoing
Bicycle and cart with herbs, tinctures, salves, and plants
38¼ × 28¼ × 78 in.

Growing Abolition, 2024
Pressed plants on paper
Thirty-six sheets: 13½ × 9½ in., each

The Abolitionist's Apothecart is one in a series of mobile herbal medicine carts created by artist jackie sumell with assistance from students at the Tulane School of Architecture's Small Center for Collaborative Design. The carts have been pedaled across the city of New Orleans to distribute natural medicines, teas, tinctures, steams, and salves, designed by people who are incarcerated to heal communities they are often accused of harming. The carts and plant medicines are also used to catalyze public conversations at the intersection of health care, social justice, public art, and prison abolition.

The Apothecarts are part of the larger Solitary Gardens project, which sumell established in 2015, utilizing the tools of prison abolition, permaculture, contemplative practice, and transformative justice to facilitate exchanges between persons subjected to solitary confinement and volunteer proxies. In New Orleans' Lower Ninth Ward, where the project is based, and at other sites hosted by art institutions and universities, garden beds planted in the dimensions of prison cells are remotely tended by those inside through written exchanges with volunteers and the use of growing calendars and design templates. The herbs harvested from these gardens are mixed into medicines, distributed by the Apothecarts, and pressed onto paper for the *Growing Abolition* installation. Through the act of

shared gardening, sumell learns from the wisdom of plants and the natural world's embrace of abolition as a strategy for liberation, producing plants that address the health of both our individual and collective bodies. Solitary Gardens act both as a call to end the inhumane conditions of solitary confinement and as an invitation to cultivate the care and compassion necessary to dismantle systems of punishment and control.

jackie sumell, born 1973 in Brooklyn, New York, currently lives and works in New Orleans.

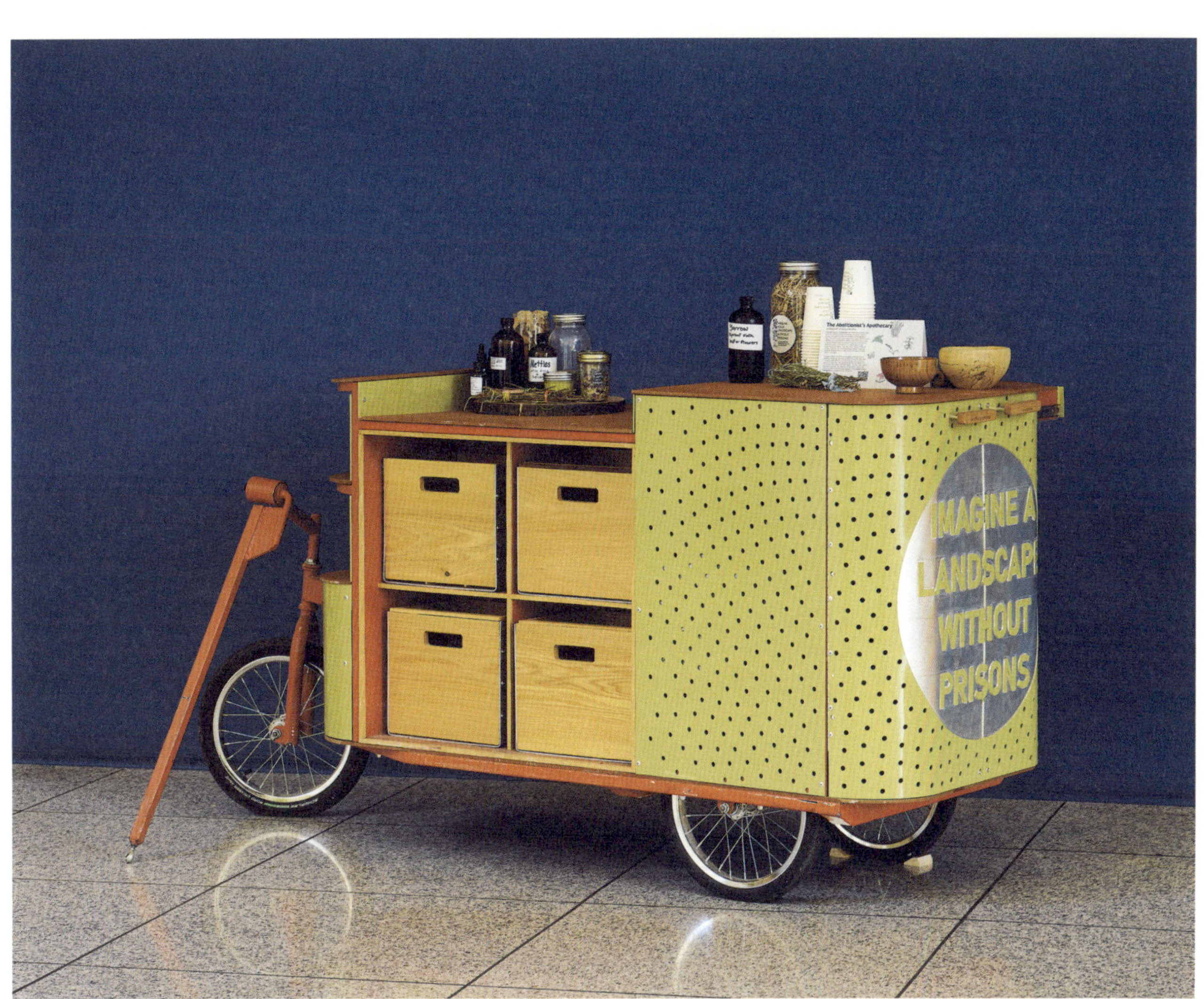

IMAGINE A
LANDSCAPE
WITHOUT
PRISONS

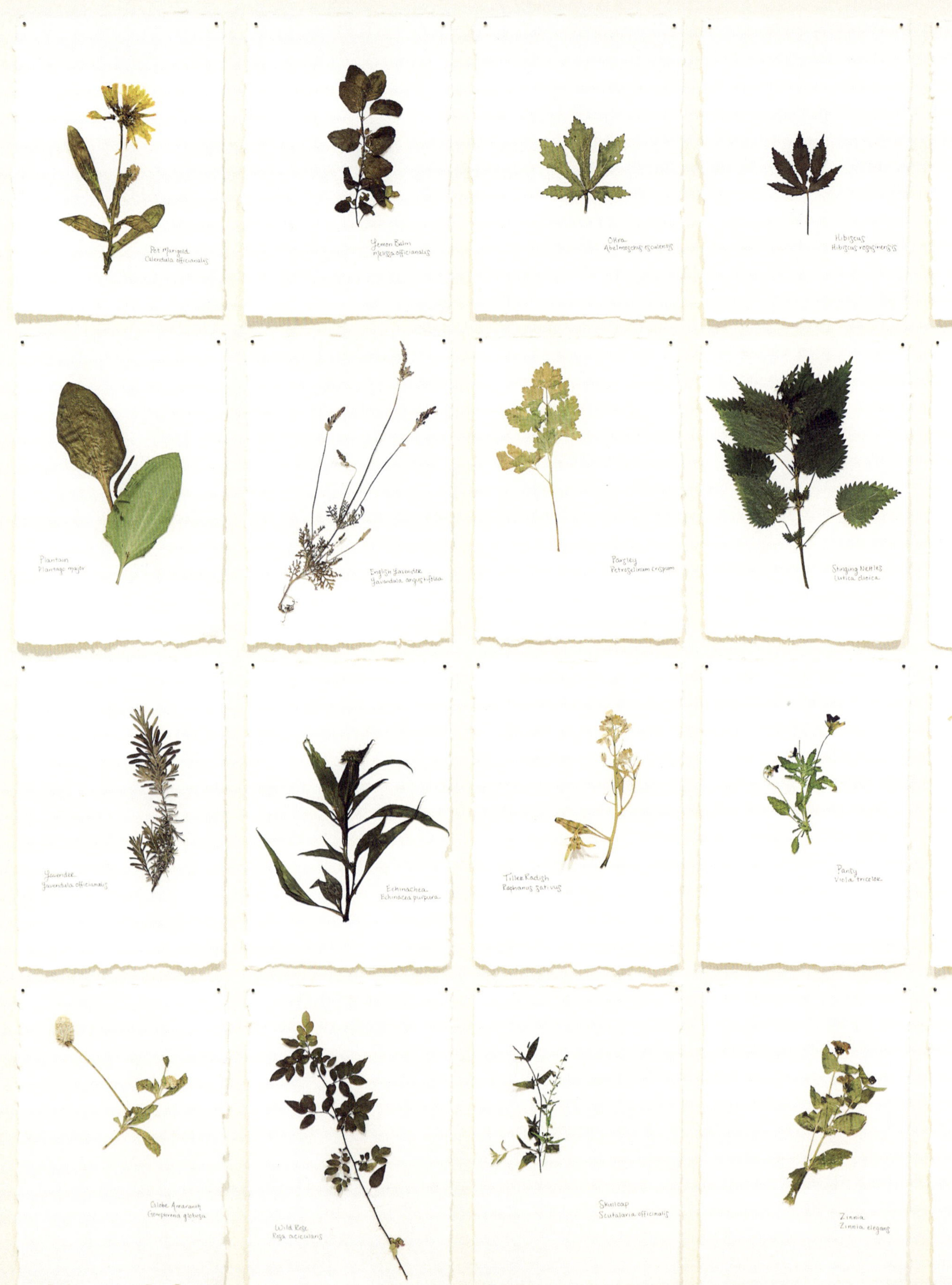

Pot Marigold
Calendula officinalis
Lemon Balm
Melissa officinalis
Okra
Abelmoschus esculentus
Hibiscus
Hibiscus rosa-sinensis
Plantain
Plantago major
English Lavender
Lavandula angustifolia
Parsley
Petroselinum crispum
Stinging Nettles
Urtica dioica
Lavender
Lavandula officinalis
Echinacea
Echinacea purpurea
Tillee Radish
Raphanus sativus
Pansy
Viola tricolor
Beggars Ti
Bidens pil
Globe Amaranth
Gomphrena globosa
Wild Rose
Rosa acicularis
Skullcap
Scutellaria officinalis
Zinnia
Zinnia elegans
Rosemary
Salvia ros

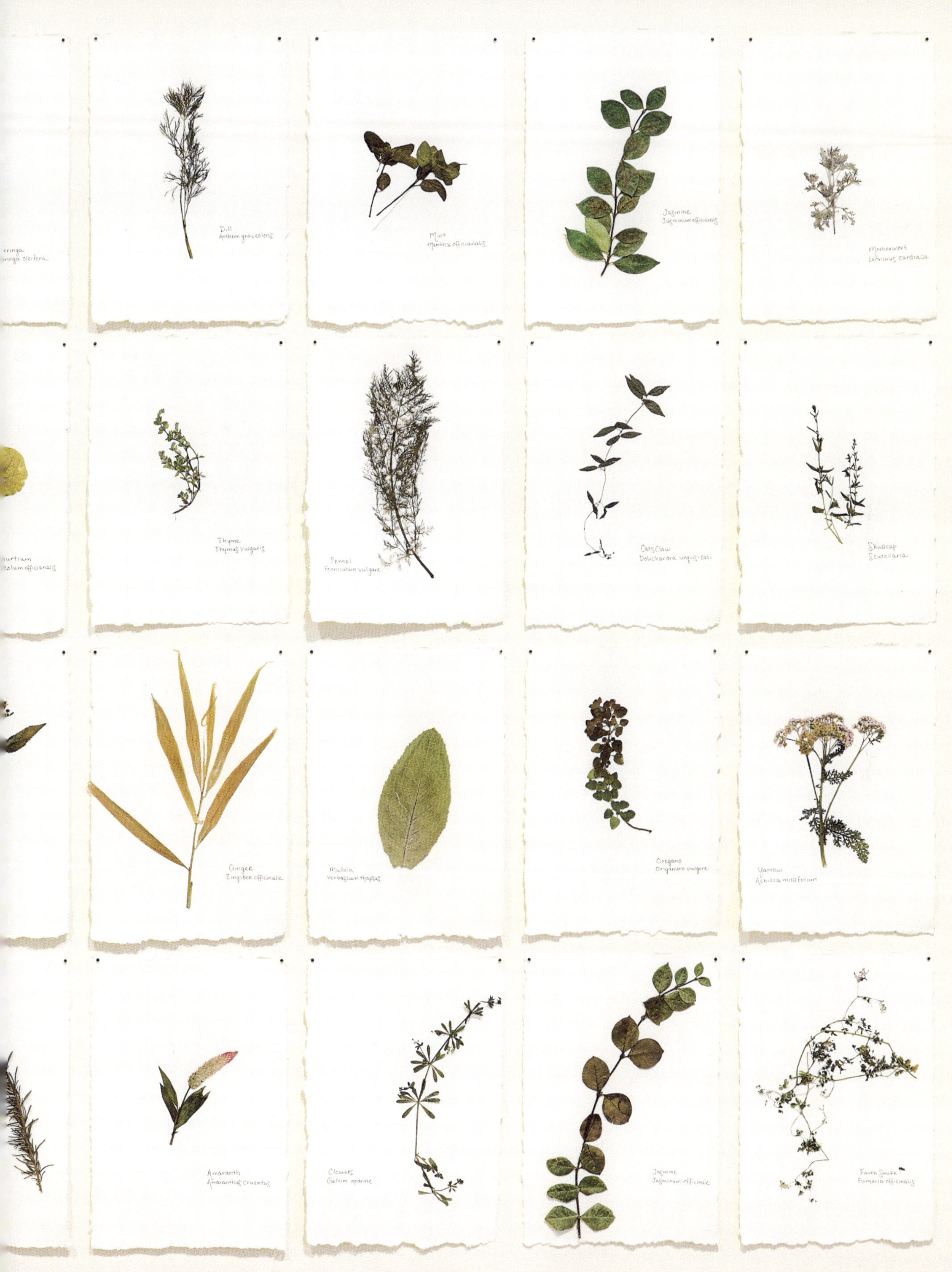
Moringa
Moringa oleifera
Dill
Anthem graveolens
Mint
Mentha officinalis
Jasmine
Jasminum officinalis
Motherwort
Leonurus cardiaca
Nasturtium
...olum officinalis
Thyme
Thymus vulgaris
Fennel
Foeniculum vulgare
Cats Claw
Dolichandra unguis-cati
Skullcap
Scutellaria
Ginger
Zingiber officinale
Mullein
Verbascum thapsus
Oregano
Origanum vulgare
Yarrow
Achillea millefolium
Amaranth
Amaranthus cruentus
Cleavers
Galium aparine
Jasmine
Jasminum officinale
Earth Smoke
Fumaria officinalis

Tea Project (Amber Ginsburg and Aaron Hughes) with Ghaleb Al-Bihani, Khalid Qasim, and Moath al-Alwi
Ode to the Sea, 2023/24
Unstitched US military Desert Camouflage Uniforms (made by people imprisoned in the US working for Federal Prison Industries [UNICOR]), tea stain, gesso, canvas, rope, antique sail pulley, embroidery thread, and oak toggle
180 × 210 × 72 in., overall

Moath al-Alwi
Untitled (GIANT), 2017
Cardboard, rope, fabric, plastic, and acrylic
24 × 36 × 9 in.

Ghaleb Al-Bihani
Untitled, 2015
Pastel on paper
24 × 18 in.

Untitled, 2015
Pastel on paper
17 × 14 in.

Untitled, 2014
Charcoal on paper
9¾ × 11⅞ in.

Tea Project
Tracing the Torture Tree | Chicago to Guantánamo | The ecosystem of police and military violence from John Burge and his co-accused to Richard Zuley, 2022
Screenprint on Rives BFK paper
20 × 30 in.

La Amistad, Like the Waters from 19.9031°N, 75.0967°W to 41°52′04.5″N 87°42′39.4″W on January 11, 2002, 2022
Screenprint on Rives BFK paper
20 × 30 in.

Khalid Qasim
Untitled, 2016
Acrylic on paper
16 × 12 in.

Untitled, 2016
Instant coffee and paint on paper
17 × 14 in.

The Tea Project traces the ongoing relationship between the military and global policing practices, connecting torture in Chicago's jails to the United States Guantánamo Bay detention camp, the Global War on Terror, and the long history of empire. Drawing on the image of the "torture tree," developed by the writer Laurence Ralph as a metaphor for torture reaching across borders,[1] the Tea Project focuses on uncovering the moments of beauty and shared humanity that emerge when technologies of violence are co-opted or converted into systems of community building.

Ode to the Sea is a new installation in this ongoing project that maps a network as wide and complex as the stars. The installation is set against a ship's sail made of stitched-together military uniforms, of the type worn by guards in Guantánamo and made in US prisons by Federal Prison Industries (UNICOR). Against this grim backdrop, artworks made by men currently and formerly held in Guantánamo assert beauty and humanity. *Ode to the Sea* is anchored by a remarkable replica ship made of materials scavenged from Guantánamo by Moath al-Alwi. Using wooden skewers, prayer beads, thread from his shirt and prayer cap, and other bits, he fashioned an emancipatory transport to sail the sea, which, like the sky, sun, and stars, prisoners living in stone boxes are never allowed to see. Nearby is Khalid Qasim's haunting seascape toned with instant coffee.

Brought together in forced proximity by the United States' Global War on Terror, the artists in this installation are a small selection of individuals involved in the larger Tea Project, who forged new connections in Guantánamo through art and creativity. With dozens of nationalities and languages in a single block, Mansoor Adayfi, a Guantánamo survivor who participated in the wider project, notes how, "from shared recitation of the Quran and exchanged greetings, a new language was born at Guantánamo, mixed with words from other languages . . . We were now part of each other's lives, and gradually built what I call 'Guantánamo culture.'"[2] Adayfi recounts being punished and deprived of meals if caught drawing in his first years of incarceration; when the first art classes were introduced in 2010, he was forced to paint while shackled to the ground. The artworks of resistance, witness, and transformation are pivotal to the movement to abolish Guantánamo, and part of the lineage of freedom movements branching ever wider.

Amber Ginsburg and Aaron Hughes work collaboratively as the **Tea Project**. **Aaron Hughes**, born

Tea Project
Speculative Reparations Ordinance for Guantánamo Torture Survivors, 2022
Ink on silk
121 × 39 in.

Speculative Reparations Ordinance for Chicago (Burge) Police Torture Survivors, 2012
In collaboration with Chicago Torture Justice Memorials, Joey Mogul, and Carla Jean Mayer
Ink on cotton
104½ × 39 in.

Selections from the series "Remaking the Exceptional," 2022:
Tracing Torture | Rumsfeld, Miller, Zuley, and Burge
What Kind of Spring Is This? | From POW to Forever Prisoner
A Decade Later | Importing and Exporting the Torture Trades
Circuit of Violence | From Ohio to Afghanistan, Iraq, Guantánamo . . .
People Rise Like the Water
The Making of One Long Night
Extraordinary Rendition of Mohamedou Ould Slahi
One Long Night | Barbed Wire (1874) and Maxim Machine Gun (1884)
Reparations Now! | The Dynamo and The Black Box
Screenprints on Rives BFK paper
20 × 30 in., each

1982, is an artist, curator, organizer, teacher, anti-war activist, and Iraq War veteran living in Chicago. **Amber Ginsburg**, born 1967, is an artist and teacher living and working in Chicago. **Ghaleb Al-Bihani**, born 1979 in Tabuk, Saudi Arabia, was held at Guantánamo for nearly fifteen years before being transferred to Oman in 2017. **Khalid Qasim**, born 1977, is a citizen of Yemen who has been held in extrajudicial detention at Guantánamo since May 2002. **Moath al-Alwi**, born 1977, is a citizen of Yemen who has been held in extrajudicial detention at Guantánamo since January 2002.

1. Laurence Ralph, *The Torture Letters* (Chicago: The University of Chicago Press, 2020).

2. Tea Project, "Remaking the Exceptional," p. 265.

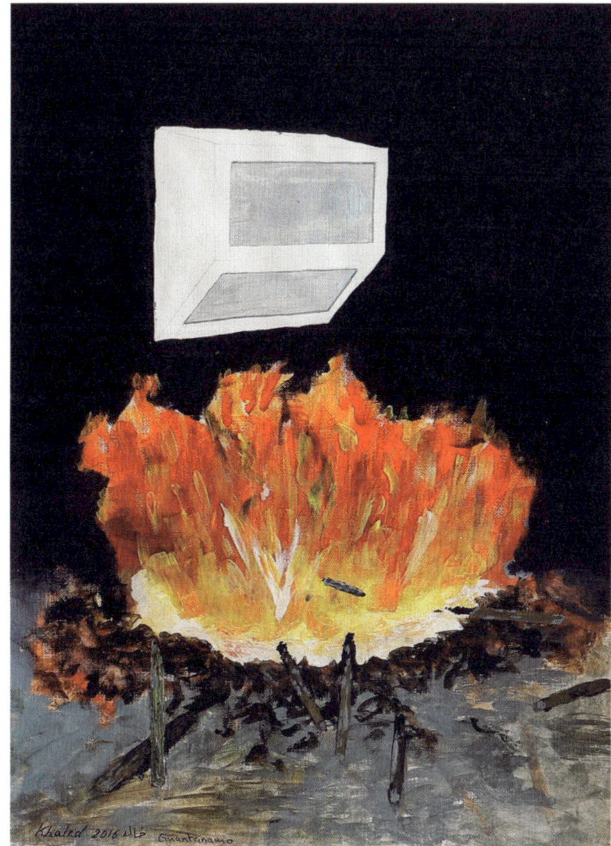

Khalid Qasim, *Untitled*, 2016
Acrylic on paper

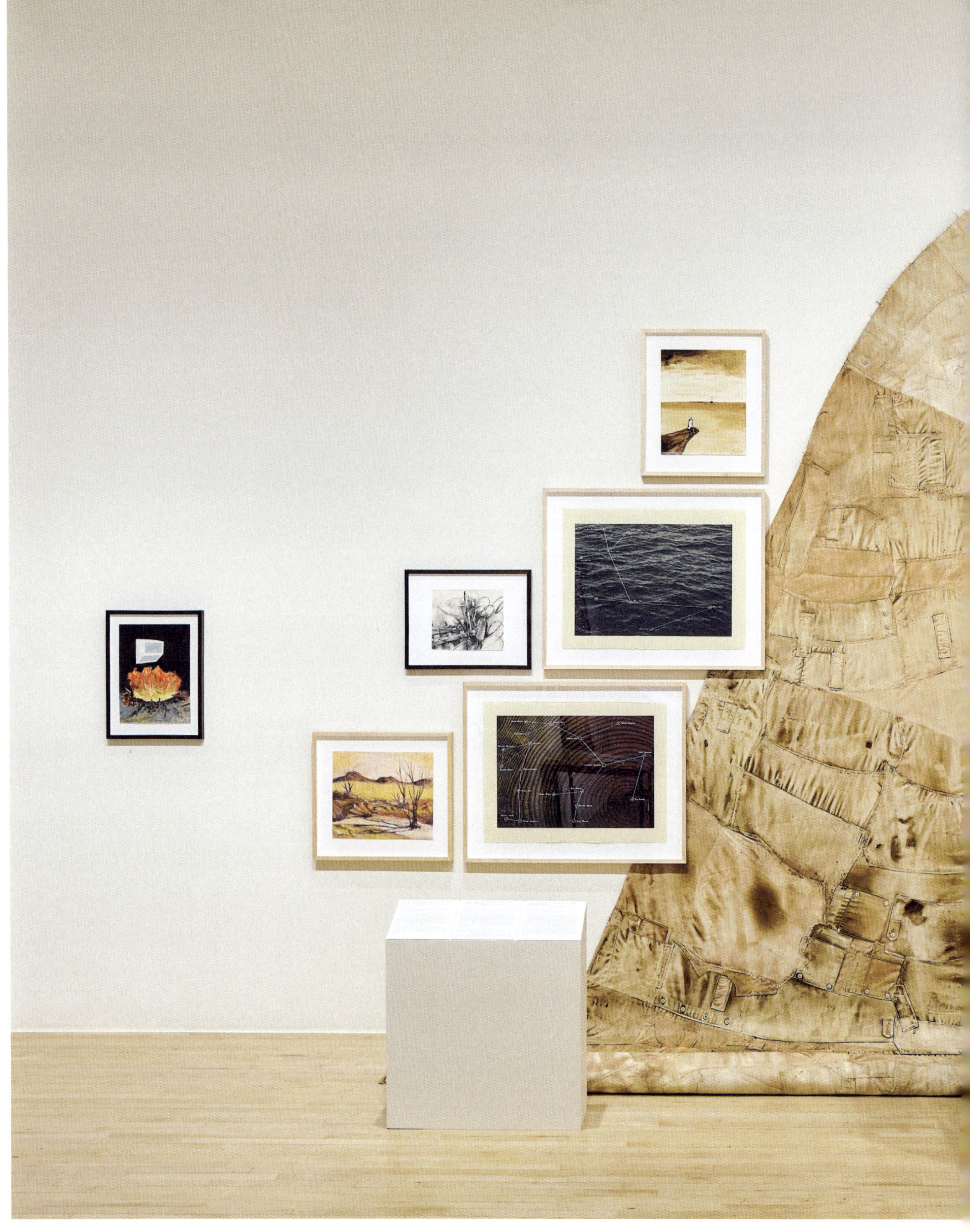

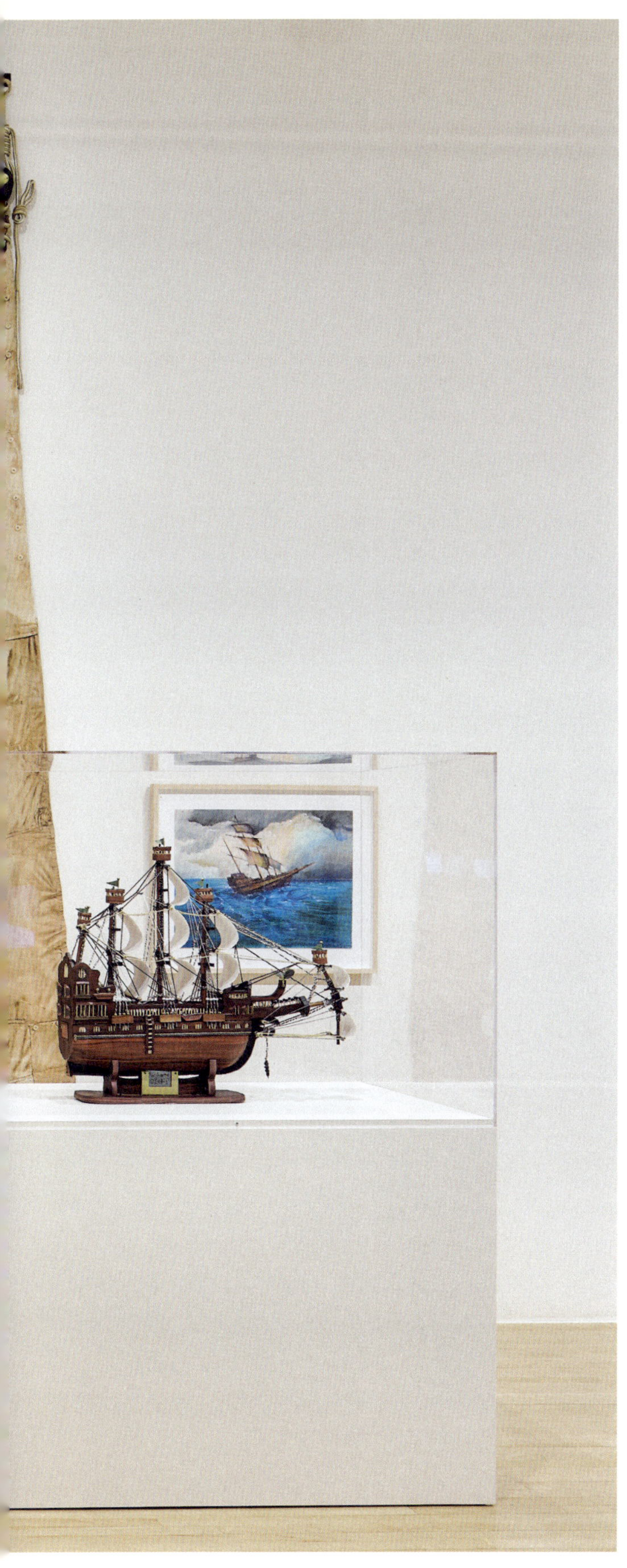

Ode to the Sea, 2023/24

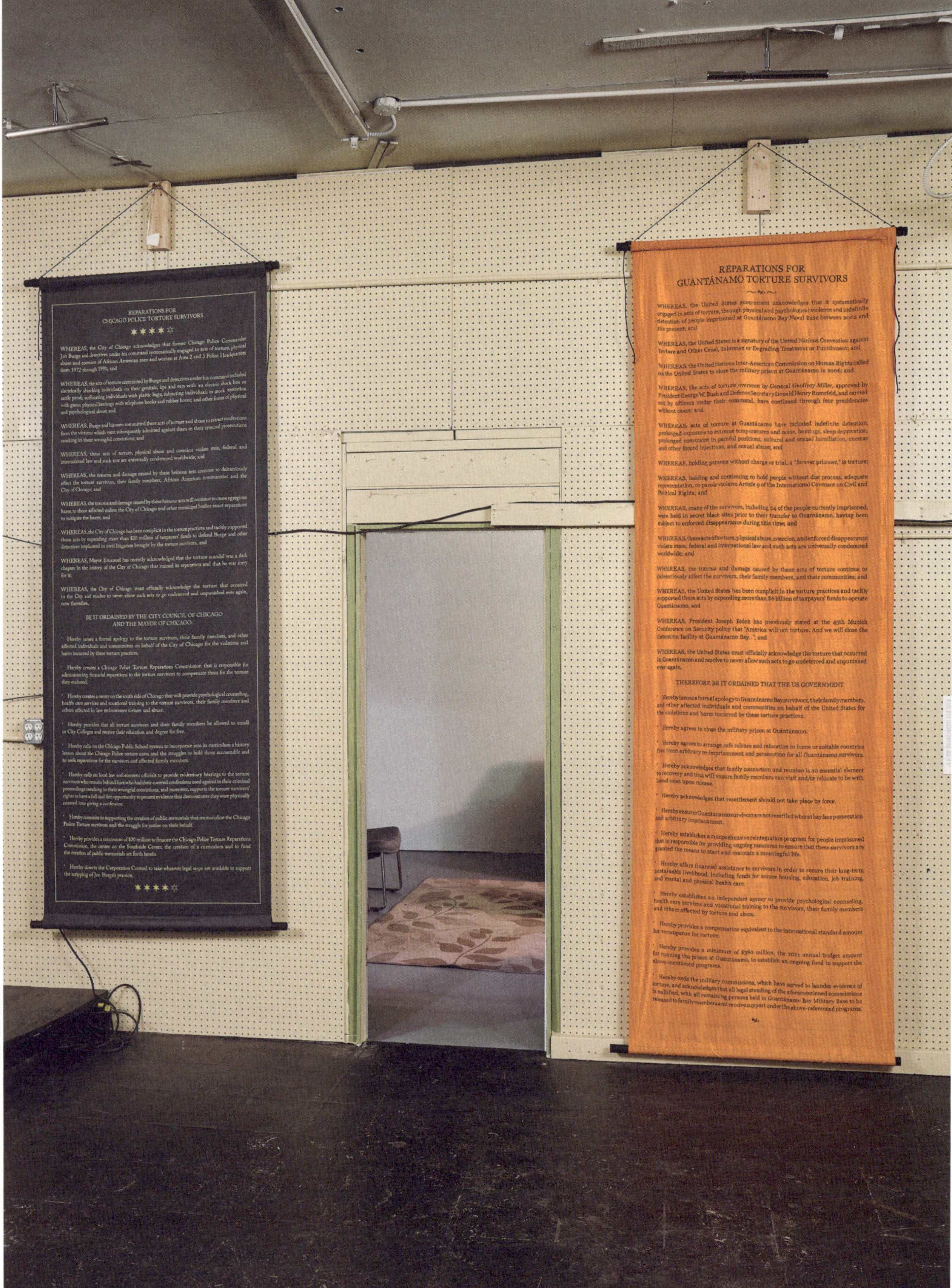

REPARATIONS FOR
CHICAGO POLICE TORTURE SURVIVORS

WHEREAS, the City of Chicago acknowledges that former Chicago Police Commander Jon Burge and detectives under his command systematically engaged in acts of torture, physical abuse and coercion of African American men and women at Area 2 and 3 Police Headquarters from 1972 through 1991; and

WHEREAS, the acts of torture committed by Burge and detectives under his command included electrically shocking individuals on their genitals, lips and ears with an electric shock box or cattle prod; suffocating individuals with plastic bags; subjecting individuals to mock execution with guns; physical beatings with telephone books and rubber hoses; and other forms of physical and psychological abuse; and

WHEREAS, Burge and his men committed these acts of torture and abuse to extract confessions from the victims which were subsequently admitted against them in their criminal prosecutions resulting in their wrongful convictions; and

WHEREAS, these acts of torture, physical abuse and coercion violate state, federal and international law and such acts are universally condemned worldwide; and

WHEREAS, the trauma and damage caused by these heinous acts continue to deleteriously effect the torture survivors, their family members, African American communities and the City of Chicago; and

WHEREAS, the trauma and damage caused by these heinous acts will continue to cause egregious harm to those affected unless the City of Chicago and other municipal bodies enact reparations to mitigate the harm; and

WHEREAS, the City of Chicago has been complicit in the torture practices and tacitly supported those acts by expending more than $20 million of taxpayers' funds to defend Burge and other detectives implicated in civil litigation brought by the torture survivors; and

WHEREAS, Mayor Emanuel has recently acknowledged that the torture scandal was a dark chapter in the history of the City of Chicago that stained its reputation and that he was sorry for it;

WHEREAS, the City of Chicago must officially acknowledge the torture that occurred in the City and resolve to never allow such acts to go undeterred and unpunished ever again, now therefore,

BE IT ORDAINED BY THE CITY COUNCIL OF CHICAGO
AND THE MAYOR OF CHICAGO:

· Hereby issues a formal apology to the torture survivors, their family members, and other affected individuals and communities on behalf of the City of Chicago for the violations and harm incurred by these torture practices.

· Hereby creates a Chicago Police Torture Reparations Commission that is responsible for administering financial reparations to the torture survivors to compensate them for the torture they endured.

· Hereby creates a center on the south side of Chicago that will provide psychological counseling, health care services and vocational training to the torture survivors, their family members and others affected by law enforcement torture and abuse.

· Hereby provides that all torture survivors and their family members be allowed to enroll in City Colleges and receive their education and degree for free.

· Hereby calls on the Chicago Public School system to incorporate into its curriculum a history lesson about the Chicago Police torture cases and the struggles to hold those accountable and to seek reparations for the survivors and affected family members.

· Hereby calls on local law enforcement officials to provide evidentiary hearings to the torture survivors who remain behind bars who had their coerced confessions used against in their criminal proceedings resulting in their wrongful convictions, and moreover, supports the torture survivors' rights to have a full and fair opportunity to present evidence that demonstrates they were physically coerced into giving a confession.

· Hereby commits to supporting the creation of public memorials that memorialize the Chicago Police Torture survivors and the struggle for justice on their behalf.

· Hereby provides a minimum of $20 million to finance the Chicago Police Torture Reparations Commission, the center on the Southside Center, the creation of a curriculum and to fund the creation of public memorials set forth herein.

· Hereby directs the Corporation Counsel to take whatever legal steps are available to support the stripping of Jon Burge's pension.

REPARATIONS FOR
GUANTÁNAMO TORTURE SURVIVORS

WHEREAS, the United States government acknowledges that it systematically engaged in acts of torture, through physical and psychological violence and indefinite detention of people imprisoned at Guantánamo Bay Naval Base between 2002 and the present; and

WHEREAS, the United States is a signatory of the United Nations Convention against Torture and Other Cruel, Inhuman or Degrading Treatment or Punishment; and

WHEREAS, the United Nations Inter-American Commission on Human Rights called on the United States to close the military prison at Guantánamo in 2006; and

WHEREAS, the acts of torture overseen by General Geoffrey Miller, approved by President George W. Bush and Defense Secretary Donald Henry Rumsfeld, and carried out by officers under their command, have continued through four presidencies without cease; and

WHEREAS, acts of torture at Guantánamo have included indefinite detention, prolonged exposure to extreme temperatures and noise, beatings, sleep deprivation, prolonged constraint in painful positions, cultural and sexual humiliation, enemas and other forced injections, and sexual abuse; and

WHEREAS, holding persons without charge or trial, a "forever prisoner," is torture;

WHEREAS, holding and continuing to hold people without due process, adequate representation, or parole violates Article 9 of the International Covenant on Civil and Political Rights; and

WHEREAS, many of the survivors, including 24 of the people currently imprisoned, were held in secret black sites prior to their transfer to Guantánamo, having been subject to enforced disappearance during this time; and

WHEREAS, these acts of torture, physical abuse, coercion, and enforced disappearance violate state, federal and international law and such acts are universally condemned worldwide; and

WHEREAS, the trauma and damage caused by these acts of torture continue to deleteriously affect the survivors, their family members, and their communities; and

WHEREAS, the United States has been complicit in the torture practices and tacitly supported those acts by expending more than $6 billion of taxpayers' funds to operate Guantánamo, and

WHEREAS, President Joseph Biden has previously stated at the 45th Munich Conference on Security policy that "America will not torture. And we will close the detention facility at Guantánamo Bay..."; and

WHEREAS, the United States must officially acknowledge the torture that occurred in Guantánamo and resolve to never allow such acts to go undeterred and unpunished ever again,

THEREFORE BE IT ORDAINED THAT THE US GOVERNMENT

· Hereby issues a formal apology to Guantánamo Bay survivors, their family members, and other affected individuals and communities on behalf of the United States for the violations and harm incurred by these torture practices.

· Hereby agrees to close the military prison at Guantánamo.

· Hereby agrees to arrange safe release and relocation to home or suitable countries free from arbitrary re-imprisonment and persecution for all Guantánamo survivors.

· Hereby acknowledges that family connection and reunion is an essential element to recovery and thus will ensure family members can visit and/or relocate to be with loved ones upon release.

· Hereby acknowledges that resettlement should not take place by force.

· Hereby ensures Guantánamo survivors are not resettled where they face persecution and arbitrary imprisonment.

· Hereby establishes a comprehensive reintegration program for people imprisoned that is responsible for providing ongoing measures to ensure that these survivors are granted the means to start and maintain a meaningful life.

· Hereby offers financial assistance to survivors in order to secure their long-term sustainable livelihood, including funds for secure housing, education, job training, and mental and physical health care.

· Hereby establishes an independent agency to provide psychological counseling, health care services and vocational training to the survivors, their family members and others affected by torture and abuse.

· Hereby provides a compensation equivalent to the international standard amount for recompense for torture.

· Hereby provides a minimum of $380 million, the 2021 annual budget amount for running the prison at Guantánamo, to establish an ongoing fund to support the above-mentioned programs.

· Hereby ends the military commissions, which have served to launder evidence of torture, and acknowledges that all legal standing of the aforementioned commissions is nullified, with all remaining persons held in Guantánamo Bay Military Base to be released to family members and receive support under the above-referenced programs.

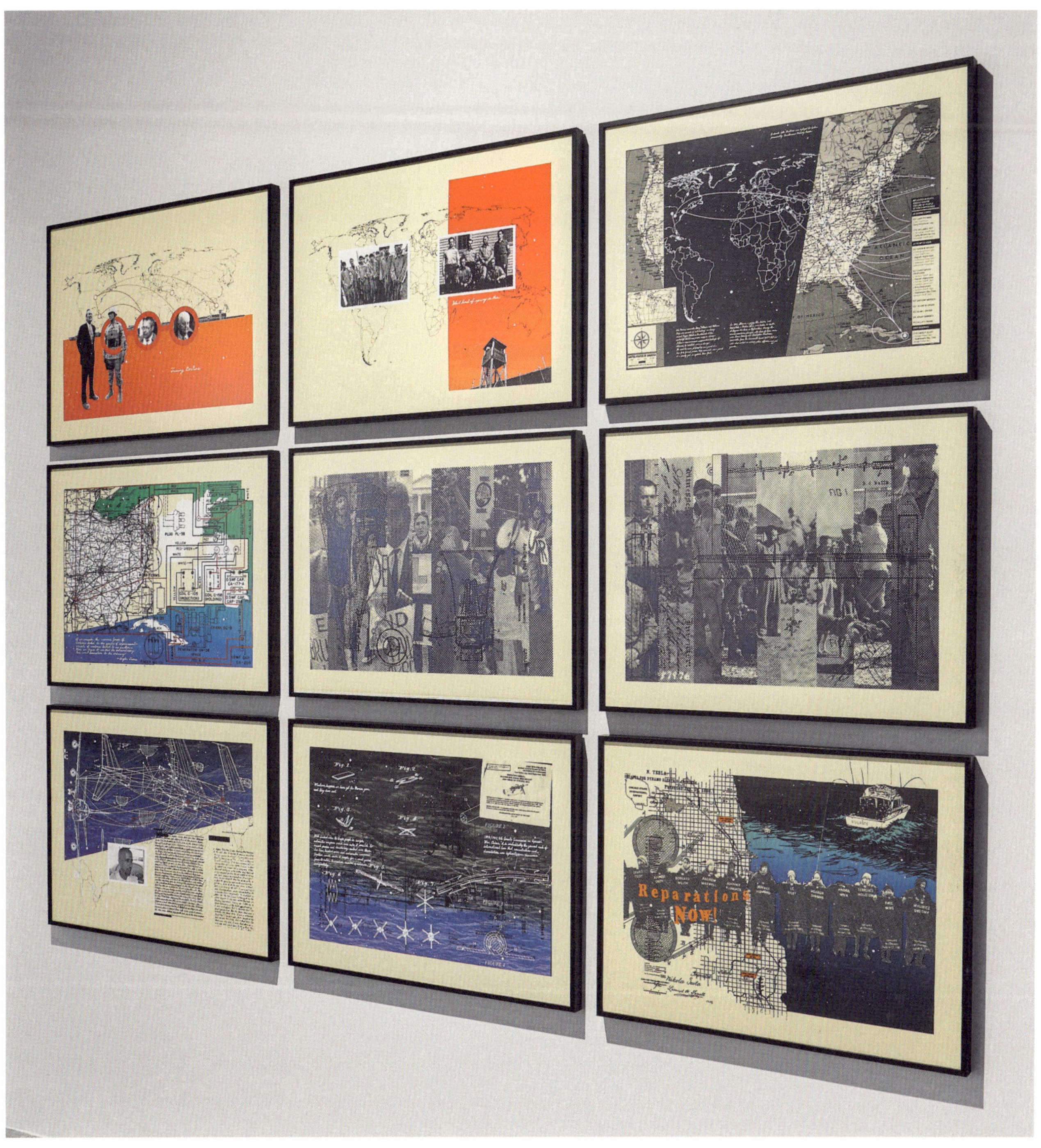

Selections from the series "Remaking the Exceptional," 2022

Speculative Reparations Ordinance for Guantánamo Torture Survivors, 2022

Speculative Reparations Ordinance for Chicago (Burge) Police Torture Survivors, 2012

Timesfive (Moira Murdock and jackie sumell)
Color the Skies Fallen Prisons, 2024
Lens, fenestration, and light box
1 × 1 in.

What if iron could learn? What would it choose to become instead of the material used to build our prisons, jails, and detention centers?

For *Color the Skies Fallen Prisons*, the artist collective Timesfive worked with iron to unlearn the violences to which the material has been made complicit. Iron, the most abundant element on earth, has the power to change; it can become steel, bronze, titanium, or even a shade of blue. Prussian blue, the first modern synthetic pigment, was created in 1704, when a chemist accidentally mixed animal blood, potash, and iron sulfate and formed the distinctive hue. It has since adorned paintings and been used to create blueprints, as well as for its powerful medicinal properties.

Color the Skies Fallen Prisons realizes the potential for prison bars to become pigment. A fenestration in the gallery wall is both a peephole and a portal through which to view the night sky above Santa Cruz on the day the last prison falls. The stars in this sky shine against a background painted blue. Collaborating with Dr. Elliot S. Williams, a chemist based in New Orleans, the artists identified a synthetic process to convert prison steel into the vibrant Prussian blue dye ($Fe_7[CN]_{18}$). The artists present this route as an alternative to the approximate calculated amount of time required to corrode a single steel prison bar under natural conditions, which ultimately returns the metal alloy to its original ferrous oxide (FeO) composition.

Timesfive is a collaboration between Moira Murdock and jackie sumell. **Moira Murdock** lives and works in the San Francisco Bay Area. **jackie sumell** lives and works in New Orleans.

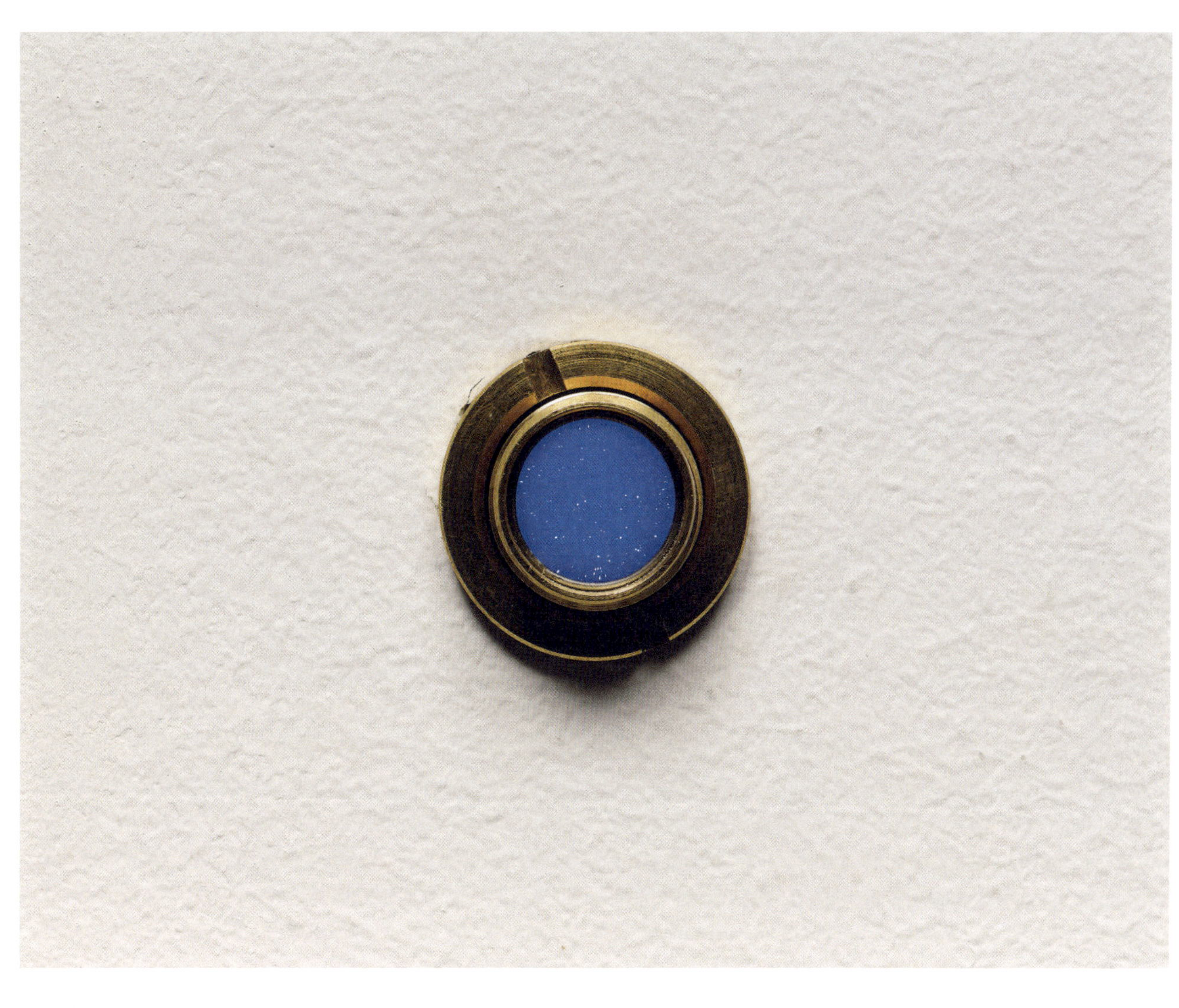

Hajra Waheed
Walls, Ladders and Roads, 2019
Glazed porcelain
Nine sculptures: approx. 8½ × 5½ × 5½ in., each

The landscape presented in *Walls, Ladders and Roads* comprises a litany of border walls, prison fences, and security gates in miniature—the myriad ways in which security and surveillance structure human life around the world. In each vignette, these barriers are transgressed by precariously placed ladders and poles, the aftermath of escape. Crafted in hand-formed porcelain, these means of escape might be delicate and seemingly insubstantial on their own, but together they become a poetic representation of the vastness of radical resistance across time and geography, serving as models for future action. Displaying a limited formal vocabulary, almost abstract in its simplicity, *Walls, Ladders and Roads* proposes a long view of resistance, molding possible exits from seemingly immovable extractive power structures.

Hajra Waheed spent the first twenty-two years of her life living in the gated headquarters of Saudi Aramco, the largest transnational oil company in the world. The artist refers to the headquarters as a "central extractive point for [the] US military industrial empire,"[1] heavily monitored by US and Saudi air bases and the CIA through aerial reconnaissance. Her paintings, sculptures, and installations reflect this reality, revealing operations of covert power from intimate perspectives, as well as moments of oppression and resistance that are enacted in response.

Hajra Waheed, born 1980 in Calgary, Canada, lives and works in Montreal.

1. Hajra Waheed, "Crisis and Creativity: Artists Speak Series," Isas Departmental, February 8, 2022, YouTube video, 1:21:19 hours, https://www.youtube.com /watch?v=8kG__oLdzPs&ab _channel=IsasDepartmental.

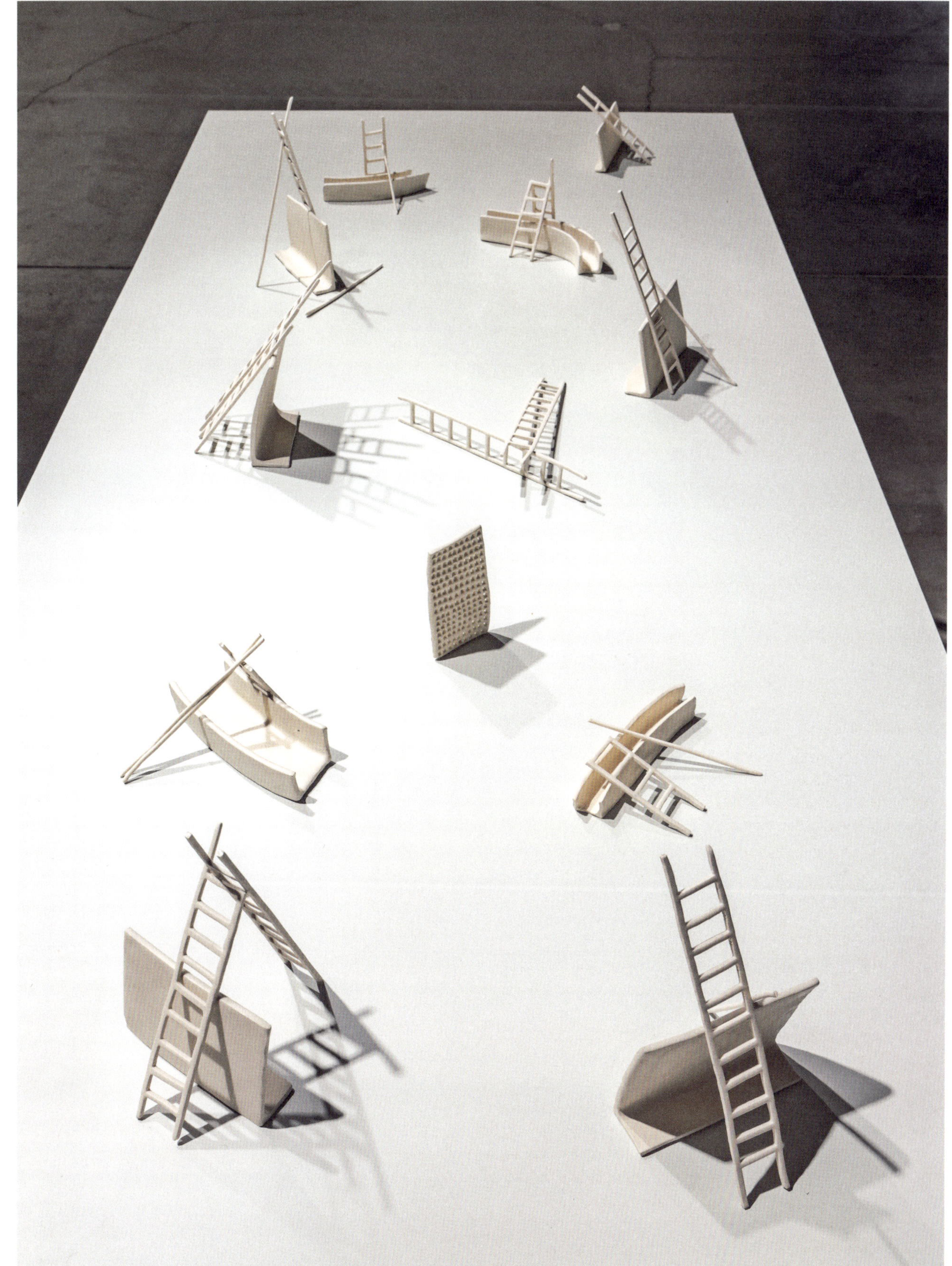

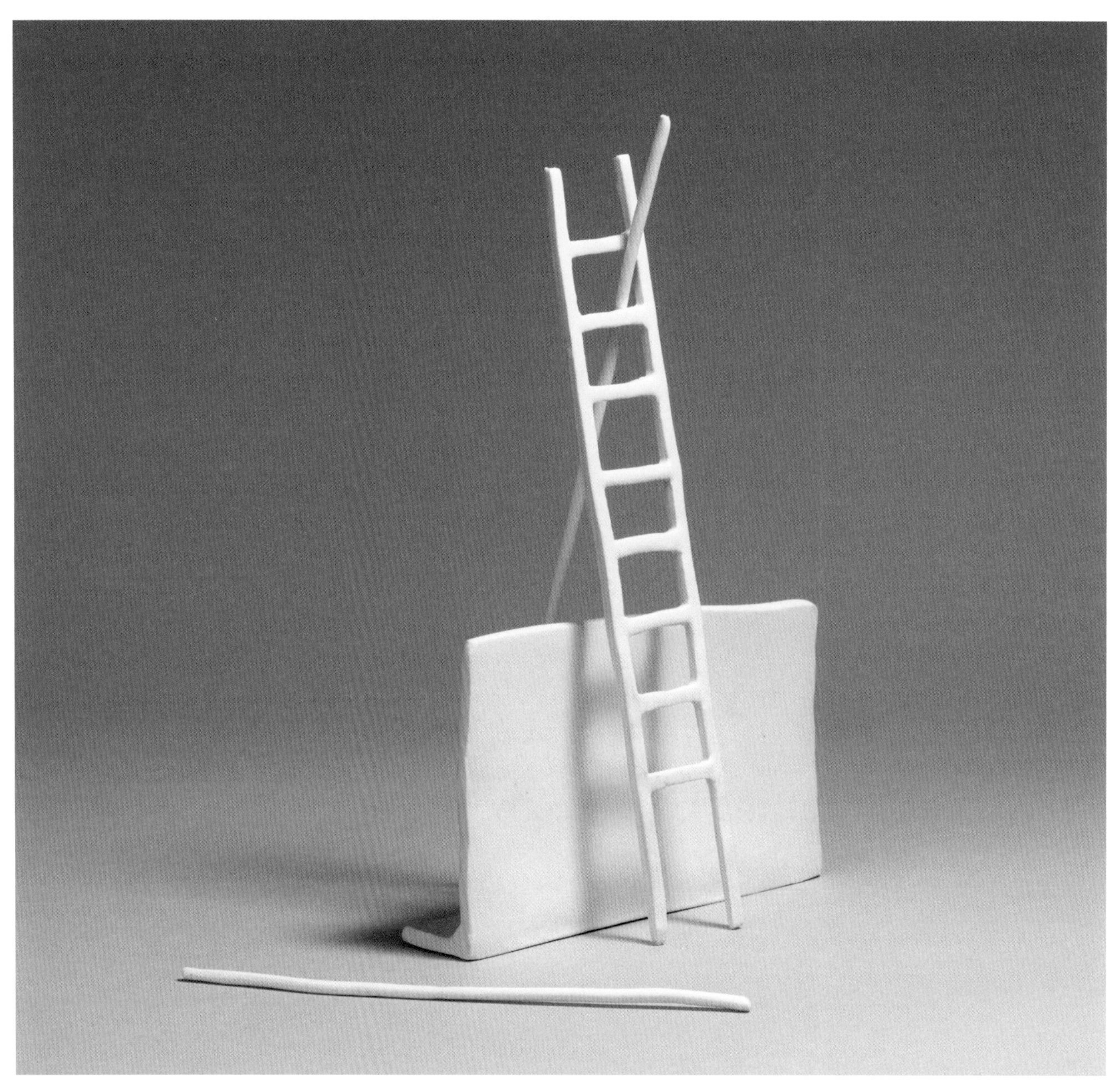

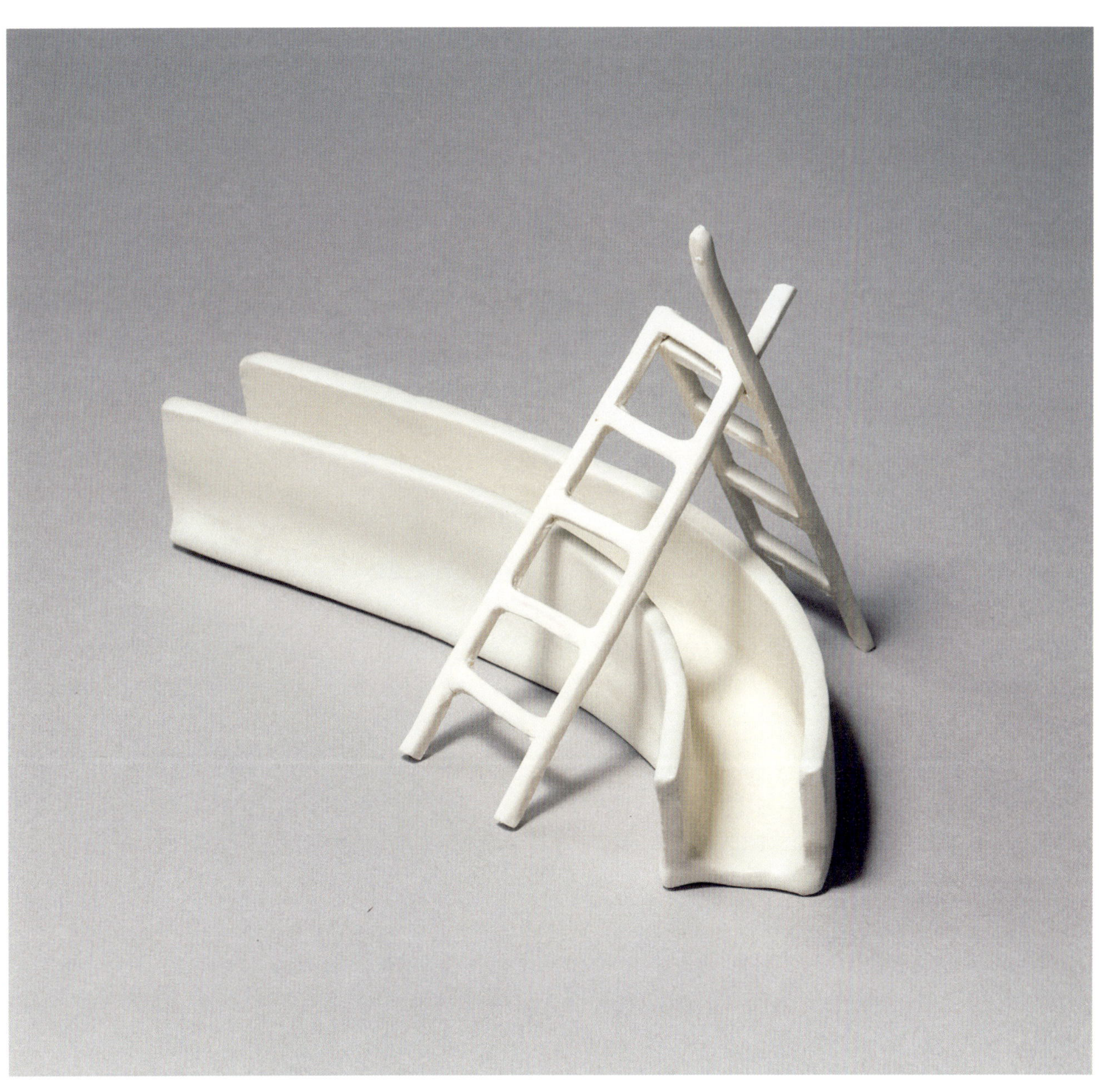

Rachel Wallis with Mariame Kaba
Anguilla Quilt, 2021

Plant-dyed, linoleum block printed, and digitally printed cotton; hemp
and linen fabric; embroidery and hand-quilting thread; glass beads; block
printing ink; and cotton batting

90 × 60 in.

Sewn across the front of the *Anguilla Quilt* is what the artists call "a roadmap of oppression" in the United States.[1] The 1947 murder of a group of prisoners by the warden and guards at a labor camp outside of Anguilla, Georgia, lies at the center of the quilt, depicted through an image of a chain gang around which the names of the men killed are delicately sewn. The quilt is made of a rough-spun hemp and cotton blend, materializing the long history of forced labor and racist exploitation, from slavery to labor camps, that has shaped the state. This history is further charted in the four corners of the quilt: A map of the enslaved population in Georgia on the eve of the Civil War. A map of jails and prisons across Georgia today. A map of lynchings, by county, between 1877 and 1950 (on which the Anguilla prison massacre is not counted). And a map of police killings between 2010 and 2020.

The violent history traced in this road map, however, is not unchangeable, inevitable, or absolute. The back of the quilt shows a map of resistance. Printed on fabric and sewn together are dozens of documents revealing the organizing by the NAACP that brought the murders to light, as well as the years of struggle for justice in Georgia and across the country that the killings inspired. In the center is a map of actions taken against racial injustices and police brutality across Georgia in 2020. Together, these ephemera trace a history of collective struggles and dreams of freedom that can provide the building blocks of a future world.

Rachel Wallis is a community-taught crafter, artist, and activist living in Chicago. **Mariame Kaba** is an organizer, educator, archivist, and curator living in New York.

1. "Process," The Anguilla Prison Massacre Quilt, June 1, 2021, https://www.anguillamassacre.com /process.

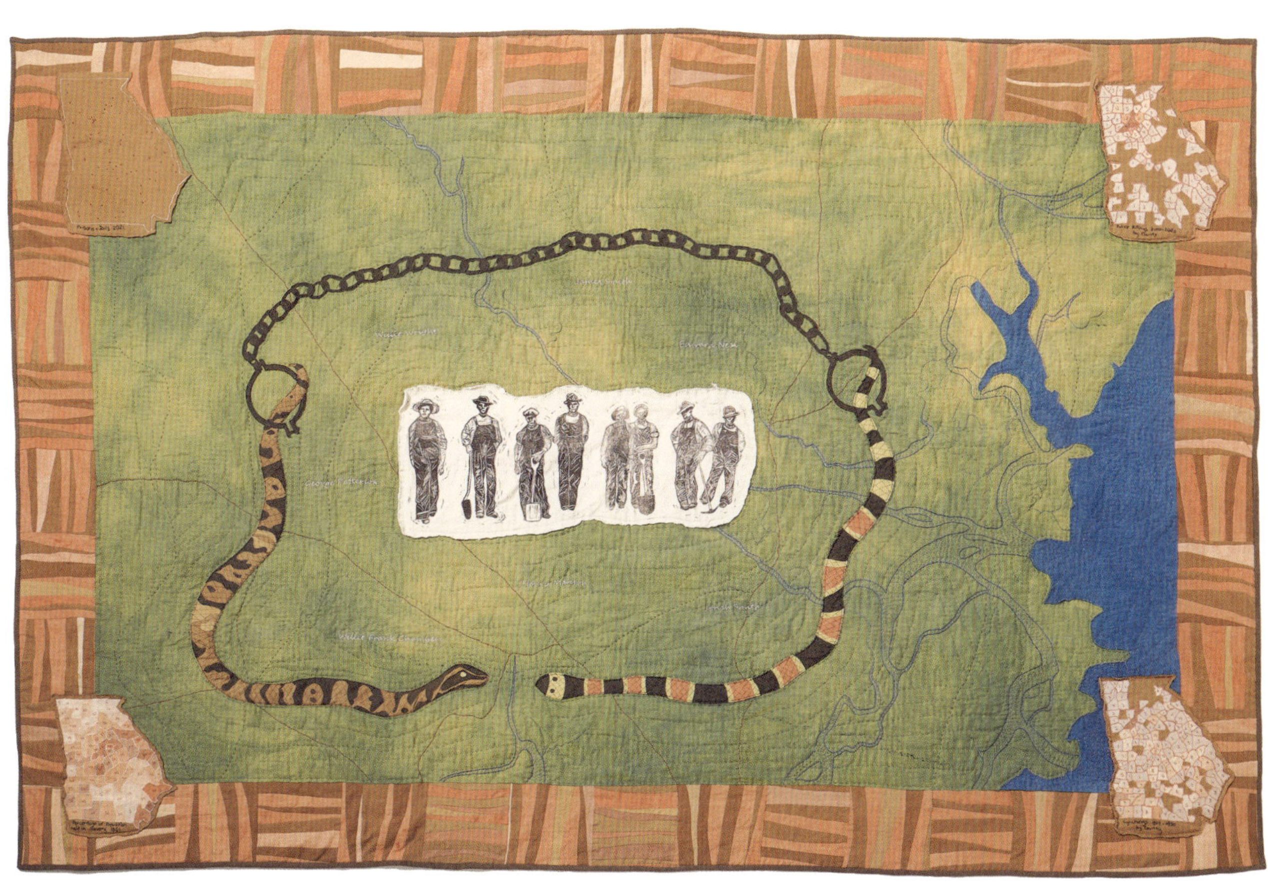

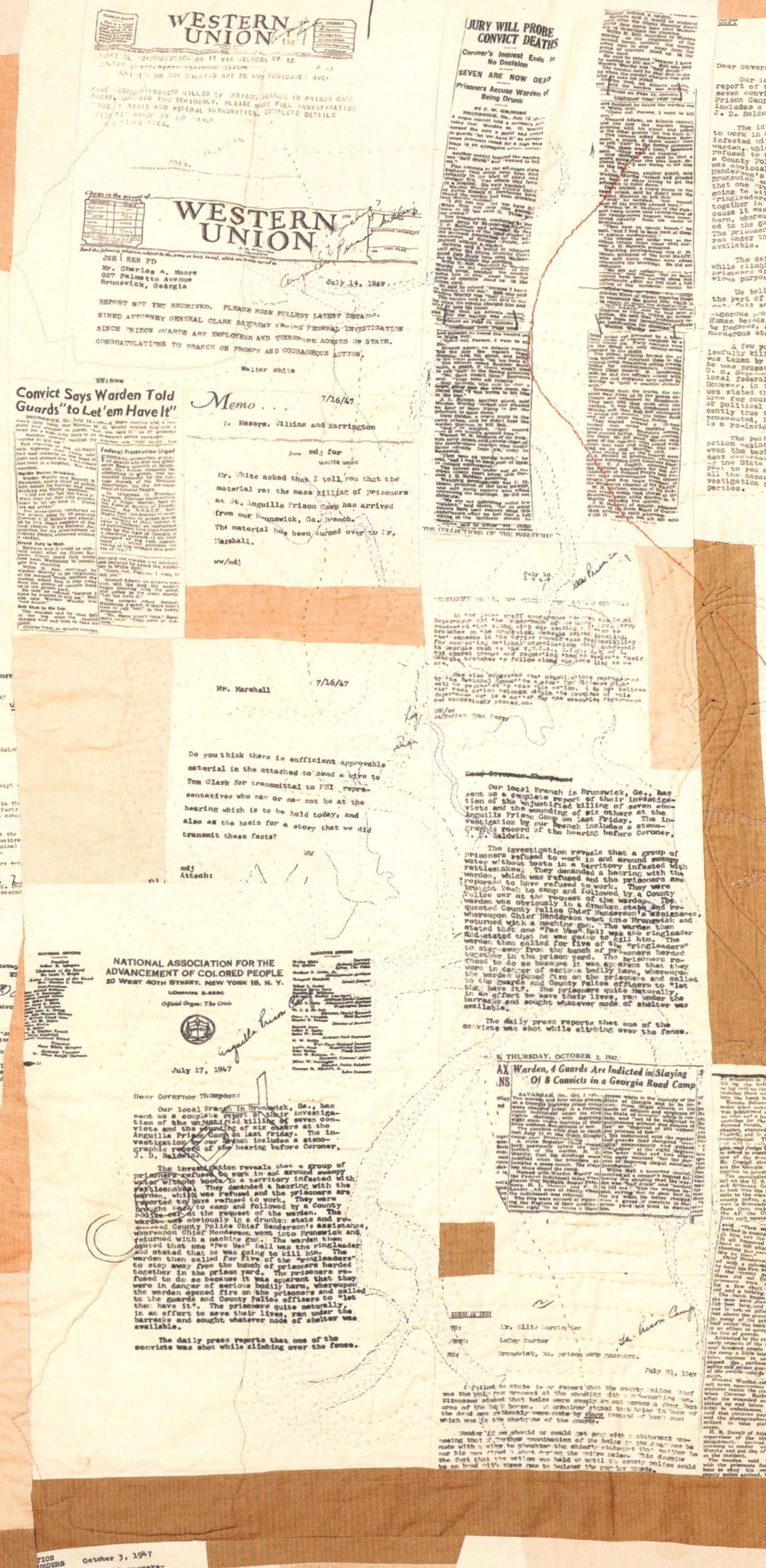

WESTERN UNION

FIVE NEGRO PRISONERS KILLED BY PRISON GUARDS IN PRISON CAMP TODAY. WOUNDED TWO SERIOUSLY. PLEASE HAVE FULL INVESTIGATION MADE BY STATE AND FEDERAL AUTHORITIES. COMPLETE DETAILS FOLLOW ARMED BY AIR MAIL.
A. MOORE PRES.

WESTERN UNION

JNE SER PD
Mr. Charles A. Moore
927 Palmetto Avenue
Brunswick, Georgia
July 14, 1947

REPORT NOT YET RECEIVED. PLEASE RUSH FULLEST LATEST DETAILS. WIRED ATTORNEY GENERAL CLARK SATURDAY URGING FEDERAL INVESTIGATION SINCE PRISON GUARDS ARE EMPLOYEES AND THEREFORE AGENTS OF STATE. CONGRATULATIONS TO BRANCH ON PROMPT AND COURAGEOUS ACTION.
Walter White

JURY WILL PROBE CONVICT DEATHS
Coroner's Inquest Ends; No Decision
SEVEN ARE NOW DEAD
Prisoners Accuse Warden of Being Drunk

Convict Says Warden Told Guards "to Let 'em Have It"
Federal Prosecution Urged

Memo . . .   7/16/47
To Messrs. Wilkins and Harrington
from mdj for WALTER WHITE
Mr. White asked that I tell you that the material re the mass killing of prisoners at St. Anguilla Prison Camp has arrived from our Brunswick, Ga. branch. The material has been turned over to Mr. Marshall.
wv/mdj

Mr. Marshall   7/16/47
Do you think there is sufficient approvable material in the attached to send a wire to Tom Clark for transmittal to FBI representatives who may or may not be at the hearing which is to be held today, and also as the basis for a story that we did transmit these facts?
mdj
Attach:

NATIONAL ASSOCIATION FOR THE ADVANCEMENT OF COLORED PEOPLE
20 WEST 40TH STREET, NEW YORK 18, N. Y.
LOngacre 3-8890
Official Organ: The Crisis
July 17, 1947

Dear Governor Thompson:
Our local Branch in Brunswick, Ga., has sent us a complete report of their investigation of the unjustified killing of seven convicts and the wounding of six others at the Anguilla Prison Camp on last Friday. The investigation by our Branch includes a stenographic record of the hearing before Coroner, J. D. Baldwin.

The investigation reveals that a group of prisoners refused to work in and around swampy water without boots in a territory infested with rattlesnakes. They demanded a hearing with the warden, which was refused and the prisoners are reported to have refused to work. They were brought back to camp and followed by a County Police car at the request of the warden. The warden was obviously in a drunken state and requested County Police Chief Henderson's assistance, whereupon Chief Henderson went into Brunswick and returned with a machine gun. The warden then stated that one "Pee Wee" Bell was the ringleader and stated that he was going to kill him. The warden then called for five of the "ringleaders" to step away from the bunch of prisoners herded together in the prison yard. The prisoners refused to do so because it was apparent that they were in danger of serious bodily harm, whereupon the warden opened fire on the prisoners and called to the guards and County Police officers to "let them have it." The prisoners quite naturally, in an effort to save their lives, ran under the barracks and sought whatever mode of shelter was available.

The daily press reports that one of the convicts was shot while climbing over the fence.
The daily press reports that one of the convicts was shot while climbing over the fence.

COPY
July 17, 1947

Dear Governor Thompson:
Our local Branch in Brunswick, Ga., has sent us a complete report of their investigation of the unjustified killing of seven convicts and the wounding of six others at the Anguilla Prison Camp on last Friday. The investigation by our Branch includes a stenographic record of the hearing before Coroner, J. D. Baldwin.

The investigation reveals that a group of prisoners refused to work in and around swampy water without boots in a territory infested with rattlesnakes. They demanded a hearing with the warden, which was refused and the prisoners are reported to have refused to work. They were brought back to camp and followed by a County Police car at the request of the warden. The warden was obviously in a drunken state and requested County Police Chief Henderson's assistance, whereupon Chief Henderson went into Brunswick and returned with a machine gun. The warden then stated that one "Pee Wee" Bell was the ringleader and stated that he was going to kill him. The warden then called for five of the "ringleaders" to step away from the bunch of prisoners herded together in the prison yard. The prisoners refused to do so because it was apparent that they were in danger of serious bodily harm, whereupon the warden opened fire on the prisoners and called to the guards and County Police officers to "let them have it." The prisoners quite naturally, in an effort to save their lives, ran under the barracks and sought whatever mode of shelter was available.

The daily press reports that one of the convicts was shot while climbing over the fence. It should be pointed out that the prisoners did not run until they were running for the obvious purpose of trying to save their lives.

We believe that this brazen disregard for human rights on the part of officers of the State of Georgia demands an independent, full and complete investigation by your office, followed by vigorous prosecution of the parties guilty of this offense. Human beings, even though they be convicts, and even though they be Negroes, are entitled to full and complete protection from murderous state officials.

A few years ago, Claude Screws, of Baker County, Ga., unlawfully killed a Negro prisoner, Robert Hall. After no action was taken by the State of Georgia to prosecute Sheriff Screws, he was prosecuted in the federal courts and the case reached the U. S. Supreme Court. The case was reversed and returned to the local federal court where Sheriff Screws was subsequently acquitted. However, in the dissenting opinion in the U. S. Supreme Court, it was stated that: "We are told local authorities cannot be relied upon for courageous and prompt action, that often they have personal or political reasons for refusing to prosecute. If it be significantly true that crimes against local law cannot be locally prosecuted, it is an ominous sign indeed. In any event, the outcome is a re-invigoration of state responsibility."

The policy of the State of Georgia not to take affirmative action against Sheriff Claude Screws and the daily disregard for even the basic rights of Negroes is high-lighted by the most recent occurrence at the Anguilla Prison Camp. The responsibility of the State of Georgia in this case is clear. We therefore appeal to you as the Chief Executive of the State of Georgia to take all the necessary steps to bring about a full and complete investigation from your office and the prosecution of the guilty parties.

Very truly yours,
Walter White
Secretary

SIX NEGRO CONVICTS KILLED AT LOCAL CAMP
Seven Others Injured By Guards Who Open Fire When Prisoners Attempt To Make Escape
List of Dead

Warden, 4 Guards Are Indicted in Slaying of 8 Convicts in a Georgia Road Camp

ACTION from Department
NATIONAL ASS

A MILLION

Black

NAACP Here In Shooting

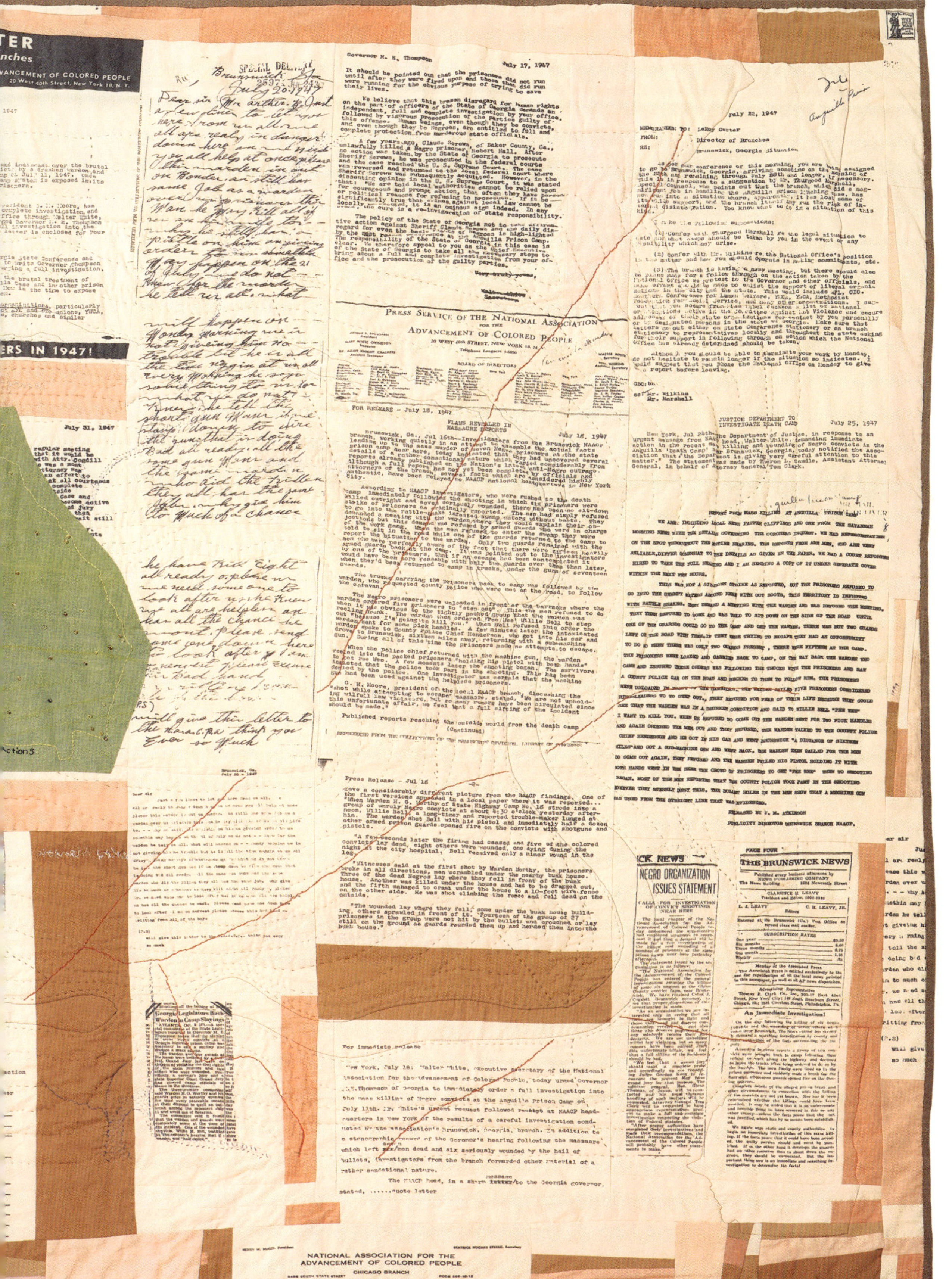
NATIONAL ASSOCIATION FOR THE
ADVANCEMENT OF COLORED PEOPLE
20 West 40th Street, New York 18, N. Y.

Governor M. E. Thompson
July 17, 1947

PRESS SERVICE OF THE NATIONAL ASSOCIATION
FOR THE
ADVANCEMENT OF COLORED PEOPLE
20 WEST 40th STREET, NEW YORK 18, N. Y.

FOR RELEASE - July 18, 1947

PLANS REVEALED IN
MASSACRE REPORTS

Brunswick, Ga., Jul 16th

July 18, 1947

July 22, 1947

MEMORANDUM TO: LeRoy Carter
FROM: Director of Branches
RE: Brunswick, Georgia Situation

JUSTICE DEPARTMENT TO
INVESTIGATE DEATH CAMP
July 25, 1947

New York, Jul 25th

Press Release - Jul 18

THE BRUNSWICK NEWS
Published every business afternoon by
NEWS PUBLISHING COMPANY

NEGRO ORGANIZATION
ISSUES STATEMENT

CALLS FOR INVESTIGATION
OF COUNTY'S SHOOTINGS
NEAR SITE

PAGE FOUR

For immediate release

NATIONAL ASSOCIATION FOR THE
ADVANCEMENT OF COLORED PEOPLE
CHICAGO BRANCH

Levester Williams
To hold us all dear, 2015
Unclean bed sheets from a Virginia adult penitentiary and poplar wood
76½ × 46½ × 3 in., each

In *To hold us all dear*, unwashed bed sheets from an adult penitentiary in Virginia are stretched taut across poplar framing. At first glance, the large rectangles exhibit the formal elements of abstraction, which could seem to be a reference to the workings of a carceral system in which people are made to disappear into the numbers that identify them—and turn them into abstractions.

Yet this quietly tender work magnifies the absence of the people who occupy the beds of the penitentiary, made present in the muted stains of sleep. Abstraction here serves to counteract the dehumanizing effects of incarceration, bringing into focus the details and humanity often lost within carceral bureaucracy. *To hold us all dear* is care work—a monument to those who "hold dear" and refuse to lose family and friends to the obliterating void of incarceration.

Levester Williams, born 1989, lives and works in Philadelphia.

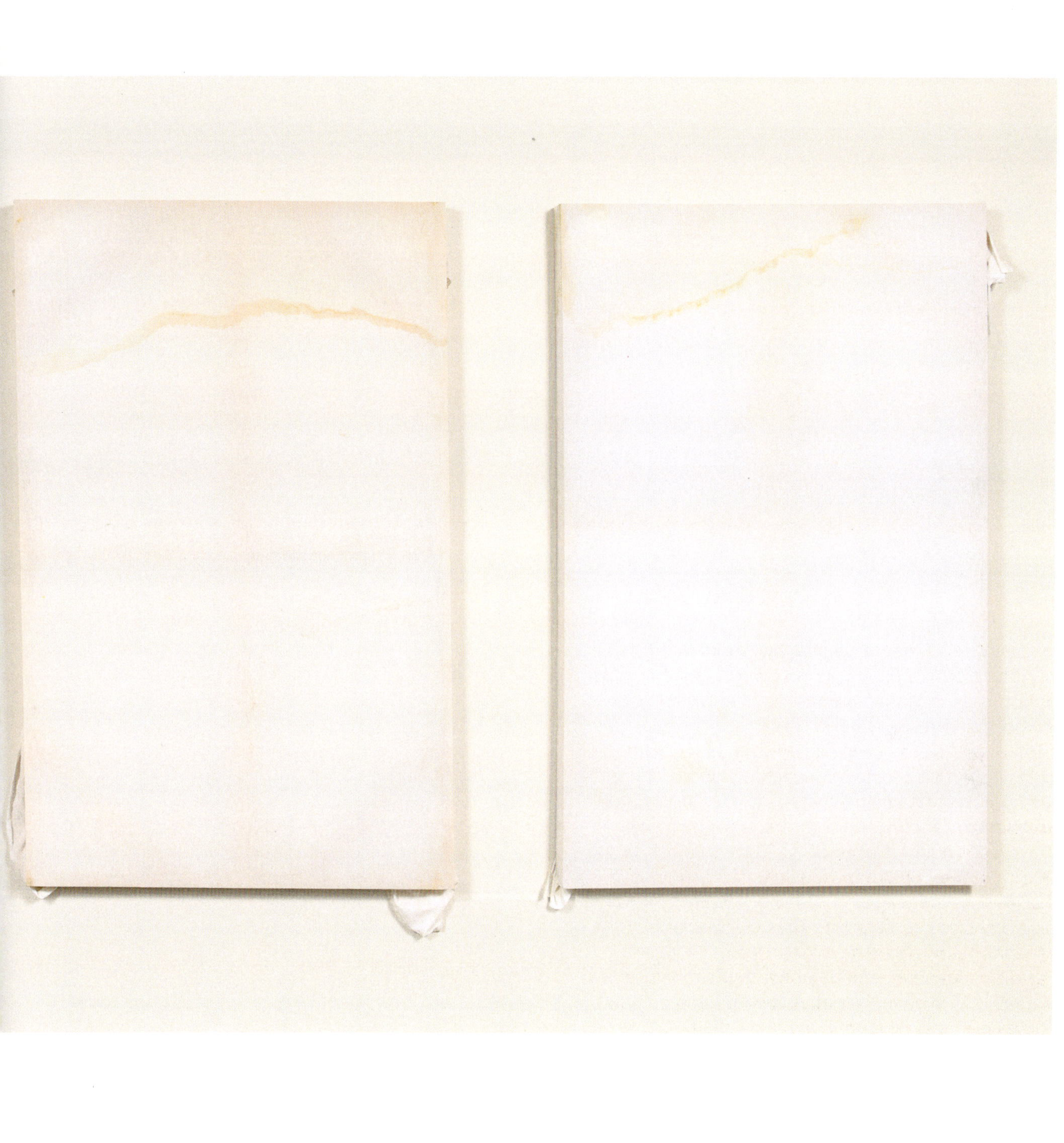

Timothy James Young
Disposition, 2024
Documents and wood frames
Fifteen documents: 11¼ × 8¾ × 1¼ in., each

Disposition is composed of some of the 602 appeals and hundreds of grievances, complaints, and writs Timothy James Young has filed over his almost three decades of incarceration. The bureaucratic paperwork records requests for medical care, adequate legal representation, and repairs to damaged property. It also documents the conditions and policies of the California Department of Corrections and Rehabilitation—and the processes and bureaucracies of repression to which Young is subjected and which he is actively resisting.

As Young describes it, *Disposition* "is the collection, reflection, and archival expression of my decades-long resistance to systemic racism, oppression, and carceral inequalities."[1] The title of the work refers to the legal meaning of the word: a disposition on a criminal record is the current status or final outcome of an arrest or prosecution. Through these grievances and appeals, Young has created his own record of the systemic oppression hidden within the bureaucracy of the criminal legal system, to reveal and impede its workings.

Timothy James Young, born 1970, is currently incarcerated at Pelican Bay State Prison, a supermax prison facility in Crescent City, California.

1. Timothy James Young, in discussion with exhibition curators.

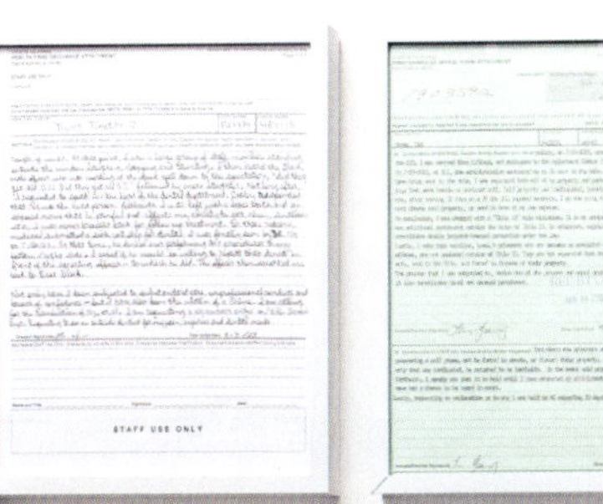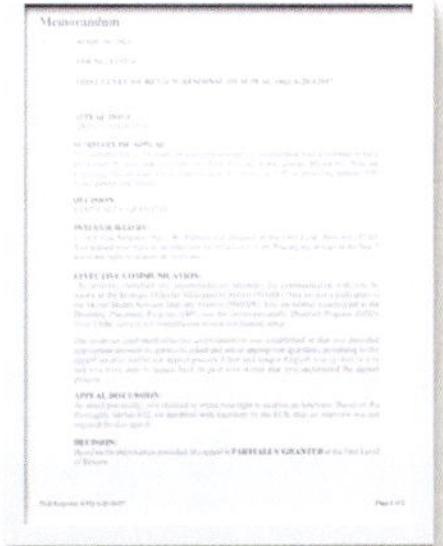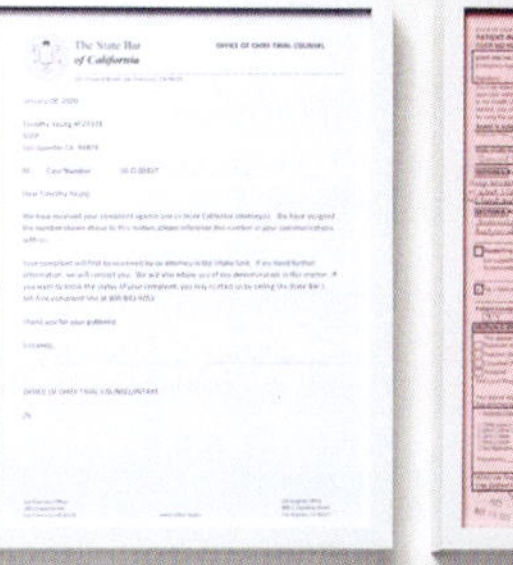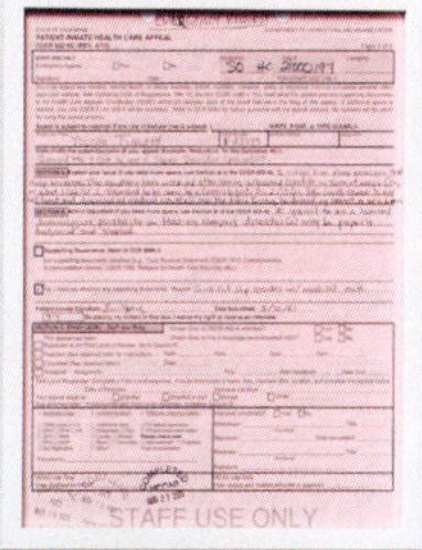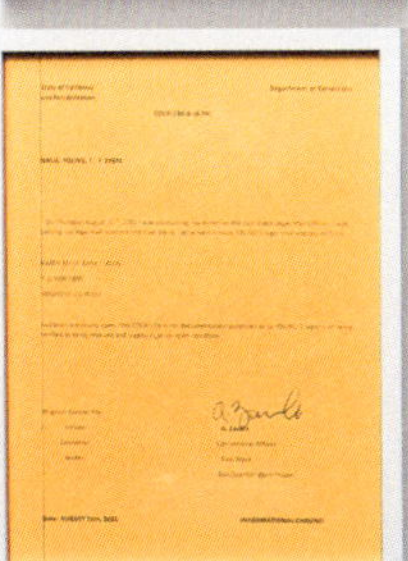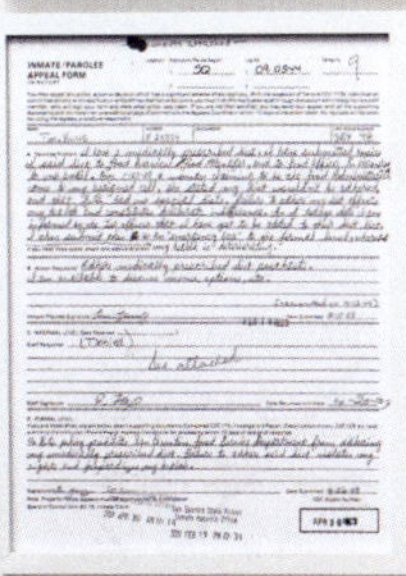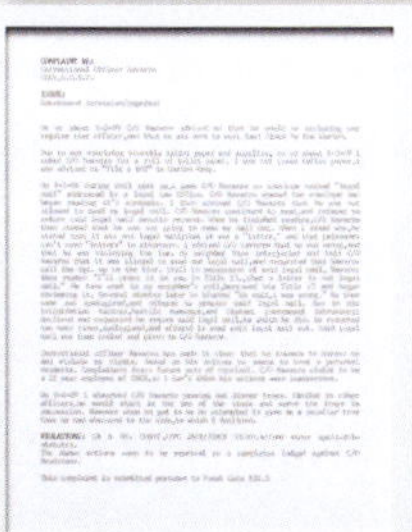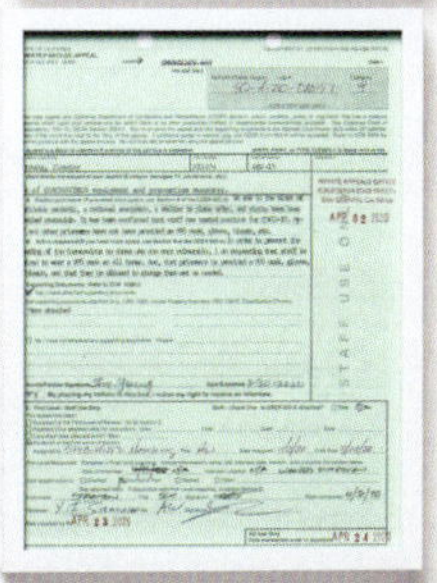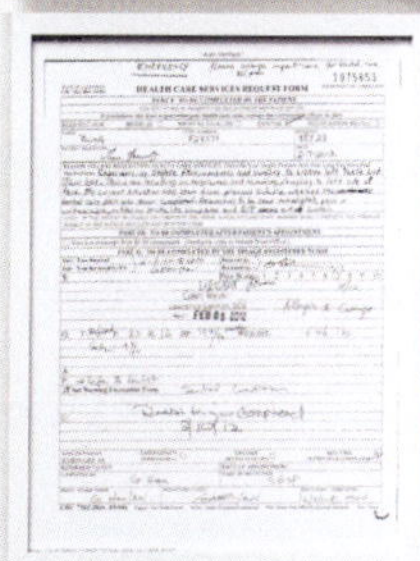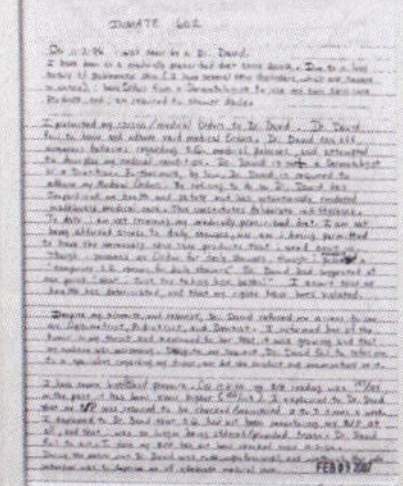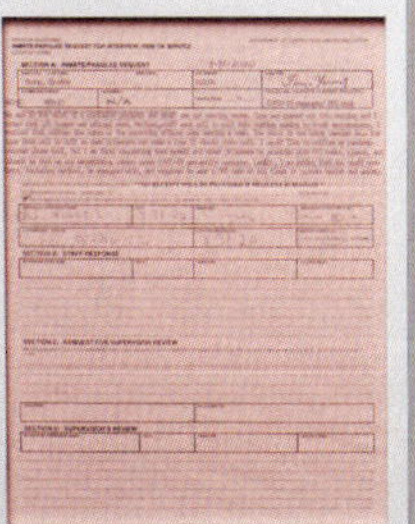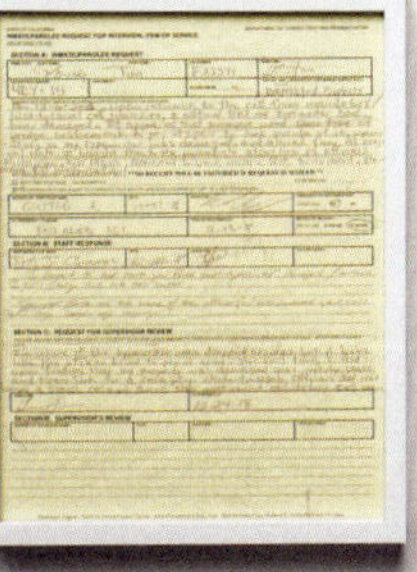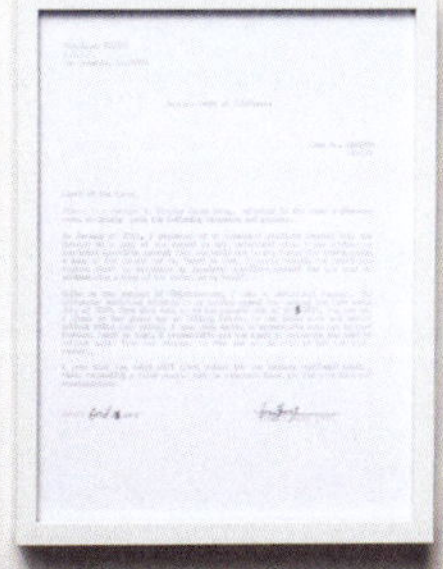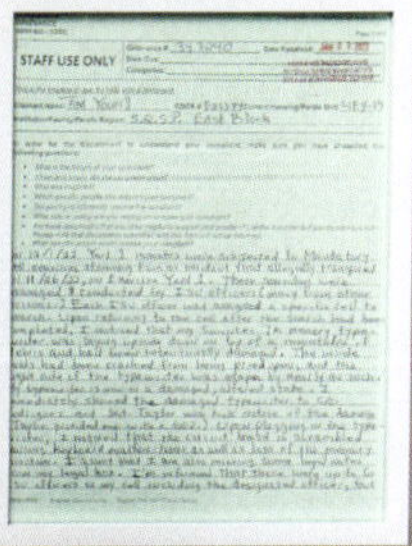

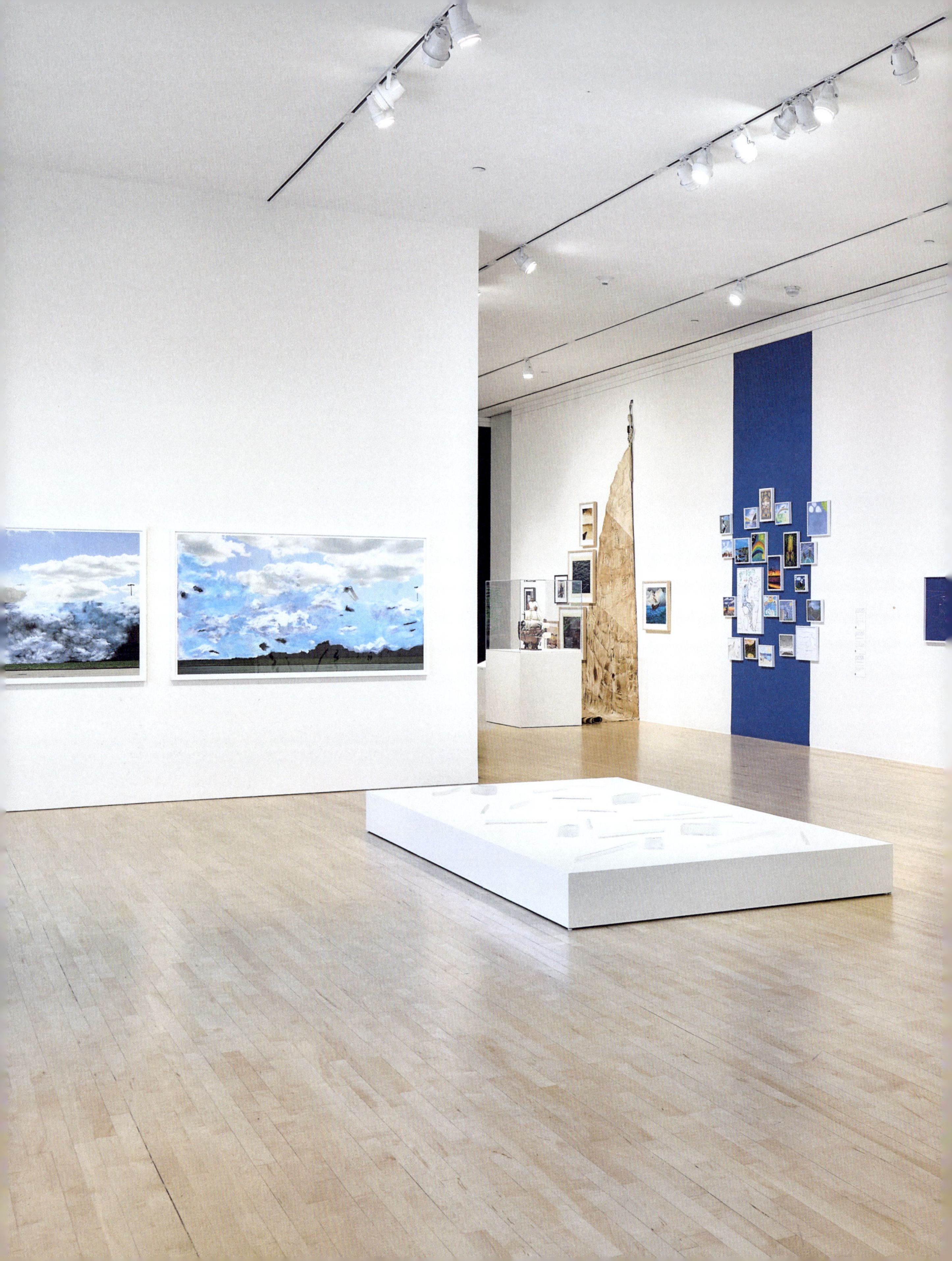

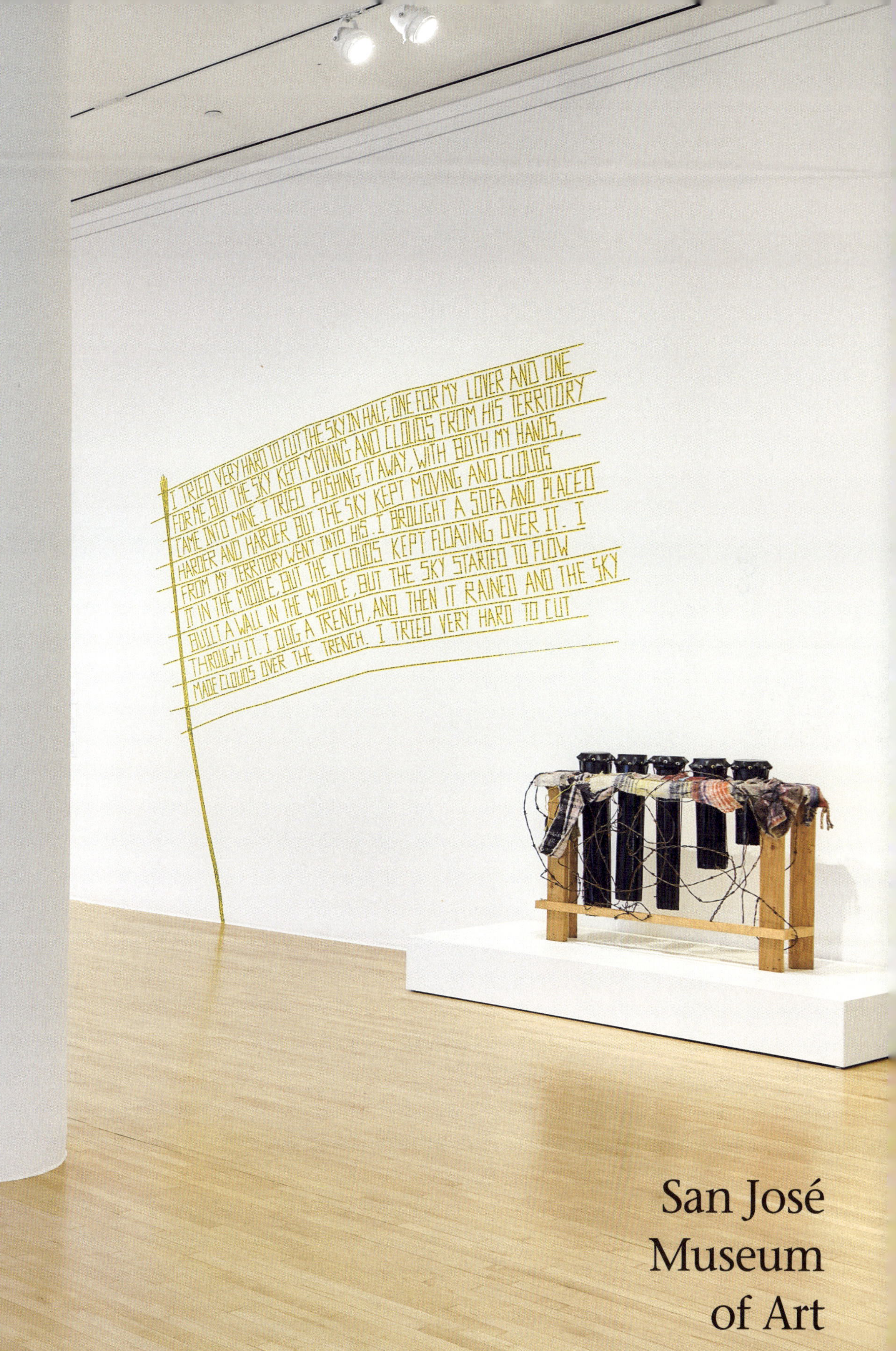

San José
Museum
of Art

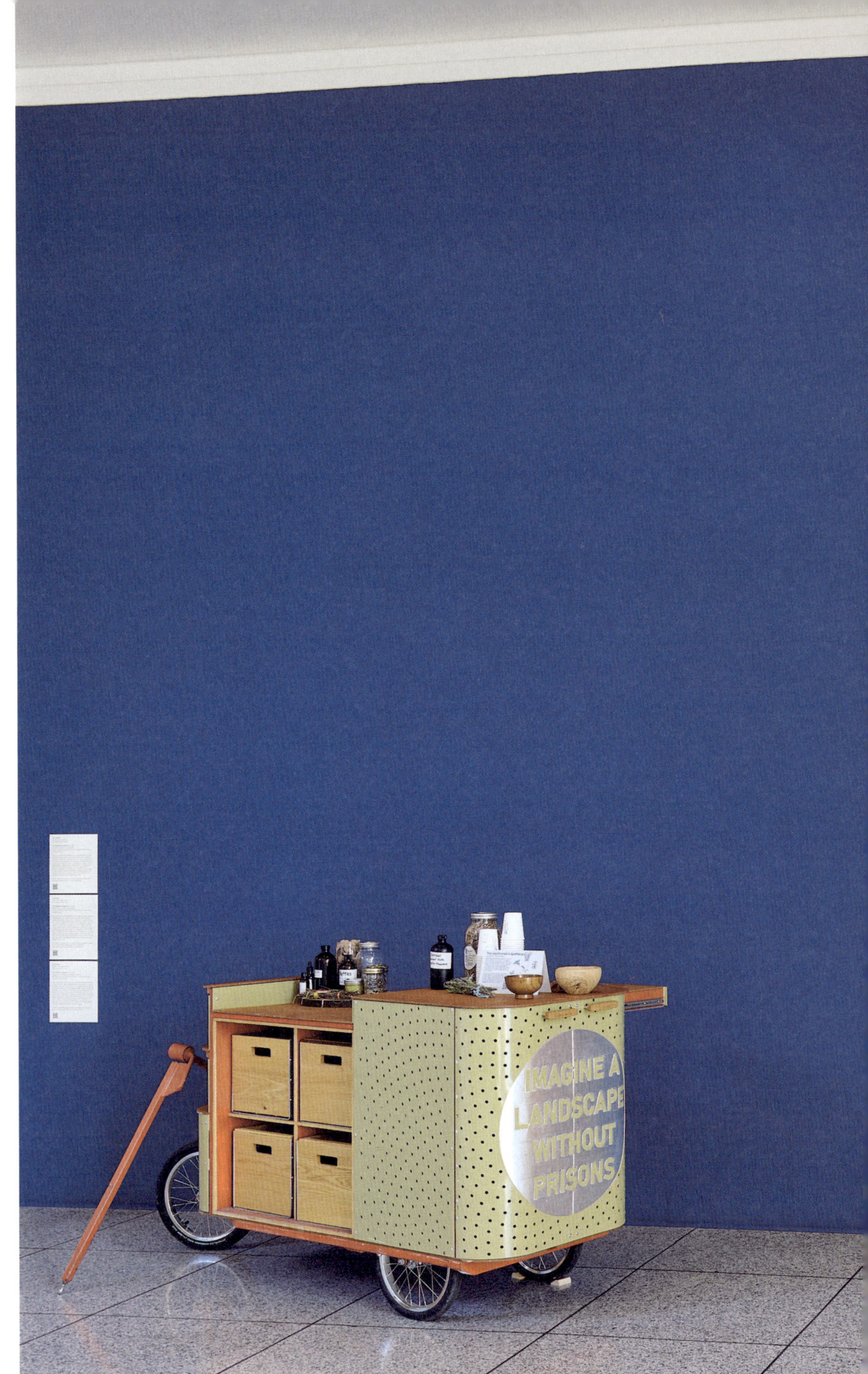

IMAGINE A LANDSCAPE WITHOUT PRISONS.

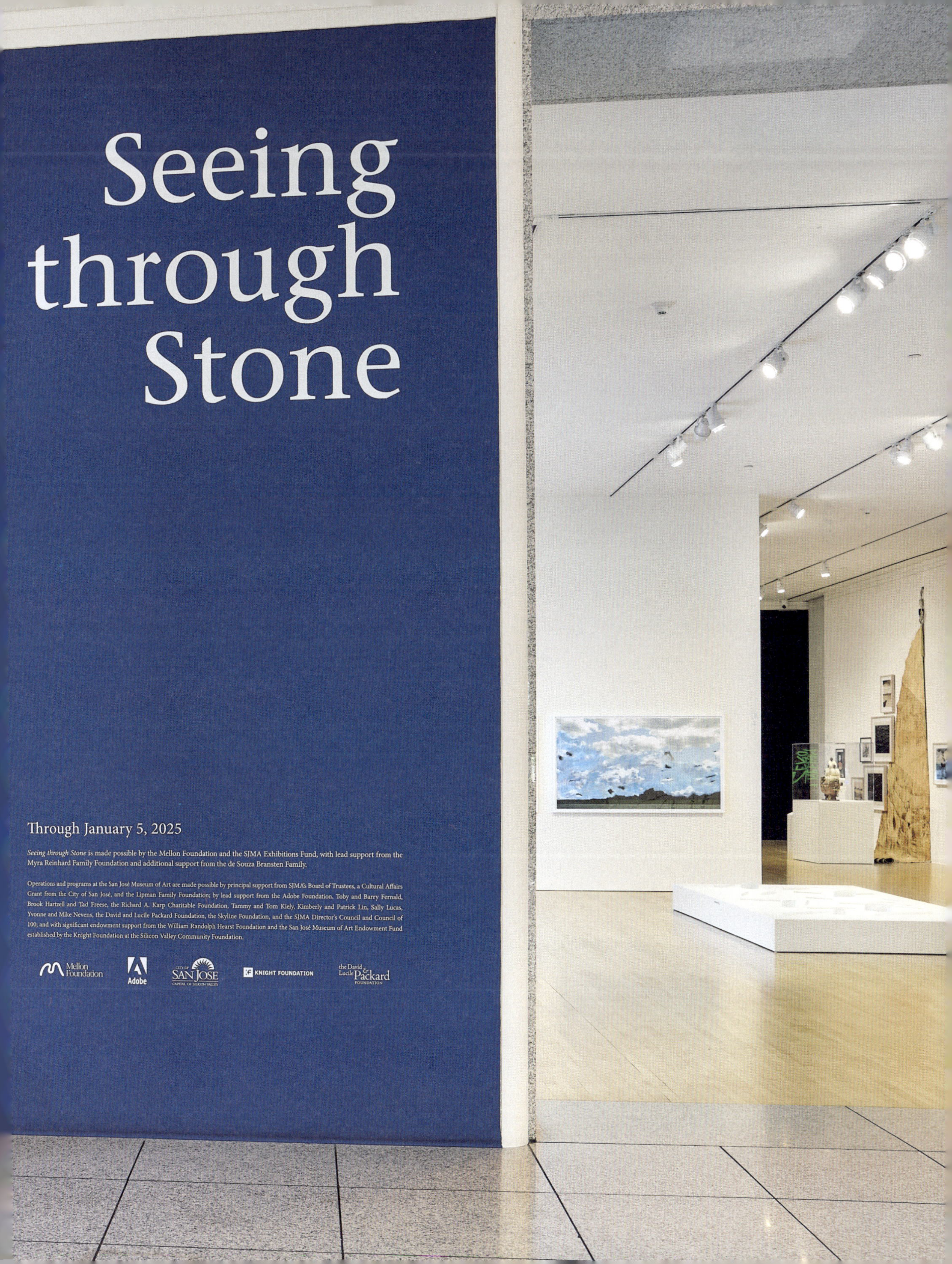

Seeing through Stone

Through January 5, 2025

Seeing through Stone is made possible by the Mellon Foundation and the SJMA Exhibitions Fund, with lead support from the Myra Reinhard Family Foundation and additional support from the de Souza Bransten Family.

Operations and programs at the San José Museum of Art are made possible by principal support from SJMA's Board of Trustees, a Cultural Affairs Grant from the City of San José, and the Lipman Family Foundation; by lead support from the Adobe Foundation, Toby and Barry Fernald, Brook Hartzell and Tad Freese, the Richard A. Karp Charitable Foundation, Tammy and Tom Kiely, Kimberly and Patrick Lin, Sally Lucas, Yvonne and Mike Nevens, the David and Lucile Packard Foundation, the Skyline Foundation, and the SJMA Director's Council and Council of 100; and with significant endowment support from the William Randolph Hearst Foundation and the San José Museum of Art Endowment Fund established by the Knight Foundation at the Silicon Valley Community Foundation.

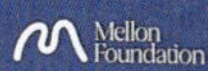
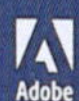
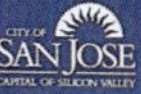
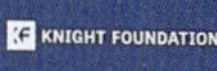
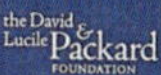

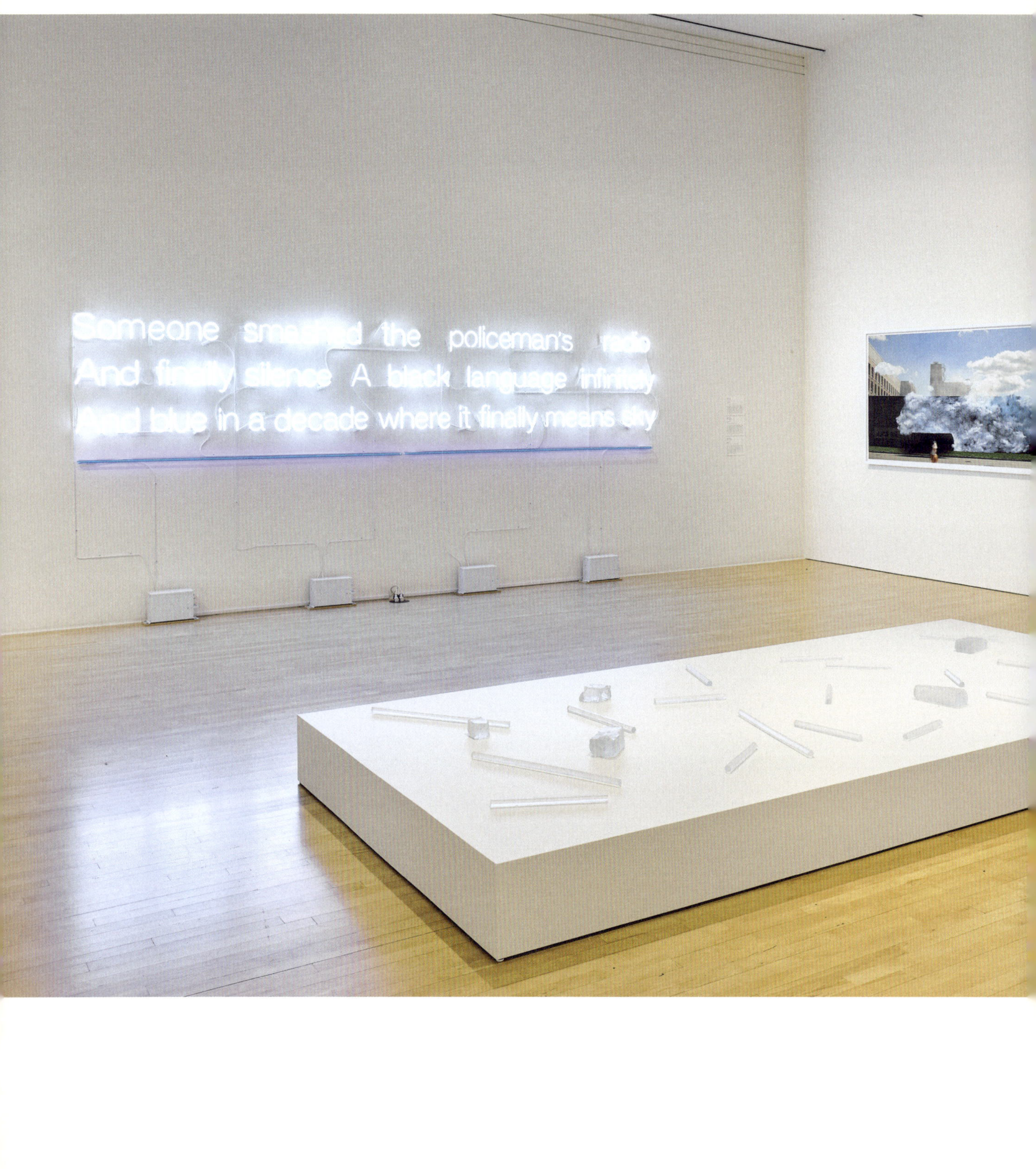
Someone smashed the policeman's radio
And finally silence A black language infinity
And blue in a decade where it finally means sky

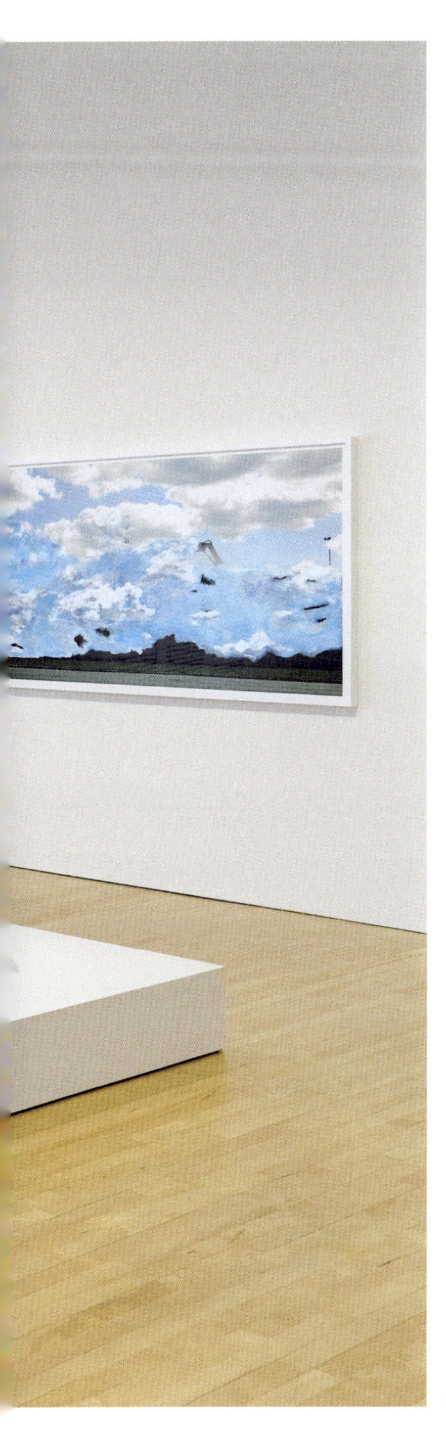
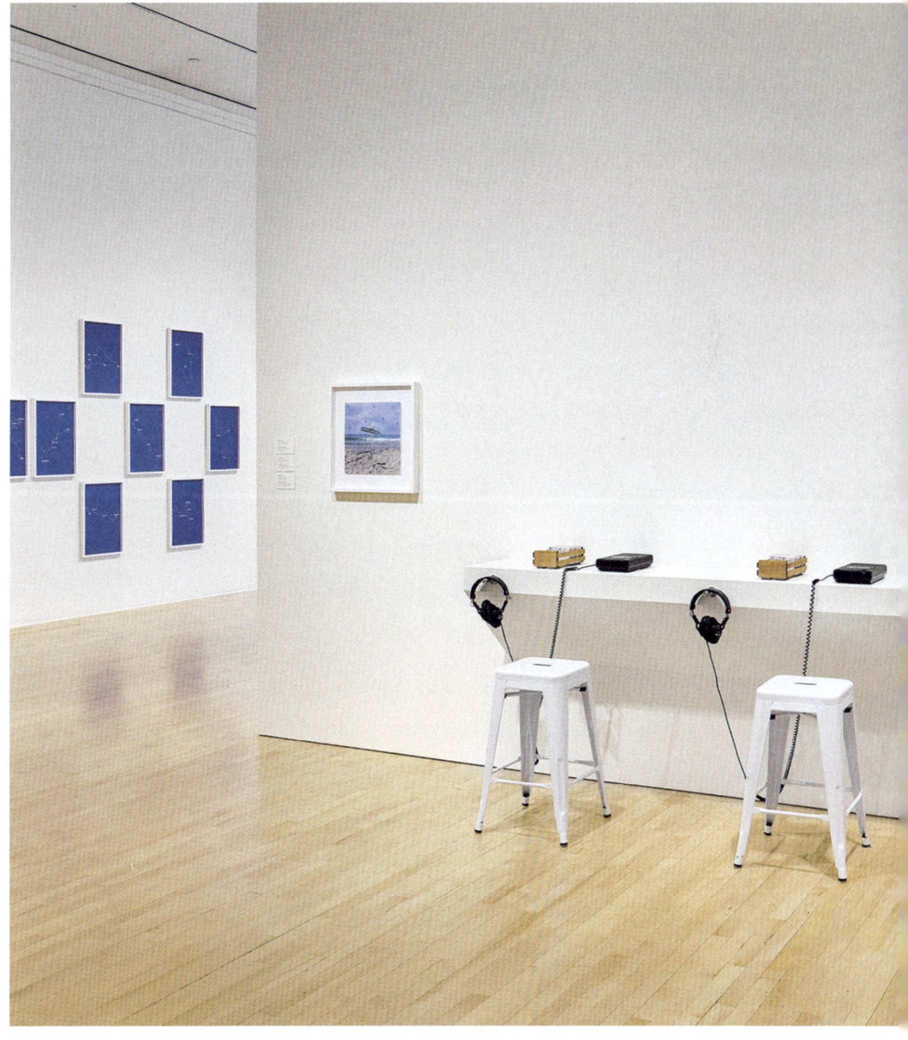

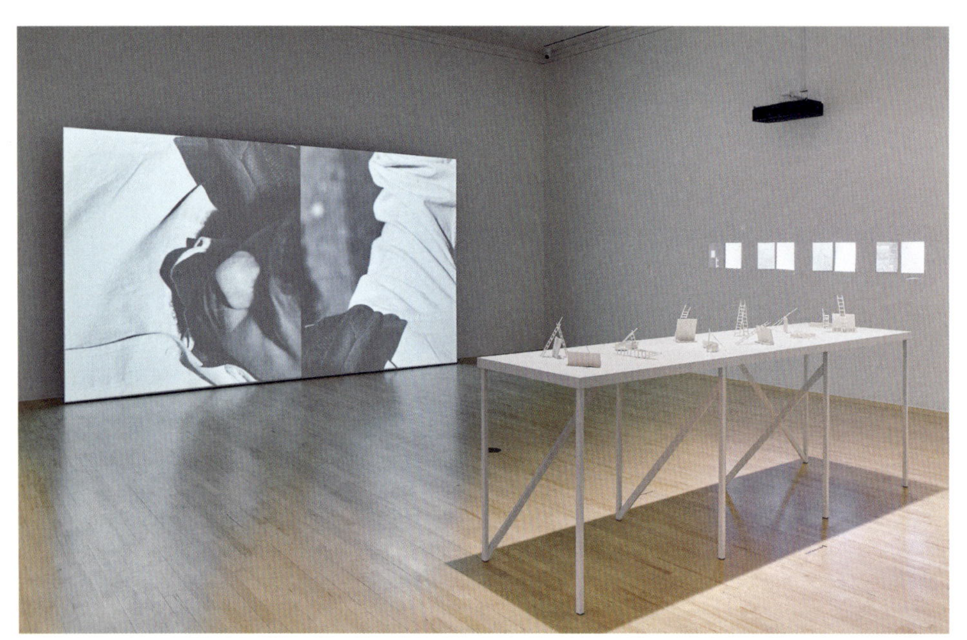

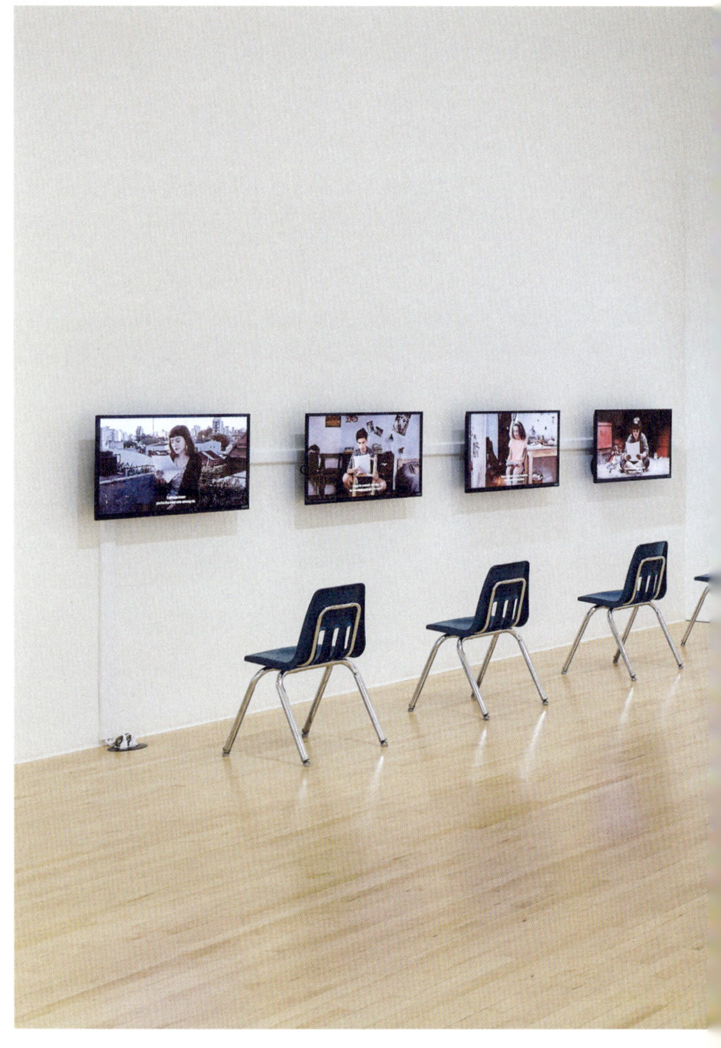

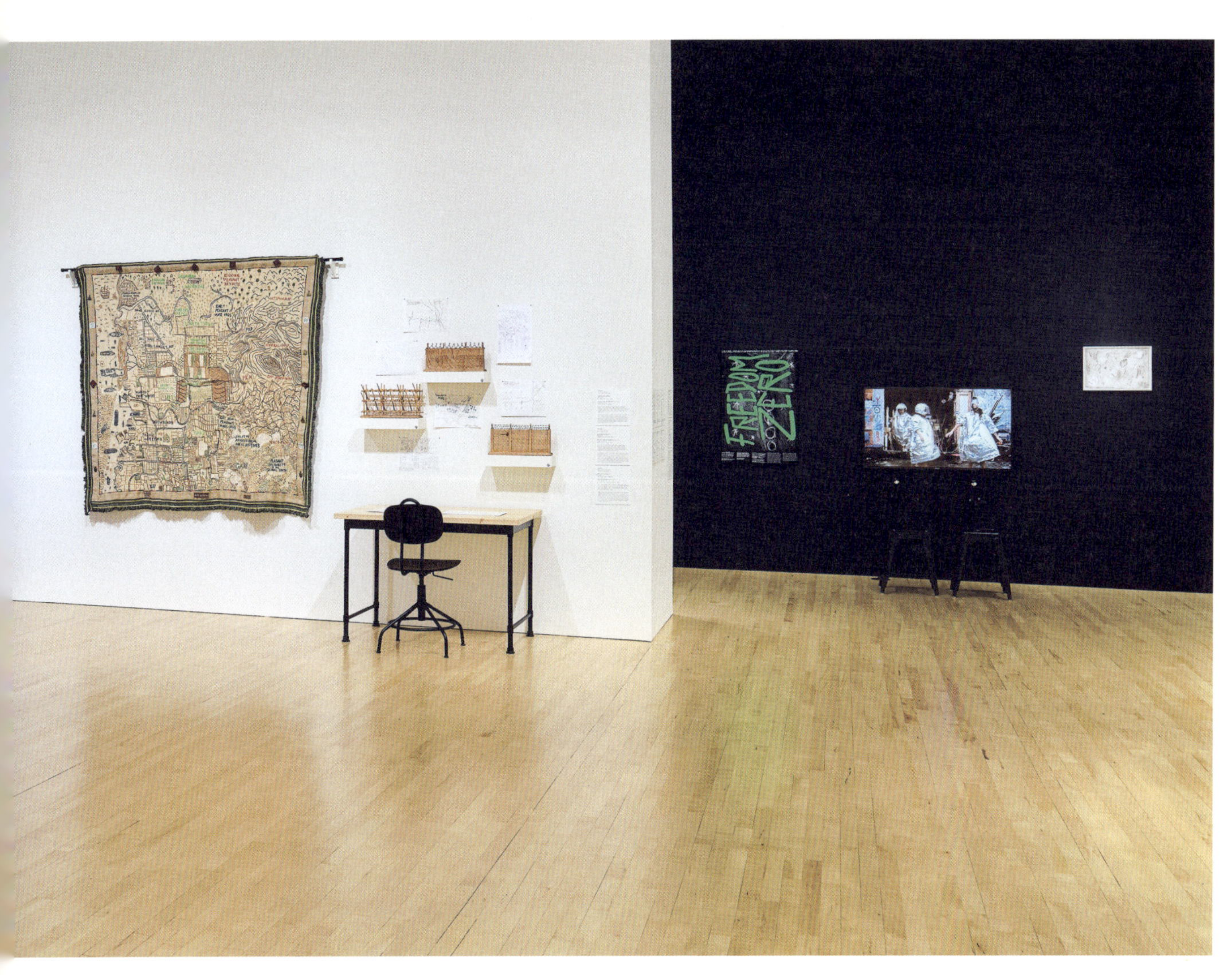

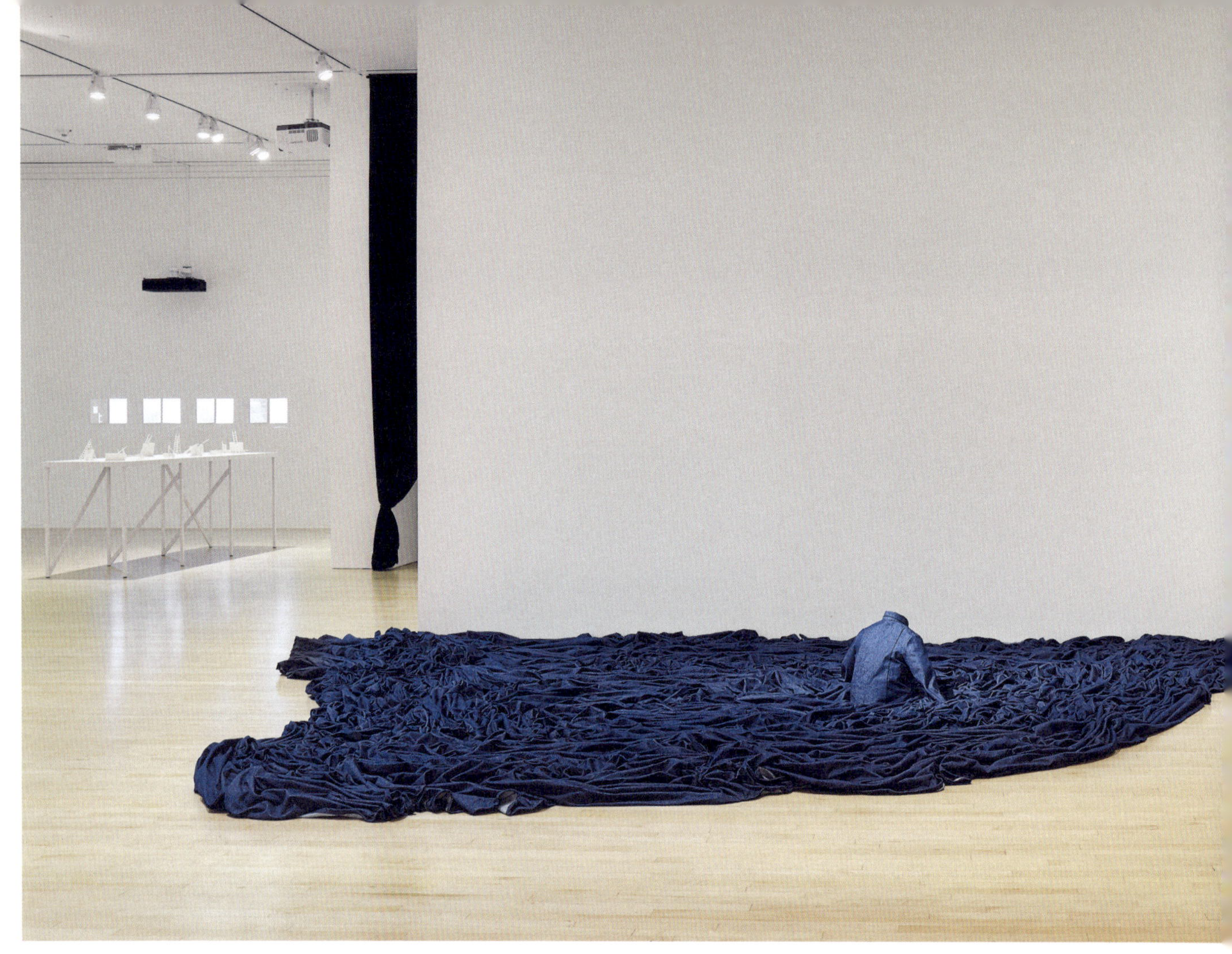

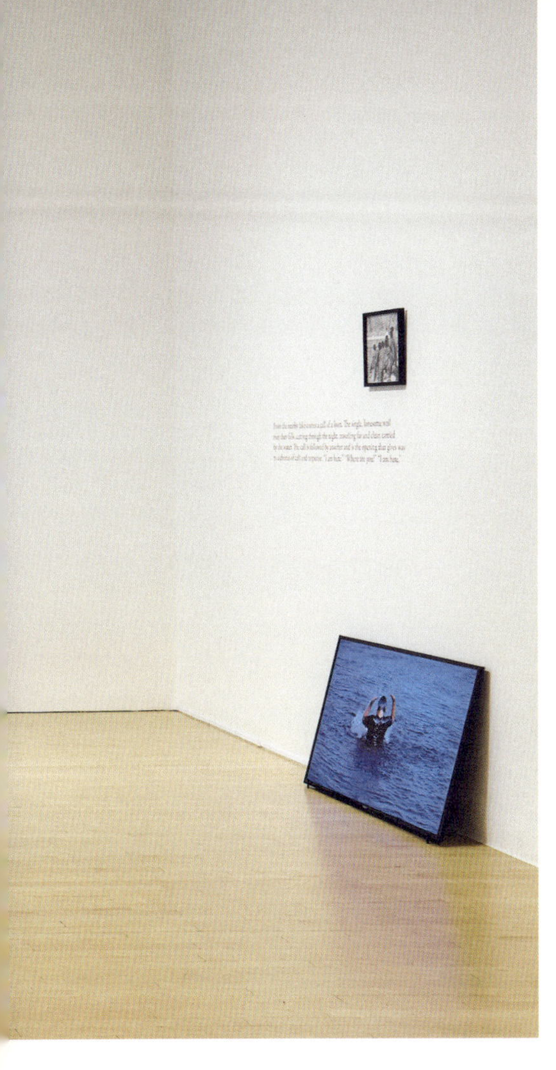

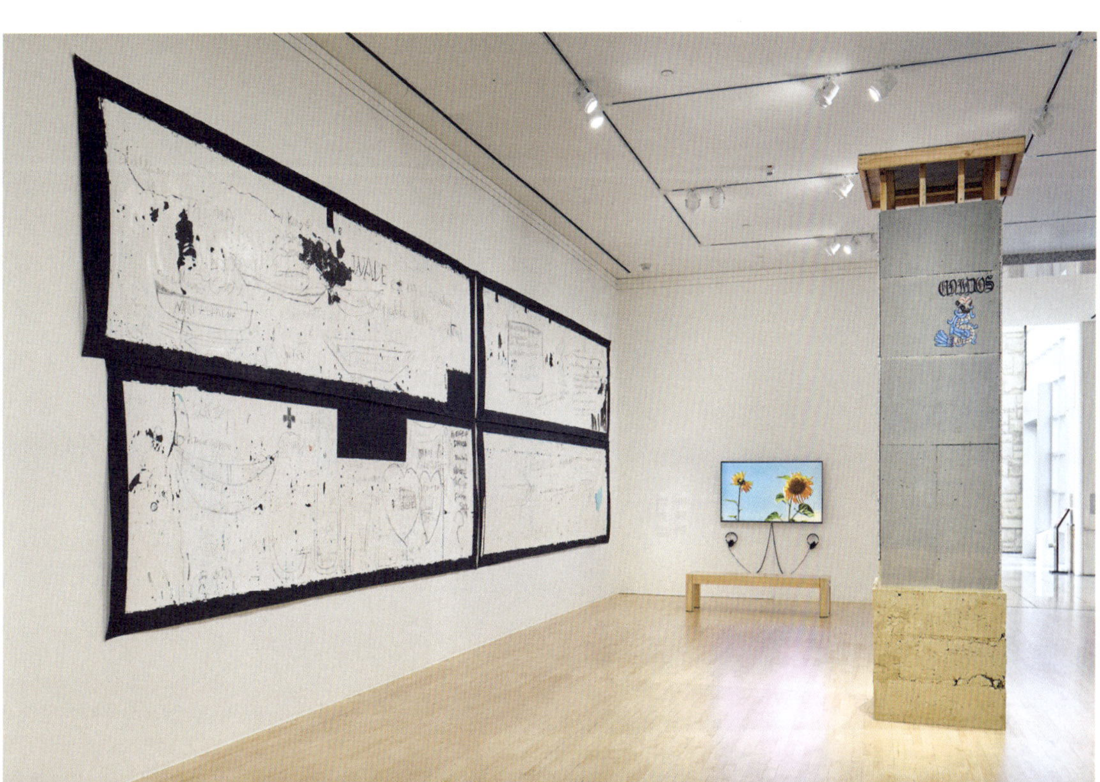

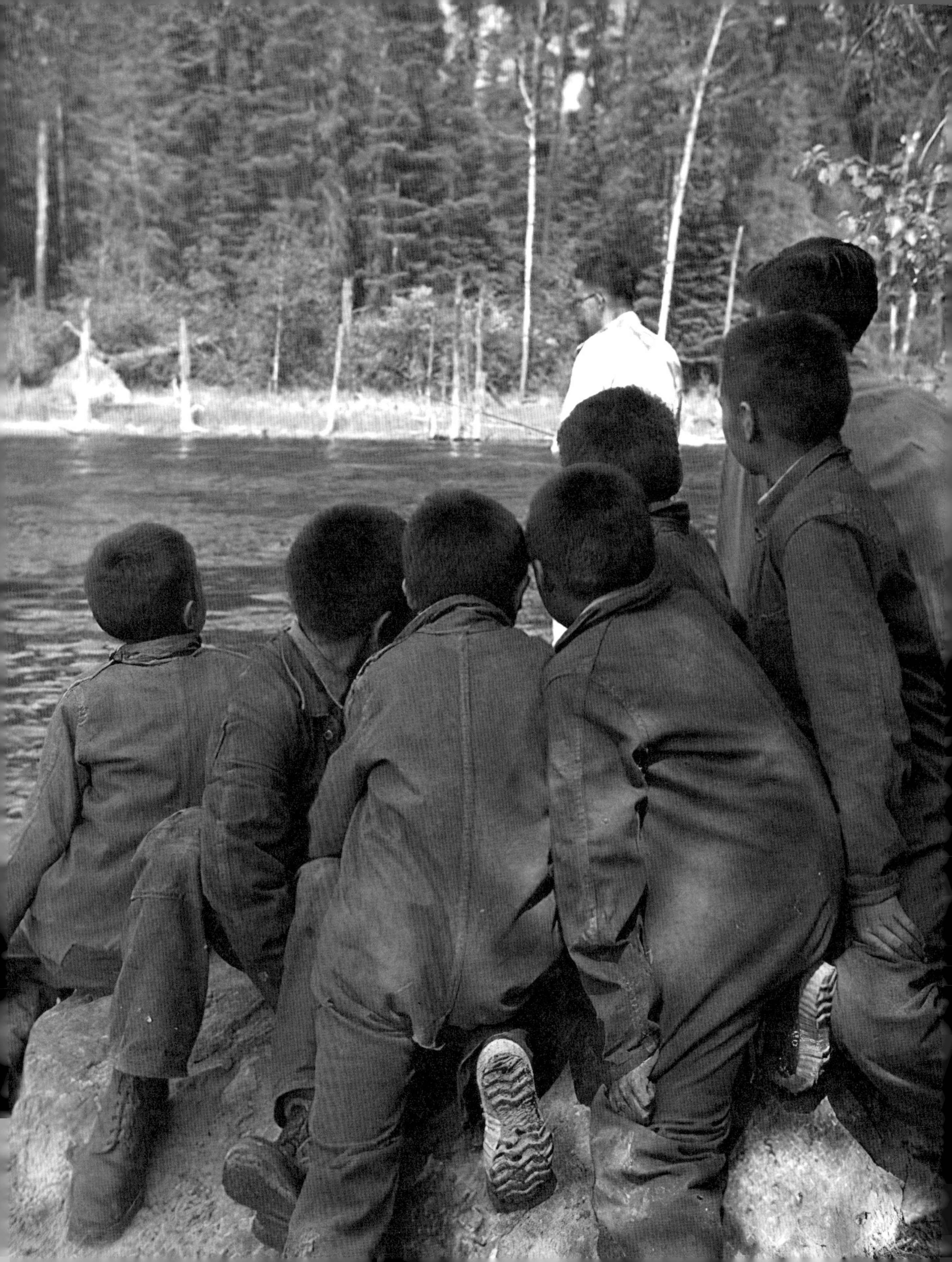

The Practice of Seeing through Stone

Leanne Betasamosake Simpson

When I learned the title of this exhibition, *Seeing through Stone*, I immediately thought of a story my elder Doug Williams used to tell me. The story is about a man named Chi'Niibish—or, in English, Big Leaf— who lived at the narrows on Zhooniyaagamig, or Silver Lake, about a hundred miles north of Toronto, Ontario, in Canada.[1] Chi'Niibish was a visionary, which meant he had the ability to see beyond current circumstances, sometimes through dreams and other times through ceremony. In Anishinaabe culture, dreams are important sources of knowledge for everyone, but visionaries have particular spiritual gifts that allow them to transcend the present moment and life on earth to visit other realms and times, generating new knowledge by communicating with spirits and ancestors. In our language, there are many different words for different kinds of dreams and visions, some of which have an embedded responsibility to share and to actualize what is seen.

Doug Williams writes that Chi'Niibish's dream was one of peace, setting out a set of daily practices to assist individuals, families, and peoples in moving together through difference, disagreement, and even violence toward transforming our relationships into ones that generate more life. Peace, along with accountability and consent, is part of a daily routine in which individuals and groups sort through not just conflict but also what they can give up to promote good relationships.[2] According to Doug, Chi'Niibish chose to work with the Nadaweg, or the Kanien'-kehá:ka [Mohawks], neighbors with whom we share Lake Ontario and with whom we've had times of peace and times of great conflict. He learned Wendat, or Huron, a language related to theirs, so he could communicate with them. He dreamed how to build a special birchbark canoe for his journey across Lake Ontario to the heart of their homeland. The canoe had the white side of the bark on the outside. As a result, from a distance, it appeared to be made of stone. Inverted canoes like this, in our culture, are used to travel to the spirit world. Chi'Niibish took his clan symbol, the eagle sitting atop a pine tree, with him on his journey.

Sometimes I imagine Chi'Niibish telling his friends that he had dreamed of making an inverted canoe to travel across the big lake to talk peace with kin we didn't always get along with. I imagine he would have been met with curiosity because the idea sounded so strange, and because my people are careful with criticism. I imagine there would have been ethical questions, because it could sound arrogant to decide to go, uninvited, to teach another people about peace, and/or it could be an act of generative accountability to face the conflict that existed between our two peoples. There would have been a few jokes, because the

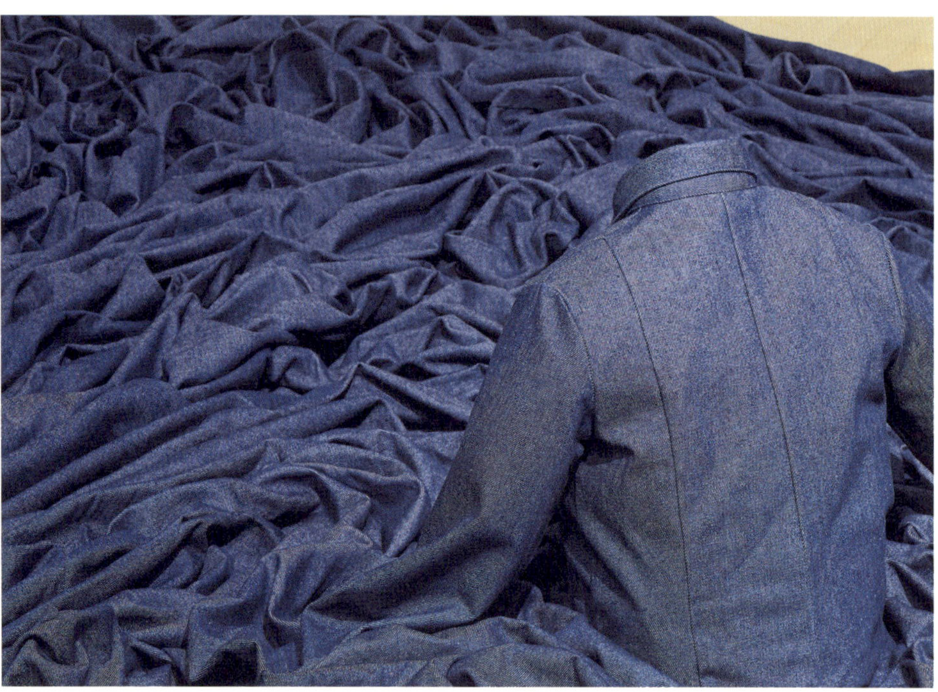

idea sounded preposterous. There would have been more laughter as they went about gathering spruce roots and making pitch. The kids would want to help. Someone would show them how to split the roots, and when they got bored, they'd abandon the job and run shrieking around the camp. Someone would be boiling tea and cooking over the fire to feed the group that had gathered.

I imagine they started small, making a toyish replica of the canoe to learn how to work with heat and water to encourage the bark to bend backward. I imagine there were prototypes that didn't quite work, and they had to rally past their failures and trouble-shoot the problems they encountered. I imagine them scaling the replicas up gradually, until they had one that could fit Chi'Niibish and his belongings. I imag-ine that as they wove the canoe, the skeptics became invested, and if they didn't quite believe in Chi'Niibish's vision at the start, they grew more sure as they went along. They certainly believed in love and support.

I think about his departure from the shore, the gathering place where sky meets land meets water and worlds overlap and commingle.

I wonder about his first few strokes of the paddle. Was he nervous? Did he look back?

I imagine looking out into the blue of Lake Ontario, toward the lake swallowing the sky, and watching a stone canoe coming toward me. I wouldn't be able to believe what I was seeing, because of course, stone doesn't float. For a few moments, my brain and my eyes would be in conflict, as I tried to figure out a plausible explanation for this defiance of physics— venturing into a space where I'm entertaining what is possible because I'm seeing something my brain knows to be unbelievable.

I picture the moment the canoe comes into sharp focus and I realize it is made not of stone but of white birch bark: Oh. That's why it floats. But also: Oh. How did he make that? Why? Why did he put such effort into molding the bark in an unnatural way? Who is this person and why is he here, paddling toward me from the hole in the horizon?

The Michi Saagiig Nishnaabeg story of Chi'Niibish ends here. He didn't come back to our homeland. He stayed with the Kanien'kehá:ka, one of the nations of the Haudenosaunee [Iroquois] Confederacy, which has a profound oral and written archive of stories and prac-tices that came from a similar being, known in English as the Peacemaker. The Haudenosaunee people hold many different stories about the origin of this being, who helped them achieve peace through the formation of their confederacy.[3]

The story of Chi'Niibish speaks to the importance of nurturing our collective ability to see a possibility

Rebecca Belmore, *At Pelican Falls*
(detail), 2017. Collection of the
artist.

or potential, as a skill and a way of bringing people together to support our makers in their sovereign creative practices. In learning from the curators about the artists featured in *Seeing through Stone*, I got a sense that in different ways, at various times in their practices, each of these artists may have been like Chi'Niibish, alone in their visioning of elsewhere, and that they, too, may have eventually found a community that believed in love and support. I got a sense that maybe these curators were a part of that community.

Within Anishinaabewin, there are endless stories like that of Chi'Niibish. Stories of people having dreams or visions or ideas and then following through with a creative practice that is transformative to the larger community. Stories of beings actively taking on the responsibility for the idea or dream, gathering people around who can help and making something different together in the face of all kinds of adversity. It is a simple process, really—one of being present, of noticing and being curious, of believing and communing, and ultimately of making; one that has built new Anishinaabe worlds and illuminated old ones. It's a generative practice of collectively making the knowledge that we need to propel us to the next iteration of the formation. And the first step in this process is opening up to the possibility of seeing through the stone of the present situation.

Children have a knack for this because they are not bound by things like reality and how the world works. It would have been easy to convince the children who witnessed Chi'Niibish's arrival that building an inverted canoe was an excellent way to spend their time. For Anishinaabe, children are our teachers because they are fresh from the spiritual world, and so we revel in babies teaching us about gathering love together, toddlers teaching us how to say no and set boundaries, teenagers teaching us about expansion. Children are welcomed into extended families and communities when they come through the doorway to the physical earth. They are welcomed with self-determination and an ethic of non-interference, giving them freedom to explore and learn without the confines of rigid authority, violence, or the institutions of school or church. They are woven into a society that models itself as a foundational way of sharing knowledge and that long existed without police or policing. As such, our stories encode times when children's own self-determination made massive contributions to Anishinaabe politics, economics, and knowledge.

I've written a lot about Biidaaban and the origins of maple syrup as a way of demonstrating how this process of being present, of emergence, works in terms of generating new knowledge and nourishing our relationships with all the interwoven plants, animals, and humans that make up a particular ecology or place.[4] Biidaaban brought the practice of making maple sugar to the Anishinaabe after watching a squirrel find sap. Curious, they gathered the sap in a basket and shared it with their mama, who cooked meat in it for their evening meal. Together, they noticed that the sugar appeared as the water evaporated, and this became a foundation of the Anishinaabe economy, a relational one that exists within the web of life and outside the container of racial capitalism.

It is with this orientation that I first saw John Macfie's 1955 black-and-white photograph in Rebecca Belmore's installation *At Pelican Falls*. Found in the Archives of Ontario, the photograph features a group of Anishinaabe children, I'd guess between the ages of six and eight, grouped around a boulder on the shore of a river. Their backs are to the camera, and I immediately recognized their uniform buzz cuts, matching denim coveralls, and work boots as indicators that these children were students in a residential school, sorted into a colonial gender binary and labeled as "boys." The children are watching a white man fishing. We know that the man is a settler by his white skin and the way he conforms to the heteronormative dress code of the time, and perhaps because he is fishing with a pole instead of by setting a net. We don't know if he is their teacher or priest or unrelated to the kids.[5]

It strikes me how interested the children are in his activity. Their backs are to the camera, so we can't see their facial expressions, but from their body language they appear transfixed—and still, which is rare for kids of this age.

At first glance, I felt a sinister energy in this photo. These kids are among generations of Indigenous children who were stolen by the state from their families, from their culture, language, religion, and knowledge system, and placed in state- and church-run boarding schools designed to assimilate them into Canadian society. And here they are. Back in the arms of their parent, *Aki*, the earth. Back in the presence of their lifeblood, *Ziibing*, the river, surrounded by the forest. Belmore says the children reminded her of "beautiful little otters,"[6] and they remind me of the same. The invisible enclosure of intimate violence keeps them still and watching, not participating. I can almost see their spirits drawing upward into the sky to meet with their ancestors and the ones who haven't yet been born. At first look, the photograph felt to me like it captured the humiliation of the colonized— like those beautiful little otters were being mocked by the colonizer, fishing as a pastime on a beautiful summer day, while the otters themselves, confined in a million different ways, could only watch and, I hope, dream.

The Canadian residential school system was influenced in part by the industrial boarding school system in the United States. It was a network of boarding schools funded by the Department of Indian Affairs and administered by Christian churches,[7] as part of a strategy to remove Indigenous peoples from our homelands so that the state could access and extract natural resources and grow its capitalist economy and the political infrastructure it needed to replicate itself. The system was designed to convert "Indians" into heterosexual, cisgender, English-speaking, Christian workers who had the skills to participate in the lowest rungs of the wage economy. Residential schools operated for about a century and were purposefully located far away from the children's home communities as a strategy to assist in assimilation. They were poorly funded genocidal projects, and children had to cope with malnutrition and outbreaks of infectious disease on top of the trauma of forced removal. The schools were notoriously violent, creating generations of Indigenous people who are survivors of sexual, physical, and emotional abuse.

In addition to horrific individual stories of abuse, residential schools had a devastating communal impact. Parents were left mourning the loss of their children. September was the quiet time in communities, which were forced to learn to live without the laughter of any school-age children. Extended Anishinaabe families, from which children learned and participated in the political and economic lifeways of our people, were devastated, and children were no longer exposed to our ethical practices of self-determination and self-reliance, leadership, decision-making, and politics. They no longer learned the language of their parents, the language that encoded the caretaking relationality of the Anishinaabe. They no longer learned how to make and replicate Anishinaabe worlds—worlds that were braided into the network of living species they shared time and space with, worlds where individual and communal self-determination was cherished and where children were seen as teachers, fresh from the spiritual world, with gifts to share with the community. As a result, these worlds were nearly destroyed.

Residential schools were carceral. Children couldn't leave. Families couldn't visit. Parents had no choice and were threatened in various ways, including incarceration, if they resisted. Residential schools, along with the Indian Act, contained Indigenous resistance and organizing because the state used the children as human shields. The intimate violence of residential schools caused trauma that has infiltrated second and third generations of survivors' families.

Pelican Falls Indian Residential School was run by the Anglican Church. Operational from 1927 to 1978,

Rebecca Belmore, *At Pelican Falls* (detail), 2017. Collection of the artist.

194

it included a 287-acre farm for the children to work, because colonialism demanded unfettered access not only to our land but also to our bodies, which were extracted and inserted into capitalist wage labor. Boys were trained to be farmers. Girls were trained to be housewives. Two-spirit and queer children were trained to be heterosexual and cisgender and to form nuclear families that could reproduce the Canadian state.

The "beautiful little otters," or *Nigigoonsiwag*, in this photo were trapped in a series of carceral enclosures, some visible, some invisible, some opaque. We know they did not have control over any part of their lives, from the time they got up to the food they ate; from how they spent their days to what they learned; from what they wore to whom they were allowed to form friendships with, and what they could be in the future.

We know they couldn't always see the sky.

And we know they were subjected to unspeakable violence, including in some cases torture, solitary confinement, starvation, and sexual abuse.[8] Many died, and their remains were buried, often in unmarked graves, in the vicinity of the schools.[9] The records show that at Pelican Falls Indian Residential School, the following twenty-four children, from an enrollment of approximately 150, died between 1935 and 1946, just before the Nigigoonsiwag attended.[10] I assume some of these little people were older siblings and cousins of the Nigigoonsiwag.

Sybil Anishinabi
Mary Ann Ash
Uriah Baxter
Lavina Beardy
Doris Carpenter
Maggie Cromarty
Dorothy Ferries
Margaret Fox
Amos Jacob
Stoney Johnson
Daniel Masakeyash
Charles Ombash
Thomas Ombash
Mike Oombash
Mary Petawayway
Morris Rooster
Samuel Sakakeesic
Michael Jean Sapay
Margaret Singebis
Ferlin Southwind
Nancy Tooshenan
John Wapoos
Thomas Wapoos
Samuel Wesley

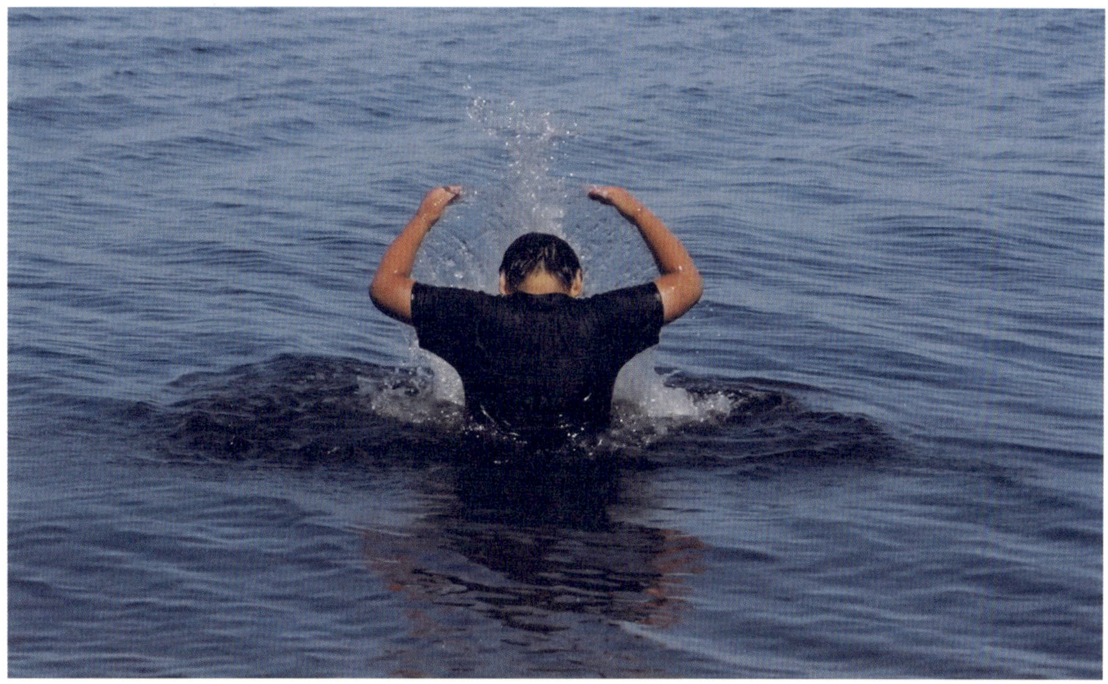

If all of these little otters had been in an Anishinaabe community, their beautiful brown bodies would not have been trapped in the summer heat and the humidity of those denim coveralls. They certainly would not have been sitting on that rock, focused on a white man fishing. They would have been running around, laughing and yelling, playing or swimming or in a boat or canoe, setting nets, or filleting fish already caught. In all of these scenarios, they would have been surrounded by other children and extended family. They would likely have been muddy from their adventures. Their gorgeous long black hair might have been braided, or matted because they couldn't sit still long enough for someone to braid it. We'd probably see a glorious diversity of gender expressions in the photo. The community would have gathered and held space around each of the Nigig as they figured out their paths in life and how to contribute to their families in ways that honored their own gifts, self-determination, and interests. The river would have taught them that they were connected to every other living being on the planet, and that we transform into different states and can travel far and still belong if we know how to weave. The sky would have bathed them in possibilities. The air would have taught them that the container that held them was leaky and connected, enhanced by deep relationality.

A few of them would have been driven by a creative practice, and this would have been noticed by their relatives. Those relatives would have been responsible for holding space around those little makers, providing encouragement and support as they learned to live within the power of their body and voice and connected that power to the world around them, making work that reflected, elevated, and challenged their community. This is a practice of love, connecting, and belonging. A few of the Nigig would have been dreamers and visionaries like Chi'Niibish, and their relatives would have been responsible for seeing their gift, helping them hone their skills and, most importantly, believing in them.

So here the Nigigoonsiwag are, on the bank of the river. Maybe their ancestors are awakening in their bones. They are feeling the heat of *Niibin*, the summer. They are seeing Ziibing. They are surrounded by trees, and perhaps they can hear the falls. They are watching a man fish, which provides a clue to another way of living. Maybe the moment we are witnessing through this photo is an instance of Nigigoonsiwag seeing through the stone of their diminished daily life in a residential school.

Maybe they are dreaming beyond their present moment.

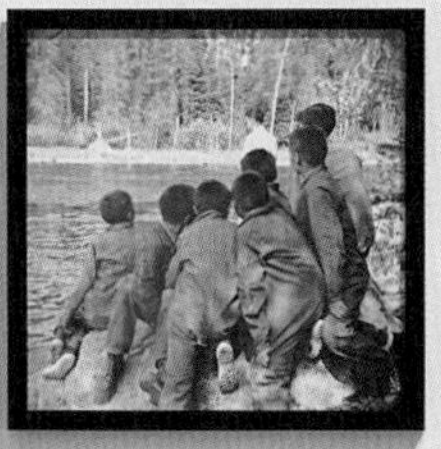

From the nearby lake comes a call of a loon. The single, lonesome wail rises then falls, cutting through the night, travelling far and clear, carried by the water. The call is followed by another and is the opening that gives way to a chorus of call and response. "I am here." "Where are you?" "I am here."

Oral stories and archival documents teach us that Indigenous children most certainly dreamed of worlds other than the ones they were forced to live in at residential schools. We know the story of Chanie Wenjack, another Nigigoonse, who escaped from Cecilia Jeffrey Indian Residential School in Kenora, Ontario, not too far from Pelican Falls.[11] In the early 1960s, Chanie tried to walk the 370 miles (600 kilometers) from Kenora to his home in Ogoki Post on the Marten Falls reserve. The twelve-year-old and two friends, Ralph and Jackie MacDonald, traveled nineteen miles (thirty-one kilometers) the first day and made it to the home of the MacDonald boys' uncle. After some days of rest, equipped with food, matches, and advice, Chanie continued his journey along the Canadian National rail lines, using a map in a passenger timetable as his guide.

He walked for thirty-six hours, covering another twelve miles (twenty kilometers). October in northern Ontario can get cold, and Chanie didn't have proper clothing for the journey. He died before he made it into the arms of his parents. By some estimates, as many as thirty thousand children in residential schools didn't make it home. Instead, they died from abuse, malnutrition, disease, or trying to walk themselves to a better life.[12]

Chanie, like so many Indigenous, Black, and Palestinian children, died seeing through the stone.

In our present moment, in the midst of the spectacular violence of the Israeli apartheid state, I must also see through the stone of colonial states and corporate media. If I shut out the noise of those intent on genocide, if I close my eyes and listen, I see those Gazan children, those beautiful little Palestinian olive seedlings, and their laughter, their press conference,[13] their hopes and dreams for a future filled with learning and trips to the beach. I see their tiny hands waving white flags as they are led away from their worlds. I see them walking through Israeli checkpoints with their siblings on their way to school in places like Hebron/ Al-Khalil. I see them mourning the loss of their parents, friends, cousins, and families. I see them mourning the loss of limbs. And I see them becoming journalists on TikTok and Instagram. I see their anger, their pain, and their resistance.

I see that their open-air prison is also full of love and belonging and schools and libraries and football games and beaches and toys and fun. I see them painting and drawing on the rubbled walls of their former homes, making worlds out of nothing. I see a "place of a million plots and a thousand narratives; where fear is the norm and joy is loud, raucous, and unapologetic; where amputees are more commonplace than washing machines and spent tear-gas grenades are used as strawberry pots."[14]

Rebecca Belmore, *At Pelican Falls* (detail), 2017. Collection of the artist.

These children in Gaza are practicing seeing through the stone of Israeli apartheid.

I am practicing seeing through the stone of colonial lies.

When the children of Gaza look up, do they see a sky that could eliminate them, or perhaps choke their lungs with smoke and debris from carpet bombing, or with white phosphorus?

> I grant you and the little ones refuge,
> the little ones who
> change the rocket's course
> before it lands
> with their smiles.[15]

The cage of spectacular violence Gazan children are living in and dreaming beyond is different from the cage that held the Anishinaabe children pictured in the photo at Pelican Falls, and from the cages holding Black and Brown children at the border.

Different and entwined.

Different and related.

Invaders   came back once again,
                      claimed the land

with   fists and fire excuses beliefs
          of the chosen and the promised
          as if God is a real-estate agent.[16]

Related through love of land, family, and culture. Related through rivers and seas, springs and trees, as long as the grass grows and the sun shines.

Related through invaders, "as if God is a real estate agent."

In her book *Undrowned*, Alexis Pauline Gumbs tells us that dolphin mothers sing to their babies while they are in the womb and after they are born so that the babies can learn their names: a way of recognizing their belonging and connection to their kin, the ones that will protect and take care of them.[17] She tells us the rest of the pod gathers quietly to support this process. I think of the baby dolphins listening through their womb home to a world they cannot yet see and perhaps cannot even imagine, hearing through stone. Learning to cut through the noise of boat traffic and capitalism to hear the frequency of belonging.

With this dolphin love story lodged in our hearts, Gumbs goes on in true Black feminist form to connect dolphin birth to captive birth, a carceral practice taking place daily in the United States and Canada, where the state shackles incarcerated people giving birth and apprehends their babies almost immediately. Gumbs

Taloi Havini, *Beroana (shell money)*, 2015. Stoneware, earthenware, porcelain, glaze, and steel wire, dimensions variable. Edition of 5. Collection of Kadist, USA, Sharjah Art Foundation, and Queensland Art Gallery.

links this, in turn, to young asylum seekers separated from their parents in cages at the border, and the over five million American children with parents in prison. This connects us to the hundreds of thousands of Indigenous and Black children apprehended by the state and placed in care.[18] It connects us to Palestinian children martyred in Gaza, walking through checkpoints in Al-Khalil, held in jails without charges in the West Bank, or displaced with their families in the diaspora.

In November 2023, I traveled to Australia to visit with Indigenous peoples who have another, related experience of colonialism and slavery. I arrived in Meanjin [Brisbane], in Yugara Country, after a long transpacific flight, to attend a day of the Sisters Inside Conference. I didn't have much time in Meanjin, and so the first thing I did after dropping off my belongings at the hotel was walk to the Queensland Art Gallery to see *sis: Pacific Art 1980–2023*, a show celebrating the work of women artists from across the Pacific. I was there specifically to see a sculpture by Taloi Havini.

Havini is from the Nakas Tribe of the Hakö people and was born in Arawa in the Autonomous Region of Bougainville. As a child, she was exiled with her family to Australia, a result of her parents' political organizing toward independence in the face of the destruction of their homeland from copper mining by the multinational Rio Tinto Company and the government of Papua New Guinea. In *sis*, Havini exhibited her 2015 sculpture *Beroana (shell money)*, a stunning visual depiction of the Hakö economy.

On entering the gallery, I saw a huge fragile spiral suspended from the ceiling, though it appeared to start at a single point near the floor and flow upward to the sky. The sculpture references the shell-based currency that Havini's people used and still use to trade with each other in a horizontal economy that privileges care and interdependence over wealth—or perhaps *as* wealth. Havini used stoneware to make replicas of this currency by hand and then strung the replicas together like beads, creating a visual representation of an exchange economy governed by individual and collective self-determination and deep reciprocity.

Experiencing *Beroana*, I felt grounded. I had a sense that I was part of something bigger than myself, experiencing economy as belonging, as a spiral pulling me out of myself and weaving into the cosmos. I was reminded that Indigenous economic practices are not a hoarding of materials and resources for the few; rather, they are a connected spiral, forming a permeable container that is expansive and responsive and designed to meet the needs of all living things. I got a sense, standing there, that my existence is part of an intimate network within my immediate environment, connected, even across vast oceans and distances, to others.

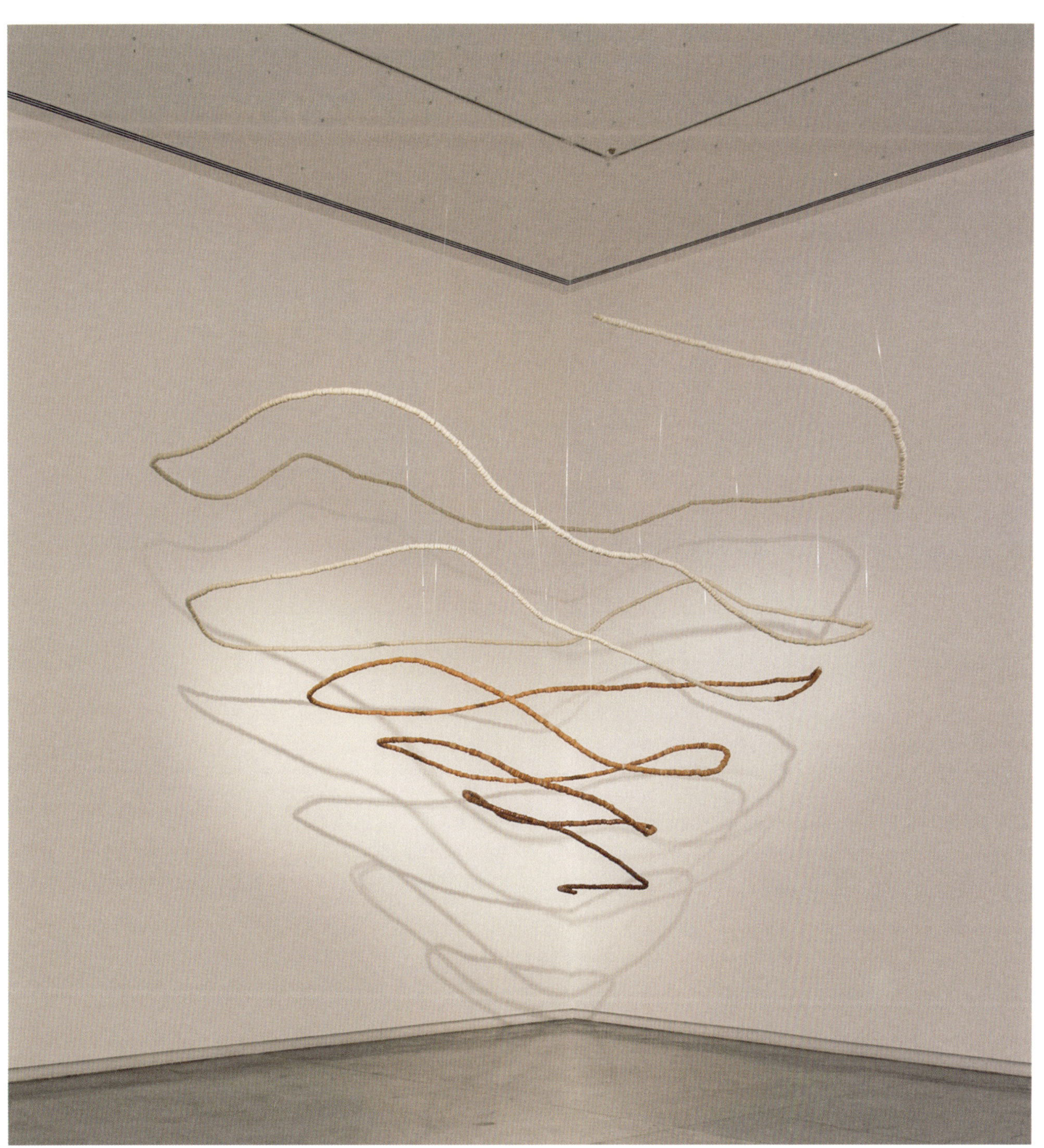

Together we spiral upward toward the sky, through difference becoming the planet and the cosmos.

In this sculpture, in this economy, in the Hakö world these practices built, there is no stone to see through.

In the world Havini and her people continue to build, putting children into cages at borders and in schools is unthinkable. Relentlessly bombing children and their families is unspeakable. Incarcerating children indefinitely and without charges is horrific. Birth is not a medical event but a ceremony, as life passes through one realm to another. The singing of parents to babies is sacred. The laughter of children playing on the beach at Beit Lahia or in Cape Town or on Manhattan Beach or at Pelican Falls is the result of cultures and politics that cherish their joy and freedom.

Colonialism is about severing relationships—to each other, to our lands, to hope, and to our futures. In its faceless face, I'm gathering the dolphins, the beautiful olive saplings, the Nigigoonsiwag, the children apprehended at all of the borders, and these *beroana* into Chi'Niibish's stone canoe, and together, along with the artists and curators in *Seeing through Stone*, we will dream and build worlds where we'll call the aesthetics of abolition normal, and we'll no longer have to vision liberation, because we'll be living it and it will be all that we know.

1. There is a written version of this story in Gidigaa Migizi (Doug Williams), *This Is Our Territory* (Winnipeg, Canada: ARP Books, 2018).

2. See Madeline Whetung, "At the Shore: Everyday Anti-violences and the Practice of Queer Creation in Michi Saagiig Nishnaabeg Territory" (PhD diss., University of British Columbia, Vancouver, BC, 2023).

3. See Susan Hill, *The Clay We Are Made Of: Haudenosaunee Land Tenure on the Grand River* (Winnipeg, Canada: University of Manitoba Press, 2017), for an account of the Peacemaker and the Great Law of Peace.

4. See Leanne Betasamosake Simpson, *As We Have Always Done: Indigenous Freedom through Radical Resistance* (Minneapolis: University of Minnesota Press, 2017), ch. 9.

5. Jessica Jacobson-Konefall tells us that Belmore's relationship to the photo shifted after a conversation with John Macfie, who took the photo. Macfie had been friends with Belmore's dad. During their conversation, Belmore learned that Macfie was out fishing on the river with his wife when he took this photo of the boys on the rock.

Placing the image in the context of a friendship between Macfie and Belmore's dad adds another layer of meaning to the work. Jessica Jacobson-Konefall, "Radiant Archives: Rebecca Belmore's *At Pelican Falls* by Dr. Jessica Jacobson-Konefall," Platform Centre, n.d., https://soundcloud.com /user-58689969/radiant-archives -rebecca-belmores-at-pelican-falls -by-dr-jessica-jacobson-konefall.

6. Jacobson-Konefall, "Radiant Archives."

7. Nishnawbe Aski Nation, "The Davin Report, 1879," accessed March 11, 2024, http://rschools .nan.on.ca/article/the-davin -report-1879–1120.asp.

8. For one example, see Jorge Barrera, "The Horrors of St. Anne's," *CBC News*, March 29, 2018, https://newsinteractives.cbc.ca /longform/st-anne-residential -school-opp-documents/. For testimonials from Pelican Falls Indian Residential School, see survivor Garnet Angeconeb's video account at Garnet's Journey: From Residential School to Reconciliation, https://garnetsjourney.com /chapters/residential-school/.

9. For one example, see Dirk Meissner, "Work to Exhume Remains at Former Kamloops Residential School Could Begin Soon, Chief Says," *CBC News*, May 20, 2022, https://www.cbc.ca/news/canada/british-columbia/tk-eml%C3%BAps-kamloops-indian-residential-school-215-exhumations-1.6460796.

10. National Centre for Truth and Reconciliation, University of Manitoba, "Pelican Lake (Pelican Falls)," National Student Memorial Register, https://nctr.ca/residential-schools/ontario/pelican-lake-pelican-falls/.

11. Ian Adams, "The Lonely Death of Chanie Wenjack," *Maclean's*, February 1, 1967, https://macleans.ca/society/the-lonely-death-of-chanie-wenjack/.

12. Ry Moran, "Truth and Reconciliation Commission," in *The Canadian Encyclopedia*, September 24, 2015, last modified October 5, 2020, https://www.thecanadianencyclopedia.ca/en/article/truth-and-reconciliation-commission.

13. Al Jazeera English, "Palestinian Children Plead for Protection in Gaza Press Conference," November 8, 2023, YouTube video, 01:10 minutes, https://www.youtube.com/watch?v=zLxHBRPLzow.

14. Sarah Wilkinson, foreword to *My Lover Was a Freedom Fighter*, by Rana Shubair (n.p.: SkyLimit Press, 2019), vii. Rana Shubair, a mother, author, and English teacher, was martyred by Israeli air strikes on December 1, 2023.

15. From Hiba Abu Nada, "I Grant You Refuge," trans. Huda Fakhreddine, *Protean Magazine* online, November 3, 2023, https://proteanmag.com/2023/11/03/i-grant-you-refuge/. A Palestinian poet, novelist, and teacher, Hiba Abu Nada wrote the poem on October 10, 2023. It is among the last pieces she composed before being martyred by an Israeli air strike on October 20. Huda Fakhreddine translated the poem from the original Arabic.

16. Mohammed El-Kurd, "Rifqa," in *Rifqa* (Chicago: Haymarket Books, 2021).

17. Alexis Pauline Gumbs, *Undrowned: Black Feminist Lessons from Marine Mammals* (Chico, CA: AK Press, 2020), 34.

18. For Indigenous children in Canada, that number is higher than at the height of the residential school system. Teresa Wright, "Foster Care Is Modern-Day Residential School System: Inuk MP Mumilaaq Qaqqaq," *CBC News*, June 4, 2021, https://www.cbc.ca/news/politics/foster-care-is-modern-day-residential-school-1.6054223.

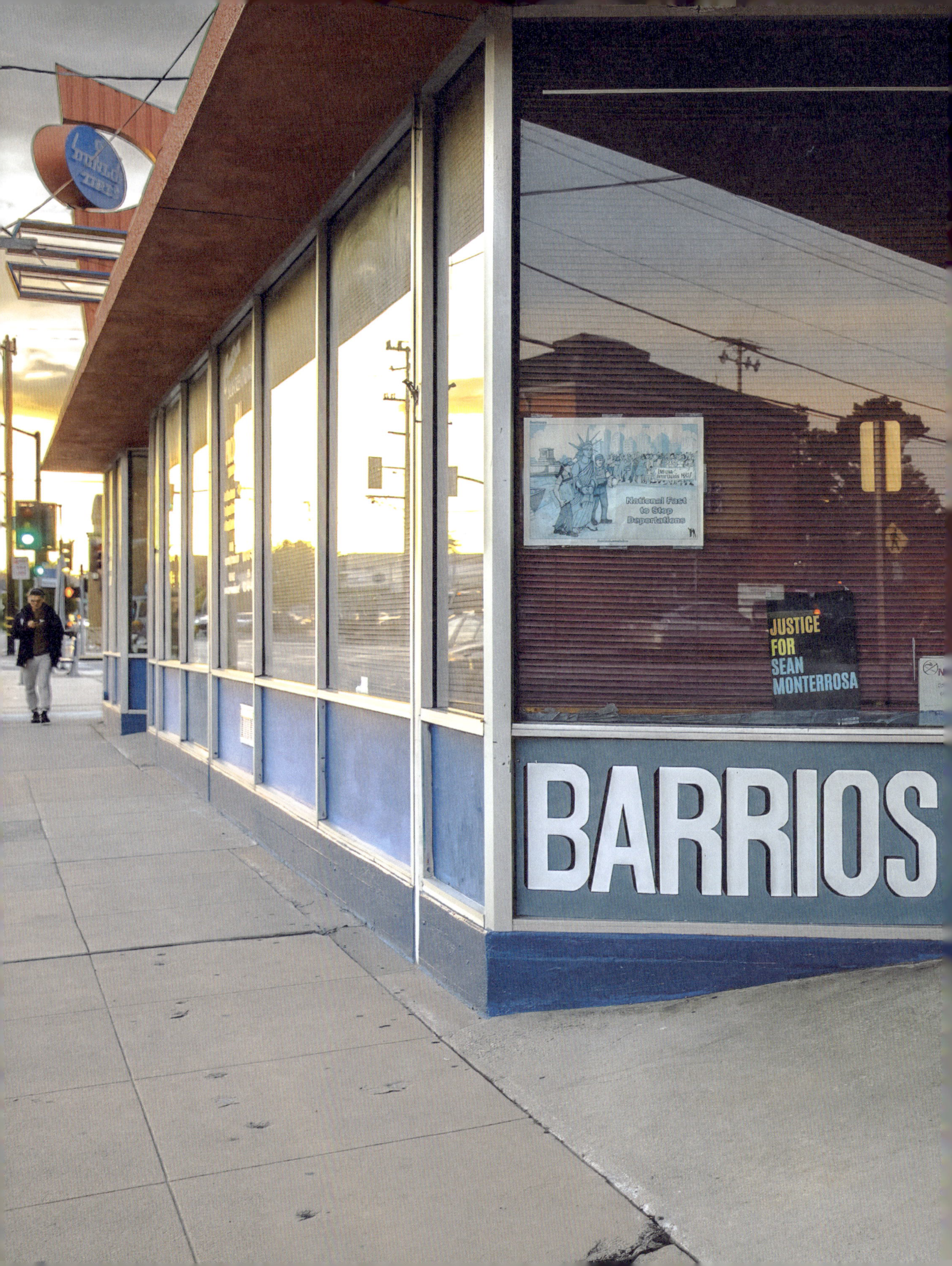

National Fast
to Stop
Deportations
JUSTICE
FOR
SEAN
MONTERROSA
BARRIOS

Abolition, Art, and Healing:
A Conversation with Nane Alejandrez

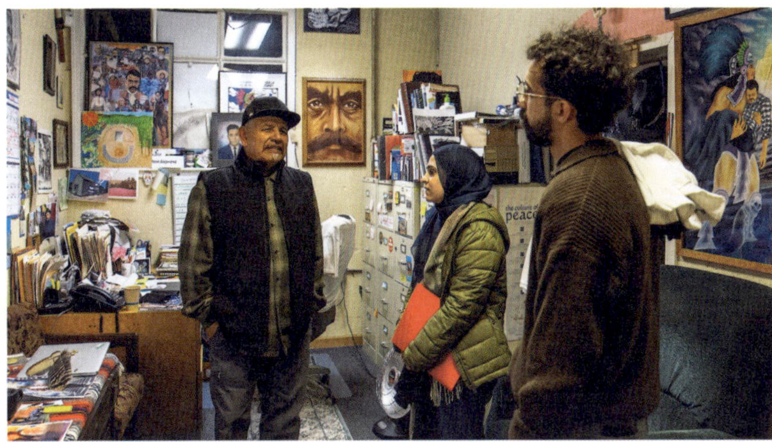

Nane Alejandrez speaks to artists at Santa Cruz Barrios Unidos, 2024.

Nane Alejandrez is the founder and executive director of Santa Cruz Barrios Unidos, a nonprofit organization dedicated to nonviolence and the end of incarceration. Founded in 1977, Barrios Unidos (referred to in this interview as SCBU) grew out of the civil rights movements of the 1960s and 1970s. The organization promotes the end of interpersonal, community, and structural violence by providing culturally driven and spiritually informed services to youth and adults. In all aspects of Nane Alejandrez's work at SCBU, he emphasizes the importance of art and culture in creating a world of peace that is just for all.

Rachel Nelson: Nane, we are truly grateful that you have offered up space at Barrios Unidos for *Seeing through Stone*, joining the Institute of the Arts and Sciences and San José Museum of Art as venues for the exhibition. Given the exhibition's orientation toward visions of a world without prisons, Gina Dent, Lauren Dickens, and I recognize the importance of centering the work that you are doing at SCBU to create that world. Can you tell me about how SCBU started?

Nane Alejandrez: In 1971, I had just come back from Vietnam, from the war. And I stepped into Fresno, California, and it was like there was another war, a street war. It was a time when we were seeing a big increase in violence in the streets. And in 1975, eleven members

of my family went to prison at the same time. I became like a transportation coordinator for my family, driving people all over the state. When I went to school at UC Santa Cruz, my wife, Jenny Alejandrez, and I were living in family housing, and we began talking about how to end the violence and fight against mass incarceration. Barrios Unidos really started in our apartment at UCSC. We came up with the idea for the name, Barrios Unidos, which means "United Neighborhoods," and for the first fifteen years we operated as a volunteer organization, selling T-shirts and burritos to fund the work.

We've always followed the philosophies of Cesar Chavez and Martin Luther King. Cesar Chavez told us to hold the land, because land is very important—you have to have a base to fight from. As Chavez put it, [we've] got to create all these little islands throughout the state, throughout the nation.

So now we have a headquarters, a center in Santa Cruz, and we offer reentry services; a juvenile transition program; after-school programming; the Prison Project, which supports people inside prisons and jails; a food pantry; a recording studio; a screenprinting shop; and other programs.

We also have five acres in the hills of Aptos [California] that we use as a retreat center. We got this land because we were having sweat lodge ceremonies and trying to learn more about our Indigenous culture. We

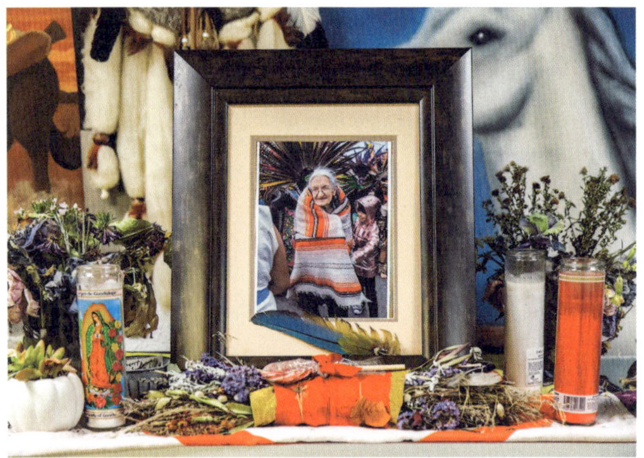

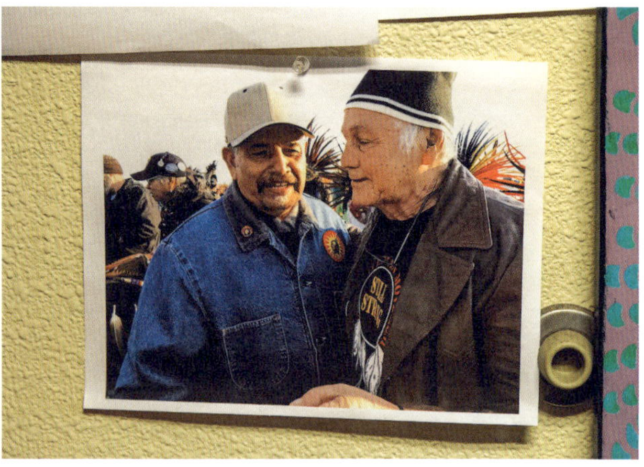

would go to a place to hold the ceremonies, but then the owners were always like, "Hey, you have too many people," or "The fire is dangerous." They didn't understand the ceremony. So we decided we needed to get our own place.

We believe in and want the abolition of all prisons. But until then, we have to be active, going into prisons and creating positive programs that are going to help our brothers and sisters come out. And when they come out, we have to develop programs to help them so that they don't go back. We understand it's very hard. People are coming out with $200 to their name after twenty-five, thirty years spent inside. Some of these individuals have done such a long, long time that they have to get used to a lot of things—like technology, driving a car, making payments. They have to re-educate themselves, and we have to be prepared to help. The community has to be prepared to welcome them back home, not only financially, but with an understanding of where they've been, so that they can succeed.

RN: SCBU is filled with murals and artworks. And as you mentioned, there is a recording studio, and I know there are regular poetry readings, concerts, and other cultural events. Can you talk about why art and culture is important to the work you do?

NA: I have met some of the greatest writers, artists, and musicians inside prisons. And I have seen how artists approach life and create the change that they want. With images or [through] songs or poetry, art has a big impact. It gives us [messages] of pain, of endurance, of resilience, and of love. Love is very hard to talk about in prison, but through the arts, you can see the love that people are showing. I can feel it through the smell of coffee coming off the drawing that I just received from the Pelican Bay security housing unit, for instance, or in the jelly beans that are used for color and give off the aroma of flowers.

We're going into an era of politics where all the gains that we've gotten throughout the last twenty years, they're in jeopardy. We've seen what has already happened to some of the national policies because of the Supreme Court. So art is more important than ever, because art helps. I don't know how to draw, but I do create things. We made a replica of the Pelican Bay security housing unit, and we bring it to different places to let people know—people who from within the prison system [would be referred] to as civilians— what is happening on the inside. We want to educate civilians, including the families of people in prisons, about what their sons or daughters have experienced. If you've been twenty-five to thirty years in the security housing unit, and then they let you out, often your

Altar and memento at Santa Cruz
Barrios Unidos, 2024.

family can't relate to you, and you can't relate to your family. Lots of families, they know the courtroom, and they know the visiting room. So we wanted to give them an experience of what it was to be inside a cell for twenty-three hours a day with no sunlight. Art allows that. And it allows us to start the conversation. And it's been really powerful. Guys that have been inside have gone into the replica and cried, because it brings up a lot of emotions.

RN: As you are describing it, art can be educational and also a source of healing—both at the individual and community level. I know that healing is an important part of the work of SCBU, and, as you mentioned, that's why you have started a retreat center. How do you define "healing"?

NA: Our approach to healing is to bring what we call the medicine to people inside, which is really just bringing humanity. To be able to go into an institution and hug a brother or sister and say, "I love you, brother. I love you, sister." This starts to break down all that hate the prison system creates. And when you start to undo that—and it can take years and years and years— then the medicine takes effect, and people become peace warriors. Nate Williams, who did thirty-two years in prison and was one of the first juveniles tried as an

adult, says, "You bring the medicine; it's up to us to take it." For Nate, the medicine has taken effect, and he is taking it back into the institutions, into juvenile facilities, and to people coming back.

To shed a tear in prison is to change that whole stereotype of "if you cry, you're weak." I've cried with a lot of men inside, and I also have cried for them out here. It is important to carry that message that it's OK to cry; tears are healing also. That's deep, deep healing, when we start to look at ourselves and others, and to begin to deal with what happened, what people experienced when they were children. What did they see?

We're on Ohlone lands, and we now have more land than the original Ohlone people here did. So we know it's not our land—we're just the caretakers of it. We have five acres in the mountains where we have sweat lodges, outdoor kitchens, outdoor classrooms, tree houses, and we have our ceremonial grounds. And that's where a lot of change has happened and a lot of healing is done.

RN: All the things that SCBU does—from feeding folks to providing housing to the healing work you are describing—this is abolition in practice. Many people think that the abolition movement is about just tearing things down. However, we know it is really about

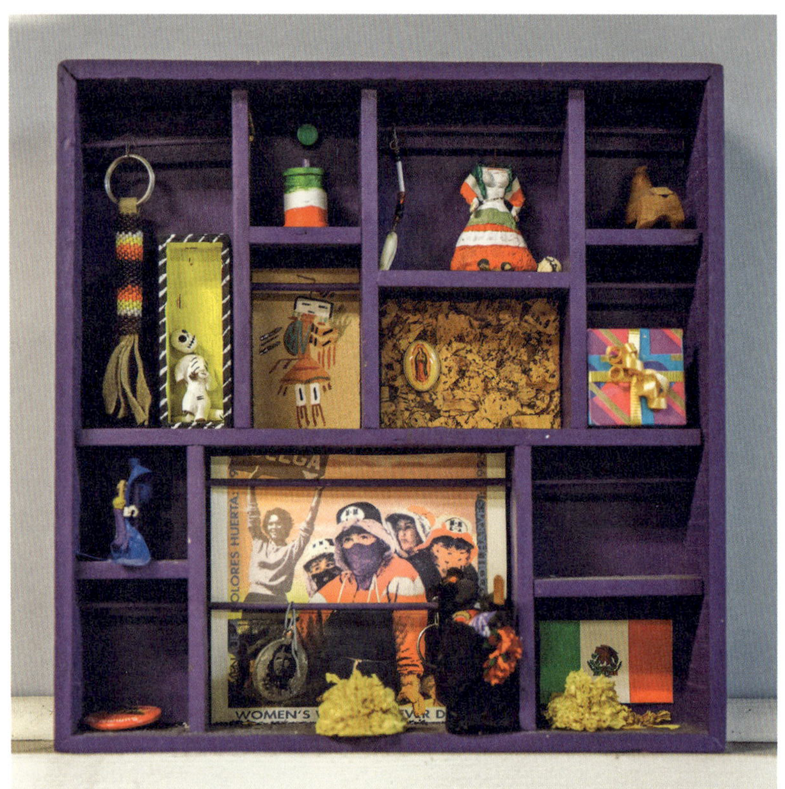

Altar and quilt at Santa Cruz
Barrios Unidos, 2024.

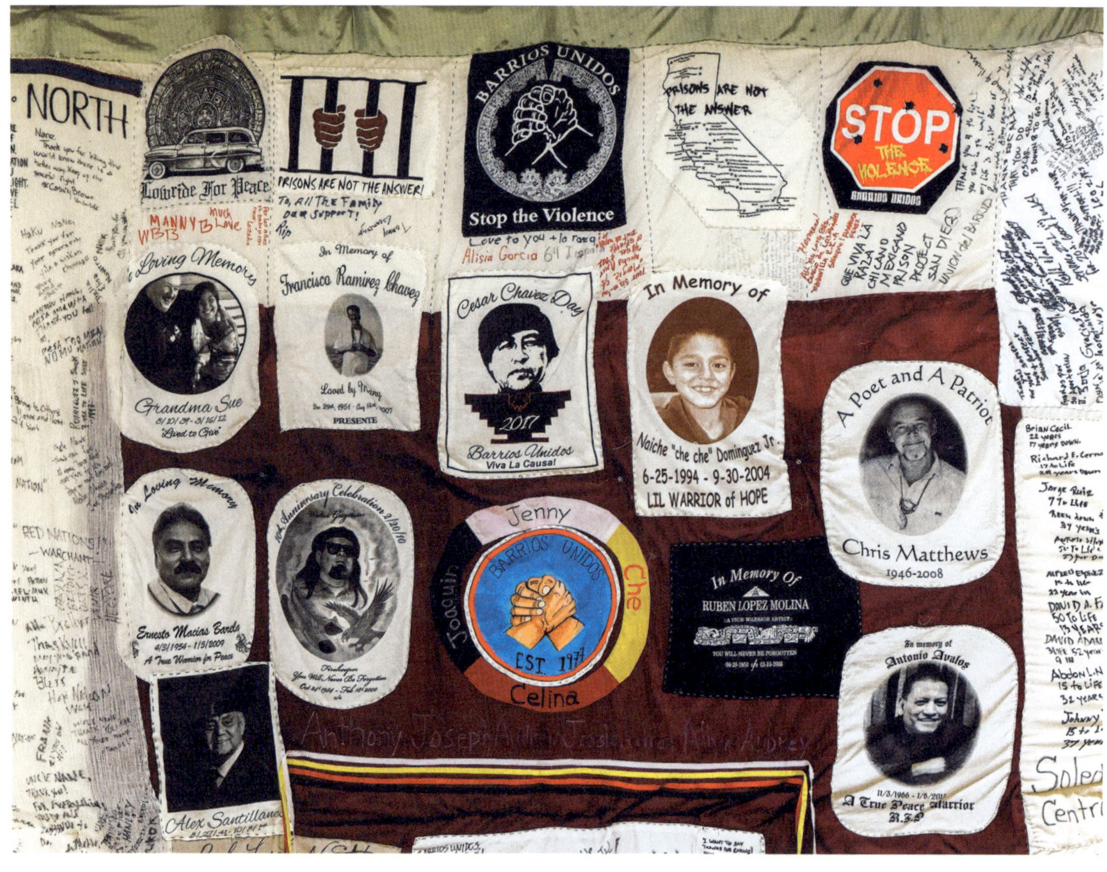

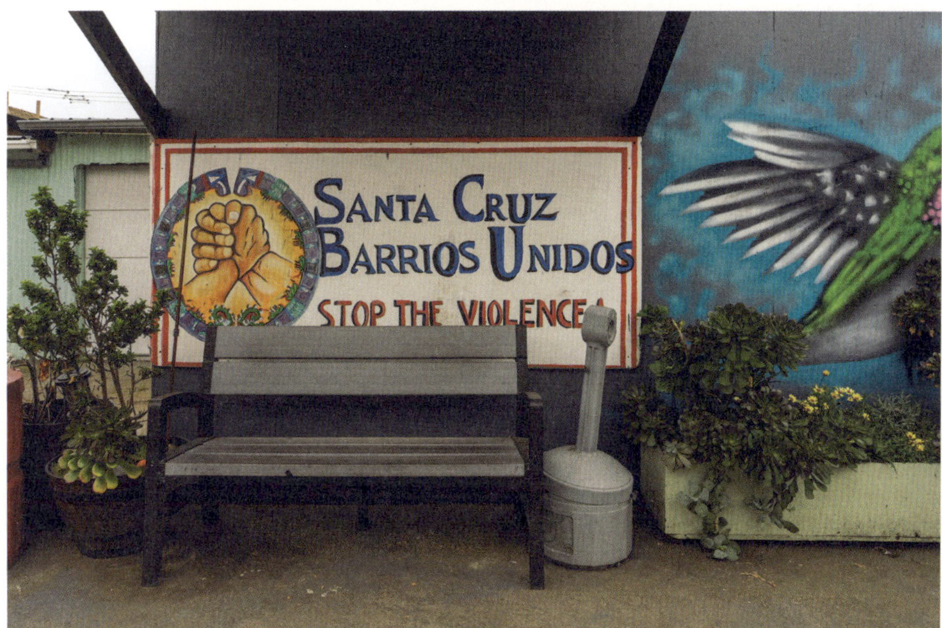

Mural outside of Santa Cruz Barrios Unidos, 2024.

building things, and providing the social structures that make prisons unnecessary.

NA: When I think of abolition, I ask myself, "Why do we have prisons?" Having been in jail myself, I know that it is important that people take responsibility for their actions. And I have heard people say, "You know what, I'm glad they took me off the street because I would have hurt somebody, or I would have been dead by now." But what I keep thinking is that we have to ask how that person got into that place where they could hurt themselves or others in the first place.

We know that some of the things that we do really work at SCBU. I can see it. I always feel like we're in practice—how do we prepare for when there is no county jail and we have to take responsibility for our actions and the actions of our community? We are moving. We're like the turtle. We're slowly moving toward abolition. So you keep doing what you're doing. I'll keep doing what we're doing. And everybody else, we all move a little bit closer to abolition. At SCBU, we're not a fly-by-night organization. We've sustained some hits, but we are here. We're committed to this for life.

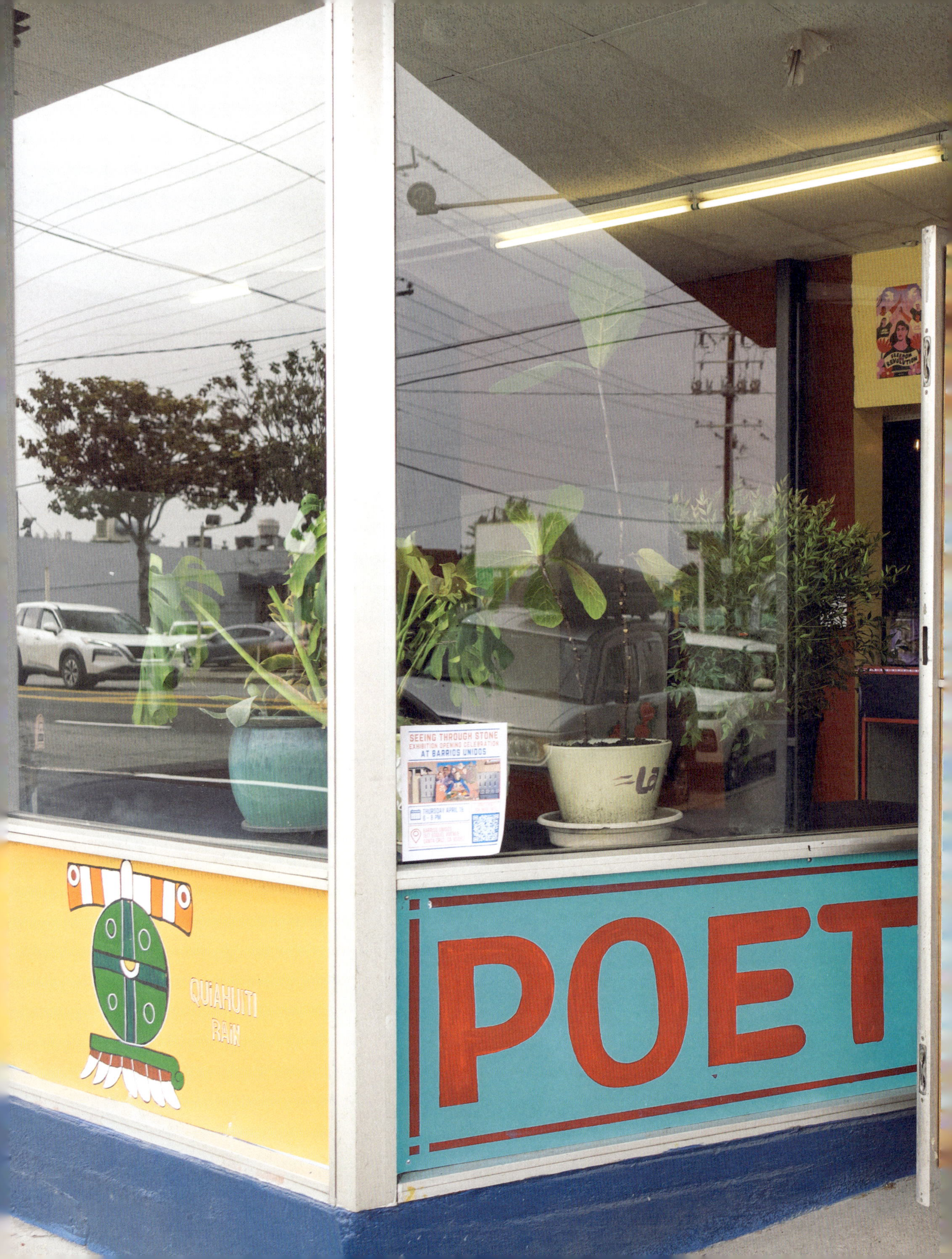

QUIAHUITL
RAIN
SEEING THROUGH STONE
EXHIBITION OPENING CELEBRATION
AT BARRIOS UNIDOS
THURSDAY APRIL 18
6 - 9 PM
POET

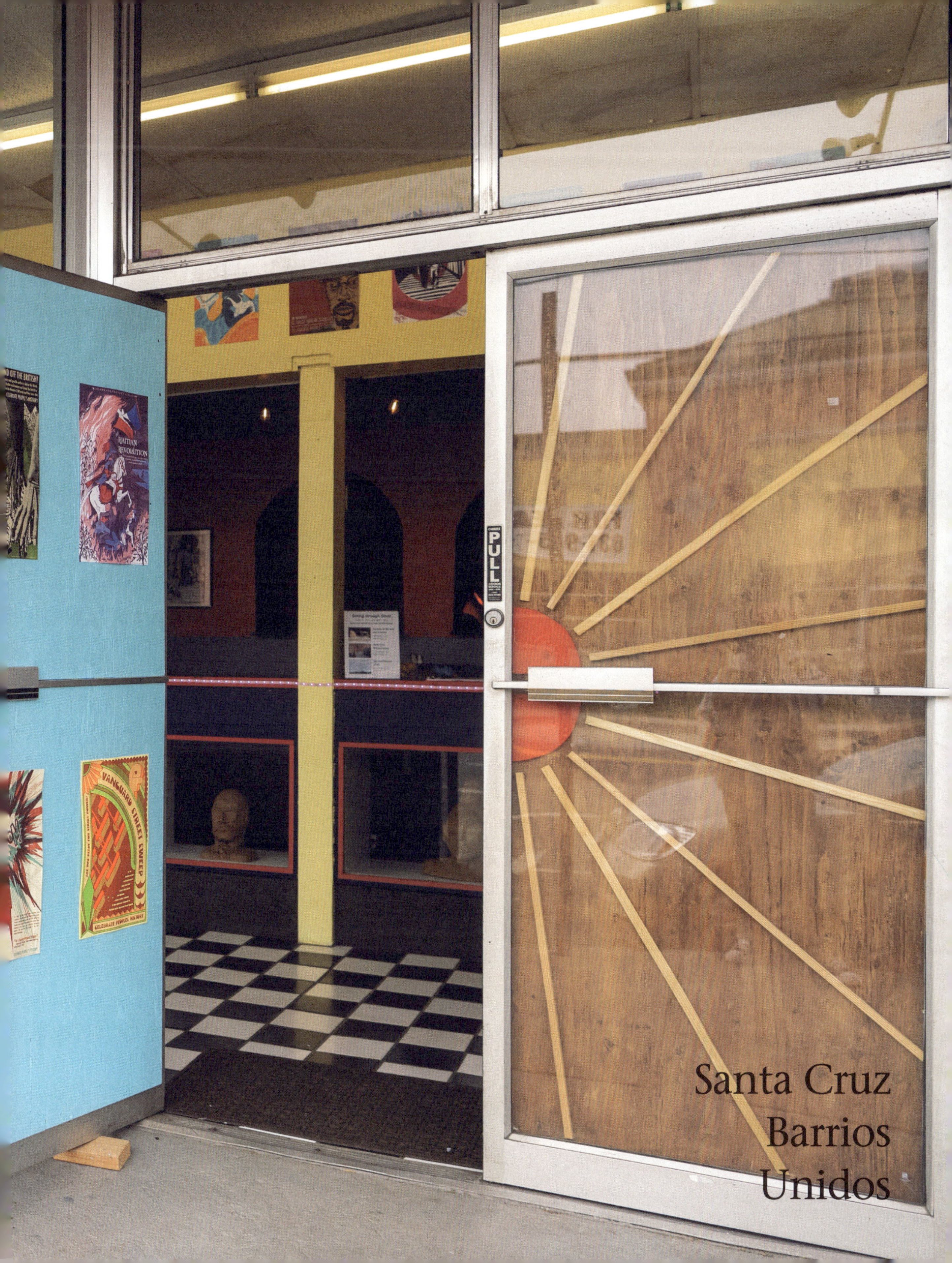

PULL
HAITIAN REVOLUTION
VANGUARD STREET SWEEP
Santa Cruz
Barrios
Unidos

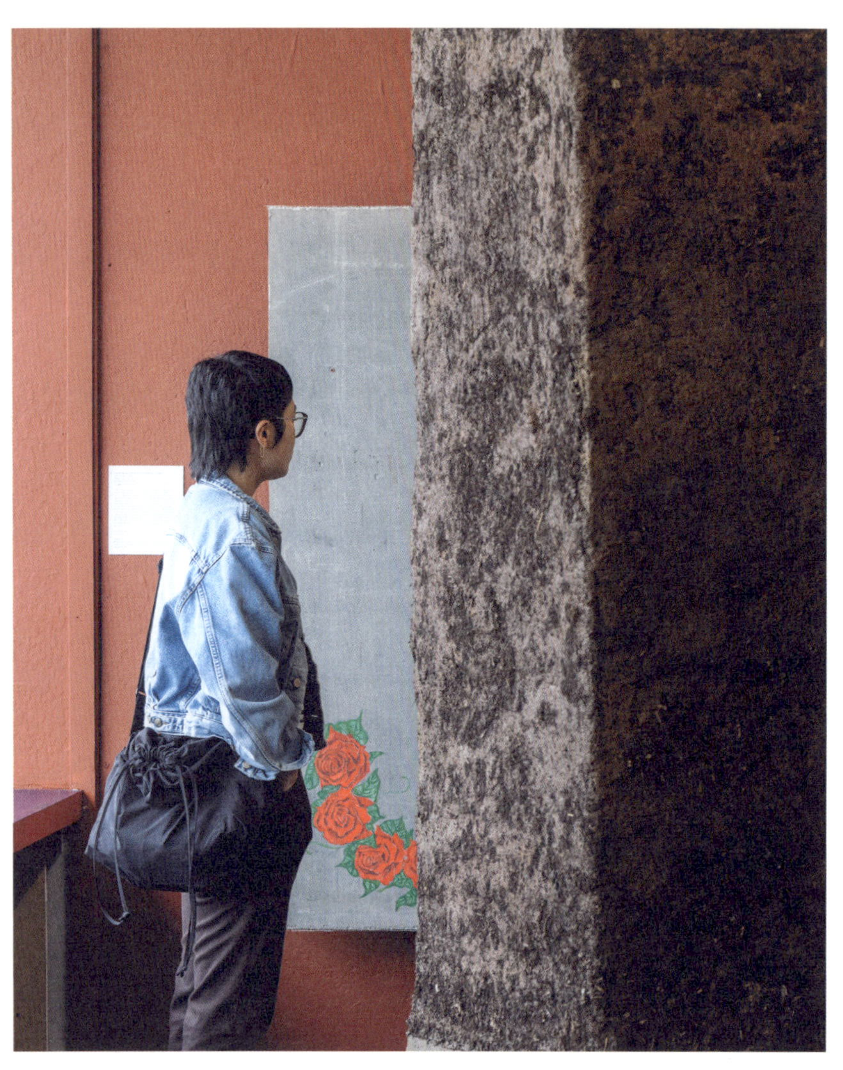

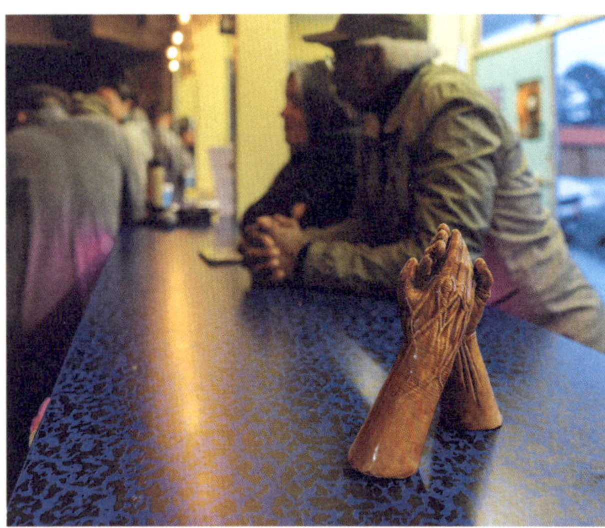

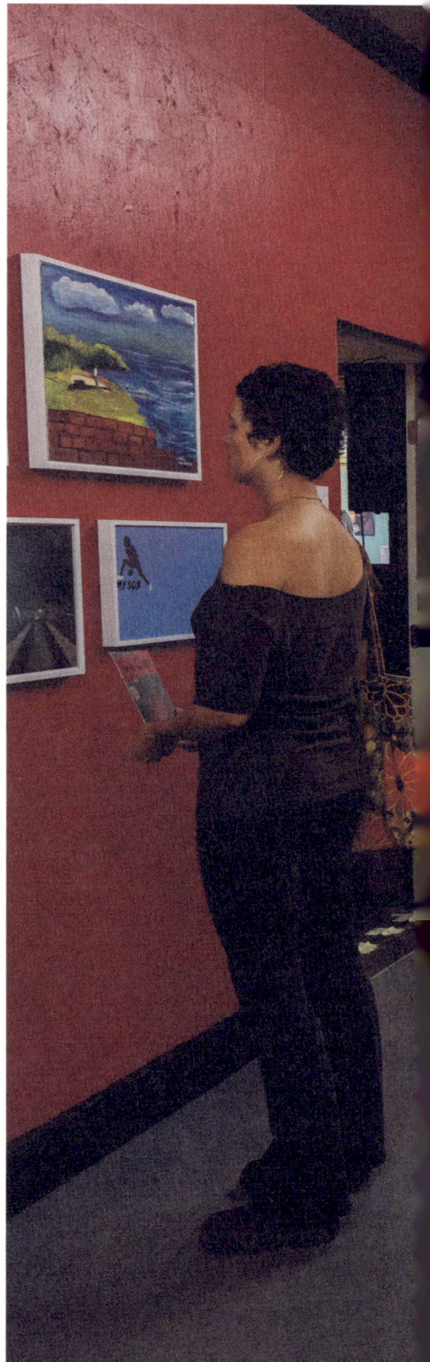

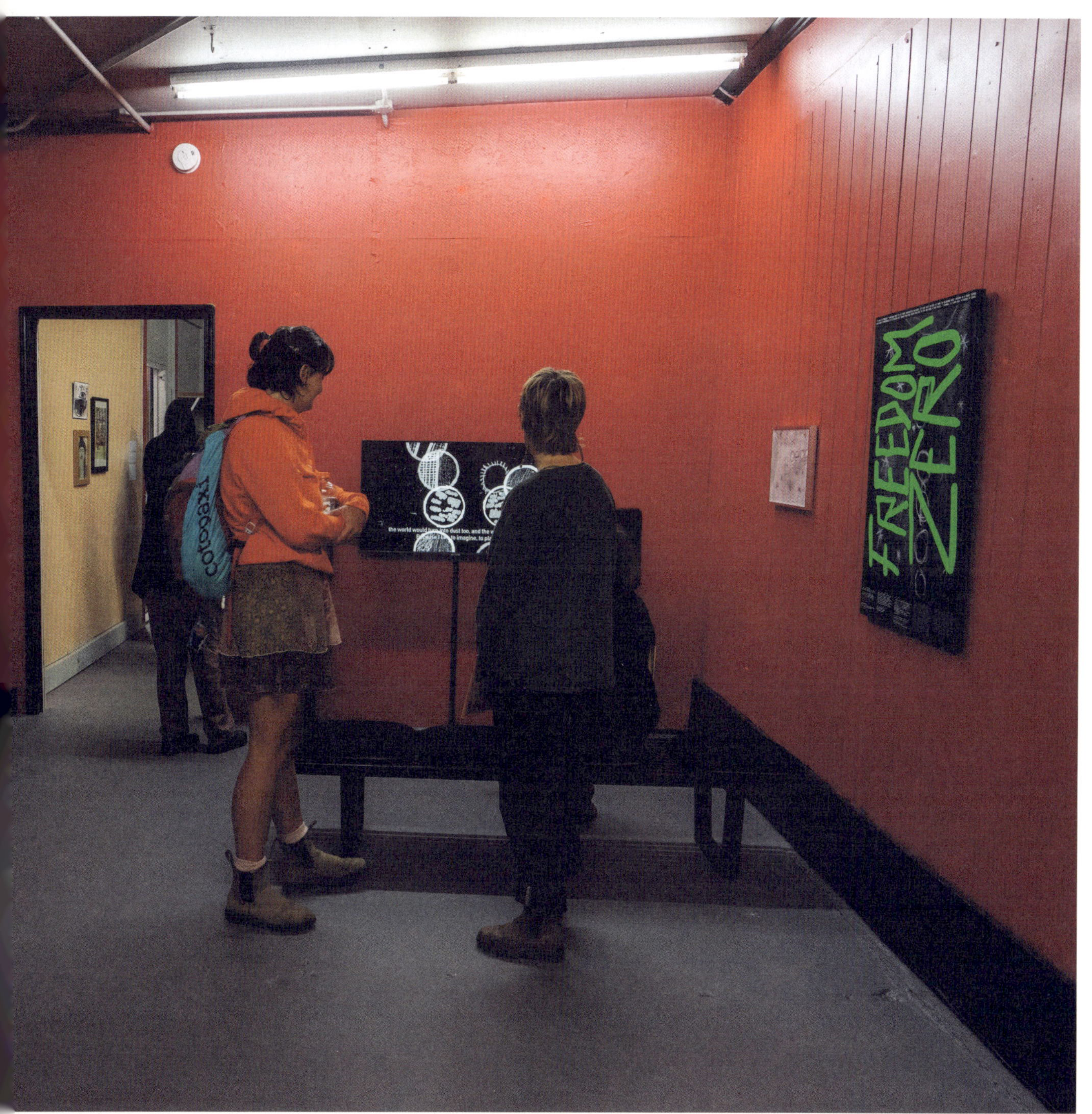

FREEDOM ZERO
the world would turn into dust too, and the
to imagine, to pla

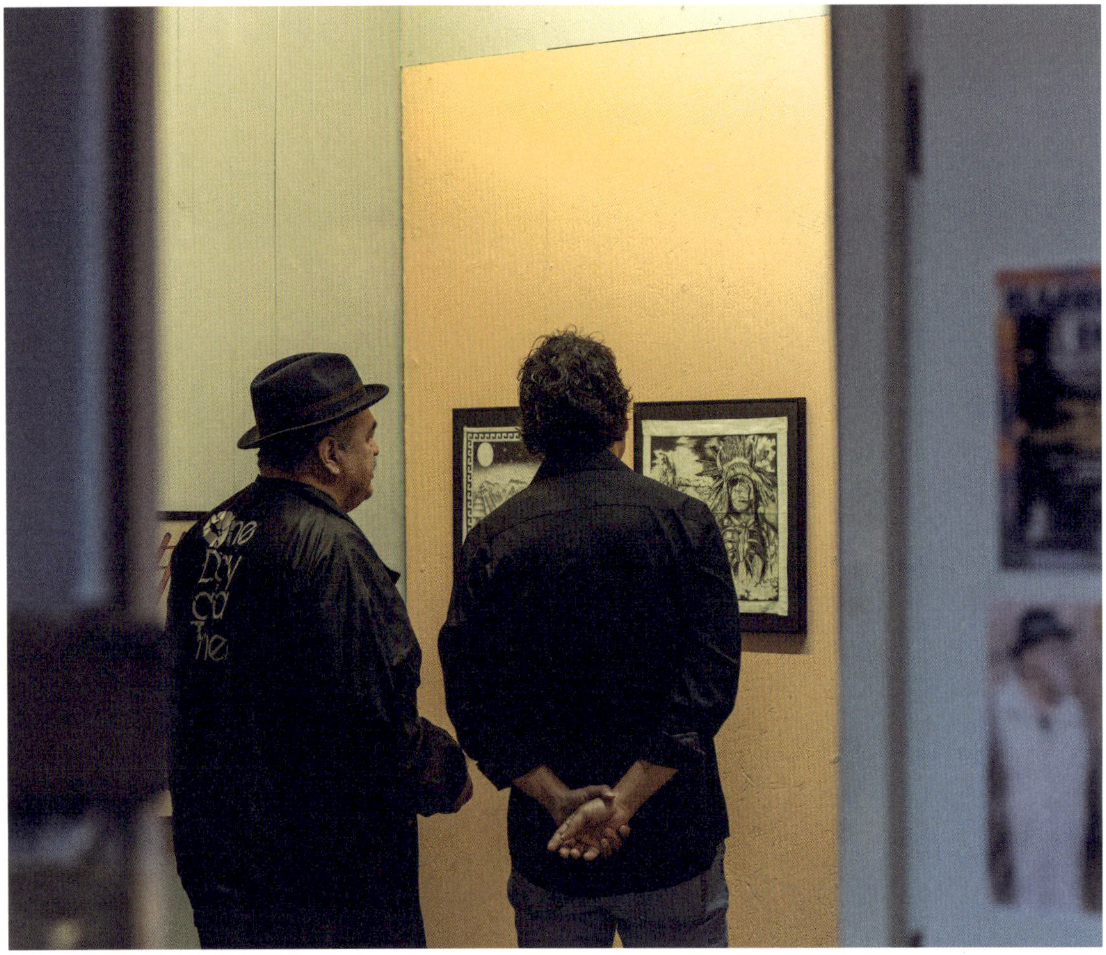

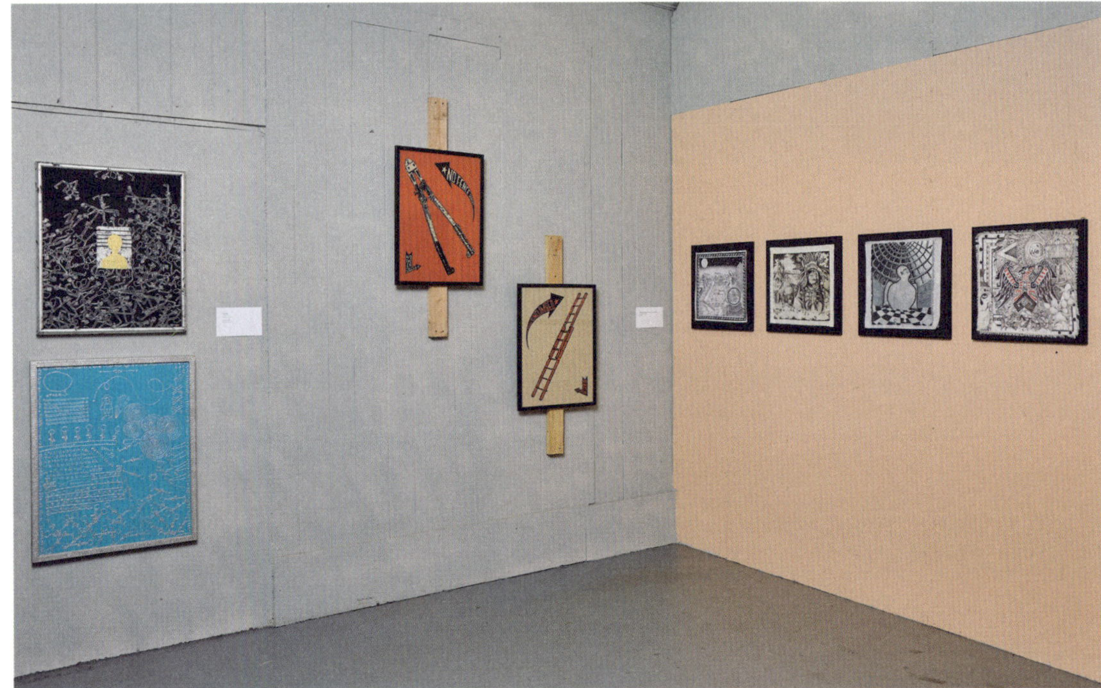

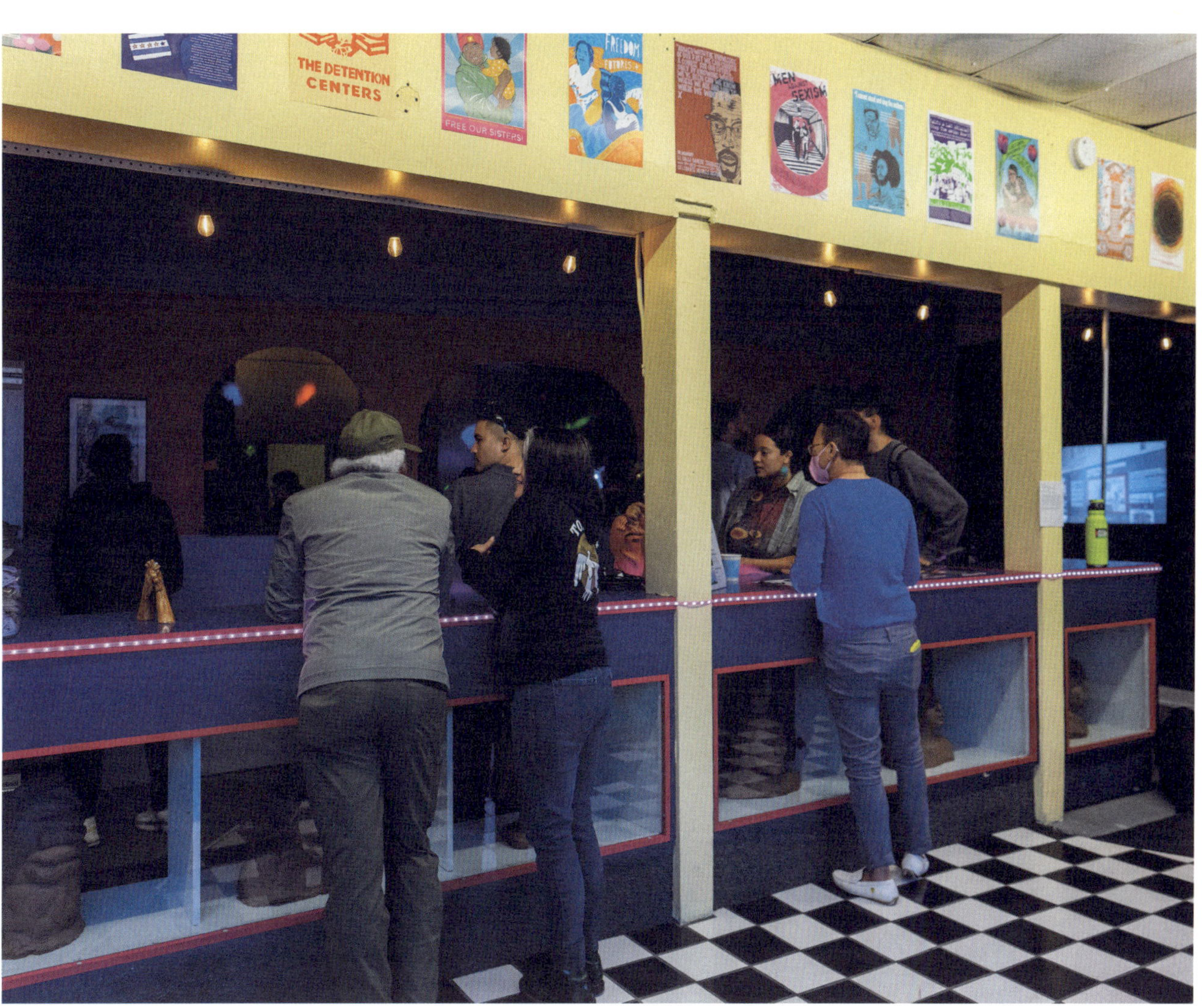
THE DETENTION
CENTERS
FREE OUR SISTERS!
FREEDOM
MEN
SEXISM

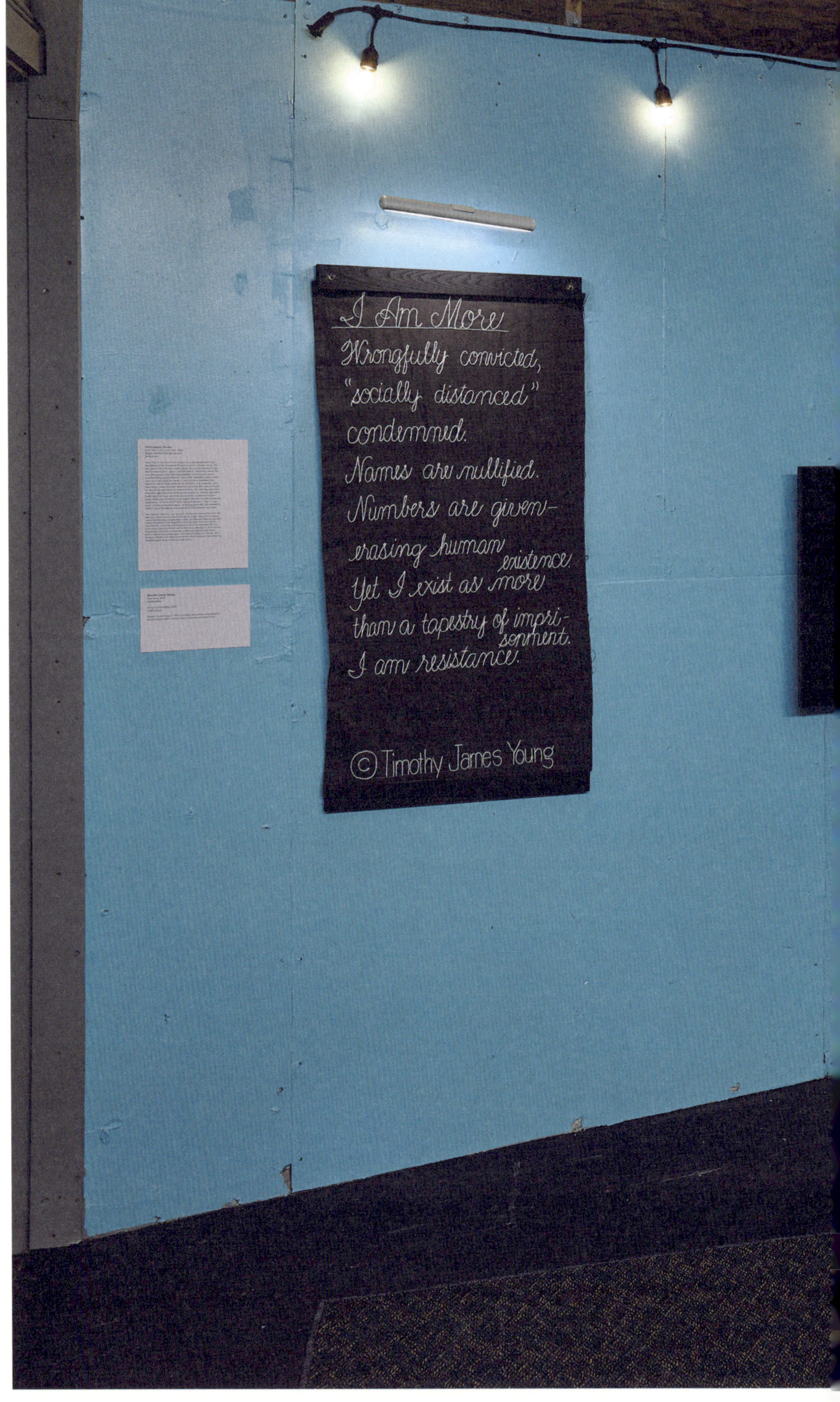

I Am More
Wrongfully convicted,
"socially distanced"
condemned.
Names are nullified.
Numbers are given—
erasing human
existence.
Yet I exist as more
than a tapestry of impri-
sonment.
I am resistance.

© Timothy James Young

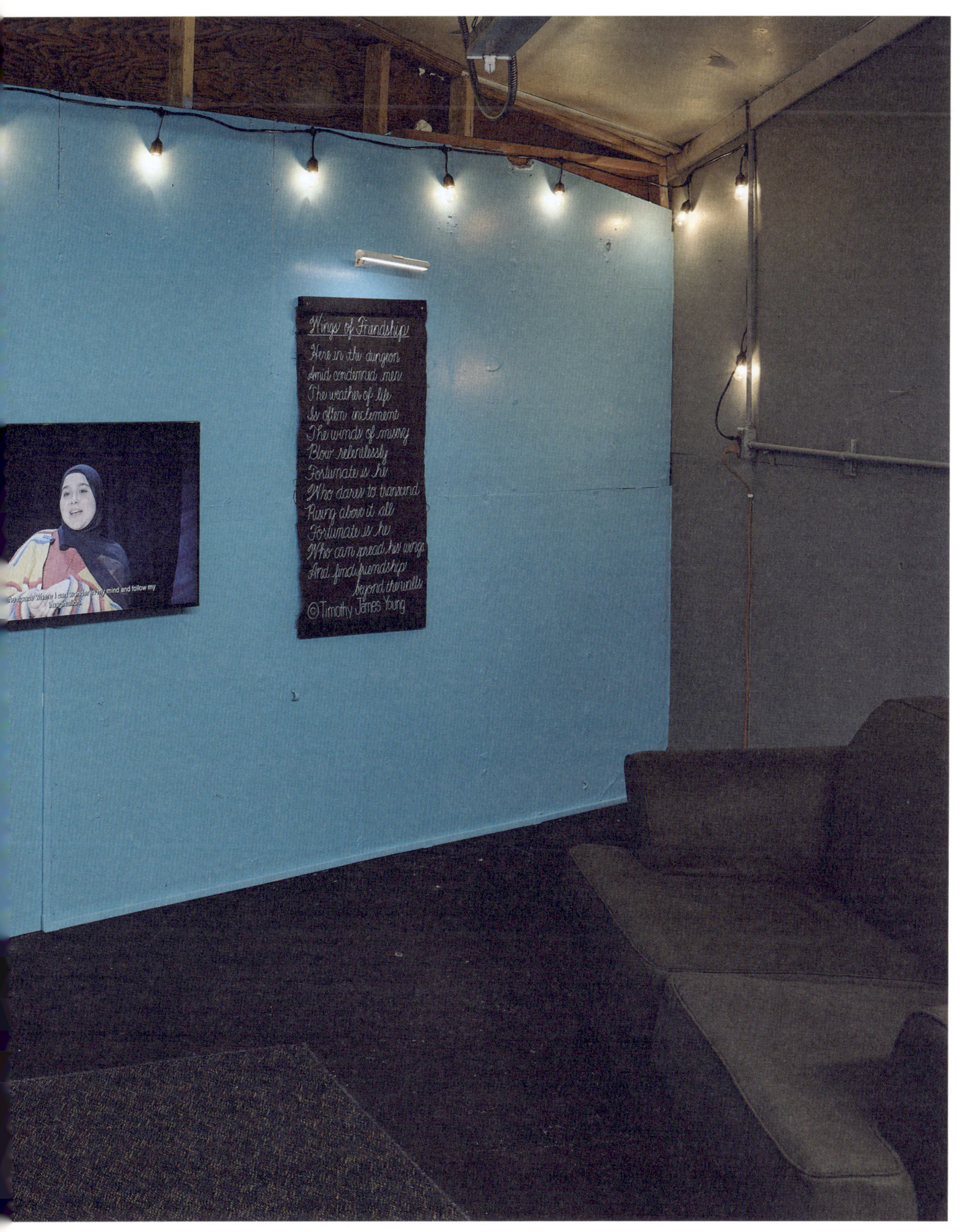

...the space where I can wonder in my mind and follow my imagination.
Wings of Friendship
Here in the dungeon
Amid condemned men
The weather of life
Is often inclement
The winds of misery
Blow relentlessly
Fortunate is he
Who dares to transcend
Rising above it all
Fortunate is he
Who can spread his wings
And find friendship
beyond the walls
©Timothy James Young

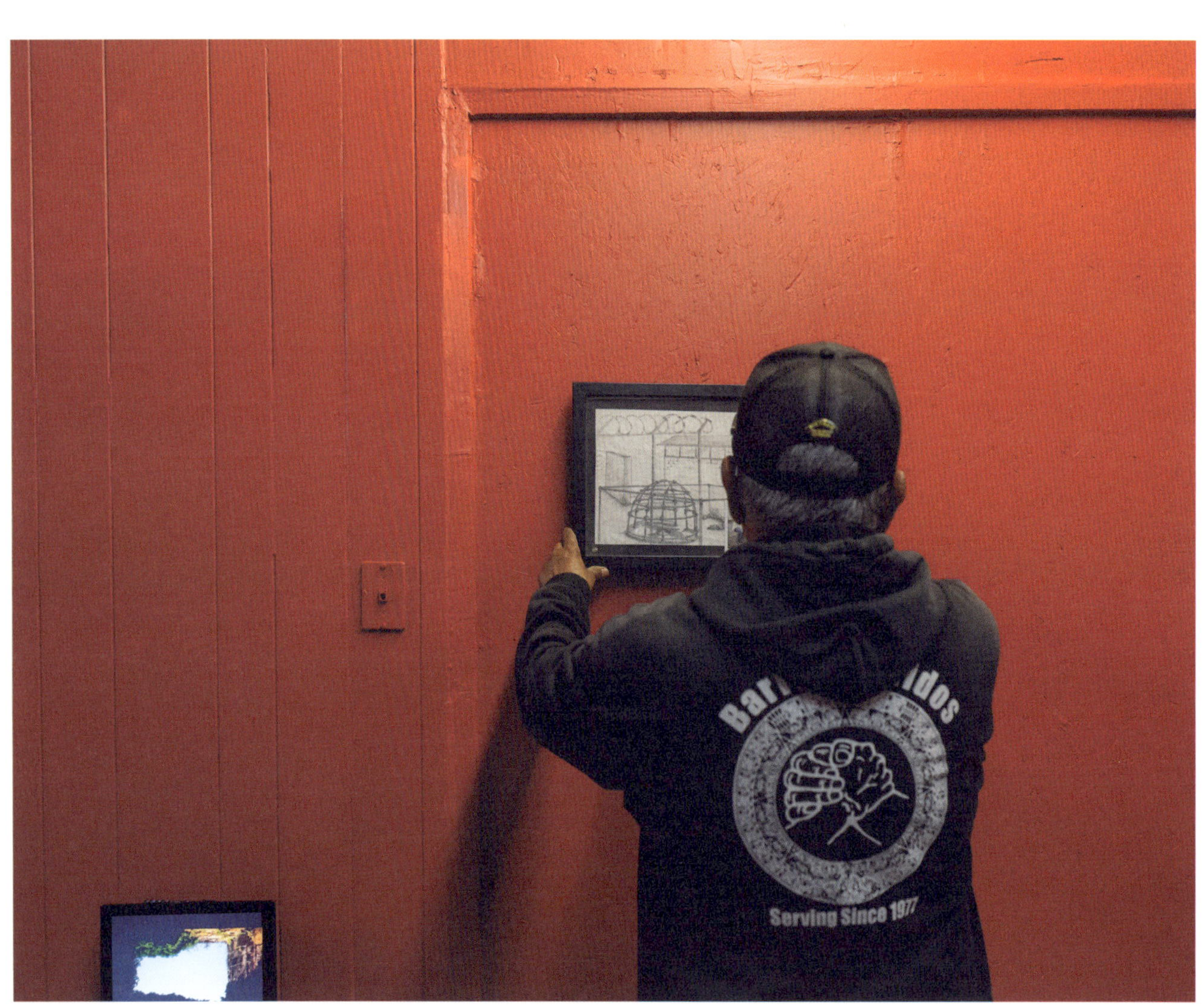
Serving Since 1977

In the Artists' Words

I'm an activist, and I'm a New Orleanian. And in New Orleans, we would never dream of organizing a march against the Iraq War or in solidarity with Palestine without a brass band. Our cultural practices are deeply political. For a long time, I've been experimenting with different ways of communicating complex information about the histories of extractivism to a broad public, whether through billboards, art installations, or different types of facilitation strategies, such as meetings and festivals.

The holes in the earth mirror the holes in our souls (and from them we can grow trees) is a video installation that is part of this pursuit for public visibility. Since 2020, I have been mapping companies' oil and gas infrastructure in Louisiana's wetlands to visualize how corporations are responsible for Louisiana's ecological collapse. I map rates of coastal erosion, which are the direct result of oil and gas extraction in the state, as well as the poisoning of Louisiana's human communities with carcinogenic emissions produced by the petrochemical plants and refineries, of which over two hundred exist along an eighty-five-mile stretch of land along the Mississippi River between Baton Rouge and New Orleans. These refineries, which account for 25 percent of the petrochemical production in the United States, occupy the formerly slave-powered sugarcane plantations in what the majority Black residents now call Cancer Alley. The industry refers to it as the petrochemical corridor. An examination of the infrastructure that I am trying to bring into visibility through mapping exercises enables an understanding of the ways in which the oil and gas industry quite literally stands on the foundations established by settler colonialism.

As I experiment with video and installation, I have also welcomed the opportunity to work in a more poetic voice. For instance, at some point, I noticed that the oil and gas configurations I mapped resemble geomechanical earthworks. They have very unique spatial signatures and look like uncanny symbols. I began staring at these constellations of pipelines, wells, and canals in my digital applications, similarly to how people stare at the skies and notice symbols in the stars, connecting them through constellating lines and understanding them somehow as reflecting different attributes of human existence. I realized that we can read these infrastructural constellations to understand something about our society and where we have come from, and to imagine where we want to go. We can read in these star charts questions about how to recover non-extractive value systems that are grounded in ecological reintegration. These constellations can help us envision a time beyond this infrastructural moment. Like when you gaze into a telescope and you're looking back in time, I imagine gazing into the future and seeing another way of being in the world.

My practice is also informed by the work of African philosophers such as Congolese scholar K. Fu-Kiau Bunseki and Malidoma Patrice Somé of the Dagara people in Burkina Faso, as well as the Descendants Project, an emerging organization committed to the intergenerational healing and flourishing of the Black descendant community in the Louisiana River Parishes. They led me to consider what happens when thousands of holes are drilled ten thousand feet deep into the body of the earth. Somé wrote about the ancestors residing as a vast pool of energy beneath the surface of the earth, and I have been haunted by this notion. I collaborated with Forensic Architecture for a 2021 project in the region, during which we developed a methodology for locating burial grounds of historically enslaved people. The burial grounds often manifest as groves of trees, partial remnants of the primordial forest that was cleared to make way for the sugarcane fields. They are also carefully cultivated ecological spaces, because enslaved people planted magnolia trees around the perimeter of their internment spaces, within the wider forest. The burial grounds, like former plantations, are now entirely contained within private property, often industrial sites or proposed industrial sites, and it's very difficult to access them on the ground—although it is very moving to see that once you enter these groves, there are families of cardinals and potentially very rare species of snakes. Some of these burial groves are featured in *The holes in the earth*, including the Houmas plantation burial grove, which is thought to be the final resting place of over a thousand people. Within the cycles and cosmologies Bunseki and Somé articulate, we can understand that the people and their spirits within the burial groves are now speaking to the current residents, calling them to action, and supporting them in their struggle to prevent the encroachment of the petrochemical industry. The groves and the ancestors and other species that inhabit them are rupturing the continuum of extractivism, and asking us to continue their work.

As we think about extractivism as a worldview, which values profit and the accumulation of profit, we understand that extractive agents have deployed the force of segregation against integral ecological communities. As human beings have been segregated from our wider ecological bodies, Black bodies and Indigenous bodies have been segregated from the body of humanity. I show the blending of data, images, and sound in this work to think of collective ways to redress this segregative violence and imagine paths to ecological reparations and reintegration.

Imani Jacqueline Brown

I grew up a few blocks away from the Cook County Jail. It was part of my psychological and physical landscape; I passed by it every day when I was going to school, or just as I was moving through my neighborhood as a teenager, as a young person. So it was always in my mind.

I went to visit Cook County Jail through a "Scared Straight" program in, I think, the sixth grade. These really strange, brutal programs still exist—children are taken to visit jails and prisons, supposedly to deter juvenile crime. I think we were deemed high risk in my elementary school because we were all Latinx kids.

I recall walking through Division I, which is the oldest part of the jail and has now been closed. I remember seeing the cells and seeing the men who looked like my neighbors, like my brother, like my uncles. I can never forget what it looked like and what it felt like. I'll never forget how obviously the white teachers hurried through, scared. I was taking in all of this information about people's behavior, about how people are confined but also the way that this space of confinement instilled a certain fear. This experience was supposed to keep me away from the detention center. In fact, it actually instilled something in me to return—but to return in a way that I'm sure none of them imagined. I teach in the jail, I organize with communities on the inside and the outside of the facility, and it is central to my art practice.

Between 2021 and 2022, I collected twenty-three pieces of debris from the demolition of the Division I building, which were cast in glass for an artwork called *Invisible Things Are Not Necessarily Not-There*

(after T.M.). When I realized that the demolition was going to happen, I decided to make a video. I stood there five days a week filming for what became *Clamour*, a sixty-hour video of the destruction. During that process, I met a lot of people who were leaving the courthouse or visiting loved ones. I met residents who were curious about what I was doing. I also met former guards who were also there to photograph the facility, and they described what it was like to work there—for instance, telling me about the facility being like an oven because there is no air-conditioning. And then one day a judge came from the courthouse and we talked and then he came back and gave me a bar from the demolition. He handed it to me and said something like, "Here you go." I felt pretty shocked, because I'd never imagined I'd be holding a bar from a cell. It felt like this was a material of harm and violence. What do I do with this? I accepted it, but I wasn't sure why. I decided that there was an opportunity here to transform the material.

Strangely enough, at the demolition site, I noticed that the guards were laying out all the bars and the bricks in a pretty orderly fashion. I think they did it so that they could come and take a moment. So every day I would go pick up two or three bars—they're pretty heavy; they are made of pure iron. And then at a certain point the guards said, "You can't take any more." And they actually didn't lay them out anymore.

I had the bars and bricks in my studio for a while, and I didn't know what to do with them. I spent a lot of time looking at them, thinking about them, talking with friends about them, and thinking about the ethical boundaries and questions about what it means to be an artist working with this material. After a while I decided to just photograph them and examine them closely. And then I cast them in glass.

There's a lot of processes that went into making these glass casts, not just in terms of fabrication but the thinking around what it means to turn jail bars made of iron that is rigid and static, and meant to confine, into another material. When cast in glass, they can be seen through, they are incredibly fragile, and you can imagine them as windows. The bars had been in that building, holding people in, for almost a hundred years. And I wanted to think of how to make something that if somebody who was locked behind those, those exact bars, were to see it, they would be moved by it, or feel like something had changed.

The glass casts are only one iteration of the bars. I have thought hard about the historical violence contained within the iron bars, and the way they were meant to take life away. And I continue to think about how, through art, I can help expose the lives that were—and are—impacted at Cook County Jail and at facilities across the US. I've continued to ask myself how they can be a window into that, without simply documenting stories in the conventional sense. I landed on sound. By tapping on them, I could hear immediately the vibrations of their histories. And I was struck by how the bars contain sound that I can't hear, that is just not audible to my ears, and I wondered how I could pull some of that out.

This led to the collaborative creation of what I think of as a sonic sculpture called *We Lit the Fire and Trusted the Heat (after Angela Davis)*. I took the bars

to an experimental sound studio in Chicago that I have worked with for some years, and we recorded them with contact mics. There was a series of experiments done by hitting the bars with different tools, different kinds of metals, or pieces of wood to hear what sounds can come out. I invited musicians to come to my studio, friends of mine or former students. Then I had the opportunity to work with composer and pianist James Gordon Williams, who was the first to publicly play and perform with the bars, opening them up to new dimensions and evoking histories of iron that trace to slavery. Musicians Samora and Elena Pinderhughes also did a public performance, and I continue to think with other musicians.

In my work, I have really gone deep into thinking about materiality, and how it encompasses the presence of something of what used to be there—people and events—while still having the ability to move beyond histories and uses. To me, thinking through the materiality of the bars, and how to rematerialize them into something beyond oppression and violence, is a way to think about—and expand—the possible.

I think so much about the ways that we can express, demonstrate, and, you know, generate life through artistic forms, whether objects or experiences or engagements. And I think it's something that I keep learning. It is the fullness of one's life and the fullness of the lives of others that I work with, and I am always striving to learn how we hold that together as much as we can and show up for each other.

Maria Gaspar

When I was wrongly incarcerated, my cell had a window. I'm roughly six foot, and it was up above my head. It was inset within the cinder block wall, and I had to tilt my head to peer up at it. But even when peering up, I could not see out of it. Through the weathering of the exterior of the window, and the fact that it was never cleaned, it was opaque. For the twenty-three hours a day I spent in that cell, there was always a suggestion, the possibility, that I should be able to look out. I was always looking for a place to peer out of, whether it was my mail slot, the sliver of window in my door, or especially that window high up on the wall. Even the gesture of looking up at the window is a hopeful thing. It is the dreamer's point of view. The window was a constant reminder of a possibility. But I never could see out.

Yet, although I couldn't see out, I did see condensation when it rained. At nighttime, there was a small luminosity of yellow, which made the window a little green. And in the daytime, if it was a good day, it was blue. If it was overcast, then it was gray.

When I began to think about making the "Forecast" series, which are neon sculptures, I was thinking about that light, that window, and how it became part of my search for something to hold on to—for some way to look out into the beyond. The artwork started out as just being the window and the colors. But I quickly found more of that architectural form surrounding the window coming into the work, and the heaviness of the cinder blocks and institutional surroundings. I wanted to show something about how the window could offer both hope and obstruction as a way to also talk about how the system can break you down even through small architectural gestures.

I named the series "Forecast" to reference the tension between planning, prediction, and the weather. You can plan a pretty picnic, but you can't predict the weather. When I was incarcerated, I was always trying to do my best to plan, to hope, but there is a constant unpredictability that's hindering, obstructing, that possibility.

I think what I'm trying to work through is those hopes and possibilities. The obstructiveness of being incarcerated is pretty obvious, and the material reality is pretty cold. And this makes it harder to see the warmth—the slight bit of warmth, or the possibility of warmth—that also exists. There's a little bit of tenderness in my work that is important. After all, you can't see the sky, but there is still light.

In the beginning when I was in my cell, I used to try to sleep my days away. But then I had other guys come in and beat on the bunk and be like, "You gotta get up. We're getting up, and we're doing something."

There are not a lot of opportunities for rehabilitation in these spaces. So the attitude from a lot of the elders was: We don't have it so it's just up to us to make it. Let's not make an excuse out of it. Let's figure it out. You want to learn a language? There's somebody here who speaks Spanish. We have nothing but time, so start a conversation with them.

Since I've been back out, all this experience and that time has been mainly devalued. Most people tell me I need to just move on. But I still hold a lot of it in me. So I'm taking these materials—these conditions—that I am told are useless and that I need to leave behind, and trying to show that there is value to be found within that coldness. As a survivor, I feel the responsibility to show that value, because there are people who are there, who are still in those spaces, who can't.

I never want to have to convince someone that prisons should be abolished by making them go through jail or prison, but somehow I want people to know that these spaces, and the individuals inside them—we're all connected.

There is a thread in most of my work: What happens when hope is taken and you're trying to search for it? Where should we look for that hope?

Sherrill Roland

Throughout the years and decades I have been incarcerated, I have gone through a lot, experienced a lot, and been subjected to a lot. People respond differently in these circumstances, but I have tried in my way to take on the system that oppresses us.

I've written hundreds of grievances, complaints, writs, and 602 appeals for things like medical care and, during the height of the COVID pandemic, hand sanitizer and face masks. I have appealed for adequate legal representation, for repairs to damaged property, and for countless other actions, conditions, and policies of the California Department of Corrections and Rehabilitation and the entire California criminal punishment system. These appeals and writs have become my documentation of the processes and bureaucracies of oppression and subjection that I am held within, and my attempts to reconcile wrongs and effect change.

These almost daily acts of resistance have become my art practice, and my ongoing artwork *Disposition* is the collection, reflection, and archival expression of my decades-long resistance to systemic racism, oppression, and carceral inequalities. It is not only a way to show what I have been subjected to, but it also shows what I have done to try to change the nature of confinement. I turn agony into art as a way to make a contribution. There are many people in similar positions, including those who came before and those who will come after, who have had to suffer the inequalities and injustices of prisons and our twisted legal system, so my practice is to reveal and impede the bureaucracy through which the system does its work.

"Disposition" is a word with multiple meanings. In the legal sense, the disposition on a criminal record is the current status or final outcome of an arrest or prosecution. Anyone who has been arrested, whether they were charged or convicted, has attached to them a list of dispositions of each time they have interacted with the system, from arrests to charges to adjudications. Dispositions are compiled into a person's criminal history record. They show only the outcomes of arrests, and erase the racialized and biased workings of the criminal legal system. My documentation is an attempt to correct this by creating a record—a disposition log—of the systemic oppression hidden within the bureaucracy.

I am also using the word "disposition" because of its use to describe the character of a person. *Disposition*,

the installation I have created out of my appeals
and grievances, not only is an indictment of the
state but also reflects on the people who have been
essential to the history of resistance—and the roles
that we can all play within the movement. I might
have spent more than two decades on death row
in solitary confinement, but I still see a place for
myself to effect change. Therefore, what I am doing
is education work—trying to show people what
struggle looks like and how it can be accomplished
regardless of where you are working from. This is a
call to other people who are on the inside and in the
so-called free world. *Disposition* tries to inspire people to work for change and to remind everyone that
change is indeed happening all around us. Sometimes it moves so slowly that it is almost imperceptible, but the system does and can change—and every
action can lead to change.

Advocacy and activism, resistance and struggle, are
art forms. Trying to change society and culture is
creative work. What I hope *Disposition* does for people on the outside is give them a vivid snapshot of
the lived experiences and harsh realities of prisons.
But I am also speaking to people on the inside, and
presenting a model or a blueprint for how resistance
might look. My hope is that I can inspire more
people to join in creating this disposition against
the realities of prison.

Timothy James Young

Daniel Lima: Frente 3 de Fevereiro is a collective that first formed in 2004, following the murder of Flávio Ferreira Sant'Ana, a young Black man, by police officers in São Paulo. This young man was "mistaken" for a thief. In Brazil, there is a very strong idea that by ascending socially, you will escape racism. Flávio had all the markers of social ascendancy: he was a dentist, he had a car, he was well-dressed, he had money. Yet he was mistaken for a thief and killed by the police. My mother, Maurinete Lima, was very touched by this case, and, as a kind of call to arms, she rallied first her sons, then the larger aggregate family of friends and activists. She motivated us to mobilize our artistic skills and knowledge to stage interventions and confront the structural issue of racism in Brazil, which this murder exposed.

Eugênio Lima: Brazilian society often frames police violence as an issue of class oppression instead of a racial issue. If you are poor, you suffer police violence, or if you dress in a way that puts you in a "suspicious group," you can be exposed to police violence. But Flávio was not poor, he didn't dress like he was part of a suspicious group. The other usual excuse, "He was in the wrong place at the wrong time," also doesn't work. Flávio wasn't even close to the location of the robbery that the police were supposedly responding to; he was in his car far away. The police put the person who was robbed in a vehicle and went out looking for someone to blame. The police approached Flávio in his car, and when he came out with his hands up, they took two shots at close range. When the police officers realized that they had committed a cold-blooded murder, they tried to bury his body, and for a while nobody knew where he was. The case unmasked the long-held idea that Brazil is a racial democracy. Flávio's father, who is Black, is a former military police officer—Flávio was killed by the institution his father dedicated his entire life to. Flávio's father gave a statement to the press: "My son was killed because he was Black." After he made that statement, the commander of the Military Police of the State of São Paulo denied that the institution is racist. This denial outraged my mother even more.

Cibele Lucena: The hegemonic press was asserting that this was a case of police violence and not of police racism. At that time, there was already a collective movement in São Paulo, formed by groups of artists in theater and in different fields. This caught Maurinete Lima's attention as a way of organizing and as a means to collectivize to confront racism.

Around 30 percent of the group is made up of artists who work in the audiovisual field, or in cinema and music.

EL: For two decades, we've staged public interventions to galvanize the public against this structural racism. For instance, the mainstream media pays a lot of attention to soccer fans during matches and broadcasts their flags and banners. So we thought, What if we replaced the soccer flags with questions and actions, such as "Hail to Black people," or "Where are the Black people?" The mainstream TV would have to broadcast these messages. So we use organized soccer as a stage to pose questions about the racism in Brazilian society.

DL: Originally commissioned for the São Paulo Biennial, *Ancestral Intelligence* is an immersive audiovisual work, which grows out of these interventions. For *Ancestral Intelligence* we challenged ourselves to re-create my mother, Maurinete Lima, who everyone called Dona Mauri. Dona Mauri passed away in 2018, and her image was never recorded in a studio. Using artificial intelligence, we created the character of Dona Mauri through a process of *presentificação*, in which an image is imbued with presence.[1] AI operates at two different levels in the work. First is the audiovisual reconstruction of Dona Mauri—her face and voice. And for that there is a technical process that requires an ethical process. Interconnecting social technology with instrumental technology, we placed an ethical value on thinking about how AI would reconstruct her voice and image. For this, we looked for the files that she recorded, texts she wrote, and the materials we have about her that could become a technical and ethical archive.

We think of the AI within *Ancestral Intelligence* as a seed—as the beginning of a process and thinking about the autonomy of intelligence. We wanted to give Dona Mauri's ancestral intelligence the autonomy to ask questions and answer to the public, giving another dimension to AI, or even altering the DNA of intelligence itself. What we call "artificial intelligence" today has been constructed in study centers, in universities, in development centers in California, for example, and by white majorities. As a result, there are biases and racist deviations that follow a preexistent structure of the world. Therefore, it is necessary to exercise and create other DNAs of artificial intelligence in this field. So we enter to dispute this field, with Dona Mauri offering a perspective on the world that can feed other knowledges.

Frente 3 de Fevereiro

CL: To create the work's script, we started with speeches and texts from the group's archive. The script's structure is not linear; it has this idea of fragments and layers that connect to and complete each other. When the public arrives at the screening room, they capture a piece of this structure at a given moment. There are many stories being told. These fragments and pieces also follow the history of our collective, incorporating texts written by the collective and images produced and records of our interventions mixed with Dona Mauri's writings. What is created is a living archive, in which today is connected with the past and the future through Dona Mauri, as an ancestor.

EL: About the word "ancestral," I would like to add that ancestry for Africa-based religions is not just about heritage. It's not like, "My grandfather passed through the world, so he is my ancestor." An ancestor is someone who comes to the *aiê* and fulfills a mission and leaves a legacy that we call *ori*.[2] This legacy is both the family relationships and genetics, but it also extends to the people who are touched by that legacy. Maurinete's intelligence is ancestral because she is an ancestor, but also because ancestry is not located in the past. Ancestry is contemporary; the ancestor is not a ghost. Maurinete is the narrator of the entire work, and she organizes the scene for the viewer. Through this presence, we create a dispute over the imaginary world. She is not the object of the story, but the agent.

DL: I think with *Ancestral Intelligence* we arrived at the idea of creating and carrying on a dialogue that is not only about the collective's history, but also thinking about the form of an instrumental technology that can be developed to affirm racialized people after death. We act into this virtual battlefield of who will tell the story of the present.

1. In Portuguese, *presentificação* means "act by which an object becomes present in the form of an image." "Presentificação," in *Dicio, Dicionário Online de Português*, accessed April 1, 2024, https://www.dicio.com.br /presentificacao/.

2. In Yoruba, *aiê* (also *àiyé* or *ayê*) means "life" or "world," and *ori* means "head" or "destiny." In Afro-Brazilian religions of Yoruba origin, such as Candomblé, *aiê* refers to the physical world of the living, while *ori* refers to the deity of each individual's "head," or their destiny.

Exhibition Checklist

Institute of the Arts and Sciences

Frank Alejandrez
Walking with Love, 2023–24
Wood
Four sticks: approx. 40 × 1½ × 1½ in.,
each
Courtesy of the artist

Juan E. Arredondo "Noodles," Joseph
Dole, Vitória Daiane Emídio dos Santos,
Darrell W. Fair, Flávia Ferreira dos Santos,
Aimee Gana, Roquelina Gomes de Souza,
Donnie Wayne Ivy, Michael Jones, Just
Me Expressions, Juan Luna, Poipi Mabo-
Harrison (Meriam, Munbarra, Poorooma,
Kokomini), Erick MacieL, Bryan Mathe-
son, Nathaniel McCray #R63745, Jessie
Milo, JOHN ORTEGA, Robert Ortiz,
George Red, Tiffanie Sedgwick (Noogar),
Gwenda Skeen (Nunckle, Kuku-Thaypan),
Kyeemah Skeen (Nunckle, Kuku-
Thaypan), Smiley, Harold "Ace" Smith,
Mark A. Stanley aka Stan-Bey, Ronald
Steele, and Ernesto Valle
*In a world without prisons, everyone would
be able to see the sky*, 2024
Various media
Dimensions variable
Courtesy of the artists

Imani Jacqueline Brown
*The holes in the earth mirror the holes in
our souls (and from them we can grow
trees)*, 2023
Media installation with soundscape
"Enbas" by Les Cenelles
218 × 127½ × 152 in., overall
Courtesy of the artist

Sharon Daniel
Reasonable Doubt(s), 2024
Three-channel film and sound
71:06 minutes
Courtesy of the artist

Cian Dayrit
Feudal Fields, 2018
Mixed media and embroidery on fabric
72 × 60 in.
Courtesy of the artist

Cian Dayrit
Feudal Fields II: Tinang, 2024
Mixed media and embroidery on fabric
72 × 60 in.
Courtesy of the artist

Caleb Duarte with Santa Cruz Barrios
Unidos
Tres Terrenos, 2024
Wood, concrete, soil, and paint
144 × 32 × 32 in.
Courtesy of the artist and Santa Cruz
Barrios Unidos

Explode! Platform (Cláudio Bueno and
João Simões)
Passagem, 2024
Installation of books, paint, metal sheets,
videos, and public program
Dimensions variable
Courtesy of the artists

Forensic Architecture Investigation Unit
at Al-Haq
Platform for Gaza, 2024–ongoing
Online database and trackpad
Courtesy of Al-Haq, Forensic Architecture,
and Al-Haq FAI Unit

The Freedom Theatre
Your Time Is Not Your Time, 2024
Single-channel film and sound
34 minutes
Courtesy of The Freedom Theatre

Frente 3 de Fevereiro
Ancestral Intelligence, 2023–24
Three-channel video and sound
49:44 minutes
Courtesy of the artists

Charles Gaines
Manifestos 4, 2020
Four graphite drawings on paper, two
monitors, four speakers, and hanging
speaker shelves
116¾ × 300 × 12 in., overall
San Francisco Museum of Modern Art.
Purchase through a gift of Amy and David
Abrams, Jim DeMare, Sarah and Jason
DiLullo, Randi and Bob Fisher, Danielle
and David Ganek, Peggy Yeoh Lee,
Michael and Jodi Price, Jonas Prince, Lu
Zhou, and the International Contempo-
rary Accessions Committee at SFMOMA

Guillermo Galindo
Ojo / Eye, 2015
Bicycle wheel, wood, steel, and amplifier
32¼ × 11¼ × 51¼ in.
Collection of Abe Tomás Hughes and
Diana Girardi Karnas

Guillermo Galindo
Voices Flag / Bandera de voces, 2017
Acrylic on beacon flags used by humani-
tarian aid group Water Stations
21½ × 47 in.
Collection of Abe Tomás Hughes and
Diana Girardi Karnas

Patricia Gómez and María Jesús González
Las 7 puertas, from "Tiempo Muerto,
Proyecto para Sección Abierta (Cárcel de
Palma de Mallorca)," 2011–13
Mural detachment on black canvas and
photographic book
Canvas: 108 × 660 in.; book: 19¾ ×
26⅜ in.
Courtesy of the artists

Sofia Karim
Diptychs, 2023
Projections on paper with text
12 × 19 in., each
Courtesy of the artist

Sofia Karim
Memories of Keraniganj Jail, 2019
3D-printed models
Nine models: approx. 6 × 9 × 6 in., each
Courtesy of the artist

Robert Hillary King
Freelines, 1962/2024
Pralines and labels
4½ × 3¾ in., each
Courtesy of the artist

Carlos Motta
The Capuchin Order, 2023
Paper architectural model, slide projector,
35 mm slides, and table
25 × 36 × 25¾ in.
Courtesy of the artist and PPOW Gallery

Mulheres Possíveis (Beatriz Cruz, Leticia Olivares, Sandra Ximenez, and Vânia Medeiros)
Lines to cross walls, 2024
In collaboration with Ana Paula, Ângela, Anísia, Caline, Caren, Cilceli, Cristiane, D., Dagma, Daniela, Eliane, Erica Fernanda, Fátima, Fernanda, Gislaine, Grazielle, Hilda, Hortência, Ingrid, Juliana, Juliana Fernanda, Juliet, Kamila, Lea, Lourdes, Maria Carmim, Maria Edivânia, Maria Gabriela, Marlyn Elizabeth, Mercedes, Miriam, Monica, Nady, Naftali, Paola, Renata, Samara, Sarah, Scheine, Shandelies, Silvia Alejandra, Suellen, Tabatha, Tanaka, Tanira, Tatiane, Thayane, Tubarão, and Uthopom
Vinyl sticker
112 × 118 in.
Courtesy of the artists

Mulheres Possíveis (Beatriz Cruz, Leticia Olivares, Sandra Ximenez, and Vânia Medeiros)
Livro de atividades, 2020/24
In collaboration with Bárbara Esmenia, Fábia Karklin, Maré de Matos, Olga Torres, and Olivia Niculitcheff
Pedagogical consultant: João Innecco
Book
6¾ × 9½ in.
Courtesy of the artists

Gabriela Mureb
Machine #4: Stone (Crank), 2017
Engine, stone, and aluminum
13¾ × 29½ × 9⅞ in.
Courtesy of the artist and Central Galeria, São Paulo

Hương Ngô
And the State of Emergency Is Also Always a State of Emergence, 2017–ongoing
Installation with black poster paper, black gaffer's tape, cyanotypes, sand, plaster, studio refuse, and framed archival pigment prints
132 × 72 × 48 in., overall
Courtesy of the artist

O grupo inteiro (Carol Tonetti, Cláudio Bueno, Ligia Nobre, and Vitor Cesar) with Vanessa Soares and Lorran Dias
Liberdade Zero (Freedom Zero), 2024
In collaboration with Centro de Estudos e Ações Solidárias da Maré and Complexo de Favelas da Maré
Video installation and charcoal drawing
Video: 13:54 minutes; drawing: 13 × 18 in.
Courtesy of the artists

Samora Abayomi Pinderhughes
Listening Station (excerpt), from *The Healing Project*, 2016–ongoing
Audiocassettes
Collection of The Healing Project

Sherrill Roland
Forecast, 2023
Steel and LED light box
66½ × 67 × 8 in.
Courtesy of the artist and Tanya Bonakdar Gallery, New York/Los Angeles

Tea Project (Amber Ginsburg and Aaron Hughes)
Selections from the series "Remaking the Exceptional," 2022:
Tracing Torture | Rumsfeld, Miller, Zuley, and Burge
What Kind of Spring Is This? | From POW to Forever Prisoner
A Decade Later | Importing and Exporting the Torture Trades
Circuit of Violence | From Ohio to Afghanistan, Iraq, Guantánamo . . .
People Rise Like the Water
The Making of One Long Night
Extraordinary Rendition of Mohamedou Ould Slahi
One Long Night | Barbed Wire (1874) and Maxim Machine Gun (1884)
Reparations Now! | The Dynamo and The Black Box
Screenprints on Rives BFK paper
20 × 30 in., each
Courtesy of the Tea Project

Timesfive (Moira Murdock and jackie sumell)
Color the Skies Fallen Prisons, 2024
Lens, fenestration, and light box
1 × 1 in.
Courtesy of the artists

Rachel Wallis with Mariame Kaba
Anguilla Quilt, 2021
Plant-dyed, linoleum block printed, and digitally printed cotton; hemp and linen fabric; embroidery and hand-quilting thread; glass beads; block printing ink; and cotton batting
90 × 60 in.
Courtesy of the artists

Levester Williams
To hold us all dear, 2015
Unclean bed sheets from a Virginia adult penitentiary and poplar wood
76½ × 46½ × 3 in., each
Collection of Darryl Atwell

Timothy James Young
Disposition, 2024
Documents and wood frames
Fifteen documents: 11¼ × 8¾ × 1¼ in., each
Courtesy of the artist

San José Museum of Art

Juan E. Arredondo "Noodles," Robert E. Barber, Albert Bell, Darwin Billingsley, C. J. Black, Mark A. Cadiz aka Rev. M. Seishin, Christopher "Khalifah" Christensen, Jessica Marie Hann, Huicho Herrera, Jeffery A. Isom, Michael Jones, Just Me Expressions, Juan Luna, Brad "Trust None" Odell, JOHN ORTEGA, Ronnie Shelton, O. Smith the Artivist, Luis Trevino, L. T2023, Unknown, and Love'ly ocean Williams
In a world without prisons, everyone would be able to see the sky, 2024
Various media
Dimensions variable
Courtesy of the artists

Sadie Barnette
West Oakland 2065, 2024
Archival pigment print and rhinestones
13 × 13 in.
Courtesy of the artist

Rebecca Belmore
At Pelican Falls, 2017
Sculpture, video, wall text, and
photograph
77 × 264 × 175 in., overall
Collection of the artist

Cian Dayrit
Agrev Algorithm, 2022
Tapestry
70⅞ × 74¾ in.
Courtesy of the artist and NOME, Berlin

Cian Dayrit
Monuments of Great Divide, 2019
In collaboration with Felman Bagalso
Wood and metal
Three sculptures: approx. 7 × 14 × 3 in.,
each
Courtesy of the artist and NOME, Berlin

Cian Dayrit
Selection of counter-maps with planta-
tion, 2017–ongoing
In collaboration with Abby Bucad, Alvin
Dimarucut, Annabelle Magana, Christine
Olado, Dagohoy P. Magaway, Ernie P.
Baratas, Fermiza and Arnold, Florinda Cal-
lena, Israel M. Axelino, Jef Alipo-on and
Jaspe Mallo, Joebert S., Johny B. Dalapan,
Manuel A. Garubat, Melche G. Balbiran,
MJ Avics, Pedro, Peter, Rafael Pallanan,
Ranel Manggatawan, Raymond Pimentel,
Rhoy Cabudoy, Roselyn B. Catampun-
gan, Salik Maguindanao, Sarah Jane T.,
Steven G., Virginia B. Jinang and Mimi
Sawoud, and Von Patlunag
Reproductions of drawings
Thirty documents: approx. 8½ × 12 in.,
each
Courtesy of the artist and NOME, Berlin

Caleb Duarte with Santa Cruz Barrios
Unidos
Tres Terrenos, 2024
Wood, concrete, soil, and paint
144 × 32 × 32 in.
Courtesy of the artist and Santa Cruz
Barrios Unidos

Charles Gaines
Sky Box II, 2020
Acrylic, digital print, aluminum, polyester
film, and LED lights
144 × 288 in.
San Francisco Museum of Modern Art.
Purchase through a gift of anonymous
donors, Ethan Beard and Wayee Chu,
Randi and Bob Fisher, Puja and Samir Kaul,
Jennifer Lamb and Chris Sharp, Bo Shan
and Catherine Dooling, Gary Steele and
Steven Rice, Mike Volpi and Toni Cupal,
and the Accessions Committee Fund

Guillermo Galindo
Caravan Variation Flag, 2015
Acrylic on beacon flag used by humanitarian aid group Water Stations, sewn on
linen backing
30 × 47 in.
San José Museum of Art. Museum purchase with funds provided by the Acquisi-
tions Committee, 2023.08

Guillermo Galindo
Llantambores, 2015
PVC pipes, immigrant tire inner tubes,
wood, cloth booties, and border barbed
wire
35½ × 53 × 17 in.
San José Museum of Art. Museum purchase with funds provided by the Acqui-
sitions Committee and Docent Council,
2023.07

Maria Gaspar
Cloud Out (Evanesce), 2023
Archival inkjet print with oil pastel on
paper
41 × 75 in.
Courtesy of the artist

Maria Gaspar
Cloud Out (Suspend), 2023
Archival inkjet print with oil pastel on
paper
41 × 75 in.
Courtesy of the artist

Maria Gaspar
*Invisible Things Are Not Necessarily Not-
There (after T.M.)*, 2023
Twenty-three glass casts
12 × 144 × 72 in., overall
Courtesy of the artist

Gabriela Golder
Cartas/Letters, 2018
Four-channel video installation with sound
Four videos: approx. 15 minutes, each
Courtesy of the artist

Patricia Gómez and María Jesús González
À tous les clandestins, from the series
"À tous les clandestins," 2019
Posters
65 × 43¼ in., each
Collection of the artists

Patricia Gómez and María Jesús González
Celda 1-3, from the series "Centro de
Retención de Migrantes de Nouadhibou
(Mauritania)," 2015–16
Mural detachment on black canvas
59 × 187 in.
Collection of the artists

Patricia Gómez and María Jesús González
Celda 3-1, from the series "Centro de
Retención de Migrantes de Nouadhibou
(Mauritania)," 2015–16
Mural detachment on black canvas
59 × 181 in.
Collection of the artists

Patricia Gómez and María Jesús González
Celda 3-2, from the series "Centro de
Retención de Migrantes de Nouadhibou
(Mauritania)," 2015–16
Mural detachment on black canvas
59 × 181 in.
Collection of the artists

Patricia Gómez and María Jesús González
Celda 5-3, from the series "Centro de
Retención de Migrantes de Nouadhibou
(Mauritania)," 2015–16
Mural detachment on black canvas
59 × 185 in.
Collection of the artists

Shilpa Gupta
Untitled (There Is No Border Here),
2005–06
Wall drawing with self-adhesive tape
118 × 118 in.
Courtesy of the artist and Tanya Bonakdar
Gallery, New York/Los Angeles

Sky Hopinka
*I held the ancestor in my arms and took
them far away from here*, 2022
Inkjet print with hand-scratched text
40 × 40 in.
San José Museum of Art. Museum purchase with funds provided by the Acquisi-
tions Committee, 2023.09

Ashley Hunt
And Water Brings Tomorrow, 2024
Single-channel film and sound
38 minutes
Collection of the artist

Steffani Jemison
In Succession (2019), 2019
Black-and-white HD video with sound
18:19 minutes
Courtesy of the artist and Greene Naftali,
New York

Sofia Karim
Diptychs, 2023
Projections on paper with text
12 × 19 in., each
Courtesy of the artist

Bouchra Khalili
The Constellation Series, 2011
Eight silkscreen prints on paper, mounted
on aluminum and framed
24 × 16 in., each
Courtesy of mor charpentier, Paris

Robert Hillary King
Freelines, 1962/2024
Pralines and labels
4½ × 3¾ in., each
Courtesy of the artist

O grupo inteiro (Carol Tonetti, Cláudio
Bueno, Ligia Nobre, and Vitor Cesar) with
Vanessa Soares and Lorran Dias
Liberdade Zero (Freedom Zero), 2024
In collaboration with Centro de Estudos e
Ações Solidárias da Maré and Complexo
de Favelas da Maré
Video installation, poster, and charcoal
drawing
Video: 13:54 minutes; poster: 36 × 24 in.;
drawing: 13 × 18 in.
Courtesy of the artists

Samora Abayomi Pinderhughes
Listening Station (excerpt), from *The Heal-
ing Project*, 2016–ongoing
Audiocassettes
Collection of The Healing Project

Sherrill Roland
Forecast, 2023
Steel and LED light box
66½ × 67 × 8 in.
Courtesy of the artist and Tanya Bonakdar
Gallery, New York/Los Angeles

Sable Elyse Smith
Landscape V, 2020
Neon
37 × 178 in.
Courtesy of the artist and Regen Projects,
Los Angeles

jackie sumell
The Abolitionist's Apothecart,
2021–ongoing
Bicycle and cart with herbs, tinctures,
salves, and plants
38¼ × 28¼ × 78 in.
Courtesy of the artist

jackie sumell
Growing Abolition, 2024
Pressed plants on paper
Thirty-six sheets: 13½ × 9½ in., each
Courtesy of the artist

Tea Project (Amber Ginsburg and Aaron
Hughes) with Ghaleb Al-Bihani, Khalid
Qasim, and Moath al-Alwi
Ode to the Sea, 2023/24
Unstitched US military Desert Camouflage
Uniforms (made by people imprisoned in
the US working for Federal Prison Indus-
tries [UNICOR]), tea stain, gesso, canvas,
rope, antique sail pulley, embroidery
thread, and oak toggle
180 × 210 × 72 in., overall
Courtesy of the Tea Project

Tea Project
*La Amistad, Like the Waters from
19.9031°N, 75.0967°W to 41°52′04.5″N
87°42′39.4″W on January 11, 2002*, 2022
Screenprint on Rives BFK paper
20 × 30 in.
Courtesy of the Tea Project

Tea Project
*Tracing the Torture Tree | Chicago to
Guantánamo | The ecosystem of police and
military violence from John Burge and his
co-accused to Richard Zuley*, 2022
Screenprint on Rives BFK paper
20 × 30 in.
Courtesy of the Tea Project

Ghaleb Al-Bihani
Untitled, 2015
Pastel on paper
24 × 18 in.
Courtesy of the Tea Project

Ghaleb Al-Bihani
Untitled, 2015
Pastel on paper
17 × 14 in.
Courtesy of the Tea Project

Ghaleb Al-Bihani
Untitled, 2014
Charcoal on paper
9¾ × 11⅞ in.
Courtesy of the Tea Project

Khalid Qasim
Untitled, 2016
Acrylic on paper
16 × 12 in.
Courtesy of Khalid Qasim's attorney,
Shelby Sullivan-Bennis

Khalid Qasim
Untitled, 2016
Instant coffee and paint on paper
17 × 14 in.
Courtesy of Khalid Qasim's attorney,
Shelby Sullivan-Bennis

Moath al-Alwi
Untitled (GIANT), 2017
Cardboard, rope, fabric, plastic, and
acrylic
24 × 36 × 9 in.
Courtesy of the artist

Hajra Waheed
Walls, Ladders and Roads, 2019
Glazed porcelain
Nine sculptures: approx. 8½ × 5½ ×
5½ in., each
Courtesy of the artist

Santa Cruz Barrios Unidos

Nane Alejandrez
Walking the Corridor at Pelican Bay, 2024
Metal gate, mannequin, clothing, banner,
and plywood
Dimensions variable
Courtesy of the artist

Ben Chandler, Darrell W. Fair, J. Huynh,
Nathaniel McCray #R63745, JOHN
ORTEGA, Mesro Dhu Rafa'a, and Ernesto
Valle
*In a world without prisons, everyone would
be able to see the sky*, 2024
Various media
Dimensions variable
Courtesy of the artists

Caleb Duarte with Santa Cruz Barrios
Unidos
Tres Terrenos, 2024
Wood, concrete, soil, and paint
144 × 32 × 32 in.
Courtesy of the artist and Santa Cruz
Barrios Unidos

The Freedom Theatre
Your Time Is Not Your Time, 2024
Single-channel film and sound
34 minutes
Courtesy of The Freedom Theatre

Ashley Hunt
And Water Brings Tomorrow, 2024
Single-channel film and sound
38 minutes
Collection of the artist

Ashley Hunt
I Have a Dream of a Different Army, 2012
Single-channel film and sound
2:57 minutes
Collection of the artist

Robert Hillary King
Freelines, 1962/2024
Pralines and labels
4½ × 3¾ in., each
Courtesy of the artist

Kali mBula
Park Your Car before You Drive Your Phone,
2013/23
Acrylic, collage, and watercolor on canvas
39 × 40 in.
Courtesy of the artist

Kali mBula
Siblings Celebrate Dance, 2013
Acrylic and wood on canvas
48 × 30 in.
Courtesy of the artist

O grupo inteiro (Carol Tonetti, Cláudio
Bueno, Ligia Nobre, and Vitor Cesar) with
Vanessa Soares and Lorran Dias
Liberdade Zero (Freedom Zero), 2024
In collaboration with Centro de Estudos e
Ações Solidárias da Maré and Complexo
de Favelas da Maré
Video installation, poster, and charcoal
drawing
Video: 13:54 minutes; poster: 36 × 24 in.;
drawing: 13 × 18 in.
Courtesy of the artists

Josh Patstone, Kali mBula, Frank Alejan-
drez, and participants
Self Portraits (Intensive workshop), 2023
In collaboration with Caleb Duarte during
a multi-day workshop at Santa Cruz
Barrios Unidos
Clay
Dimensions variable
Courtesy of the artists

Tea Project (Amber Ginsburg and Aaron
Hughes)
*Speculative Reparations Ordinance for Chi-
cago (Burge) Police Torture Survivors*, 2012
In collaboration with Chicago Torture
Justice Memorials, Joe Mogul, and Carla
Jean Mayer
Ink on cotton
104½ × 39 in.
Courtesy of the Tea Project and Chicago
Torture Justice Memorials

Tea Project (Amber Ginsburg and Aaron
Hughes)
*Speculative Reparations Ordinance for
Guantánamo Torture Survivors*, 2022
Ink on silk
121 × 39 in.
Courtesy of the Tea Project

Timothy James Young
I am more, 2020
Embroidery
41 × 22 in.
Courtesy of the artist

Timothy James Young
Wings of friendship, 2020
Embroidery
41 × 22 in.
Courtesy of the artist

Curators' Acknowledgments

The work of abolition is necessarily a collaborative effort toward a collective vision, and *Seeing through Stone*, developed across three separate institutions—a university art gallery, a city art museum, and a community-based nonprofit—embodies this reality. Despite the distinct organizational frameworks, missions, and funding structures of the Institute of the Arts and Sciences (IAS), San José Museum of Art (SJMA), and Santa Cruz Barrios Unidos (SCBU), joining together to chart the multiple ways in which the work of abolition manifests across different social and political realities created a crucial opportunity for us to find and nourish the seeds of this collective vision within our own institutions.

This has been a vital and hopeful endeavor, and one that continues the long-term partnerships between the institutions established through Visualizing Abolition, a public scholarship initiative launched at the IAS in 2019 to shift the social attachment to prisons through art and education. *Seeing through Stone* is the largest exhibition to date in the yearslong partnership between the IAS and SJMA, building on multi-site exhibitions, art commissions, and educational programming that have been key to the Visualizing Abolition initiative. The artist residency program produced collaboratively by the IAS and SCBU has also been essential, providing support for artists coming out of prison to develop their practices.

All of these efforts have been a learning experience for everyone involved, and we owe an immense debt of gratitude to the Andrew W. Mellon Foundation for allowing us this opportunity to learn and grow together.

Our gratitude extends to everyone who took part in creating not only *Seeing through Stone* but also the larger Visualizing Abolition program.

At Barrios Unidos, we thank Nane Alejandrez and Jenny Alejandrez, Sam Cunningham, Mary Lou Alejandrez, Josh Patstone, and Anna Fonk, as well as every member of the staff and every volunteer—not only for the time and effort they have spent with and on us, but also for providing a daily example of abolition in practice.

We are grateful to all of our collaborators on the inside, who have given their time, guidance, and creative works to *Seeing through Stone* and Visualizing Abolition; we especially thank Timothy James Young, Frank Alejandrez, and Reginald BoClair. We also appreciate everyone who has helped facilitate our work across prison borders, including Laurie Brooks, Denise Carrascosa, Cherie Hacker, Debbie Kilroy, Christine Lashaw, Carol Newborg, Sarah Ross, and Meital Yaniv.

Beyond the support from the Mellon Foundation, Visualizing Abolition received early, critical funding from the Ford Foundation as well as Peter Coha,

240

Nion McEvoy and family, James Gunderson, Wanda Kownacki, Pat and Rowland Rebele, Jock Reynolds and Suzanne Hellmuth, and Randy and Celia Wedding. Our gratitude also goes to the *Seeing through Stone* sponsors at SJMA: the SJMA Exhibitions Fund, the Myra Reinhard Family Foundation, and the de Souza Bransten Family.

We are immensely grateful to S. Sayre Batton, Oshman Executive Director at SJMA, for her early and unwavering support of this institutional partnership, and her many behind-the-scenes efforts in the slow work of reimagining museum structures as a crucial part of abolition.

The support we have received at the University of California, Santa Cruz, has also been essential and welcome, and we thank Chancellor Cindy Larive, Campus Provost and Executive Vice Chancellor Lori Kletzer, Arts Dean Celine Parreñas Shimizu, Humanities Dean Jasmine Alinder, and the many others who have championed this work.

This exhibition would not have been possible without the dedication and support of staff at our institutions. At the IAS, we thank Louise Leong, head of exhibitions; Tatiane Santa Rosa, Visualizing Abolition program manager; Veriche Blackwell, preparator; Maia Kamehiro-Stockwell, program coordinator; tam welch, program coordinator; and Alex Moore, manager of education programs. Extra thanks go to Tatiane Santa Rosa for her translations of Portuguese into English. Thanks also to Luke Fidler, who provided early curatorial assistance. Our gratitude also goes to the IAS student staff.

At SJMA, we especially thank the exhibitions team for their tireless and nimble work in bringing this complex project to fruition: Richard James Karson, director of design and operations; Daniel Becker, associate exhibition designer; Aaron Lee, preparator; and Anamarie Alongi, registrar. Thanks to Nidhi Gandhi, curatorial and programs associate, for sharing her organizational skills. Our deepest thanks to Jennifer Sime, chief philanthropy officer; Jeff Bordona, director of education; Karen Rapp, deputy director; and Melanie Samay, director of marketing and communications.

Our sincere appreciation goes to Robin D. G. Kelley and Leanne Betasamosake Simpson for their contributions to this book, and to Pristone and the team at Marquand Books—Kestrel Rundle, Tom Eykemans, Leah Finger, and Gina Broze—for their beautiful book design and enthusiasm for this project. Thank you to Kristin Kearns for her sensitive eye.

Finally, profound gratitude to the artists who help us dream of a world without prisons.

—Gina Dent, Lauren Schell Dickens, and Rachel Nelson

Contributors

Nane Alejandrez is founder and executive director of Santa Cruz Barrios Unidos, a grassroots organization promoting cultural uplift, racial justice, community healing, policy initiatives, and restorative justice work in youth and adult facilities as well as state and local communities. Alejandrez established the violence prevention organization in 1977 in an effort to provide opportunities to at-risk youth and to cultivate pathways for people who have been incarcerated to reenter society. In 1993, Alejandrez organized the first transcultural incarcerated gang prevention summit, known as the Kansas City Peace Summit, resulting in a peace plan that has been adopted by the incarcerated community across Missouri. He is the recipient of numerous awards, including the Chief Justice Earl Warren Civil Liberties Award, the Fellowship of Reconciliation Martin Luther King Jr. Award, and the Sankofa Lifetime Achievement Award. As an organization, Barrios Unidos has received the Letelier-Moffitt Human Rights Award from the Institute for Policy Studies.

Gina Dent, PhD, is professor of humanities and faculty research director of the Institute of the Arts and Sciences at the University of California, Santa Cruz. Dent is also principal investigator and co-director of Visualizing Abolition (a project at the University of California, Santa Cruz) and works in the fields of cultural studies, carceral studies, and postcolonial and legal theory. She is the editor of *Black Popular Culture* (1992), named *Village Voice* Best Book of the Year, and author of articles on race, feminism, popular culture, and visual art. Her recent co-authored book—*Abolition. Feminism. Now.* (2022)—grows out of her decades-long work as an advocate for prison abolition. Dent has taught internationally, in Brazil, Colombia, and Sweden, as well as at the European Graduate School, and lectures and consults widely on culture and justice-related concerns.

Lauren Schell Dickens is chief curator at the San José Museum of Art. She has been collaborating with the Institute of the Arts and Sciences on exhibitions for Visualizing Abolition since 2020, including producing solo exhibitions with Sky Hopinka, Sadie Barnette, and Forensic Architecture. In addition, she has organized major group exhibitions including *Our whole, unruly selves* (2021), *With Drawn Arms: Glenn Kaino and Tommie Smith* (2019), *Other Walks, Other Lines* (2018), and *The House Imaginary* (2018), and solo exhibitions with Diana Al-Hadid, Kelly Akashi, Rina Banerjee, Woody De Othello, Jay DeFeo, and others. Her public project with the Propeller Group and El Mac was awarded the 2018 Creative Impact Award by the City of San José. She is a 2019 Andy Warhol Foundation Curatorial Research Fellow and recipient of the Fellows of Contemporary Art 2022 Curators Award.

Robin D. G. Kelley, PhD, is the Distinguished Professor and Gary B. Nash Endowed Chair of American History at the University of California, Los Angeles, and a contributing editor to the *Boston Review*. His many books include *Africa Speaks, America Answers: Modern Jazz in Revolutionary Times* (2012); *Thelonious Monk: The Life and Times of an American Original* (2009), which received the PEN Open Book Award and was selected as one of the *New York Times Book Review*'s "100 Notable Books of 2009"; *Freedom Dreams: The Black Radical Imagination* (2002); *Three Strikes: Miners, Musicians, Salesgirls, and the Fighting Spirit of Labor's Last Century* (2001); *Yo' Mama's Disfunktional! Fighting the Culture Wars in Urban America* (1997), which was named "Outstanding Book on Human Rights" by the Gustavus Myers Center for the Study of Human Rights; and *Hammer and Hoe: Alabama Communists during the Great Depression* (1990), which won the Elliott Rudwick Prize from the Organization of American Historians. Kelley's essays have appeared in professional journals as well as general publications, including the *Journal of American History*, the *American Historical Review*, the *Black Music Research Journal*, the *African Studies Review*, the *New York Times*, the *New York Times Magazine*, *Souls*, *Colorlines*, and the *Nation*.

Rachel Nelson, PhD, is director and chief curator of the UC Santa Cruz Institute of the Arts and Sciences. Nelson serves as co-director of two major public scholarship initiatives: Visualizing Abolition, an art-based project designed to shift the social attachment to prisons, and An Aesthetics of Resilience, an art and science collaboration focused on climate change. Since joining the Institute of the Arts and Sciences, Nelson has curated and organized exhibitions with artists including Carlos Motta, Sky Hopinka, Sadie Barnette, Al-Haq's Forensic Architecture Investigation Unit, Carolina Caycedo and David de Rozas, and Futurefarmers. Nelson has published widely on contemporary art, including book chapters, exhibition catalog essays, journal articles, and reviews, in such outlets as the *Brooklyn Rail*, *Nka*, *Third Text*, *Savvy*, and *African Arts*.

Leanne Betasamosake Simpson, PhD, is a writer, activist, faculty member at the Dechinta Centre for Research and Learning, and Distinguished Visiting Professor in the Faculty of Arts at Toronto Metropolitan University. Simpson has lectured and taught extensively at universities across Canada and the United States and has over twenty years' experience with Indigenous land-based education. She is the author of eight books, including *A Short History of the Blockade: Giant Beavers, Diplomacy, and Regeneration in Nishnaabewin*

(2021), *The Gift Is in the Making: Anishinaabeg Stories* (2013), *Islands of Decolonial Love* (2013), and *Dancing on Our Turtle's Back: Stories of Nishnaabeg Re-creation, Resurgence and a New Emergence* (2011). Her project *Rehearsals for Living* (2022), a collaboration with Robyn Maynard, was a national bestseller and was shortlisted for the Governor General's Literary Award for non-fiction. Her novel *Noopiming: The Cure for White Ladies* (2022) was shortlisted for the Governor General's Literary Award for fiction and the Dublin Literary Award. *This Accident of Being Lost* (2017) was a finalist for the Rogers Writers' Trust Fiction Prize and the Trillium Book Award. She is Michi Saagiig Nishnaabeg and a member of Alderville First Nation.

This book is published in conjunction with the exhibition *Seeing through Stone*, co-organized by the Institute of the Arts and Sciences and San José Museum of Art, and presented at the Institute of the Arts and Sciences (April 12, 2024–January 5, 2025), Santa Cruz Barrios Unidos (April 19, 2024–January 5, 2025), and the San José Museum of Art (April 26, 2024–January 5, 2025).

Seeing through Stone is made possible by the Mellon Foundation and the SJMA Exhibitions Fund, with lead support from the Myra Reinhard Family Foundation and additional support from the de Souza Bransten Family.

Operations and programs at the San José Museum of Art are made possible by principal support from the SJMA Board of Trustees, a Cultural Affairs Grant from the City of San José, and the Lipman Family Foundation; by lead support from the Adobe Foundation, Toby and Barry Fernald, Brook Hartzell and Tad Freese, the Richard A. Karp Charitable Foundation, Tammy and Tom Kiely, Kimberly and Patrick Lin, Sally Lucas, Yvonne and Mike Nevens, the David and Lucile Packard Foundation, the Skyline Foundation, and the SJMA Director's Council and Council of 100; and with significant endowment support from the William Randolph Hearst Foundation and the San José Museum of Art Endowment Fund established by the Knight Foundation at the Silicon Valley Community Foundation.

Copyright © 2024 Visualizing Abolition at the Institute of the Arts and Sciences and San José Museum of Art
Individual texts © 2024 the authors
All rights reserved. No part of this publication may be reproduced or transmitted in any form or by any means, electronic or mechanical, including photocopy, recording, or any information storage or retrieval system, without permission in writing from the publisher.

Library of Congress Control Number: 2024943371
ISBN: 978-1-64657-045-4

Published by
Institute of the Arts and Sciences
100 Panetta Drive
Santa Cruz, CA 95060
ias.ucsc.edu

San José Museum of Art
110 South Market Street
San José, CA 95113-2383
sanjosemuseumofart.org

Available through:
ARTBOOK | D.A.P.
75 Broad Street, Suite 630
New York, NY 10004
artbook.com

Produced by Marquand Books, Seattle
marquandbooks.com

Edited by Kristin Kearns
Designed by Thomas Eykemans
Typeset in ITC Stone Sans and Serif by Maggie Lee
Proofread by Ted Gilley
Color management by I/O Color, Seattle
Printed and bound in Singapore by Pristone

Cover: Maria Gaspar, *Cloud Out (Suspend)*, 2023. Archival inkjet print with oil pastel on paper, 41 × 75 in. Courtesy of the artist.

p. 6: Ghaleb Al-Bihani, *Untitled* (detail), 2015, from the Tea Project's *Ode to the Sea*, 2023/24. Pastel on paper, 24 × 18 in. Courtesy of the Tea Project.

p. 18: Hajra Waheed, *Walls, Ladders and Roads* (detail), 2019. Courtesy of the artist.

pp. 26–27: Caleb Duarte with Santa Cruz Barrios Unidos, *Tres Terrenos*, 2024. Wood, concrete, soil, and paint, 144 × 32 × 32 in. Courtesy of the artist and Santa Cruz Barrios Unidos.

p. 48: Bouchra Khalili, *The Constellation Series* (detail), 2011. Courtesy of mor charpentier, Paris.

p. 188: John Macfie, *Students of the Anglican Residential School at Pelican Falls Near Sioux Lookout, Watching a Fisherman*, ca. 1955. Archives of Ontario, C 330-8-0-0-5.

p. 202: Facade of Santa Cruz Barrios Unidos, 2024.

Photograph Credits
Individual images appearing in this publication may be protected by copyright in the United States of America, or elsewhere, and may not be reproduced without the permission of the rights holders. In reproducing the images contained in this publication, the San José Museum of Art obtained permission of the rights holders whenever possible. Should the Museum have been unable to locate the rights holder, notwithstanding good faith efforts, it requests that any contact information concerning such rights be forwarded so that they may be contacted for future editions.

Cover, pp. 106–7: Courtesy of Maria Gaspar. Photos by Clare Britt.
pp. 6, 24: Courtesy of Ghaleb Al-Bihani and the Center for Constitutional Rights. Photos by Zoey Dalbert/DePaul Art Museum.
pp. 18, 167–69: Courtesy of Hajra Waheed. Photos by Paul Litherland.
pp. 21–23, 26, 28, 35–36, 38–48, 51, 53–57, 59, 61–63, 66–67, 71, 72 (top), 73–75, 77–79, 81–83, 90–91, 94–97, 99, 102–3, 108, 114–15, 117, 119, 125, 127 (bottom), 132, 135, 137, 139, 141, 144–45, 147, 152–53, 155–57, 160–63, 165, 174–75, 178–87, 190, 196, 214–15: Photos by Glen Cheriton.
pp. 27, 89, 133, 207–13, 216: Photos by Daris Jasper, @ culturesaving.
pp. 29, 126, 127 (top left, top right), 128: Courtesy of Sofia Karim. Photos © Shahidul Alam.
pp. 31, 159: Courtesy of Khalid Qasim and Shelby Sullivan-Bennis. Photos by Zoey Dalbert/DePaul Art Museum.
p. 65: © Imani Jacqueline Brown.
pp. 68–69: © Sharon Daniel.

p. 72 (bottom): Courtesy of Cian Dayrit and NOME, Berlin. Photo by Gianmarco Bresadola.
p. 85: © Al-Haq, Forensic Architecture, and Al-Haq FAI Unit.
p. 87: © The Freedom Theatre.
p. 93: © Charles Gaines. Photo by Katherine Du Tiel.
p. 100: © 2015 Guillermo Galindo. Courtesy of the artist and Magnolia Editions. Photo by Magnolia Editions.
p. 101: © 2017 Guillermo Galindo. Photo by Richard Misrach.
p. 105: Courtesy of Maria Gaspar. Photos by Phillip Maisel.
p. 109: © Gabriela Golder.
p. 111: © Patricia Gómez and María Jesús González.
pp. 112–13: Courtesy of Levi Fanan/Fundação Bienal de São Paulo. Photo by Levi Fanan/Fundação Bienal de São Paulo.
p. 116: © Shilpa Gupta. Courtesy of Shilpa Gupta and Tanya Bonakdar Gallery, New York/Los Angeles.
pp. 120–21: © Sky Hopinka.
p. 123: © Ashley Hunt.
p. 129: © Sofia Karim.
pp. 130–31: Courtesy of Bouchra Khalili and mor charpentier, Paris. Photo © François Doury.
p. 136: Courtesy of the Mulheres Possíveis Archive. Photos by Ierê Papá.
p. 140: Courtesy of Hương Ngô. Photo by Tom Van Eynde.
p. 143: Courtesy of O grupo inteiro.
p. 149: Courtesy of Sherrill Roland and Tanya Bonakdar Gallery, New York/Los Angeles.
p. 151: © Sable Elyse Smith. Courtesy of the artist, Regen Projects, Los Angeles, and Carlos/Ishikawa, London. Photo by Charles Benton.
pp. 171–73: Courtesy of Rachel Wallis and Mariame Kaba. Photos by Bryce Laughlin Photography.
p. 177: Photo by Mickey Ta.
p. 195: Courtesy of PLATFORM: centre for photographic + digital arts. Video by Scott Benesiinaabandan.
p. 199: Courtesy of Taloi Havini. Photo by Sharjah Art Foundation.
pp. 202–4, 206: Photos by Andrew J. O'Keefe.